P9-ELH-548

1983-84

2195383

September 1983—August 1984

TARBELL'S
Teacher's Guide
to the International Sunday School Lessons
Includes the RSV and KJV

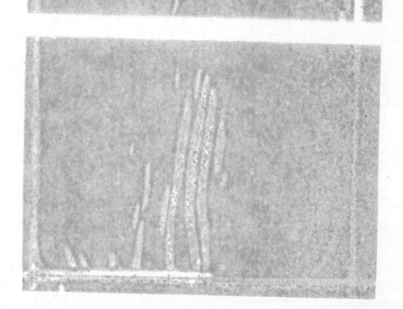

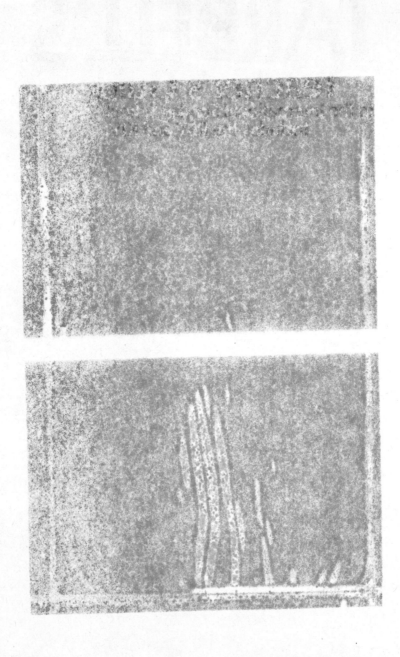

79th Annual Volume
September 1983—August 1984

TARBELL'S
Teacher's Guide
to the International Sunday School Lessons
Includes the RSV and KJV

**Edited by FRANK S. MEAD
and WILLIAM P. BARKER**

Fleming H. Revell Company
Old Tappan, New Jersey

This volume is based on The International Sunday School Lessons; the International Bible Lessons for Christian Teaching, copyright © 1970 by the Committee on the Uniform Series.

The text of the Revised Standard Version of the Bible and quotations therefrom are copyright 1946 and 1952 by the Division of Christian Education, National Council of Churches, and used by permission.

Unless otherwise identified all biblical quotations in the material used by the author to illustrate the lesson are from the King James Version.

Scripture quotations from The Living Bible are copyright © 1971 by Tyndale House Publishers, Wheaton, Illinois. Used by permission.

ISSN: 0730-2622
ISBN: 0-8007-1347-8

CONTENTS

Foreword 9
A Word to the Teacher, by Frank S. Mead 11

2195383

LIST OF LESSONS
SEPTEMBER, OCTOBER, NOVEMBER 1983
OUR BIBLICAL FAITH

Lesson				Page
I.	Sept.	4.	*God of Creation* .... Genesis 1:1; Psalms 19:1–4; Acts 17:24–28; Romans 1:20	15
II.	Sept.	11.	*God of History* .... Psalms 105:4–11, 37–45	21
III.	Sept.	18.	*God of Inspired Prophets* .... Deuteronomy 18:15–22; Amos 5:21–24; Micah 6:8	26
IV.	Sept.	25.	*God in Christ* .... John 14:8–11; Hebrews 1:1–4; 1 John 1:1–4	32
V.	Oct.	2.	*The Problem: Sin* .... Jeremiah 2:9–13; Romans 1:18, 28–2:1, 11	39
VI.	Oct.	9.	*The Motive: God's Love* Hosea 11:1–4, 8; 14:4–7; 1 John 4:8, 9	45
VII.	Oct.	16.	*The Means: God's Son* .. Romans 3:21–26; 5:6–11; Colossians 1:13, 14	51
VIII.	Oct.	23.	*The Result: New Persons* .... Ephesians 4:17–5:2; 2 Corinthians 5:17	57
IX.	Oct.	30.	*God's Gracious Covenant* .... Exodus 19:5, 6; Hebrews 8:6–13	64
X.	Nov.	6.	*God's Steadfast Love* ... Psalms 103:1–12; Ephesians 1:5–10 ...	69
XI.	Nov.	13.	*God's Indwelling Spirit* John 14:25, 26; Romans 8:9–17, 26–28	75
XII.	Nov.	20.	*God's Called-Out People* Colossians 3:1–3; 4:5, 6; 1 Peter 2:9–17 ...	81

Lesson   Page
XIII. Nov. 27. *God's Witnessing People* Matthew 5:13–16;
                                           28:18–20; 2 Corin-
                                           thians 5:18–21; 2
                                           Timothy 4:1, 2   87

DECEMBER 1983, JANUARY, FEBRUARY 1984
STUDIES IN ISAIAH

I. Dec.   4. *A New Day for God's*
              People . . . . Isaiah 2:2–4; 62:1–3 . . .   93
II. Dec.   11. *Good News for the*
              Afflicted . . . . Isaiah 61:1–7   99
III. Dec. 18. *Preparing for God's*
              Coming . . . . Isaiah 40:3–11   105
IV. Dec.   25. *A Reign of Righteous-*
              ness . . . . Isaiah 9:2–7; 11:1–3 . . .   111
V. Jan.   1. *God's Case Against His*
              People . . . . Isaiah 1:2–6, 18–20   117
VI. Jan.   8. *Song of the Vineyard* . . . Isaiah 5:1–7   123
VII. Jan. 15. *Vision and Mission* . . . . . Isaiah 6:1–8   128
VIII. Jan. 22. *Turn to the Lord* . . . . Isaiah 31:1–7   133
IX. Jan.   29. *A Day of Joy and*
              Gladness . . . . Isaiah 35:1–6, 8–10   139
X. Feb.   5. *I Am the Lord* . . . . Isaiah 43:1–7   145
XI. Feb.   12. *The Servant of the Lord* Isaiah 42:1–4; 49:5, 6;
                                           53:4–6   151
XII. Feb. 19. *Come to the Feast* . . . . . . Isaiah 55:1–3, 6–11   157
XIII. Feb. 26. *The Service God Seeks* . . Isaiah 58:5–11   162

MARCH, APRIL, MAY 1984
THE GOSPEL OF MARK

I. Mar.   4. *Jesus Begins His*
              Ministry . . . . Mark 1:14–28   168
II. Mar.   11. *Jesus Encounters*
              Hostility . . . . Mark 2:15–17, 23–3:6   174
III. Mar. 18. *Jesus Uses His Power* . . . Mark 4:37–41; 5:35–43   181
IV. Mar.   25. *Jesus Calls Persons to*
              Minister . . . . Mark 8:27–38   186
V. Apr.   1. *The Way of the Servant* Mark 10:32–45   192
VI. Apr.   8. *Confrontation in*
              Jerusalem . . . . Mark 11:8–10, 15–19,
                                           27–33   198
VII. Apr. 15. *In the Shadow of the*
              Cross . . . . Mark 14:22–36   204

CONTENTS

Lesson   Page

VIII. Apr. 22. *Crucified and Raised From Death* .... Mark 15:31–39; 16:1–7   210

IX. Apr. 29. *Be a Doer of the Word* .. James 1:1–6, 19–27   216

X. May 6. *Showing Your Faith Through Works* ...... James 2:1–7, 14–24   221

XI. May 13. *Be Careful What You Say* .... James 3:1–10, 13–18 ..   227

XII. May 20. *Be Responsible to God* .. James 4:1–10, 13–17 ..   232

XIII. May 27. *Be Patient Before God* .. James 5:7–18   238

JUNE, JULY, AUGUST, 1984
THE RISE AND FALL OF A NATION

I. June 3. *The People's Demand for Monarchy* .... 1 Samuel 12:14–25   244

II. June 10. *When Jealousy Dominates* .... 1 Samuel 18:5–16   250

III. June 17. *An Anointed Shepherd* .. 2 Samuel 5:1–3; 7:8–16   255

IV. June 24. *Family Rebellion* .... 2 Samuel 15:2–12   261

V. July 1. *Sowing Seeds of Destruction* .... 1 Kings 9:1–7; 11:9–12   266

VI. July 8. *Why Division Came* .... 1 Kings 11:29–33; 12:15, 16   271

VII. July 15. *An Era of Evil* .... 1 Kings 16:21–25, 29–33; 22:37–39   277

VIII. July 22. *Reform: By Force?* ...... 2 Kings 10:18, 19, 24–31   283

IX. July 29. *War Between the Kingdoms* .... 2 Kings 14:1–3, 8–14 ..   289

X. Aug. 5. *Last Days of a Kingdom* 2 Kings 17:5–9, 11–15, 17, 18   294

XI. Aug. 12. *Reform in Religion* ..... 2 Kings 18:1–8, 19:29–31; 20:20   300

XII. Aug. 19. *Measured by the Word* 2 Kings 22:10–13, 15, 16; 23:1–3   306

XIII. Aug. 26. *Into Exile* .... 2 Kings 25:1–12   312

FOREWORD

Here is your copy of TARBELL'S TEACHER'S GUIDE—lesson material printed on pages, bound in book form. A book, yes, but this Guide is more than just a book. It is the seventy-ninth annual edition of what has been acclaimed as a *teaching tradition*—one established by Martha Tarbell and edited by Dr. Tarbell for forty-four years. For the past thirty-five years, this Guide has been edited by Frank S. Mead, ably assisted in recent editions by William P. Barker.

Following a lifetime of service in the Lord, Dr. Mead—teacher, author, pastor, editor, and truly one of God's very special children—was called Home on June 16, 1982.

Dr. Mead is greatly missed by his loved ones, by his friends in Christian education and in the pastorate, and by his co-workers here at Revell. Consistent with Dr. Mead's plan for the ministry of TARBELL'S teaching tradition to continue, Dr. Barker has been named to serve as editor of this Guide next year and in the years to follow.

As they endeavored to make this Guide especially useful to its teacher users, Dr. Mead and Dr. Barker wrote with five objectives in mind:

1. To lead our readers to an awareness of God through His self-revelation in the Bible—that God was not only present at Eden and Sinai, but that in Christ He walks and wins in our world from Seattle to South Africa.
2. To know that He calls us to respond to Him in faith and love—a response in which action follows oral declaration of our faith or recitation of the Apostles' Creed.
3. To know who we are and what we are in fellowship with the God who gave us life.
4. To inspire growth in spirit and in knowledge of our Lord, maturing in development from the days when we spoke as children to the days of full spiritual maturity.
5. To lead us to abide with Him in Christian trust and faith, even unto the end.

In a challenge to teachers, Dr. Mead recently wrote, "An old, gnarled dead tree fell to the ground just beyond my study window. Men came and took it away, leaving a part of the stump, hardly visible in the growing grass. And lo, as the months and years passed, I saw a totally new tree growing from the stump, and I sit in my study and watch it grow. If God can do that with a tree, what more can He do for us!

"You are a sower of the seeds of the tree of faith, teacher! Your job, with the help of these lessons, is to teach awareness of this creative God, response to His love, fellowship with Him and His disciples, growth, and trust that with Him the old and outworn may be replaced with new and abiding faith. TARBELL'S may help you as you do this; God will help you more."

THE PUBLISHER

A WORD TO THE TEACHER

Opening the letters that come to us from teachers using TARBELL'S is something like opening Pandora's box: we never know whether the letter will be a blessing or a blast. Most of them are blessings, and we are grateful for that. But every now and then we get one that hits us like a blockbuster and makes us reach for our smelling salts.

One fine old lady, some years back, wrote us three times to ask the same question: "Why do you go on and on with those Uniform Lesson Outlines? Why can't you write your own outlines?" Well, if we could, we might do just that, but up to now we have found no better outlines. We have three reasons for saying that.

One is that the Uniform Lesson Outlines appeal all across the board to teachers in all of our churches. They are used in every "main line" denomination in the country, and many outside the main line; they are interdenominational. Second: they are Bible-based; if they were not, we would never use them. That is the base, the foundation of it all. Cecil B. DeMille said once, "After more than sixty years of almost daily reading of the Bible, I never fail to find it always new and marvelously in tune with the changing needs of every day."

Third: these Outlines are carefully prepared to lead out from the Bible to apply the Good News in every walk of life. The Lessons they prepare are not so much concerned with learning factual material of two thousand years ago so much as they are concerned with responses to the teachings of the Bible—responses, growth, fulfillment, acknowledgement of who we are (as children of God). It is Bible teaching plus biblical living *now*. The teacher must have a "follow up"; after he has led his students to memorize the verses of the Bible, he must convince them of the all-important value of *application*.

Years ago, we knew a fine young boy who was justly proud of his attendance record in the church school; he wore a long string of fifteen medals on his chest; he had not missed a session of Sunday School in fifteen years. That is good: we could use a few more like that. But his wise pastor said to him, "That's fine, Jerry, I'm proud of you. But tell me, Jerry, what has it *done* to you?"

Aye, that *is* a question we should all ask. We once heard the great evangelist Gypsy Smith say, "What makes the difference is not how many times you have been through the Bible, but how many times and how thoroughly has the Bible been through you?" That concept, that idea of reading-and-doing, should well be the aim and purpose of the church-school teacher. Study that Bible, yes: read it for its sheer beauty, a beauty unmatched by any other book. Read it as food for the hungry soul, read it for its stirring, haunting hymns and Psalms. But above all, read it to find and to put your feet in the footprints of a Master of life who can make of your life not a grinding, exhausting experience but an experience of beauty and high purpose—with Him.

Other books were given us for information; the Bible was written for our transformation. Whatever else the teacher may do, he or she *must* be, with Christ, a transformer. Otherwise, why teach at all?

God bless you all.
Frank S. Mead

79th Annual Volume
September 1983—August 1984

TARBELL'S
Teacher's Guide
to the International Sunday School Lessons
Includes the RSV and KJV

SEPTEMBER, OCTOBER, NOVEMBER 1983

OUR BIBLICAL FAITH

LESSON I—SEPTEMBER 4

GOD OF CREATION

Background Scripture: Genesis 1:1; Psalms 19:1–6; 136:3–9; Acts 17:24–28;
Romans 1:20
Devotional Reading: Psalms 136:1–9

KING JAMES VERSION

GENESIS 1   1 In the beginning God created the heaven and the earth.

PSALMS 19   1 The heavens declare the glory of God; and the firmament sheweth his handywork.

2 Day unto day uttereth speech, and night unto night sheweth knowledge.

3 *There is* no speech nor language, *where* their voice is not heard.

4 Their line is gone out through all the earth, and their words to the end of the world.

ACTS 17   24 God that made the world and all things therein, seeing that he is Lord of heaven and earth, dwelleth not in temples made with hands;

25 Neither is worshipped with men's hands, as though he needed any thing, seeing he giveth to all life, and breath, and all things;

26 And hath made of one blood all nations of men for to dwell on all the face of the earth, and hath determined the times before appointed, and the bounds of their habitation;

27 That they should seek the Lord, if haply they might feel after him, and find him, though he be not far from every one of us:

28 For in him we live, and move, and have our being; as certain also of your own poets have said, For we are also his offspring.

ROMANS 1   20 For the invisible things of him from the creation of the world are clearly seen, being understood by the things that are made, *even* his eternal power and Godhead; so that they are without excuse:

REVISED STANDARD VERSION

GENESIS 1   1 In the beginning God created the heavens and the earth.

PSALMS 19   1 The heavens are telling the glory of God;
and the firmament proclaims his handiwork.

2 Day to day pours forth speech,
and night to night declares knowledge.

3 There is no speech, nor are there words;
their voice is not heard;

4 yet their voice goes out through all the earth,
and their words to the end of the world.

ACTS 17   24 The God who made the world and everything in it, being Lord of heaven and earth, does not live in shrines made by man, 25 nor is he served by human hands, as though he needed anything, since he himself gives to all men life and breath and everything. 26 And he made from one every nation of men to live on all the face of the earth, having determined allotted periods and the boundaries of their habitation, 27 that they should seek God, in the hope that they might feel after him and find him. Yet he is not far from each one of us, 28 for 'In him we live and move and have our being'; as even some of your poets have said, 'For we are indeed his offspring.'

ROMANS 1   20 Ever since the creation of the world his invisible nature, namely, his eternal power and deity, has been clearly perceived in the things that have been made. So they are without excuse;

KEY VERSE: The heavens are telling the glory of God; and the firmament proclaims his handiwork. Psalms 19:1 (RSV).

HOME DAILY BIBLE READINGS

Aug. 29.   M.   *The Great Deeds of the Creator.* Psalms 136:1–9.
Aug. 30.   T.   *The Glory of the Creator.* Psalms 19:1–6.
Aug. 31.   W.   *The Word of the Creator.* Genesis 1:1–13.
Sept.   1.   T.   *The Incomparability of the Creator.* Isaiah 40:18–26.

Sept. 2. F.   *The Wisdom of the Creator.* Proverbs 8:22–31.
Sept. 3. S.   *The Majesty of the Creator.* Psalms 8:1–9.
Sept. 4. S.   *God of Creation and Resurrection.* Acts 17:24–31.

BACKGROUND

The thirteen sessions for this quarter gives us a study of some (not all) of the great basic affirmations of our Christian faith. It all begins with a consideration of things and thoughts and convictions that start with "the beginnings," with the great creative acts of the Creator. *Genesis* is the Greek word for "birth."

Actually, in the Scriptures, there is not just one but three accounts of the "birth" (beginning) of the universe and all within the universe. In Genesis 1, we see the Creation taking place in six days with the "creatures" (animals, birds, etc.) created *first* and man *last.* In Genesis 2, the story is different; here we find the act of Creation performed in one day, with man created first, and the animals last. Again, in Psalm 104 we see Creation as God's *continuing* activity, and God often working through the helping hands of men.

The background of the biblical creation stories clearly reflect a Babylonian influence. The old Babylonians had a Creation story which, in some places, closely resembles the Hebrew stories in Genesis. But the Genesis account is a great improvement over the Babylonian, and of far greater value to us. "Here," said the great Christian scholar Charles R. Erdman, "Here is the revelation of one God, infinitely powerful, wise and good, and an account of His relation to the origin of the world and to the history of nations. Here are recorded the beginnings of life, of sin, of apostasy, of punishment, of atonement, of worship, of prophecy, and of salvation. Genesis forms the first chapter in the history of redemption, which is the substance of the entire Bible. It points forward from a Paradise Lost to a Paradise Regained."

NOTES ON THE PRINTED TEXT

"In the beginning, God created the heaven and the earth." The earth was "Without form, and void." Another word for it is *chaos.* There was no established order; it was all desolation and emptiness, shrouded in darkness. But God was there! His Spirit (breath) brooded over the chaos, ready and able to give it order and beauty—and *life.*

Life! That was a lot more important than just establishing order; God's *purpose* in it all was to give to man a place to live and to grow in the knowledge and *love* of God. The act of Creation was a revelation of God's presence, power, and mercy. "When we say that Genesis means 'the beginning,' . . . we should think of it rather as the book that begins the story of God's intervention to save us from the consequences of our own pride and folly"—William Neil; in *Harper's Bible Commentary.*

The author of Psalms 19 tells us to forget our little man-made problems and look up at the heavens to see the mystery and the glory of God: "The heavens declare the glory of God; and the firmament sheweth his handiwork." It is good advice. There is a celestial harmony over all the heavens and the earth which reaches our hearts and makes us rejoice in the majesty of our Creator. The voice of the singing spheres go "through all the earth, and their words are heard to the end of the world."

Once we sat on a horse behind a Colorado cowboy; he was "a tough one," but he taught us a great lesson. As we sat on a high hill, we watched the sun rise in all its glory; he sat there speechless, with his hat in his hand. When it was over, we asked him, "Pete, were you praying while you sat there?" He replied, "Of course, I was praying. Can you watch a thing like that and *not* pray?"

An unknown poet has put it in these words:

> When I am with God
> My fear is gone
> In the great quiet of God.
> My troubles are as the pebbles in the road,
> My joys are like the everlasting hills.

This is the *continual* creation of God; it plants within us an awareness of God and a sense that when we are with Him, all life is changed—without Him—chaos!

In Acts 17, we have the famous sermon of Paul in Athens—the intellectual capital of the world. Athens laughed at Paul; he laughed right back at them in this startling sermon.

The Athenians, he said in effect, seemed to know everything about everything—except the true God. They carved on their altars the words, "To the Unknown God." They worshiped a God of whom they knew nothing. In their many temples, they bowed to graven images and idols which were helpless to satisfy their needs and longings. That, said Paul, was nonsense, if not blasphemy.

There was, he told them, but one *true* God, the God who made the world and everything in it, a God living not in temples but in the human heart. Powerful enough to create all the nations of men, this God was merciful enough to reach out to all manner of men everywhere and give them what idols and temples made with hands could never give them. He was not far from *any* man, anywhere. And this God stood ready to lighten every man's ignorance about these things provided they put away their idols and sought Him in spirit and in truth.

Your unknown god, and all the lesser gods of your temples in Athens, has never and never will accomplish that! There *must* be a God above all lesser gods; there *must* be but one all-powerful Creator.

If God were not this Creator, if He did not create the world and all within it—who *did?*

In Romans 1:20, Paul gives us his final word on salvation through the *true* God. Certainly there must have been Greeks who heard him and laughed at him and asked the question, "How could God blame (punish, or cast out) those heathen who did not *know* God. Paul never says that God has sent or will send people to hell for these or other sins. He says something more terrible: 'God gave them up.' He just took His hand away and let man do as he pleased. He let them create their own hell, living in a world they preferred to *His* world. . . . Paul's answer . . . is a short one: they were without excuse, because God's power and deity (Godhood) have been clearly perceived in the things He has made. In other words, the creation speaks to us of our Creator. To take for a god anything less than the Creator is to take the wrong turn."—Kenneth J. Foreman in vol. 21, *The Layman's Bible Commentary.*

SUGGESTIONS TO TEACHERS

Scientist Carl Sagan skillfully presented "Cosmos" on television a few years ago. The TV series and the book by the same title showed Sagan's appreciation of the ordered beauty of the universe. However, Sagan also insisted that blind chance made all of this possible. Sagan dismissed, even tried to discredit any notion of a Creator God bringing the universe and all its creatures into being and continuing to have a personal relationship with its human inhabitants.

Many persons share Sagan's philosophical worldview. "Cosmos's" blend of nature-mysticism, materialism, and scientism is both pervasive and persuasive. It, of course, contradicts the biblical story.

This series of lessons lays out the biblical story. Beginning today with the God of Creation, these Sundays are intended to help those in your class to understand better what God has done—and continues to do—as He reveals Himself.

1. *CREATES*. Have your class examine carefully the opening lines of the Bible: "In the beginning, *God*. . . ." Before anything was brought into being, behind all that is, stands the Creator. Note that there are no arguments for God's existence. Unlike the Greek philosophers, the biblical writers never tried to use human reason to "prove" God. Furthermore, these biblical authors understand that God is more than One who "is." This God creates, they emphasize. The purpose for which this God exists is to create!

2. *CARES*. Move your class discussion into a look at the lovely litanies about God's Creation in Psalms 136:1–9. In the face of scientist Sagan's claims of blind chance or mere accident governing the universe, help your class to understand better that God creates because He cares. There is a loving direction behind God's activities. Have your class share their perceptions of the universe, whether it is friendly or unfriendly, whether life is basically good or evil. Ask each on what basis are formed his or her viewpoints.

3. *COMPLETES*. Although some may wring their hands because the world seems so hopelessly messed up, the biblical claim is that God has not given up on His Creation. Moreover, this Creator concludes what He starts. He completed what He initiated. He never quits in disgust, as Acts 17:24–28 says, but perseveres with His Creation, especially through Jesus Christ. Try to draw out from your class times when each member felt that it was useless to continue. Remind your class that the Creator God insists on continuing His creative work in the life of each of the members of your class.

4. *CLARIFIES*. Romans 1:20, your class should take time to note, rings out the bold claim that the Creator shows His power and divine nature to everyone. Even the most irreligious person has some sense that he or she was created by a creator. Even the most insensitive man or woman is given hints that this universe is the handiwork and property of Another. Have your class list some of these hints, such as the beauties of nature, the miracle of birth, etc.

TOPIC FOR ADULTS
GOD OF CREATION

Elephants All the Way Down? A little boy once wondered what supports the world. So, he asked his father what holds up the world. The father answered that the world rests upon the back of a very large turtle. The answer sufficed for a day or two, but presently the son came back to ask what holds up the turtle. The turtle, said the father, rests upon the back of a very large tiger. The boy accepted this for a while, then wanted to know what holds up the tiger. The father, now committed to this line of thought and beginning to panic, said that the tiger rests upon the back of a very large elephant. Inevitably, the question arose: What holds up the elephant? The father was annoyed and finally sputtered, "Son, it's elephants all the way down!"

Is this silly nonsense—a universe without God as Creator—what do you think? You may not literally talk of "elephants all the way down," but you may forget that the Genesis story announces that the God of Creation made possible all that is. You may live with the assurance also that this same caring Creator continues to support the world.

Need to Understand God's Revelation. "George Gallup, Jr., has reported some 'worrisome findings' on the future of religion in America. The pollster said that while 94 percent of polled Americans claim a belief in God and nearly half of all adults attend church regularly, 'most Americans pray, but in an unstructured and superficial manner. . . . Prayers are usually prayers of petition rather than prayers of thanksgiving, intercession, or seeking forgiveness. God for some is viewed as a "divine Santa Claus." ' "

"Gallup said that 'many of the most deeply believing people are found outside our churches.' He added that the most ominous trend of all was 'the sorry state of biblical knowledge in our nation and the shocking lack of knowledge about the basics of our faith.'

"Six in ten teen-agers are unable to name any of the four Gospels of the New Testament; four in ten teens who attend church cannot do so.

"Three in ten teens say they do not know what religious happening is celebrated at Easter.

"One-third of teens do not know the number of disciples Jesus had, while one in five among regular churchgoers flunks this question."—Copyright 1981 Christian Century Foundation. Reprinted by permission from the May 13, 1981 issue of *The Christian Century.*

These facts underscore the need for this series of lessons. We must inform ourselves about the basics of our faith, starting at the beginning with the God of Creation.

Belief Problems. If the thought comes to you that everything that you have thought about God is mistaken and that there is no God, do not be dismayed. It happens to many people. But do not think that the source of your unbelief is that there is no God. If you no longer believe in the God in whom you believed before, this comes from the fact that there was something wrong with your belief, and you must strive to grasp better that which you call God. When a savage ceases to believe in his wooden god, this does not mean that there is no God, but only that the true God is not made of wood.

Questions for Pupils on the Next Lesson. 1. Do you think, with old Henry Ford, that "history is bunkum"? 2. Why must God's people remember His wonderful works? 3. Should we live mostly in the past, or mostly in the present, or mostly in the future, or what? 4. What happens to a group that forgets its heritage? 5. What are the "Roots" of the Church?

TOPIC FOR YOUTH
DO YOU SEE WHAT I SEE?

Einstein's Respect for God of Creation. Some young persons express great admiration for Carl Sagan, the eminent science teacher and television personality who speaks so condescendingly about belief in God. But the greatest scientist of our century, Albert Einstein, wrote, "My religion consists of a humble admiration of the illimitable superior Spirit who reveals himself in the slight details we are able to perceive with our frail and feeble minds. That deeply emotional conviction of the presence of a superior reasoning power, which is revealed in the incomprehensible universe, forms my idea of God."

Idea of God. "Sigmund Freud considered the idea of God an infantile illusion. Man, the oversized child, thought Freud, felt threatened and frustrated by the mystery of life and looked for a supernatural 'motherly' protection and an assurance of a Utopia.

"Some of Freud's immediate successors in the developing field of psychoanalysis didn't quite agree with his premises. The idea of illusion, however, persists today among atheists and cynics who regard the idea of God as caused by human inadequacy and wishful-thinking.

"The nonbelievers, of course, would never have us think that they ever feel inadequate or have illusions.

"Is the idea of God an illusion? And why do the majority of people believe there is a God?

"The Bible implies that man doesn't seek, find, or invent God, but that God seeks and finds man. The idea of God comes from God himself. The Bible records how God has dealt with humanity and also contains the record of how man has dealt with primary revelation."—Rev. Joseph Mohr. Reprinted with permission from *The Morning Call Weekender,* Allentown, PA; Saturday, July 18, 1981.

"See What I See?" A famous heart specialist was asked about his faith. How, his young questioner asked, could this noted surgeon-researcher take seriously a Creator-God?

The noted authority on cardiac problems replied, "If you saw what I see every time I work on a heart, you'd agree with me. The heart is one of God's master-pieces. Think of it! An organ no bigger than a fist, yet it beats over 100,000 times each day. And it pumps enough blood over a lifetime through the 60,000 miles of the average human circulatory system to fill 13 million barrels. In all this, I see the mind and energy of the God of Creation at work!"

Sentence Sermon to Remember: The universe is a thought of God.—Johann von Schiller.

Questions for Pupils on the Next Lesson. 1. Why do most youth seem to focus on the present? 2. Why is it important to remember our "Roots"? 3. What are the "Roots" of your church? 4. Do you think that God is still involved in human history? Why, or why not? 5. Where should a Christian put the most emphasis—on the past, or on the present, or on the future?

LESSON II—SEPTEMBER 11

GOD OF HISTORY

Background Scripture: Deuteronomy 26:5–10; Psalm 105; Acts 7:2–53
Devotional Reading: Deuteronomy 26:5–10

KING JAMES VERSION

PSALMS 105   4 Seek the LORD, and his strength: seek his face evermore.

5 Remember his marvellous works that he hath done; his wonders, and the judgments of his mouth;

6 O ye seed of Abraham his servant, ye children of Jacob his chosen.

7 He *is* the LORD our God: his judgments *are* in all the earth.

8 He hath remembered his covenant for ever, the word *which* he commanded to a thousand generations.

9 Which *covenant* he made with Abraham, and his oath unto Isaac;

10 And confirmed the same unto Jacob for a law, *and* to Israel *for* an everlasting covenant:

11 Saying, Unto thee will I give the land of Canaan, the lot of your inheritance:

37 He brought them forth also with silver and gold: and *there was* not one feeble *person* among their tribes.

38 Egypt was glad when they departed: for the fear of them fell upon them.

39 He spread a cloud for a covering; and fire to give light in the night.

40 *The people* asked, and he brought quails, and satisfied them with the bread of heaven.

41 He opened the rock, and the waters gushed out; they ran in the dry places *like* a river.

42 For he remembered his holy promise, *and* Abraham his servant.

43 And he brought forth his people with joy, *and* his chosen with gladness:

44 And gave them the lands of the heathen: and they inherited the labour of the people;

45 That they might observe his statutes, and keep his laws. Praise ye the LORD.

REVISED STANDARD VERSION

PSALMS 105   4 Seek the LORD and his strength, seek his presence continually!

5 Remember the wonderful works that he has done,
his miracles, and the judgments he uttered,

6 O offspring of Abraham his servant, sons of Jacob, his chosen ones!

7 He is the LORD our God;
his judgments are in all the earth.

8 He is mindful of his covenant for ever, of the word that he commanded, for a thousand generations,

9 the covenant which he made with Abraham,
his sworn promise to Isaac,

10 which he confirmed to Jacob as a statute, to Israel as an everlasting covenant,

11 saying, "To you I will give the land of Canaan
as your portion for an inheritance."

37 Then he led forth Israel with silver and gold,
and there was none among his tribes who stumbled.

38 Egypt was glad when they departed, for dread of them had fallen upon it.

39 He spread a cloud for a covering, and fire to give light by night.

40 They asked, and he brought quails,
and gave them bread from heaven in abundance.

41 He opened the rock, and water gushed forth;
it flowed through the desert like a river.

42 For he remembered his holy promise, and Abraham his servant.

43 So he led forth his people with joy, his chosen ones with singing.

44 And he gave them the lands of the nations;
and they took possession of the fruit of the peoples' toil,

45 to the end that they should keep his statutes,
and observe his laws.
Praise the LORD!

KEY VERSE: Remember the wonderful works that he has done.
Psalms 105:5 (RSV).

HOME DAILY BIBLE READINGS

Sept. 5.   M.   *Mighty Acts Recited.* Deuteronomy 26:5–10.
Sept. 6.   T.   *Deliverance Praised.* Exodus 15:1–10.

21

Sept. 7.   W.   Deliverance Forgotten. Micah 6:3–8.
Sept. 8   T.   Deliverance Hymned. Psalms 135:1–14.
Sept. 9   F.   Creation of Nation Remembered. Psalms 114:1–8.
Sept. 10   S.   Divine Purposes Resisted. Acts 7:51–60.
Sept. 11. S.   Faithfulness Required. Psalms 105:37–45.

BACKGROUND

The Psalms are hymns, religious songs; most of them are addressed to God, most of them used in public worship, some but not all of which are said to have been written by David. It is more likely that they were written over a long space of time by different and generally unknown poets or authors. It is probable that our Old Testament Book of Psalms is made up of small collections written at different times and places.

There is a great variety in these Psalms. A few of them seem to have been written in hatred, calling in bitterness for vengeance on Israel's enemies, but this is outweighed by the number of Psalms written to call the worshipers' attention to praising God and expressing their complete trust in Him. (Notice that Psalm 105, our Scripture for today, begins with the words, "O give thanks unto the Lord ..." and ends with the words "Praise ye the Lord.")

There is another arrangement here that we must understand as we begin to study this lesson. Some of the Psalms have a *personal* note: "The Lord is my shepherd; I shall not want." Others have a *national* significance and reference: they refer to what God has done with His nation Israel in the past. You will find the word *Remember* more than once in Psalm 105. (*See* verses 8, and 37–45.) God, says the Psalmist, "remembered" His covenant (with Israel) forever. So Israel is called upon to remember what God has done for them, and praise Him for His loving guidance of a people who were peculiarly His people.

What exactly was it that they should remember? *Why* should they praise Him? Why should we in twentieth-century America praise Him?

NOTES ON THE PRINTED TEXT

To prove his contention that God had constantly blessed Israel in her long history, the Psalmist goes all the way back to the beginning—back to Abraham, a seventy-five-year-old obscure man in Ur. To Abraham, He made a promise: "Get thee out of thy country, and from thy kindred, and from thy father's house, unto a land that I will shew thee: And I will make of thee a great nation ..." (Genesis 12:1). That was the "covenant." Abraham must have wondered why God had picked *him. Why me?* But he went! "... he went out, not knowing whither he went" (Hebrews 11:8). Canaan? Where was Canaan? Where was this promised land? Never mind that, said God to Abraham: He would guide them there. Go! It was no accident, this entry of Abraham into Canaan; God planned it that way. God in history!

Have you ever stopped to consider the fact that whenever a great crisis has risen in man's history, God has sent a man to resolve it? When religion in old England became unbearable, He sent the Pilgrim to a land in cold winter, a land of which they knew little or nothing, to found in the name of God, a great new nation. When the Continental army of the American Revolution was about ready to give up, God had a man named Washington on his knees in the snows of Valley Forge. Someone has said of Napoleon, who bathed Europe in blood, that "When God wearied of Napoleon, He took him!"

When Israel, in Canaan, seemed likely to die in famine, God raised a man named Joseph, a slave in mighty Egypt, and raised him from a prison cell to become "ruler over of all his (Pharaoh's) possessions." That was God's way of keeping His covenant—by filling Egypt's barns for Israel's sake.

Then came Moses! He came in the nick of time—God's time. Moses didn't exactly *want* to lead Israel out of Egypt; he ran from Egypt—but under the command of God, he went back to Egypt crying out to a tyrant Pharaoh, "Let my people go!" Pharaoh didn't want to let them go, but he was helpless before the enraged and consecrated Moses and the God of Moses.

Out into the wilderness they went. They were not so much a well organized people as they were a mob. More than once, in their wilderness wanderings, they were a petulant, complaining people who thought it might be better to go back to Egypt than to die in that wilderness. But before them, always, there was a pillar of cloud by day and a pillar of fire by night, guiding them. God overwhelmed their petty complaints and their lack of faith, and led them on, in spite of themselves. When they were hungry, He gave them manna and quails to eat; when they thirsted, He gave them water. They forgot their covenant; God never forgot it, nor them. He saw them through. "Praise the Lord," cried the Psalmist.

We make a mistake when we think that this happened only to Israel. What happened to them has happened time and again later to other men and nations. Says the Psalmist, "He is the Lord *our* God; his judgments are in *all* the earth." To put that in the present tense, we might say that God has had and still has a hand in the history of every nation in our world.

The poet Shelley called history "that record of crimes and miseries." He was wrong; J. A. Froude was nearer the truth when he said that history is "A voice forever sounding across the centuries the laws of right and wrong."

We vote for Mr. Froude. Being Christians, and the inheritors of the faith of Abraham, Moses, and Joseph, we believe that history is the slow and painful march toward the kind of world that God intended it to be.

SUGGESTIONS TO TEACHERS

J. B. Phillips as a pastor in London used to ask the teen-agers in his parish if they thought that God understood radar. Almost without exception, his young people answered *No*. Phillips, dismayed at their notions of such a tiny and trivial God, went on to make a fresh translation of the Scriptures.

You could start today's lesson by asking your class the same kind of question; however, you may discover that many regard the Lord in the category of a senile grandparent in a distant nursing home. Contrast this notion with the biblical material in this lesson in which God acts in history!

1. *EMPHASIS ON EVENTS.* Unlike most of the other world's religions, the biblical faith does not rest on myths and legends, fantasies and speculation. The Creator God of Scripture is not like Zeus cavorting with goddesses and toying with humans. Nor is the God of the Bible like the divinities of Eastern philosophies, remote and cool, and disinclined to bother with human affairs. From Genesis to Revelation, the Bible stresses that God acts in history. It emphasizes events. Reread Deuteronomy 26, Psalm 105, and Acts, selections in today's Scripture readings, and note the way these widely diverse writings accent incidents from human lives in which God was present and at work. Ask your class whether God is still at work in events today.

2. *INTEREST IN THE OPPRESSED.* In each of the passages selected from a wide variety of sources in the Bible, the message is the same: God is obsessively concerned about those who are hurting, especially the poor and the downtrodden. Have your class relate the story of the Hebrews' sufferings and injustices under the Pharaoh. Ask your class to examine the passages in today's lesson—the "creed" recited at the dedication of the harvest festival (Deuteronomy 26:5–10), the beautiful hymn chanted in worship (Psalm 105), the speech by Stephen at his trial (Acts 7:2–53)—which underscore God's interest in the oppressed. If God is acting in history today (as the Bible insists!) have your class identify the oppressed in which He must be interested at this time.

3. *ACCENT ON ACTION.* "All religions are the same" is the claim of many well-intended but misinformed people. The story of the Bible is simply not the same as, say, the story of the Buddhists or the Hindus. Without trying to find flaws or pick fights with Eastern religions or others, you should remind your class that the biblical God is busy. He is not merely "being"; He is actively *doing.* He creates. He makes and keeps promises to humans, including Abraham and his descendants. He gives land. He protects the weak. He frees the enslaved. He sends deliverers. He hears the cries of those in trouble. He feeds. Encourage your class to comment on ways in which this same God has been in action in our lives today.

4. *INSISTENCE ON INVOLVEMENT.* Move your lesson to its climax in God's greatest involvement in our stories through the Crucifixion and Resurrection of Jesus Christ. Look carefully at Stephen's recapitulation of the acts of God in history, culminating in Christ. Stephen was confident that the Lord continues to involve Himself in human affairs. Are your people? Ask your class to describe what God is busy doing now.

TOPIC FOR ADULTS
GOD OF HISTORY

Need the Christian Hope. Over twenty years ago, Dr. Phillip Potter, the ecumenical leader, was on a brief visit to Christian church leaders in Czechoslovakia. Late one night, a group of Marxist intellectuals came to his hotel room in Prague.

"Is it true," they asked Potter, "that the 'death of God theology' is sweeping through the West?"

Dr. Potter was taken aback that a group of Marxist intellectuals would be asking about the "death of God theology," and asked in turn, "But why is this of such concern to you?"

The spokesman for the Marxist delegation replied, "Because there is no future without transcendence. You are Christians. God is the basis of transcendence. If you have lost God, you have no transcendent principle to transform the present. We are in the same business of creating a new world. We need your companionship to build that future. And you need God, because we need the principle of hope."

Even some Marxist thinkers must acknowledge that God is at work in history. Without our awareness that the Lord is the Ruler of history, we Christians lose hope.

Forgetting God's History. On Sunday, June 29, 1981, Bill Maupin announced that he and his followers in the Lighthouse Gospel Tract Foundation would be bodily lifted up to heaven within the following twenty-four hours. Maupin, then fifty-one years old, had quit his wrought-iron business the previous year to "get the message out" and prepare for the ascension. He served as head of the group of forty to fifty people who belong to his Lighthouse Gospel Tract Foundation, and insisted that true believers in Jesus Christ, living or dead, would be taken up to heaven in the process known as *rapture* on or before noon, June 29, 1981. Maupin and his followers were so certain of the date of their ascension to heaven that he and many others sold their homes and belongings. "We're going," Maupin announced. "I'm more sure of that than anything I know."

Sadly, Bill Maupin and his followers have not read the rest of their Bibles. They fail to understand that God is the God of history. They ignore the biblical story of God's past, present, and future involvement in our human story. Instead of focusing morbidly on present ills and imagining a dramatic future intervention for a favored few, they could better "remember the wonderful works that He has done" (Psalms 105:5) and work with God in history. Christians never try to escape history. They learn from it and work within it.

Reconnecting to the Past. The word *religion* comes from the Latin word *reli-*

gare. It means to bind back, to link again, to reconnect. Early Christians thought of religion as reconnecting them to the Lord who works in history. Religion was binding them to the divine story which is still unfolding.

Do you think of your religion as linking you with Abraham, Moses, the prophets, with Jesus and the disciples, the reformers and the saints?

Questions for Pupils on the Next Lesson. 1. What, frankly, do you think a *Prophet* is? 2. Are there prophets speaking God's Word today? If so, who are they? 3. Who in your church has unique gifts for communicating? Would you call them prophets? 4. What kind of leaders do you follow? 5. What are the standards of leadership that you hold most important?

TOPIC FOR YOUTH
LISTEN AND LEARN

God's Monument. "Where is God today? What evidence do we have of Him?" Perhaps you hear people asking these questions, or are asking them yourself.

In St. Paul's Cathedral in London, a marker with a Latin inscription gives the epitaph for the architect, Sir Christopher Wren, who designed the magnificent cathedral. The marker states: "Lector, Si Monumentum Requiris, Circumspice" ("Reader, if you seek his monument, look around you").

The same could apply for the Lord. If you want to see evidence of His involvement and presence, look into the biblical story. Look around you now. He is still the Lord of history!

God Above Kings. Thomas à Becket was the trusted crony of Henry II, king of England in the turbulent twelfth century. Henry wanted dependable yes-men in his service, and made Becket Lord Chancellor of the realm. Later, the temperamental, moody king appointed Becket Archbishop of Canterbury. Becket resisted. King Henry II, however, commanded. Against his will, Thomas à Becket was installed as archbishop.

Becket then fought to defend the role and realm that had been thrust upon him. "You are indeed my Lord," he reminded the king, "but Almighty God is your Lord as well as mine." Thomas à Becket remembered that God is Lord of all and works in history. Inevitably, he and the king clashed repeatedly.

Henry II pouted that no one could cut the archbishop down to size, and four knights rode to Canterbury Cathedral. As they waved their swords and confronted Thomas à Becket before the altar, Becket told them, "I am ready. I die for my Lord, that in my blood the Church may obtain liberty and peace." When the attackers approached to slay him, he said, "Here I am, no traitor, but a priest of God." He was martyred for his unswerving allegiance to the Lord of History. He had listened and learned that God is involved in human affairs.

Listening and Learning From Fun Costs. What do you think God is thinking in the light of what fun-loving Americans are spending on leisure activities?

From 1965 to 1981, the outlays for sports, recreation, and entertainment went from $58 billion to $244 billion. In real terms, after allowing for inflation, leisure spending shot up 47 percent during this period. While fun-seeking Americans laid out those billions of leisure dollars, 70 percent of the world's people still have no access to uninfected water and therefore experience chronic disease and death for their infants.

Sentence Sermon to Remember: God never sleeps; He is eternally awake, and busy.—J. E. Barnes.

Questions for Pupils on the Next Lesson. 1. What is your definition of a prophet? 2. Are there phony prophets? 3. What do you look for in a leader? 4. Who should speak for God? 5. What are your leadership qualities?

LESSON III—SEPTEMBER 18

GOD OF INSPIRED PROPHETS

Background Scripture: Deuteronomy 18:15–22; Amos 7:10–15, 5:21–24;
Micah 6:8
Devotional Reading: Amos 7:1–9

KING JAMES VERSION

DEUTERONOMY 18 15 The LORD thy God will raise up unto thee a Prophet from the midst of thee, of thy brethren, like unto me; unto him ye shall hearken;

16 According to all that thou desiredst of the LORD thy God in Horeb in the day of the assembly, saying, Let me not hear again the voice of the LORD my God, neither let me see this great fire any more, that I die not.

17 And the LORD said unto me, They have well *spoken that* which they have spoken.

18 I will raise them up a Prophet from among their brethren, like unto thee, and will put my words in his mouth; and he shall speak unto them all that I shall command him.

19 And it shall come to pass, *that* whosoever will not hearken unto my words which he shall speak in my name, I will require *it* of him.

20 But the prophet, which shall presume to speak a word in my name, which I have not commanded him to speak, or that shall speak in the name of other gods, even that prophet shall die.

21 And if thou say in thine heart, How shall we know the word which the LORD hath not spoken?

22 When a prophet speaketh in the name of the LORD, if the thing follow not, nor come to pass, that *is* the thing which the LORD hath not spoken, *but* the prophet hath spoken it presumptuously: thou shalt not be afraid of him.

AMOS 5 21 I hate, I despise your feast days, and I will not smell in your solemn assemblies.

22 Though ye offer me burnt offerings and your meat offerings, I will not accept *them;* neither will I regard the peace offerings of your fat beasts.

23 Take thou away from me the noise of thy songs; for I will not hear the melody of thy viols.

24 But let judgment run down as waters, and righteousness as a mighty stream.

MICAH 6 8 He hath shewed thee, O man, what *is* good; and what doth the LORD require of thee, but to do justly, and to love mercy, and to walk humbly with thy God?

REVISED STANDARD VERSION

DEUTERONOMY 18 15 "The LORD your God will raise up for you a prophet like me from among you, from your brethren—him you shall heed—16 just as you desired of the LORD your God at Horeb on the day of the assembly, when you said, 'Let me not hear again the voice of the LORD my God, or see this great fire any more, lest I die.' 17 And the LORD said to me, 'They have rightly said all that they have spoken. 18 I will raise up for them a prophet like you from among their brethren; and I will put my words in his mouth, and he shall speak to them all that I command him. 19 And whoever will not give heed to my words which he shall speak in my name, I myself will require it of him. 20 But the prophet who presumes to speak a word in my name which I have not commanded him to speak, or who speaks in the name of other gods, that same prophet shall die.' 21 And if you say in your heart, 'How may we know the word which the LORD has not spoken?'—22 when a prophet speaks in the name of the LORD, if the word does not come to pass or come true, that is a word which the LORD has not spoken; the prophet has spoken it presumptuously, you need not be afraid of him.

AMOS 5 21 "I hate, I despise your feasts, and I take no delight in your solemn assemblies.

22 Even though you offer me your burnt offerings and cereal offerings,
I will not accept them,
and the peace offerings of your fatted beasts
I will not look upon.

23 Take away from me the noise of your songs;
to the melody of your harps I will not listen.

24 But let justice roll down like waters, and righteousness like an everflowing stream.

MICAH 6 8 He has showed you, O man, what is good;
and what does the LORD require of you
but to do justice, and to love kindness,
and to walk humbly with your God?

KEY VERSE: *I will raise up for them a prophet like you from among their brethren; and I will put my words in his mouth, and he shall speak to them all that I command him.* Deuteronomy 18:18 (RSV).

HOME DAILY BIBLE READINGS

Sept. 12. M. *The Prophetic Role.* Deuteronomy 18:15–22.
Sept. 13. T. *The Prophetic Call.* Jeremiah 1:4–10.

Sept. 14. W. *The Prophetic Commission.* Ezekiel 3:16–21.
Sept. 15. T. *The Prophetic Responsibility.* Amos 7:10–15.
Sept. 16. F. *The Prophetic Cry for Justice.* Amos 5:21–27.
Sept. 17. S. *The Prophetic Cry of Woe.* Amos 6:1–7.
Sept. 18. S. *The Prophetic Cry of Hope.* Habakkuk 3:16–19.

BACKGROUND

In the early days of Israel, there were leaders appointed by the people or chosen of God. There were local judges (another word for them was *clerks*), who were heads of families in the various clans or tribes; there were local judges and superior judges, who rendered justice; local courts and a superior court; priests— and prophets. The prophets, beginning with Moses, had a highly important place in God's dealings with Israel. They might be diviners or "seers," or predictors of future events, or ecstatics who prophesied in a state of ecstasy. But their particular function was to hear, and speak; they were to hear messages from God and then proclaim those messages to the people. In the Hebrew, the word for prophet is *nabi,* which meant "to bubble forth," like a fountain; in the Greek language, the word meant "one who speaks for another" or "who speaks for a god." Our English word was borrowed from the Greek.

They were men of great power in Hebrew society; the Prophet Nathan pointed his finger in shame at King David, and Moses defied a Pharaoh in Egypt. Certain that God spoke to him personally, the prophet relayed God's message and commandments to the people, fearlessly and unconcerned as to how painful might be the result of his speaking. The prophets had a way of making people mad, and that was good for Israel.

NOTES ON THE PRINTED TEXT

The word *Deuteronomy* comes from a word in the Greek translation which means "repetition of the law" given to Moses on Mount Horeb nearly forty years earlier. Israel is encamped in the great wilderness somewhere south of the Dead Sea, just before the death of Moses and Israel's entry into Canaan. Knowing that he will shortly die, Moses gave three long speeches (1:1–4:43, 4:44–28:69, and 29:1–30:20). *The Living Bible* puts the whole book in quotation marks. Moses speaks as a prophet as well as an interpreter of laws laid down by God. In our Scripture for this lesson, he speaks of the coming of a future Prophet (better, the coming of a whole line of prophets) "like unto me; unto whom ye shall hearken." And he tells his people what these prophets shall be like and whether or not they are to be "hearkened" to. There will come false prophets, as well as true ones. How shall the Israelites know "which is which"? What is the test of a true, God-accepted prophet?

The first and primary test is this: listen to all the prophets, *but wait and see whether or not the prophecy will come to pass.* If a prophet predicts that God will desert His people at such and such a date, and then does not desert them, it is false prophecy. If some hocus-pocus magician poses as a prophet and promises a miracle that doesn't happen, don't listen to him! Yes, a true prophet just might predict events which do not happen, but that may be because of a change in the morality of the people he is speaking to. But prophecy in the biblical sense is something far more than predictions of the future; it is a declaration of the will of God in relation to the practical (and moral) conduct of men (as, for instance, in the prophecies of the Prophet Amos).

Amos! He was the last man we might expect to become a prophet; he was an obscure herdsman in Tekoa, a wilderness desert near Bethlehem with a sun that could drive a man mad. He came roaring out of Tekoa with a torch in his hand, and he set Israel aflame. He told the Israelites that they were a disgrace to God: they pretended to love Him, and they lied: their actions betrayed their lack of faith and their hypocrisy. They oppressed the poor, selling them for a pair of shoes; they prayed—and persecuted; they stored up violence and robbery in their palaces; they offered sacrifices to gain the favor of God, and God was outraged at that. They celebrated feast days ("for the Lord!") and the smoke of their false feasts was a stench in the nostrils of their God. Amos despised it, and all their (hypocritical) assemblies. God's punishment for all this would fall upon them. This was prophecy based upon the immorality of a people who had forgotten that faith must be proved in *action*. Amos prophesied punishment for that. They were punished.

Change your ways, Israel, before it is too late. Seek again the Lord you once honored—seek God, and not evil, that you should live as your God commanded. "Let judgment (justice) run down as waters, and righteousness as a mighty stream" (Amos 5:24).

Could that be aimed at us as well as to the Israelites? Shall we, in the mightiest nation in the world, live only to become rich and richer, to the neglect of the laws of God?

The Prophet Micah appeared after Amos, and he added what might be called a postscript, or an addition, to the prophecy of the man from Tekoa. He summed it all up in one short sentence (in Micah 6:8). What, he asked, did the Lord require of His people, of every man, everywhere, at any date? The Lord required that man "do justice"; that he do what was right and fair and just between men; he who deals not justly is not acceptable as a worshiper of God. He should "love mercy." The RSV says he should "love kindness" and that may be the better translation. Mercy may be better than justice in many cases; kindness may be better than both. Lastly, man should "walk humbly with your God." James V of England put it well: "God resisteth the proud, but giveth grace to the humble." There is no better definition of true faith than in that one line in Micah 6. If a man not live justly, friendly, and humble, he has no right to call himself a Christian.

SUGGESTIONS FOR TEACHERS

Cartoonists depict anyone dealing with prophecy as wearing a tattered robe and sandals, having a shaggy beard and staring eyes, and carrying a sandwich board stating, THE END IS NEAR. To many, that's a prophet: a sort of religious crackpot who claims to foretell the future.

Today's lesson, continuing the series in which God reveals Himself, centers on the way He reveals Himself through inspired persons. The cartoonists' picture of a prophet may be the notion many have, so you may as well start the lesson by asking what your class members think a prophet is. Move on quickly to comparing their misconceptions of prophets and prophecies to the biblical accounts.

1. *AUTHORIZED AS INTERMEDIARIES.* Instruct your class in the way prophets in the Bible were called and used by God as divine go-betweens. Prophets were to let God's people know what God intended them to be and to do. Take a few minutes in your lesson to urge your class to consider who God's intermediaries or prophets are today. Ask whether the Church should have such a role. If the Church is to be a prophet, is your congregation carrying out its task as intermediary for the Lord?

2. *SELECTED AS SPOKESMEN.* Technically, in Hebrew, the word *prophet* means one who speaks for God. "God's spokesman," not a weirdo-fortuneteller type, is who a biblical prophet is. Point out to the class that God's spokesmen never talked in pious generalities. Nor did God's spokesmen pretend to foretell what's happening in September, 1983. The prophets spoke forcefully about God's activity in their times, and called God's people to be obedient to Him. Discuss whether God's prophets today are necessarily always in the organized church. Who are some of the prophetic voices in our land?

3. *SUSPECTED AS SUBVERSIVES.* If God's prophets were truly tuned in on what God had in mind for their times, and if these spokesmen acted faithfully, they usually discovered they were not always welcome. Being a prophet, in fact, rarely won a popularity contest. To the contrary, most prophets learned that people don't want God interfering with their human plans. Take Amos as an example. Devote enough lesson time with this doughty intermediary and spokesman for the Lord to illustrate the point that prophets are almost always disliked and rejected. Remind your class that Christians may also expect to encounter opposition whenever they live as prophets. The Church will be suspected also as "subversive" by those who resent its prophetic role.

4. *CONSISTENT AS CLARIFIERS.* Budget plenty of class time to work with Micah 6:8. Have your class take note of what the Lord wants of each member of His community *now!* Prophets like Micah consistently clarify what God expects us, His people, to be and to do in our times. Have your class members talk over how exactly Christians are to "do justice," to "love mercy," and to "walk humbly with your God."

TOPIC FOR ADULTS
GOD OF INSPIRED PROPHETS

Prophet Without Profit. "No great prophet ever decided, 'I've nothing better to do this afternoon, so I'll offer the Lord my service as an immortal missionary, with financial profit, of course.' With rare exceptions, the prophets were originally reluctant to obey the call, and after they obeyed they were neither happy nor financially affluent. They had to march to the beat of a different drummer and face opposition. They suffered and died, something which few would do for illusions."—Rev. Joseph Mohr. Reprinted with permission from *The Morning Call Weekender,* Allentown, PA; Saturday, July 18, 1981.

Historian as Prophet. A prophet is one who sees what God is doing in the world. The truly prophetic voices tell what God has in mind for us, and call us to account. In *Christianity and History,* written shortly after the conclusion of World War II, Herbert Butterfield, professor of modern history at the University of Cambridge, insists on a moral factor in history, one which does react upon those flouting it. Thus he vindicates the insight of the Old Testament prophets. "Though some offenses may pass at first without a reckoning," he wrote, "yet if we presume upon such immunity, these old debts may accumulate at compound interest and may still have to be met when the moment comes for the final settlement of the account."

Remember! Prophets remind God's people to recall their duties to God. Rudyard Kipling assumed such a prophetic role at the time of Queen Victoria's Diamond Jubilee. In attendance for the celebration were an empress, a crown prince, twenty-three princesses, a grand duke, three grand duchesses, four ordinary duchesses, forty Indian potentates (riding three abreast, gorgeously decorated) and the papal nuncio sharing a carriage with a representative of the emperor of China.

Fifty thousand troops tramped through London. The British Empire spanned the globe. Victoria reigned in splendor over one quarter of the human race. The British proudly assumed that they would continue to rule indefinitely over a world map on which "the sun never sets on the British Empire." Kipling, as the popular and premier writer of the day, was asked to write a poem commemorating the magnificent celebration on June 22, 1897. It was assumed that he would produce a stirring epic praising Imperial power. Instead, Kipling wrote a humble hymn, warning his countrymen to remember the Lord of nations. Kipling's prophetic lines were not appreciated at the time. Nonetheless, the world pays little attention to the pomp and memory of Queen Victoria today, but repeats with reverent whisper Kipling's prayer:

God of our fathers, known of old,
    Lord of our far flung battle line
Beneath whose awful hand we hold
    Dominion over palm and pine:
Lord God of hosts, be with us yet,
    Lest we forget—lest we forget.
The tumult and the shouting dies,
    The captains and the kings depart;
Still stands thine ancient sacrifice,
    an humble and contrite heart.
Lord God of hosts, be with us yet,
    Lest we forget—lest we forget.

Questions for Pupils on the Next Lesson. 1. What is God's fullest revelation of Himself? 2. Why was God's revelation in Jesus Christ not immediately obvious? 3. In what ways does Jesus reveal the nature of God? 4. What was the Hebrew people's understanding of the spoken Word? 5. Was there any inconsistency between Jesus' words and actions?

TOPIC FOR YOUTH
TUNE IN TO THE MESSENGERS

Prophet on Horseback. Two hundred years ago, there was bitter rivalry between Christian groups, often centering on theological dogma or interpretation. In the midst of the narrowing emphasis, Francis Asbury came preaching. He was one of John Wesley's missionaries to the New World and became the first bishop of the infant American Methodist Church. In 1782, when he was thirty-seven years old and out on horseback encouraging the conversions that formed the Methodist societies, he wrote in his journal:

"I see God will work among Mennonites, Dunkers, Presbyterians, Lutherans, Episcopalians, Dutch, English—no matter: the cause belongs to God."

Like his spiritual mentor, Paul, he put emphasis on the work of God—not the work of humans. Therein he found the source of unity: our common life in Christ. Asbury is revered as a prophet in the American Church.

God's Orders. Many Christians were disappointed when the Vatican appointed Monsignor Oscar Arnulfo Romero as Archbishop of El Salvador in 1977. Archbishop Romero was not one of the "liberation theologians." He had never been known to speak out. When the violence which has wracked El Salvador continued, Archbishop Romero began criticizing the repression and violence by both leftist and rightist extremists. He also tried to get the government security forces to cease killing innocent civilians. In March, 1980, he declared from his pulpit: "No soldier is obliged to obey an order contrary to the law of God. It is time you come to your senses and obey your conscience rather than follow sinful commands."

A few days later, while celebrating mass in his cathedral in San Salvador, gunmen burst in and assassinated him. God's messenger might have been killed, but his message has not been stilled. Other prophets in San Salvador have been inspired to speak out.

Prophet for Peace. The world aches for world political leaders to reduce the idiotic confrontation between nuclear superpowers. Most Americans want U.S. defenses strengthened, yet at the same time for arms control negotiations to go on between us and the Russians. Nobody has put this better than a veteran diplomat and student of Russia, former ambassador George F. Kennan. His words are those of a biblical prophet: "The superpowers are on a collision course. Communication between them seems almost to have broken down. We are building a type and volume of weaponry which could not possibly be used without utter disaster. . . .

"What I would like to see the President do, after due consultation with the Congress, would be to propose to the Soviet government an immediate across-the-boards reduction by 50 percent of the nuclear arsenals now being maintained by the two superpowers—a reduction affecting in equal measure all forms of the weapon, strategic, medium-range and tactical, as well as all means of their delivery—all this to be implemented at once and without further wrangling among the experts, and to be subject to such national means of verification as now lie at the disposal of the two powers."—*Parade*, July 19, 1981.

Sentence Sermon to Remember: A prophet is not without honour, save in his own country, and in his own house.—Matthew 13:57.

Questions for Pupils on the Next Lesson. 1. How does God show us what He is like? 2. Do you take seriously the claim that Jesus Christ is God's fullest revelation? 3. How does Jesus reveal God's nature? 4. Can you think of any inconsistencies between what Jesus said and what He did? 5. If God is like Jesus, why are some people afraid of Him?

LESSON IV—SEPTEMBER 25

GOD IN CHRIST

Background Scripture: John 1:14–18; 14:8–11; Hebrews 1:1–4; 1 John 1:1–4
Devotional Reading: John 1:14–18

KING JAMES VERSION

JOHN 14   8 Philip saith unto him, Lord, shew us the Father, and it sufficeth us.

9 Jesus saith unto him, Have I been so long time with you, and yet hast thou not known me, Philip? he that hath seen me hath seen the Father; and how sayest thou *then,* Shew us the Father?

10 Believest thou not that I am in the Father, and the Father in me? the words that I speak unto you I speak not of myself: but the Father that dwelleth in me, he doeth the works.

11 Believe me that I *am* in the Father, and the Father in me: or else believe me for the very works' sake.

HEBREWS 1   1 GOD, who at sundry times and in divers manners spake in time past unto the fathers by the prophets,

2 Hath in these last days spoken unto us by *his* Son, whom he hath appointed heir of all things, by whom also he made the worlds;

3 Who being the brightness of *his* glory, and the express image of his person, and upholding all things by the word of his power, when he had by himself purged our sins, sat down on the right hand of the Majesty on high;

4 Being made so much better than the angels, as he hath by inheritance obtained a more excellent name than they.

1 JOHN 1   1 THAT which was from the beginning, which we have heard, which we have seen with our eyes, which we have looked upon, and our hands have handled, of the Word of life;

2 (For the life was manifested, and we have seen *it,* and bear witness, and shew unto you that eternal life, which was with the Father, and was manifested unto us;)

3 That which we have seen and heard declare we unto you, that ye also may have fellowship with us: and truly our fellowship *is* with the Father, and with his Son Jesus Christ.

4 And these things write we unto you, that your joy may be full.

REVISED STANDARD VERSION

JOHN 14   8 Philip said to him, "Lord, show us the Father, and we shall be satisfied." 9 Jesus said to him, "Have I been with you so long, and yet you do not know me, Philip? He who has seen me has seen the Father; how can you say, 'Show us the Father'? 10 Do you not believe that I am in the Father and the Father in me? The words that I say to you I do not speak on my own authority; but the Father who dwells in me does his works. 11 Believe me that I am in the Father and the Father in me; or else believe me for the sake of the works themselves.

HEBREWS 1   1 In many and various ways God spoke of old to our fathers by the prophets; 2 but in these last days he has spoken to us by a Son, whom he appointed the heir of all things, through whom also he created the world. 3 He reflects the glory of God and bears the very stamp of his nature, upholding the universe by his word of power. When he had made purification for sins, he sat down at the right hand of the Majesty on high, 4 having become as much superior to angels as the name he has obtained is more excellent than theirs.

1 JOHN 1   1 That which was from the beginning, which we have heard, which we have seen with our eyes, which we have looked upon and touched with our hands, concerning the word of life—2 the life was made manifest, and we saw it, and testify to it, and proclaim to you the eternal life which was with the Father and was made manifest to us—3 that which we have seen and heard we proclaim also to you, so that you may have fellowship with us; and our fellowship is with the Father and with his Son Jesus Christ. 4 And we are writing this that our joy may be complete.

KEY VERSE: In many and various ways God spoke of old to our fathers by the prophets: but in these last days he has spoken to us by a Son. Hebrews 1:1, 2 (RSV).

HOME DAILY BIBLE READINGS

Sept. 19.   M.   *The Word Made Flesh in Christ.* John 1:9–18.
Sept. 20.   T.   *God Well-Pleased in Christ.* Mark 1:1–11.
Sept. 21.   W.   *The Hidden Mystery in Christ.* Ephesians 3:7–21.
Sept. 22.   T.   *The Way in Christ.* John 14:1–14.
Sept. 23.   F.   *Servanthood Exalted in Christ.* Philippians 2:5–10.
Sept. 24.   S.   *God's Glory Reflected in Christ.* Hebrews 1:1–14.
Sept. 25.   S.   *God Made Manifest in Christ.* 1 John 1:1–10.

BACKGROUND

We are studying doctrines in the lessons for this quarter. What is a doctrine? It is a teaching, a belief, which expresses an article of faith. The basic doctrine of our Christianity is our doctrine of belief in Jesus Christ. Who and what was Jesus Christ?

There has always been confusion about that—even at the Last Supper among disciples who, we think, should have known by that time who and what He was. When Jesus told them that He was about to leave them by way of crucifixion, Peter blurts out, "But *where* are you going?" Peter would say that! Thomas the Doubter was in that group; he, too, had his doubts (John 14:5). When Jesus said that His Father, who has been among them, would be with them after He (Jesus) has gone, Philip says, "Lord, shew us the Father, and it sufficeth (satisfies) us."

We should not ridicule Philip for asking that. At one time or another, we all ask ourselves that, and we should; if we ask no questions, we will never find any answers!

NOTES ON THE PRINTED TEXT

Jesus called God *Abba* (Mark 14:36), and *Abba* is the word by which a Jewish child calls his father—a father great in wisdom and love. Our children often say to their playmates, "My father is better than your father!" The father is the ruler of their homes; he provides for them, guides them, teaches them. Just so the Father, to Jesus, was the God who created man and his world, who seeks to guide us His children. What the word really means is that it settles the problem of our relationship to God, the supreme Father of all, and to look at Jesus is for us to see God the Father. In 2 Corinthians 4:6 we read of "the knowledge of the glory of God in the face of Jesus Christ." "The two are so bound together that to be in touch with one is to be in touch with the other"—Floyd V. Filson.

Jesus did not work independently of God; "My meat is to do the will of him that sent me, and to finish his work"; "Not my will, but thy will be done"; "he that hath seen me hath seen the Father" (working through Christ).

John goes further; he has Jesus saying that if they would really know Him, they should *look at what He has done and that He still does.* He healed, He brought men back to allegiance with God. He taught as no other teacher had ever taught. He did great works. He changed the face of the world. He promised that His disciples would do yet greater works—by which He meant that they would gather great flocks of believers into the one flock to which He looked forward (John 10:16).

As God in the flesh, Jesus was and is the greatest revelation of God ever to visit our earth. Says Dr. William Barclay, "If we call Jesus the divine Word, we are saying that He is the means of God's communication with us and that He is the expression of the thought of God. In Jesus, God communicates with people; in Jesus we can see the perfect expression of the mind of God."—From *Who Is Jesus,* The World Methodist Council, publishers.

In Paul's Epistle to the Hebrews (possibly written jointly by Paul and Apollos about A.D. 67) we have another glorious picture of Jesus, another explanation of what and who He was. It starts with the declaration that God, long before Jesus came, gave the Jews many different glimpses of His Truth. *Glimpses* is a good word for it. The early Jewish prophets provided views and ideas and revelations that were inspiring and utterly sincere. But the prophets differed, considerably, about all this. Their revelations were fragmentary, lacking in unity. It was a series of revelations given in different ways; it came through dreams or visions, or through a burning bush, or through the angel of the covenant, or in a "still small voice," or in some other way. It was good, but not good enough. We call it the *old* revelation. But now, with Jesus, we find a totally "new revelation."

It was one and the same God who gave us both revelations, but the latter was far better than the former: God now speaks to man through "a Son." Jesus, as the Son of God, "bears the stamp of the 'glory of God'—a phrase which in both Hebrew and Greek stands for the showing forth of God's real nature"—John Wick Bowman. The two revelations, old and new, are linked together as the chapters of a story are linked together, with the Christ becoming the ultimate conclusion, the last chapter in the drama of the Father.

It is this Son who was the fulfillment of all the hopes and promises of God to Israel—". . . the creative power that shaped the universe, the human embodiment of the essential being of God, who has made us at one with God by His offering of Himself, and has now taken His rightful place as Lord of all."—William Neil.

Far greater than any other at any time, far greater than the angels of heaven, is this Christ. His name in none other than Him lies our salvation: "for there is none other name under heaven given among men, whereby we must be saved" (Acts 4:12).

First John 1 is a call to fellowship with the Christ who was present "from the beginning." The Gospel According to John (the Apostle) starts with the same declaration. Before anything else existed, there was Christ with God—which means that Christ is *eternal.* The power, the divinity which worked within Him, is as old as time! The mind of God *which we saw* in Him as He walked the earth, which offered us redemption through the Son, is the same mind which was behind Creation. Knowing that, how can we not believe in both God *and* Son? We have *seen* Him, said Paul, seen Him with our own eyes. Some have even *touched* Him. He intimates that it is foolishness to argue about that. Having understood that, we are obligated to have fellowship with Him, the eternal, living Christ, to accept Him for what He was and did.

To quote Dr. Barclay again—"He was, He is, He will be. He came, He comes, He will come." Knowing this, and in fellowship with Him, our joy shall be *full.*

SUGGESTIONS TO TEACHERS

A college student doing a term paper on Islam was surprised to learn that there is a reference to Jesus in the Koran. Supposing that this reference (which she had not bothered to look up for herself) reinforced her notion that "all religions boil down to the same thing," the student jubilantly wrote that Jesus, Mohammed, Gautama Buddha, Confucius, and Zoroaster are all part of a "hall of fame of great religious leaders." Had the young woman investigated the reference to Jesus in the Muslim Koran, she would have been startled to discover that the Koran downgrades Jesus and distorts His message. Sincere Muslims would be the first to disagree with her thesis that Jesus and Mohammed are look-alikes in her hall of fame.

Your lesson for today is to help your class members clarify their thinking about Jesus Christ. This means guiding them into a deeper understanding of Jesus Christ as the supreme revelation of God. Working with the scriptural material for this lesson, call attention to the following key points about Jesus:

1. *SUMMARIZES THE DIVINE.* Jesus is God's Word enfleshed. If one takes the claims of the writers of the New Testament seriously, Jesus must be regarded as more than one more great guru, or even the greatest of anything, whether teacher, leader, thinker, idealist or whatever. Although Jesus is, of course, the "greatest" in any category of human greatness, He simply cannot be pegged. John's Gospel must be taken seriously when it makes the astonishing claim that God Himself became incarnate or took human form in the person of Jesus. As teacher of this lesson, you may wish to have each class member write a brief statement of who Jesus is, in order to stir some thinking.

2. *SUSTAIN THE UNIVERSE.* Little boys like to play with models of cars, trains, airplanes, etc. These tiny replicas may satisfy children, but they are hardly the real thing. The same thing is true with God. Many church people have a match-box toy version of the Lord. They have scaled down the Almighty. The biblical writers insist that Jesus Christ has cosmic importance. For example, Hebrews 1:2, 3 shouts about Jesus Christ as sustainer of the universe. How big is the God of people in your class?

3. *STANDS AS SUPREME.* Point out the way each New Testament writer in his own unique way insists that Jesus surpasses every other. This includes John the Baptist, and also the angels and heavenly beings. The litmus test of Christ's supremacy, however, lies in the realm of the everyday life of the people in your class. Bring this to focus by asking whether Jesus is supreme when it comes to deciding how one spends his or her money, or uses free time, or selects a job, or deals with disagreeable persons.

4. *SHARES GOD'S LIFE WITH US.* The passages in the Gospel of John and the Letter of John all underline the friendship God wants to have with each of us, and which He has initiated through Jesus Christ. Draw out your class on the relationship each person has with Jesus Christ personally.

TOPIC FOR ADULTS
GOD IN CHRIST

How God Lives in the World. Christians must look to Jesus who is the "promise that God is for us and that God will not bail us out. We might wish to escape the world, but it would be good news to have God's pledge that God will not leave us or withdraw the divine presence. And that is exactly what God in Christ makes plain (Romans 8:30).

"In the presence of Jesus in the experience of the first witnesses, we discern what God is doing, how God lives in the world, how God rules in such a way that his involvement is good news, that the presence of God is a source of power and not only a sympathetic presence. Jesus is the final norm for experiencing the way God lives and rules in the world.

"Thus the suffering and the oppressed people of the world have a special access to experiencing God's presence because, by virtue of the Incarnation, God has opened himself to suffering. When Jesus was crucified, God suffered the loss of the beloved Son . . . God's suffering is the consequence of God's loving involvement in the world. Suffering is often what happens to lovers. It is good news, then, to know that when we fail, or suffer loss, or experience oppression, we are not thereby isolated from God, but, in fact, brought into fellowship with all fellow sufferers through the experience."—Lee E. Shook, LCA/Partners, June 1981.

The Approachable God. When Prince Charles was married to Lady Diana Spencer in July, 1981, millions watched the fairy-tale wedding and celebrations. Many were awed by the elaborate etiquette required of those who were presented to the Queen. Some of those who met the Queen had to consult *Buel's Manual of Self Help: A Book of Practical Counsel, Encouraging Advice and Invaluable Information.*

In *Buel's Manual,* they learned that the following protocol was expected of a lady in a long dress: "Upon leaving her carriage she must carry nothing in her hands, for both will be needed to manage her train. As she enters the ante-room and meets there the lord-in-waiting, she drops her train, which has been carried thus far folded carefully over her left arm. At this juncture the lords-in-waiting adjust and spread her train by the use of their wands and then direct her to the presence chamber, taking her card at the same time and passing it on to the royal attendant, who reads it aloud.

"The lady being thus announced goes forward until she approaches within a few feet of the royal person, usually to the edge of the dais, and then bows as low as possible. At this the Queen will present her hand to be kissed, but if it be a king, he merely returns the courtesy, whereupon the lady retires, with her face toward the sovereign until she has passed through the exit door.

"Great presence of mind and not a little dexterity are necessary to prevent awkwardness, if not mishap, in thus moving backward, for the lady must not pick up her train, but must manage it as best she can with her feet."

Taking their cue from earthly monarchies, some persons think that they dare not approach the Almighty without going through impossibly complicated rituals. They assume the Lord is offended if the necessary distance and awe are not maintained. They also take it for granted that basically God just does not care to be approached. He chooses to remain aloof and regal.

The supreme revelation of God is in Jesus Christ. In Jesus, we see the Lord of all the universe who lays aside all splendor and chooses to be among us because He loves us!

Heart Knowledge. A young agricultural expert and his wife prepared to serve Christ's Church as missionaries in rural India. They prepared themselves carefully by going to language school to study Marati, the local language. They immersed themselves in reports so that they knew an incredible number of statistics about the health and deaths, production and per capita income. They were particularly well versed in the facts about infant mortality: that 240 out of every 1,000 live births died before they reached their fifth birthday. Their intellectual knowledge impressed many, but they did not seem to be able to gain acceptance by the villagers they were trying to serve. One afternoon, after being in India for two years, their little three-year-old daughter complained of not feeling well, and was found to have a high fever. That evening, in spite of valiant efforts to save her, the child died. The heartbroken couple buried her the following day, as is customary in that area.

Suddenly, children's deaths were more than a statistic. The missionary couple learned the personal significance of losing a child in India. With insiders' knowledge of the meaning of grief over the death of a little one, they were able to relate to the villagers in ways they never had before.

God comes to us with an insider's understanding of our hurts and needs. He also knows the meaning of suffering and loss. God was in Christ, experiencing our humanity in every way.

Questions for Pupils on the Next Lesson. 1. How would you define sin? 2. Should Christians speak of "Sin" or "sins"? 3. Is anyone free of sin? 4. What are some of the capacities for evil that you see in yourself? 5. Why do we tend to ignore the seriousness of sin?

TOPIC FOR YOUTH
MEET GOD IN PERSON

Known by Name. Helen Keller was a famous writer and speaker who suffered from being completely blind and deaf from an early age. Although severely handicapped and forced to live in a world with no sounds or light, Miss Keller became one of the best loved and respected personalities in the late nineteenth and early twentieth century. One time when she was very young, Phillips Brooks tapped out a message on her hand about Jesus. Miss Keller nodded and replied, "Yes, I always felt there must be Somebody. So now I know His name."

The Somebody we all have always felt must be present is named Jesus. God comes to meet us in person through Jesus Christ!

Became One of Them. God came as one of us. In Jesus, He meets us in person. We, in turn, are to be extensions of the Incarnation.

Mary Slessor was one who understood the Good News that God was in Christ. She was a self-educated lass from the slums of Dundee who had a brilliant mind and who became one of the most remarkable women the world has known. She went to work in Calabar which is now a province of modern Nigeria.

Calabar had for two centuries been a center of the slave trade. Over a million slaves had been shipped out of its anchorage and thousands of others had died there or been butchered because they were too sick to travel. The trade had jumbled up different tribes, destroyed their old way of life and their culture, and had perverted their religion. Its cruelty had spread like a virus from the anchorage up the rivers and through the forests. To bring order out of chaos the Egbo secret society had been founded to rule the area by terror. The people accepted that appalling cruelties were part of everyday life, that they always had been, and that they always would be.

As Nigerian historians agree, scores of slaves were slaughtered at the funerals of chiefs to provide an escort into the spirit world, women had no personal rights as citizens and could be flogged or killed with impunity, and unwanted children were thrown out to die.

The Scottish Mission had been working in the anchorage townships since 1845. But the ruling tribe, the Efik, had barred it from going to live among the up-river tribes, and the forest tribes had chased out its numbers. They were a handful of dedicated people. Twenty-eight of them had died of fever over the years and about the same number were sent home with their health ruined. In the anchorage, they had achieved a great deal: slaves were no longer slaughtered, or babies thrown out to die, and the conditions under which the women and the slaves lived were much improved. But they were trapped in the anchorage and unable to help all the hundreds of thousands of people beyond it who were still living under the cruel legacy of the slave trade.

Mary Slessor brought a new dimension to their work. When she had helped her local minister to tackle the problems of the slums of Dundee she had not been an outsider but one of the slum people. In Calabar, she decided not to go on being an outsider but to become an African. Over twelve years she studied their language, their religion, laws, and customs, and prepared herself to do without European food, mosquito nets, and water-filters, and to live in mud huts and go barefoot. Then she broke out of the anchorage and went into the forests to live with the tribes and to put herself beyond any law but theirs.

They could have killed her. Instead, within a few months, she had become a respected member of her first tribe and, during the twenty-eight years in which she lived and worked in the forests, she became so special to them all that in a world of cruelty and killing no one offered violence to her of any kind. She stopped battles, executions, and floggings, rescued unwanted children, treated the sick and set up community groups round the little mud churches-cum-schools which she built and which she encouraged the people to run themselves. She could only do this because she did not live in a different world, but in theirs, as one of them.

Gradually she took much of the cruelty and violence out of their lives. She was often near to death from fever and malnutrition and crippled in her later years by rheumatism, while her possessions would not have filled a suitcase. But her influence was felt over hundreds of square miles.

The True Person. Hans Küng, one of the most distinguished and highly regarded theologians of today, wrote in his book, *Does God Exist?*: "As the true man (Jesus), in whom theory and practice, being and action, teaching and life, form a unity, by His proclamation, His behavior and His whole fate, He is for me a model of being human. If I trustingly rely on this model, it enables me to discover and realize the meaning of my being human and of my freedom in existing and involving myself for my fellow men."—From DOES GOD EXIST? by Hans Kung. Copyright © 1978, 1979, 1980 by Doubleday & Company, Inc.

Sentence Sermon to Remember: As the print of the seal on the wax is the express image of the seal itself, is Christ the express image—the perfect representation of God.—St. Ambrose.

Questions for Pupils on the Next Lesson. 1. What is your definition of "sin"? 2. Why do most people smile when "sin" is mentioned? 3. What are your loyalties in life at this time? On what basis do you choose these? 4. What are some of the gods which youth create? 5. What, as you see it, is the main human predicament?

LESSON V—OCTOBER 2

THE PROBLEM: SIN

Background Scripture: Jeremiah 2:9–13; Romans 1:18–2:29
Devotional Reading: Romans 2:5–11

KING JAMES VERSION

JEREMIAH 2 9 Wherefore I will yet plead with you, saith the LORD, and with your children's children will I plead.

10 For pass over the isles of Chittim, and see; and send unto Kedar, and consider diligently, and see if there be such a thing.

11 Hath a nation changed *their* gods, which *are* yet no gods? but my people have changed their glory for *that which* doth not profit.

12 Be astonished, O ye heavens, at this, and be horribly afraid, be ye very desolate, saith the LORD.

13 For my people have committed two evils; they have forsaken me the fountain of living waters, *and* hewed them out cisterns, broken cisterns, that can hold no water.

ROMANS 1 18 For the wrath of God is revealed from heaven against all ungodliness and unrighteousness of men, who hold the truth in unrighteousness;

28 And even as they did not like to retain God in *their* knowledge, God gave them over to a reprobate mind, to do those things which are not convenient;

29 Being filled with all unrighteousness, fornication, wickedness, covetousness, maliciousness; full of envy, murder, debate, deceit, malignity; whisperers,

30 Backbiters, haters of God, despiteful, proud, boasters, inventors of evil things, disobedient to parents,

31 Without understanding, covenant-breakers, without natural affection, implacable, unmerciful:

32 Who knowing the judgment of God, that they which commit such things are worthy of death, not only do the same, but have pleasure in them that do them.

2 1 Therefore thou art inexcusable, O man, whosoever thou art that judgest: for wherein thou judgest another, thou condemnest thyself; for thou that judgest doest the same things.

11 For there is no respect of persons with God.

REVISED STANDARD VERSION

JEREMIAH 2 9 "Therefore I still contend with you, says the LORD, and with your children's children I will contend.

10 For cross to the coasts of Cyprus and see, or send to Kedar and examine with care; see if there has been such a thing.

11 Has a nation changed its gods, even though they are no gods? But my people have changed their glory for that which does not profit.

12 Be appalled, O heavens, at this, be shocked, be utterly desolate, says the LORD,

13 for my people have committed two evils: they have forsaken me, the fountain of living waters, and hewed out cisterns for themselves, broken cisterns, that can hold no water.

ROMANS 1 18 For the wrath of God is revealed from heaven against all ungodliness and wickedness of men who by their wickedness suppress the truth.

28 And since they did not see fit to acknowledge God, God gave them up to a base mind and to improper conduct.

29 They were filled with all manner of wickedness, evil, covetousness, malice. Full of envy, murder, strife, deceit, malignity, they are gossips,

30 slanderers, haters of God, insolent, haughty, boastful, inventors of evil, disobedient to parents,

31 foolish, faithless, heartless, ruthless.

32 Though they know God's decree that those who do such things deserve to die, they not only do them but approve those who practice them.

2 1 Therefore you have no excuse, O man, whoever you are, when you judge another; for in passing judgment upon him you condemn yourself, because you, the judge, are doing the very same things.

11 For God shows no partiality.

KEY VERSE: *All have sinned and fall short of the glory of God.*
Romans 3:23 (RSV).

HOME DAILY BIBLE READINGS

Sept. 26. M.   *The Evils of God's People.* Jeremiah 2:9–13.
Sept. 27. T.   *"My Sin Is Ever Before Me."* Psalms 51:1–12.
Sept. 28. W.   *No Excuse.* Romans 1:18–23.
Sept. 29. T.   *"God Shows No Partiality."* Romans 2:1–11.
Sept. 30. F.   *"Doers of the Law."* Romans 2:12–16.
Oct.   1. S.   *"Will You Not Teach Yourselves?"* Romans 2:17–24.
Oct.   2. S.   *"A Matter of the Heart."* Romans 2:25–29.

BACKGROUND

Both Judaism and Christianity have struggled for ages against one great, common plague. It is not a physical plague, but a spiritual one. It is a plague or a curse called sin, and it is as old as Eden, as current in modern times as it was in ancient times.

The time came when Israel, religiously, was almost bankrupt. To tell the people just how repulsive they had become in sin, God called a young twenty-year-old man named Jeremiah, who reared up among the Hebrews like a human cyclone. He was hated, despised, feared, persecuted, and threatened with assassination. He was a lonely voice, God's voice, speaking out in a wilderness of sin. That was about 626 B.C.

About A.D. 57, God called another man to lead the Christian fight against sin. This was Paul. Things were better in Paul's day than they were in Jeremiah's but not much. Like the old prophet, Paul roared like a lion against sin; he told the Christians in Rome that in a way, in spite of the coming of Christ, they were not much better than the pagan Romans!

Of what *kind* or manner of sin was he talking about?

NOTES ON THE PRINTED TEXT

Jeremiah prophesied during the reigns of the last five kings of Judah—a time of trouble. There had been a steady downgrade in Judah since the days when King Hezekiah and King Josiah brought about great reforms in the worship and practices of the Jewish faith, but that had all "gone down the drain." Under the kings who succeeded Hezekiah and Josiah, the people of Judah had slowly and deliberately forsaken God; they had fallen so low that they worshiped heathen gods—idols made with their own hands! Among all the crowds in Jerusalem, Jeremiah said, there was not even one "upright" (faithful) man to be found. For that desertion of God, the prophet said, Jerusalem would be destroyed. It was destroyed.

What had they done? What was their sin? They had substituted pagan gods for their true God who had so long been to them "the fountain of living waters" (verse 13). They had "built cisterns" to hold the stale, stagnant waters of heathen gods who were worth nothing. Even the heathen knew better than to do that; the heathen nations held fast to their gods worthless as they were, but the people of Judah and Israel gave up their God and went chasing after silly, pagan idols. It was fatal nonsense: the cisterns they had built to hold the waters of paganism couldn't hold any water at all!

It was, and is, an old, old story and a grim one. Shakespeare wrote well when he wrote that "There is a divinity that shapes our ends, Rough-hew them how we will." That is as true of nations as it is of men. A recent prominent Russian who fled to the United States put it in a nutshell when he said that he had fled Communism simply because "it just doesn't work." History proves his point. No nation, turning its back on God, can long endure; the fate of Jerusalem and Judah awaits any nation that tries it.

The Apostle Paul wrote a good letter to the Christians in Rome about sin. He wrote from Corinth, a wicked city, and to Rome which also was wicked.

He goes back to review some Jewish history. Back there, before Christ came, even the Hebrews had committed many grievous sins; they knew better, but they didn't care. They sinned against God, and for that God "let them go" (Romans 1:24). What else could God do with such a people? When a man makes up his mind to do whatever he wants to do, good or bad, God lets him go, so that he might discover for himself what the wages (penalties) of sin truly are.

But, someone says, "How *could* God blame the heathen, when they didn't know any better?" Ah, but they *did* know better. They had heard the early prophets condemning them for living lives that were an insult to God—lives of plain sin; they knew well what God had done for them in a past that reached all the way back to His creation of mankind. They heard those prophets predict disaster, destruction, at the hand of an outraged God. "For the wrath of God is revealed from heaven against *all* ungodliness and unrighteousness of men who hold the truth in unrighteousness" (Romans 1:18).

Now the Christian Jews were quick to condemn the unrighteous, paganized, non-Christians. They pointed the finger of shame at those awful heathen! Paul told them that before they did that, they should take a good look at themselves! Were they not, many of them, guilty of the same sins the pagans had committed? Judge not, lest ye be judged!

The sins Paul worried about were not the sins of idol worship as they were the deep-seated sins of the heart, mind, and soul. That is, sins of unrighteousness, fornication (sex), covetousness, envy . . . read the rest of the list in Romans 1:29, 30. It is almost too horrifying to read.

Paul hurled all these accusations at Christian Jews who were, he suggests, even worse in their sinning than the heathen were. Christ had come among them to make God's will and love for them plain, and they had crucified Him. Their sin was greater than that of the pagans because they had seen Him and heard Him. Their excuses were foolishness. They were never to be saved because they were God's peculiar people; God made no distinction, was no respecter of persons, shows no partiality. His judgment will fall upon unrighteous men, Jewish and Gentile alike.

It might help *us* to look to our own sins before we condemn the sins of others!

SUGGESTIONS TO TEACHERS

Writer G. K. Chesterton, who was a shrewd observer of human nature and also a good lay theologian, penned the line, "the good news of original sin." At first, some of his readers recoiled. Those raised in the pollyanna tradition that people are basically sweet and nice ("there's no such thing as a bad boy") took Chesterton to task. Chesterton, however, knew his Bible as well as the human situation. People must face up to their problem as sinners before they can be helped.

Your lesson today is to aid those in your class to have a good look at the basic human problem—to see themselves as they really are. Only when they see and accept the dark side to their lives will they be able to receive the light of salvation.

1. *DIAGNOSIS.* You will discover that some in your class may not be happy with having themselves described as sinners. Point them to the Bible passages in today's lesson, reminding them that the Lord diagnoses the case of humans like a skillful physician examining a patient who may not want to accept the seriousness of the illness, or that the Lord brings serious charges against people who scoff at all laws. Note the charges. God states that humans insist on exchanging God for gods; Jeremiah states it well: instead of drinking from a fresh flowing spring, we depend on the brackish contents of leaky, cracked cisterns!

2. *DELUSION.* Part of the destructiveness of sin is the way we will lie to ourselves and others about ourselves. Evil persuades us to live in the delusion that we

are right. The phony life follows. Allow lots of lesson time to study what Jeremiah and Romans say about the destruction which takes place when we live the lie. It is helpful even to list as many forms of delusion as can be seen in the Scripture, such as ingratitude toward God and corrupted forms of behavior.

3. *DARKNESS.* "Their senseless minds were darkened," Romans 1:21 describes those who allowed the lies about God and themselves to take hold and rule their living. Every person in your class has had times when his or her senseless mind was darkened. Here is the result of human delusions: *Darkness!* You will be doing your class a great service by helping them to identify some of the forms of the darkness resulting from human sin, including guilt, fear, anxiety, loneliness, alienation.

4. *DELIVERANCE.* Be careful, however, that you don't put your lesson on such a negative note that people think that the problem of sin makes their situation completely hopeless. The day's lesson must not close in a minor key but with the great crashing triumphant trumpet chord of "God has redeemed His people!" Through Jesus Christ, God has dealt effectively with the delusions and darkness in which every human finds himself or herself! God diagnoses the human situation accurately and precisely; God also acts to save us from the destruction which threatens us!

TOPIC FOR ADULTS
THE PROBLEM: SIN

Disease of the Soul. "Sin is a disease of the soul that keeps the wars raging in life. Such a disease eats away at the heart, separating it from God and peace.

"Sin is man's biggest problem. All other conflicts or symptoms can be traced, eventually, to man's sin, his desire to do his own thing and ignore the ways of God.

"Sin causes separation between man and his Creator. When such a separation persists, man finally falters for he was not designed by his Creator to live his life outside the ways of God.

"Sin dulls the perspective of life because it shuts out the view of God. And life that does not have the Godward-view will run off course and stall in selfish pursuits.

"Sin drains the heart, for it causes one to live against the tide. Man was intended to live in harmony with his Creator. Where sin breaks such harmony, the high tides of disharmony soon threaten the plans of life."—C. Neil Strait, *Quote,* July 1, 1981.

The Blind Spot. Thomas Nast, the well-known cartoonist, was on one occasion present with other guests at a party. He drew a caricature of everyone present and then passed them around for all to see. The result was quite interesting. Everyone present recognized the caricature of every other person and enjoyed a hearty laugh. But there was a large group who could not recognize their own pictures. So it is with all of us. Everyone has his blind spot. This is sin. We fail to see ourselves as we really are.

Threat to Our Future. "I do not believe the greatest threat to our future is from bombs or guided missiles. I do not think our civilization will die that way. I think it will die when we no longer care—when the spiritual forces that make up the wish to be right and noble die in the hearts of men. Arnold Toynbee has pointed out that nineteen of twenty-one notable civilizations have died from within and not by conquest from without. No bands were playing. No flags were waving when these decayed. It happened slowly, in the quiet, and in the dark when no one was aware. . . .

"If America is to grow great, we must stop gagging at the word, *spiritual.* Our task is to re-discover and re-assert our faith in the spiritual, non-utilitarian values on which American life has rested from its beginning."—Dr. Laurence Gould, former President of Carleton College, Northfield, Minnesota.

Questions for Pupils on the Next Lesson. 1. Does God love us because we love Him, or is it the other way around? 2. How has God shown His love for us? 3. When were you most aware of receiving love? 4. How do you reconcile God's love with His judgment? Can He be both Lover and Judge? 5. Are there any limits or restrictions on God's love?

TOPIC FOR YOUTH
YOU GOT A PROBLEM

Most Villainous of History. Recently, professors of politics and history at the Catholic University of America took a vote and came up with the "ten most villainous people in history." This collection of infamous people, in their opinion, was guilty of the most horrible sins of all. The list includes the following:

Caligula, despotic Emperor of Rome from A.D. 37 to 41: *Nero,* full-time emperor and sometime violinist who struck sour notes in Rome from 54 to 68; *Attila the Hun,* who led his barbaric tribe from 433 to 453; *Ivan the Terrible,* nogoodnik tsar of Russia from 1547 to 1584; *Catherine de Médicis,* Machiavelli-mentored queen of France from 1547 to 1589 and noted butcher of Protestants; *Abdul-Hamid II,* murderous ruler of the Ottoman Empire from 1876 to 1909; *Joseph Stalin,* Soviet leader from 1929 to 1953; *Adolf Hitler,* an automatic club member as leader of Nazi Germany from 1933 to 1945; *Mao Tse-tung,* Chinese Communist leader from 1949 to 1976; and the only living honoree, Uganda's brutish, exiled dictator *Idi Amin.*

God's list, however, would also include each of us. He knows us well enough to point out that there is something of the Caligula, Nero, Attila, Ivan, Catherine, Abdul-Hamid, Stalin, Hitler, Mao and Amin in each of us. Our problem is that each of us secretly or openly has a streak of cruelty, lust, and insensitivity in us. God sees the despot that lurks in each of us!

More Than Private Piety. A few years ago, a religious body selected what is called "The Christian Statesman of the Year." With great fanfare and publicity, the religious group presented the award to a well-known senator from a southern state primarily because he neither smoked nor drank. Elaborate attention was drawn to the way he turned his back on "sin." Although the senator's private morals were pious, his social ethic was primitive. This national leader had long opposed civil rights and campaigned for years on a segregationist platform. He had vigorously fought all legislation ending segregation and offering justice for black citizens.

Sin is more than lack of personal piety. Sin has to do with failure to work to end oppression. Sin has a societal dimension!

Remembering Our Mortality. King Philip II of Macedonia, father of Alexander the Great, was a wise man. He ordered one of his servants to come to him every morning without fail, and, no matter what the king was doing, declare loudly, "Remember, Philip, that you must die."

Today we discourage negative thoughts about ourselves—especially the fact of our mortality. We bury subversive truths about ourselves below the level of consciousness and try to forget them, but they are still there. Or we resort to euphemisms. Criminals are usually called "good boys" by their mothers; society calls them "sick." People do not commit fornication; they simply "make love." People are not poor; they are underprivileged. People do not die; they "fall asleep." We do not kill our terminally ill pets, we "put them to sleep." Soldiers in Vietnam destroyed a village to "save it."

The only other thing to do is to face the truth and tell it "like it is."

Every day God must catch our attention, and like the loud cry of Philip's servant, remind us that humans are wrongdoers, finite, and mortal.

Sentence Sermon to Remember: The deadliest sins are the consciousness of no sin.—Thomas Carlyle.

Questions for Pupils on the Next Lesson. 1. If someone from another religion asked you what example you could give of God's love, what would you tell him? 2. Which comes first: our love for God or His love for us? 3. What is an occasion when you have experienced unconditional love? 4. Does God ever draw the line when it comes to loving some people? 5. How do you know that God really cares about you?

LESSON VI—OCTOBER 9

THE MOTIVE: GOD'S LOVE

Background Scripture: Hosea 11:1–4, 8; 14:4–7; John 3:16–18; 1 John 4:8–12
Devotional Reading: John 3:16–18

KING JAMES VERSION

HOSEA 11 1 When Israel *was* a child, then I loved him, and called my son out of Egypt.

2 *As* they called them, so they went from them: they sacrificed unto Baalim and burned incense to graven images.

3 I taught Ephraim also to go, taking them by their arms; but they knew not that I healed them.

4 I drew them with cords of a man, with bands of love: and I was to them as they that take off the yoke on their jaws, and I laid meat unto them.

8 How shall I give thee up, Ephraim? *how* shall I deliver thee, Israel? how shall I make thee as Admah? *how* shall I set thee as Zeboim? mine heart is turned within me, my repentings are kindled together.

14 4 I will heal their backsliding, I will love them freely: for mine anger is turned away from him.

5 I will be as the dew unto Israel: he shall grow as the lily, and cast forth his roots as Lebanon.

6 His branches shall spread, and his beauty shall be as the olive tree, and his smell as Lebanon.

7 They that dwell under his shadow shall return; they shall revive *as* the corn, and grow as the vine: the scent thereof *shall be* as the wine of Lebanon.

1 JOHN 4 8 He that loveth not knoweth not God; for God is love.

9 In this was manifested the love of God toward us, because that God sent his only begotten Son into the world, that we might live through him.

REVISED STANDARD VERSION

HOSEA 11 1 When Israel was a child, I loved him,
and out of Egypt I called my son.

2 The more I called them,
the more they went from me;
they kept sacrificing to the Baals,
and burning incense to idols.

3 Yet it was I who taught Ephraim to walk,
I took them up in my arms;
but they did not know that I healed them.

4 I led them with cords of compassion,
with the bands of love,
and I became to them as one
who eases the yoke on their jaws,
and I bent down to them and fed them.

8 How can I give you up, O Ephraim!
How can I hand you over, O Israel!
How can I make you like Admah!
How can I treat you like Zeboiim!
My heart recoils within me,
my compassion grows warm and tender.

14 4 I will heal their faithlessness;
I will love them freely,
for my anger has turned from them.

5 I will be as the dew to Israel;
he shall blossom as the lily,
he shall strike root as the poplar;

6 his shoots shall spread out;
his beauty shall be like the olive,
and his fragrance like Lebanon.

7 They shall return and dwell beneath my shadow,
they shall flourish as a garden;
they shall blossom as the vine,
their fragrance shall be like the wine of Lebanon.

1 JOHN 4 8 He who does not love does not know God; for God is love. 9 In this the love of God was made manifest among us, that God sent his only Son into the world, so that we might live through him.

KEY VERSE: He who does not love does not know God, for God is love. 1 John 4:8 (RSV).

HOME DAILY BIBLE READINGS

Oct. 3. M. *"How Can I Give You Up?"* Hosea 11:1–9.
Oct. 4. T. *"I Will Heal Their Faithlessness."* Hosea 14:1–9.
Oct. 5. W. *"Thou Knowest Me Right Well."* Psalms 139:7–18.
Oct. 6. T. *"God So Loved the World."* John 3:16–21.
Oct. 7. F. *"The Free Gift of God."* Romans 6:15–23.
Oct. 8. S. *"No Condemnation."* Romans 7:21–8:4.
Oct. 9. S. *"Love Is of God."* 1 John 4:7–12.

BACKGROUND

In order to properly understand Hosea, we have to look back to Amos. Both were great prophets, but they differed in their prophecies. Both of them lived and worked in the northern kingdom of Israel. Both of them saw clearly what was about to happen in Israel, but they had different conceptions of the God of Israel. Amos was a thunderer, echoing the wrath of God; Hosea was a prophet speaking for a God whose other name was Love. One was the soul of fury, the other the essence of tenderness.

Only yesterday on TV, we saw a high building in New York City come crashing down. Dynamiters had placed their explosives in its foundation, and a great crowd stood on the sidewalks, waiting breathlessly for the building to come down. There was nothing the crowd could do but watch and wait. Both Amos and Hosea were like that; they knew that Israel was about to come crashing down; they watched and waited for the blow to come.

In Amos's view, there was nothing anybody could do about it; Israel deserved what was about to happen to her; all they could do was to accept the judgment of God and face extinction at the hands of the Assyrians. He scolded, and condemned; he was an angry man speaking for an angry God.

But Hosea wasn't mad; he was heartbroken. And he saw a great hope for the future which Amos never saw.

NOTES ON THE PRINTED TEXT

We have read the first three chapters of Hosea to find out why he felt the way he did about it all. In those chapters, we find a suffering, almost beaten man who mourned for an unfaithful wife, Gomer. Gomer had left him, deserted him, gone off to become a temple prostitute and finally a slave. It was out of his grief that Hosea's preaching of a God of love was born. This wife of his was a repulsive character; most husbands would have cut such a woman out of their lives or turned her over for punishment. In both Old and New Testaments, the punishment for an adulterous woman was death by stoning—and many a woman suffered that fate. Such a death was about to come to the woman taken in adultery in the story of Jesus in the eighth chapter of John: Jesus refused to condemn her; He said to her, "Go, and sin no more!" And that was about what Hosea would have said—*did* say. He never stopped loving Gomer; he forgave her, and took her back into his home.

Based on this experience, Hosea preached to doomed Israel of a God who had always loved them, and always would. In tears he spoke words of his God of love for Israel: "How can I give thee up. . . . Ephraim (Israel)." How could God destroy them, wipe them out, as He had wiped out the lost cities of Admah and Zeboim? God would *not* let Israel die, for He loved Israel, had loved them with undying love. He had taught them how to walk with Him, taken them in His arms, healed them, bound them with the bands of *love*. God, like many another father, knew that these children of His would go on sinning, but He would go on loving them. He would heal their backsliding. He would be to them what dew was to a lily in the field: He would lead them. They would return from exile, and "dwell beneath my shadow; they shall flourish as a garden" (Hosea 14:7, RSV).

Where Amos had given up on them, Hosea sought to put their hands in the hands of God and trust Him for their future. God was waiting for them to come home to Him as Hosea had waited for Gomer to come home and be forgiven.

If you would understand the Gospel of Jesus, His view of God, His love of mankind, read Hosea.

Love . . . beareth all things, hopeth . . . endureth all things. God and Hosea . . . loving, forgiving, waiting. What a long, long step this was from the Old Testament God of wrath! And what a joy it is for the Christian to know that "The love that kept us through the passing night will guide and keep us still!"

Now, teacher, sit down and read 1 Corinthians 13, the "love letter" of the Scriptures. And *memorize 1 John 4:8, 9,* so that you will never forget what love is. Note, for instance, that Paul says that after all is said and done, there are three things that "remain," three things or beliefs that matter most: they are faith, hope, and charity (love), and the greatest of these three things is not faith nor hope, but *love.* That one word is "the bottom line" in the whole of Christianity. Without love—nothing!

And John, the very old disciple, sums it all up in two brief verses. Sixty years after Jesus, he reminds us that the greatest love the world has ever known is the incomprehensible, everlasting love of *God,* and that if we would know what love really is, it is not our love for Him, but His love for us. Stumbling sinners that we are, He loved us enough to sacrifice His greatest possession, His own Son, to teach us how much, how deeply, He loves us.

Surely, if He loved us like that, the least we can do is to love each other. It just isn't enough to say that we love God; He asks us to prove it in loving others. "He who does not love (others) does not know God" (verse 8, 1 John 4). We err when we try to define love by some human standard; we are right when we see it as something divine, something that sent Jesus to Calvary *in love for us.*

Burton Hillis asks us, "Who says pull never gets you anywhere? If love tugs at your heartstrings, you're sitting on top of the world." Memorize that, too!

SUGGESTIONS TO TEACHERS

Trying to summarize the meaning of God's love in one lesson is like trying to plumb the depths of the Pacific with a length of clothesline. As teacher, you may freely acknowledge that you'll never succeed in teaching everything that needs to be said on the topic for today. Veteran teachers, like other Christian saints, will tell you that ultimately you will have to admit the mystery in God's love, and finally step aside and point silently to the Cross. Therefore, don't be intimidated by today's lesson. Although the subject may seem overwhelming, let the biblical passages speak for themselves.

1. *WHY A PARENT CARES.* Refer to Hosea's tender words about God's love. Note how the prophet compares the Lord's love to the way a caring parent looks after a small child, patiently carrying it when tired, holding it in strong, secure arms and comforting it when frightened, gently taking it by the hands as it takes its first stumbling steps. Bring the subject closer to home by asking why members of your class have a concern for the welfare of small children and babies. If they have such an interest in their well-being, how much more does God care for each of us!

2. *WHAT A GARDENER PLANTS.* Let your class see the analogy which Hosea draws between a person gently tending a delicate plant and the Lord restoring fragile, broken lives. In each of these pictures, the biblical writers are saying in effect, "God's love is like a parent's, or a gardener's, except more so." What special images can members of your class bring up to describe God's love to

them? Possibly, each will share ways in which God's caring has particular meaning in his or her life.

3. *HOW A HEALER MAKES WHOLE.* The passages from the Johannine literature in the New Testament (The Gospel of John and the letters of John) stress that God has come to bring wholeness. Jesus is Savior! You probably already know that the Greek word for *savior* and *salvation* means "wholeness," and has to do with healing or making whole. God's motive in all His dealings with us humans is to make us whole persons, not to sentence us or make us miserable. It would be useful if you would have your class dissect the familiar John 3:16 verse, phrase at a time. The "Gospel within the Gospel," as John 3:16 has been called, sums up well the meaning of the Lord's love. Make sure that everyone in your class realizes that he or she is the "whosoever" spoken about in this great verse!

4. *WHEN A PERSON LOVES.* Love compels a response. The response will be either positive or negative, but love demands some kind of reaction. In the face of God's incredible love for us through Jesus Christ, the response will be either to love others or to reject them brutally. In your lesson, assist your class members to grow in their understanding of what the response of love is. It is more than feelings. Love is what they do. Love is not seeking to be consoled, but consoling; not wanting to be understood, but understanding; not wanting to be cared for, but caring for others! Also ask whether your congregation and your class is being the seedbed for such concern for others. Specifically, what may your church do more to show it is a community of those loved by God?

TOPIC FOR ADULTS
THE MOTIVE: GOD'S LOVE

Amazing Discovery. Mary Stewart, the writer, has three significant novels featuring King Arthur, Merlin, and the Knights of the Camelot Round Table and their ladies. In *The Crystal Cave,* Merlin is reputed to be an illegitimate child, son of the Prince of Darkness. The boy is condemned because his father is unknown, and is almost put to death. The rejected youngster believes he is an unwanted, unacceptable, bastard boy. Finally, he discovers that he is really the king's accepted and cherished son. Merlin became the ruler of ancient Brittany and Wales, and brought fifth-century Britain from chaos and superstition to a point where King Arthur could reign.

When God's love is realized by us, we come to know that we are more than we dreamed we could be. We become aware that instead of being rejected and unloved nobodies, we are the cherished and beloved sons and daughters of The King!

The Sacrament of the Yellow Shoes. "The plane landed in Phoenix. I was determined that I would try to express a new kind of love toward my daughter, yet I was dreading the visit as much as she was. Later I found out that when I called to tell her that I was coming to visit her, she had turned to her best friends and said, 'What on earth will I do with Father for five hours?'

"She met me in the friend's car (obviously a clergyman's daughter could not afford one). I asked her where she would like to go to lunch, saying that I would take her anywhere. She had not often been treated in this manner by her father and could not think of a place to go; I took her to the nicest place I knew, the Arizona Biltmore. We had lunch by the pool, the waiters hovering over us. Suddenly I was seeing her as a real person, with real needs, not just as *my* child. Something of my new attitude must have broken through to her. Quite tentatively she asked me if I would like to go shopping with her in the Thomas Mall that afternoon. Although that was not exactly my idea of a Saturday afternoon in the lovely Arizona February, I paused to reflect before I answered. I thought to myself that I was not there to be taken care of but to love. And so I replied quite honestly that I would love to go shopping with her in the mall.

"We walked up and back the interminable length of the mall several times. I was aware of Myra and her reactions just as if she had been a sensitive and hurting counselee. I noticed that our pace slackened in front of a shoe store, observing that her eyes were focusing upon a pair of yellow shoes. I asked her if she should like to try on those shoes, and she replied that it would be a nice idea. Naturally they fit perfectly. This is known in theological language as divine providence. There was a yellow bag to match and I asked her if she would like to have that, assuring her that these gifts would not come out of her allowance. She thought the bag would be nice, too.

"Something happened between us that day. Myra realized that I could treat her as a person in her own right and with love. From then on neither of us dreaded our getting together. It was no longer, 'What will I do with Father for five hours,' but 'Why don't you come more often and stay longer?' I call this experience 'the sacrament of the yellow shoes.' Myra has since married and has children. Her life expresses a fine understanding of the meaning and practice of Christianity and Christian love."—Morton Kelsey, *Caring*, Paulist Press, 1981.

Indication of Immortality. "The consciousness of immortality needs no knowledge, no guarantee, no threat. It lies in love, in this marvelous reality in which we are given to ourselves. We are mortal when we are without love and immortal when we love. . . . I achieve immortality to the extent that I love. . . . I dissipate into nothingness as long as I live without love and therefore in chaos. As a lover I can see the immortality of those who are united to me in love."—Karl Jaspers, from a paper in *Death to Life*, Chicago, Argus Communications, 1968.

Questions for Pupils on the Next Lesson. 1. Does every person have the possibility of being made right with God by responding to His love through Jesus Christ? 2. How does the life as well as the death of Jesus have an impact on human life? 3. Why do we have humans require God's forgiveness? Why can't we handle our guilt and separation ourselves? 4. Do you agree with the biblical writers that God chose the right time for Christ's death? 5. What are the "powers of darkness" which the Bible claims that Christ overcame by His death?

TOPIC FOR YOUTH
YOU GOT A FRIEND

Distillation of Lifetime of Learning. After spending a lifetime studying and writing about men and events, historian-philosopher Will Durant, at ninety-two, distilled more than 2,000 years of history into three simple words: "love one another."

"My final lesson of history," says Durant, "is the same as that of Jesus.

"You may think that's a lot of lollipop," Durant adds with a laugh. "But just try it. Love is the most practical thing in the world."

History has taught Durant to be "realistic" about human nature. "I accept man as history shows him to be: good and bad, competitive and cooperative. The best I can do is take human beings as they are and assume that they are going to be decent, and I find that if I make that assumption, it helps them to be decent.

"If you take an attitude of love toward everybody you meet, you'll eventually get along."—Published in *Parade* newspaper magazine on August 6, 1978.

God Remembers. For over a century, Hart Island has served as the potter's field for the nameless nobodies among the poor and homeless of New York City. Over 700,000 humans have been buried on the 101 acre jumble of swamp grass and weeds, all without money or mourners. Louisa Van Slyke, an orphan who died in Charity Hospital in 1869 at the age of twenty-four, was the first to be dumped into a grave on Hart Island. Yellow fever victims, then sick old men, narcotics addicts, convicts—often with no more identification than "unknown white male" or "unknown black female" written on a list and scratched on a pine box—are stacked in trenches three deep, two across. Inmates from Rikers Island, New York's correctional institute, earn thirty-five cents an hour, wielding shovels and wheelbarrows and operating the payloader that digs the forty-foot long common graves. At night, the island is deserted, visited occasionally by thieves or vandals that row the one-third mile from the Bronx hoping to find something to steal or destroy. They have stripped the railings, broken the windows and defaced the walls of the few ancient buildings, even toppling the altar and stealing the bell from the chapel. The one structure on the island that has not been vandalized is the plain, thirty-foot monolith which was erected by prisoners in 1947. The simple white washed structure has a cross on one side. On the other is the single word: Peace.

The Cross is God's message of peace with Him to all the unwanted and unknown and unloved. Although humans may not love, God stands by each as if he or she is the only person in the world. He remembers us in love!

Ike's Regret. Because God loves us, we love each other. How hard it is, however, to express that love to each other. Especially in families!

Dwight D. Eisenhower tells in his memoirs how remorseful he was over not showing his father how he loved him. In spite of the genial grin and Kansas friendliness, "Ike" felt pathetically sad when his father died without realizing how deeply Ike loved him. "My only regret," wrote Eisenhower, "is that it was always so difficult to let him know the great depth of my affection for him."

Sentence Sermon to Remember: Tell me whom you love, and I will tell you what you are.—Arsene Houssaye.

Questions for Pupils on the Next Lesson. 1. Have you ever been really forgiven by someone you have hurt? 2. Have you discovered how hard it is to forgive someone who has hurt you? 3. Why did God have to take the initiative in forgiving us? 4. Are there any persons that God will not forgive? 5. Have you ever tried to live with guilt?

LESSON VII—OCTOBER 16

THE MEANS: GOD'S SON

Background Scripture: Romans 3:21–26; 5:6–11; Hebrews 9:11–15; Colossians
1:11–14
Devotional Reading: Hebrews 3:1–6

KING JAMES VERSION

ROMANS 3   21 But now the righteousness
of God without the law is manifested, being
witnessed by the law and the prophets;

22 Even the righteousness of God *which is*
by faith of Jesus Christ unto all and upon all
them that believe: for there is no difference:

23 For all have sinned, and come short of the
glory of God;

24 Being justified freely by his grace through
the redemption that is in Christ Jesus:

25 Whom God hath set forth *to be* a propi-
tiation through faith in his blood, to declare his
righteousness for the remission of sins that are
past, through the forbearance of God;

26 To declare, *I say,* at this time his righteousness: that he might be just, and the justifier
of him which believeth in Jesus.

5   6 For when we were yet without
strength, in due time Christ died for the ungodly.

7 For scarcely for a righteous man will one
die: yet peradventure for a good man some
would even dare to die.

8 But God commendeth his love toward us,
in that, while we were yet sinners, Christ died
for us.

9 Much more then, being now justified by his
blood, we shall be saved from wrath through
him.

10 For if, when we were enemies, we were
reconciled to God by the death of his Son, much
more, being reconciled, we shall be saved by his
life.

11 And not only *so,* but we also joy in God
through our Lord Jesus Christ, by whom we
have now received the atonement.

COLOSSIANS 1   13 Who hath delivered us
from the power of darkness, and hath translated
us into the kingdom of his dear Son:

14 In whom we have redemption through his
blood, *even* the forgiveness of sins:

REVISED STANDARD VERSION

ROMANS 3   21 But now the righteousness
of God has been manifested apart from law, although the law and the prophets bear witness to
it, 22 the righteousness of God through faith in
Jesus Christ for all who believe. For there is no
distinction; 23 since all have sinned and fall
short of the glory of God, 24 they are justified by
his grace as a gift, through the redemption
which is in Christ Jesus, 25 whom God put
forward as an expiation by his blood, to be received by faith. This was to show God's righteousness, because in his divine forbearance he
had passed over former sins; 26 it was to prove
at the present time that he himself is righteous
and that he justifies him who has faith in Jesus.

5   6 While we were still weak, at the right
time Christ died for the ungodly. 7 Why, one
will hardly die for a righteous man—though
perhaps for a good man one will dare even to
die. 8 But God shows his love for us in that while
we were yet sinners Christ died for us. 9 Since,
therefore, we are now justified by his blood,
much more shall we be saved by him from the
wrath of God. 10 For if while we were enemies
we were reconciled to God by the death of his
Son, much more, now that we are reconciled,
shall we be saved by his life. 11 Not only so, but
we also rejoice in God through our Lord Jesus
Christ, through whom we have now received
our reconciliation.

COLOSSIANS 1   13 He has delivered us
from the dominion of darkness and transferred
us to the kingdom of his beloved Son, 14 in
whom we have redemption, the forgiveness of
sins.

*KEY VERSE: While we were still weak, at the right time Christ died for the un-
godly.* Romans 5:6 (RSV).

HOME DAILY BIBLE READINGS

Oct. 10.   M.   *The Gift of Grace.* Romans 3:21–26.
Oct. 11.   T.   *Mediator of a New Covenant.* Hebrews 9:11–15.
Oct. 12.   W.   *We Are Made Alive With Christ.* Colossians 2:8–15.
Oct. 13.   T.   *Christ the Cornerstone.* Ephesians 2:11–22.
Oct. 14.   F.   *The Faithfulness of Christ.* Hebrews 3:1–6.
Oct. 15.   S.   *Reconciled Through Christ.* Colossians 1:13–23.
Oct. 16.   S.   *While We Were Yet Sinners.* Romans 5:6–11.

BACKGROUND

Before Christ came, the Jews sought to find fellowship with God by way of obedience to their Law. They called for strict obedience to that Law; when and if they broke it, they sought the approval of God in repenting by way of sacrifices on their altars—*animal* sacrifices. Having so sacrificed, they went on to break the Law again—and sacrificing again, and again, and again. No wonder Amos protested against that in words of fire: "Though ye offer me burnt offerings, and your meat offerings, I will not accept them" (Amos 5:22). He realized that God's people, in this sad performance, had cut themselves off from the true God.

So the question arises: how could His people come to terms with God? How could they reestablish that old fellowship with Him? Paul told them how in his letters to the Romans and the Colossians.

NOTES ON THE PRINTED TEXT

As a Pharisee, Paul had undoubtedly accepted the Jewish faith in the Law and the custom of sacrifice. But when he met Jesus on the Damascus Road, a new view of sacrifice and salvation became clear to him. Christ did not try to wipe out the Jewish Law or obedience to it, but He offered a better and more certain way. It was as though He threw open a new gate to heaven for *all* men.

It was not enough, Paul told his fellow Hebrews, just to obey the Law. It was not enough just to go about doing good deeds or "good works." (Thieves have been known to give stolen money to the poor; does that wipe out *their* sin?) Not by works are men saved, but by faith in a Christ who came to die for *their* sins! If we put our trust in the sacrificed Christ, our sins will be blotted out, forgiven and forgotten. By faith and faith alone is a man "justified." Justification is God's verdict of "Not Guilty" upon all sinners, His forgiveness. All of us, without exception, must plead guilty of sin. "For all have sinned, and come short of the glory of God" (Romans 3:23). This justification, or forgiveness, comes to us by the grace (goodness, righteousness) of God as a *gift;* it cannot be bought, or earned.

Paul uses two words here that we must understand: *redemption* and *expiation.* Redemption is a word that reaches back into ancient Jewish history. If a Hebrew was made a slave, he could be "redeemed"—bought free—by his next of kin. Just so, Paul reasoned, mankind has been "bought free of sin" in the sacrifice of Jesus on the cross. It was a terrible price, but it accomplished a great thing: it was the final, powerful sacrifice which brings sinning man back to God.

Jesus paid for *our* sins on that cross. Someone has written of the unrepentant Judas looking up at the Master dying on the cross and saying, "God! That is my cross he's dying on."

On the cross, Jesus "expiated," or "atoned" (which means "at-oneness" with God) for *our* sins, not His; it was a redemption offered even to such as Judas! Judas dies a sinner. There were others about Him who lived on as sinners, weak, unrighteous, hopeless, utterly helpless to "find a way out." Then, just at the right moment, Paul says, Jesus came (Romans 5:6), came to die for sinners who had no use for Him. (We heard an atheist say only yesterday, "I don't need anybody to die for me"!) Nevertheless, God sent His Son, "while we were yet sinners" (Romans 5:8). Was there ever a greater love? In *The Living Bible,* we read a transliteration of Romans 5:10: "And since, when we were his enemies, we were brought back to God by the death of his Son, what blessings must he have for us now that we are his friends, and he is living within us!" There are a hundred good sermons in that.

At the time of Jesus, men still "walked in darkness." It was a world in which evil (the devil) held dominion over them. Sinister and superhuman forces menaced their lives. And while *we* would not admit that this is true today, we still are talking about evil political and economic forces which are threatening our very existence! The cynic smiles at the thought of Jesus driving the forces of evil out of a Gadarene demoniac, but we still have our "healers" going up and down the land offering to "exorcise" the evil spirits out of the mentally and spiritually ill. Or we sit and moan that our world is about to be blown into extinction by Russian bombs (so we make the same bombs!).

Paul takes exception to this state of mind, this fear and discouragement: "He (God in Christ) has delivered us from the dominion of darkness . . ." (Colossians 1:13). No man, thanks to Christ, needs to sit and wail in our modern darkness; the blazing light of the Prince of Peace is his for the asking. Jesus offered us the way out; in faith in Him, we have the only antidote to darkness and despair. He has given us a light to guide us to a better world and a better life. His way out of the darkness is our only way out—provided that we have the faith and courage to try it. He has bought our freedom from disaster with His blood and already forgiven us our sins committed in the dark night of sinful rejection of both Him and His way.

SUGGESTIONS TO TEACHERS

Fortunately, they found Jim in time and rushed him to the emergency room. He had closed the garage doors and turned on the engine of his car. Only twenty-nine, he had survived two tours in Vietnam, but had drifted from job to job, place to place. After two failed marriages and a series of brief affairs, life for Jim seemed to evaporate into a dreary wandering through a haze of marijuana smoke and drinking binges. Occasionally his rage boiled over, and he had been arrested twice for barroom violence. At first, after his suicide attempt, Jim was angry at himself for failing to kill himself and told the hospital chaplain so. When the chaplain patiently tried to explain that God accepted Jim and his bungled life, Jim blurted, "How can I ever be right with God or the world again?" Happy to report, because of the grace of Christ and the skills and insights of a caring thera-pist, Jim gradually changed from being the angry young veteran to an active young Christian.

His question to the chaplain, "How can I ever be right with God or the world again?" is what lies behind your lesson today. That question is also asked by those in your class, although they might not have been driven to the brink of self-destruction like Jim. Your lesson for this Sunday must hold up Jesus Christ as the means by which God has brought a new and loving relationship between Himself and all the Jims of this world.

The Scripture material in today's lesson will provide so much for you to work with that, if you listen carefully to these passages, you will discover lesson ideas for a year of Sundays. Here are a few for starters:

1. *RESCUES US FROM POWERS OF DARKNESS.* Take a few minutes to look up the meaning of the old biblical word *deliver*. Help your class to recover some of the experience Paul had when he states that Christ "delivered us from the dominion of darkness," or "rescued us" as other translations put it. If Christ has rescued us, remind your class that we are meant to be about the task of being actively involved in the divine rescue operation for the human race. We must rescue individuals like Jim. We as Christ's people must also rescue persons from destruction by war or injustice.

2. *RETURNS US TO GOD'S PRESENCE.* Hebrews repeatedly insists that Jesus Christ has offered us access directly to the Almighty. Jesus Christ ushers us into the very presence of the Eternal. As our "High Priest," He brings us into the holiest of all realms, to an encounter with the Lord God, Creator of all. Have your class ponder the meaning of this extraordinary claim! The guesswork about God's nature has been taken away. We now see that the Lord means to be on friendly terms with Jim and each of His sons and daughters!

3. *RELIEVES US FROM USELESS RITUAL.* Our consciences are eased through the sacrifice of Christ, and we need not continue hating ourselves or trying to remove the guilt through drink, drugs, sex, fake religion, compulsively overworking at the job, or any other ritual in our society. Through Jesus Christ, we are made right with God! It would be helpful to take a few minutes to have your people tell some of the ways they or others sometimes try to relieve themselves of the pangs of alienation from God, from others, from life, and from ourselves. But make sure you conclude the lesson with the ringing affirmation that Jesus Christ is God's means of redeeming His people.

TOPIC FOR ADULTS
THE MEANS: GOD'S SON

Remembered Two Things. John Newton, the author of the beloved hymn "Amazing Grace," was a shipmaster who engaged in the slave trade before he was confronted by Jesus Christ. He regretted deeply his involvement in the horrors of slavery. Remembering his own part in the monstrous crime, he frequently said, "My heart shudders that I was ever engaged in it." He determined to make amends and joined others working to abolish slavery in the British Empire. Newton became something of a pest to many persons in Parliament and other high offices as he campaigned continuously against slavery. When a university wrote that he was being awarded an honorary Doctor of Divinity degree, John Newton refused to use the title, stating that the dreary coast of Africa had been his university and that he would never accept any diploma "except from the poor blacks." By the time the British Parliament ended the British slave trade in March, 1807, Newton was worn out. He knew that he was dying and considered it another "amazing grace" from God that he had been permitted to live to see the abolition of slavery in Britain. William Jay, leaning over Newton's bed to catch his last words, heard the old repentant slaveship skipper whisper, "My memory is nearly gone. But I remember two things: That I am a great sinner . . ." he paused a long time to get his breath . . . "And that Christ *is* a great Saviour!"

"We Must Forgive." Speaking at a meeting of the Church of the Brethren about repression in El Salvador and the church's response, theologian Jorge Lara-Braud related this advice given to him by the late Salvadoran archbishop, Oscar Romero:

"Please don't be bitter. Our persecutors have the right to be confused. They have never seen the face of the converted Catholic Church. They are very confused because they used to have us in their back pocket. Now we have read the Gospel, and the minimum translation is the defense of the poor. We don't like this violence (against us) but we must forgive. . . . If we lose the hope that the persecutors can be converted, then there is no other way but to act like they do."

Freed at Last. After twenty-nine years of imprisonment without ever being convicted of a crime, Emmanuel Treadway walked out of jail.

A small, humpbacked man, Treadway, forty-six, was "lost in the system," for years. He entered prison as a "defective delinquent" at seventeen, when he was charged with attempted assault.

With no family, or attorney to press for his release, he remained at Chester County Prison, Chester, Pennsylvania.

"Someone lost a paper on me a long time ago," said Treadway.

"This man was lost in the system, I think they forgot about him," said public defender R. Kerry Kalmback, who became Treadway's lawyer in 1977, got the charge dismissed and began working for his release.

Treadway didn't speak when he was transferred to the prison in 1977. "It wasn't that he couldn't speak, but it took a while to adjust," said Kalmback. "The prison officials really went out of their way to assist him once the charges were dropped and he began to come out of his shell."

God's mercy in Jesus Christ comes like a reprieve from a hopeless imprisonment. Just as this prisoner felt lost for years until "found" by an energetic young public defender, you may think that you must endure being shut in a lonely cell of guilt. God has found you. In Jesus Christ, He has made a way to restore you to the world, to Him, to others, to yourself. He has overcome the system of the "powers of darkness" that have tried to destroy you. Through Jesus Christ, you are freed to live!

Questions for Pupils on the Next Lesson. 1. How does Paul contrast the old and new natures of humans? 2. What are Paul's standards for Christian living in Ephesians 4 and 2 Corinthians 5? 3. What is the best model we have of God's kindness? 4. What does it mean to "grieve the Holy Spirit"? 5. How does a Christian find the balance between responsible anger and improper anger?

TOPIC FOR YOUTH
GOD MADE A WAY

Manson Family Member Meets the Master. Tex Watson was once one of Charles Manson's most loyal followers. Tex took part in the rituals of violence which culminated in the orgy of mass murder in which movie actress Sharon Tate and others were brutally stabbed to death. Recently, Tex Watson was interviewed by a TV station on the West Coast. The reporters discussed Tex's exploits while he was part of the Manson "Family." Tex Watson did not hide or evade his part in the cultic brutality. Before the interview finished, however, he told the interviewer and the large listening audience that Jesus Christ had found him in prison. The young man convicted of killing for kicks calmly described the meaning of God's mercy through Jesus Christ. Tex Watson testified that he knew that he had been forgiven by Jesus Christ. He further stated that through Jesus Christ, he was even finding a sense of purpose to his life in the midst of serving his long sentence. Serving Christ who had forgiven even him, Tex Watson expressed the joy and serenity Christ brought him as he worked to share the Gospel with others behind bars!

Have you discovered that the God who made a way to forgive Tex Watson has also made a way to accept you?

Whip Sockets on the Cars. The first automobiles were called "horseless carriages." They were designed to look like carriages, right down to the whip sockets. The first automobiles built in the United States of America had sockets mounted on them to hold the whips—whips for driving horses that were no longer there! Gradually designs were adapted to the automobile's uniqueness—but it took a while.

Although Christ brought us an entirely new relationship to God, some Christians retain empty rituals which are not necessary. Some church folks "buggy whip" believers—insisting on perpetuating useless traditions instead of relying on the Risen Lord. We live by Christ's grace, not by human goodness. Forget trying to keep the "whip sockets" in religion. Let's live boldly as forgiven persons.

Christ Rescues in the World, Not From the World. Herbert Armstrong and his son, Garner Ted Armstrong, and their World Wide Church of God carefully set the date of the Second Coming of Jesus Christ for October 6, 1962. They pleaded on the radio and television for contributions before the last great day. When the day passed, the Armstrongs recalculated and announced that the day was actually October 6, 1972. Money continued to pour in. Although Garner Ted Armstrong was forced to leave the World Wide Church of God, charged with sexual immorality, Herbert, the father, still continued to raise $65 million each year through his broadcasts, tapes, and books. When the 1972 date came and went without Jesus reappearing, Armstrong senior calmly stated that the real date was October 6, 1982. This prophecy of doomsday also proved to be in error, but the World Wide Church of God has not seemed to mind.

Jesus, however, does not come to take us away from this world. Through Jesus Christ, God has come to put us right with Him *in* this world. He does not care about having us tinker with timetables of the Second Coming. He will not be party to our efforts to remove ourselves from living responsibly in this world. Through Jesus Christ, God makes a way to have us live at peace with Him and each other, with nature and with ourselves.

Sentence Sermon to Remember: When Jesus comes, the shadows depart—Inscription on the wall of a castle in Scotland.

Questions for Pupils on the Next Lesson. 1. Do you ever wish you could be a new person? 2. Whom do you look to as an example of meaningful, happy living? 3. What can your church do to help you understand who you are and what values to choose? 4. What difference has your commitment to Jesus Christ made in your daily living? 5. What are the minimal standards of Christian living, according to Ephesians 4 and 2 Corinthians 5?

LESSON VIII—OCTOBER 23

THE RESULT: NEW PERSONS

Background Scripture: Ephesians 4:17–5:2; 2 Corinthians 5:14–21
Devotional Reading: Titus 3:3–8

KING JAMES VERSION

EPHESIANS 4 17 This I say therefore, and testify in the Lord, that ye henceforth walk not as other Gentiles walk, in the vanity of their mind,

18 Having the understanding darkened, being alienated from the life of God through the ignorance that is in them, because of the blindness of their heart:

19 Who being past feeling have given themselves over unto lasciviousness, to work all uncleanness with greediness.

20 But ye have not so learned Christ;

21 If so be that ye have heard him, and have been taught by him, as the truth is in Jesus:

22 That ye put off concerning the former conversation the old man, which is corrupt according to the deceitful lusts;

23 And be renewed in the spirit of your mind;

24 And that ye put on the new man, which after God is created in righteousness and true holiness.

25 Wherefore putting away lying, speak every man truth with his neighbour: for we are members one of another.

26 Be ye angry, and sin not: let not the sun go down upon your wrath:

27 Neither give place to the devil.

28 Let him that stole steal no more: but rather let him labour, working with *his* hands the thing which is good, that he may have to give to him that needeth.

29 Let no corrupt communication proceed out of your mouth, but that which is good to the use of edifying, that it may minister grace unto the hearers.

30 And grieve not the Holy Spirit of God, whereby ye are sealed unto the day of redemption.

31 Let all bitterness, and wrath, and anger, and clamour, and evil speaking, be put away from you, with all malice:

32 And be ye kind one to another, tenderhearted, forgiving one another, even as God for Christ's sake hath forgiven you.

5 1 Be ye therefore followers of God, as dear children;

2 And walk in love, as Christ also hath loved us, and hath given himself for us an offering and a sacrifice to God for a sweetsmelling savour.

2 CORINTHIANS 5 17 Therefore if any man *be* in Christ, *he is* a new creature: old things are passed away; behold, all things are become new.

REVISED STANDARD VERSION

EPHESIANS 4 17 Now this I affirm and testify in the Lord, that you must no longer live as the Gentiles do, in the futility of their minds; 18 they are darkened in their understanding, alienated from the life of God because of the ignorance that is in them, due to their hardness of heart; 19 they have become callous and have given themselves up to licentiousness, greedy to practice every kind of uncleanness. 20 You did not so learn Christ!—21 assuming that you have heard about him and were taught in him, as the truth is in Jesus. 22 Put off your old nature which belongs to your former manner of life and is corrupt through deceitful lusts, 23 and be renewed in the spirit of your minds, 24 and put on the new nature, created after the likeness of God in true righteousness and holiness.

25 Therefore, putting away falsehood, let every one speak the truth with his neighbor, for we are members one of another. 26 Be angry but do not sin; do not let the sun go down on your anger, 27 and give no opportunity to the devil. 28 Let the thief no longer steal, but rather let him labor, doing honest work with his hands, so that he may be able to give to those in need. 29 Let no evil talk come out of your mouths, but only such as is good for edifying, as fits the occasion, that it may impart grace to those who hear. 30 And do not grieve the Holy Spirit of God, in whom you were sealed for the day of redemption. 31 Let all bitterness and wrath and anger and clamor and slander be put away from you, with all malice, 32 and be kind to one another, tenderhearted, forgiving one another, as God in Christ forgave you.

5 1 Therefore be imitators of God, as beloved children. 2 And walk in love, as Christ loved us and gave himself up for us, a fragrant offering and sacrifice to God.

2 CORINTHIANS 5 17 Therefore, if any one is in Christ, he is a new creation; the old has passed away, behold, the new has come.

KEY VERSE: Therefore, if any one is in Christ, he is a new creation. 2 Corinthians 5:17 (RSV).

HOME DAILY BIBLE READINGS

Oct. 17.   M.   *A New Creation.* 2 Corinthians 5:14–21.
Oct. 18.   T.   *Heirs in Hope.* Titus 3:3–8.
Oct. 19.   W.   *Alive to God in Christ Jesus.* Romans 6:1–11.
Oct. 20.   T.   *Walk by the Spirit.* Galatians 5:13–26.
Oct. 21.   F.   *Put on the New Nature.* Ephesians 4:17–24.
Oct. 22.   S.   *Do Not Grieve the Holy Spirit.* Ephesians 4:25–32.
Oct. 23.   S.   *Be Imitators of God.* Ephesians 5:1–10.

BACKGROUND

Too often, in reading and thinking about the early Christians who lived in Paul's time, we get to thinking that they were a people who, after Christ and Paul came, were almost a community of saints. Wrong! They were certainly a *courageous* people; we must give them credit for that. But they were also a people living in a terrifying world, highly dangerous for anyone who came along with the suggestion that the pagans who dominated it were all wrong about their gods and should change their ways and worship Jesus Christ. The pressures put upon the Christians were appalling; it must have made many of them wonder about compromising, just a little, with the relentless enemies who surrounded them.

So Paul wrote often to the new Christians to comfort and strengthen them in their attempt to live as all converts to Christ must live, however difficult that might be. He wrote to the Christians in Ephesus just what it meant to live as "the members of Christ's body," "new men," "children of God," etc. It was a letter written not only to be read in the Church at Ephesus, but in the other churches in Asia as well. He told them what they were called to do in their everyday living. It was not easy for them to do as Paul said.

When we read it, we can see that it is not easy for us in our modern churches to do as he says, either!

NOTES ON THE PRINTED TEXT

There is an idea about conversion to Christ which calls for careful study; this is the idea that once a man is converted, his troubles are over; he is saved once and for all; from that moment of conversion he is saved from sin. Yes, he is saved—but he is not immune from the *temptation* to sin. He can fall flat on his face after the great experience has come to him. The Christian has no armor to protect him against *that.*

In 2 Corinthians 5:17, we have the immortal statement that "Therefore if any man be in Christ, he is a new creature; old things are passed away; behold, all things are become new." That would seem to justify the ridiculous pronouncement of the cynics, "Love God, and do as you please." Paul never said *that.* What he did say was that with conversion comes a change in the *nature* of the convert. Before conversion, it was natural, easy, for a man to sin. After one has accepted Christ that idea dies, and a better, natural idea takes its place: the new man *wants to live in imitation of Christ.* Thinking that, his whole life changes; he is a *new* man, and the old sinful man (nature) has died within him.

Accepting Christ, then, is *only the beginning.* From that beginning on, the Christian has a fight on his hands: he must engage in a continuing battle to live as Christ tells him to live. Christianity is not a rest camp; it is a struggle.

Paul says that the convert must make a clean break from his old life-style—the life-style of the godless. The godless live with calloused hearts, in ignorance, in licentiousness (lewdness, dissolute, unclean). They also live in a state of selfishness. They do not try to decide what is right and what is wrong; they live only for and by themselves, and they care nothing for what happens to anyone else. They oppress the poor and fight to enrich themselves.

Jesus never taught *that*. His constant emphasis was on "others." He defended the poor, the weak, and He demands that all His followers do likewise.

If we think this description of ungodliness doesn't apply to *us* now, we should read our newspapers. Our world reeks with moral and economic greed, with a ruthless assertion which cares nothing for the rights of our neighbors.

Put on a new Christlike nature, man! Put away the old practices that once ruled your hearts. Be better than the heathen enemies of God. Stop lying in untruthfulness. (There is no such thing as a white lie.) Tell the truth, even when it hurts. Put away anger—uncontrolled, unrighteous anger. Yes, there is such a thing as righteous anger, but even that can get out of control and become unrighteous. Going off in a fit of anger can give the devil his "opportunity"; opportunity, here, means making room for the devil in one's heart. Don't open any doors to the devil! Never let the sun go down on your anger; never nurse a grudge! Throw it into your wastebasket before you go to sleep.

Further, stop stealing—stealing wealth, time, advancement at the cost of losing a friend. Beware of bad language—cursing, blaspheming, *gossip!* All that can destroy a Christian, ruin his reputation and his character. Bad language is the index of a dirty mind.

In the closing of this passage, in verses 31, 32, Paul stops scolding (which his hearers deserved), and turns to charity. He says now, "Be kind to one another, forgive one another, as Christ forgave you." Stop hating and begin to *love,* for that is what God would have you do. Imitate (copy) the righteousness and truthfulness of God. And imitate your Christ, whose giving of His life pleased God.

You say that this is "a large order" for any Christian layman? The Cross was a large order, too, but the Son never hesitated to fulfill it in order to lift us from sin into glory with a loving God.

Take it or leave it, believe it or deny it, these are the standards for Christian living.

SUGGESTIONS TO TEACHERS

Recently, a woman was arrested for shoplifting in a city in South Carolina. At her hearing in court, she indignantly protested when the prosecutor commented that she was a common thief. "Why, I am no common thief," she asserted, "I've got Jesus in my heart." Because she claimed to be very religious, the woman demanded leniency. The judge, who was unmoved by her pious claims, fined her $250 plus costs and put her on probation.

Sometimes Christians think that it is enough to "have Jesus in their hearts," or to have gone through a dramatic conversion, or to experience religious feelings on certain occasions. You probably have people in your class who are inclined to think this way.

Your task as teacher today is to deepen the awareness of your students that the result of God's deliverance through Christ means becoming new persons. This lesson's background Scripture in Ephesians and 2 Corinthians offers magnificent possibilities for you to get this across.

1. *ACCEPTANCE.* Start at the beginning by reminding your people that God has acted decisively on our behalf by coming to us in Christ, God has loved us; we respond by loving and serving Him.

2. *ATTITUDE.* A person's response to God's graciousness means a completely different attitude toward God, toward other human beings, toward the world and even toward himself or herself. Instead of hostility, one has hospitality. Try as teacher to probe gently to discover what the basic attitudes toward God, people,

life, and self are. Are they negative? If so, how can the attitude of God in Christ toward us help change those negative attitudes?

3. *AMBITION.* Belonging to Christ brings an entirely new series of goals for a person. A Christian's ambition, if he or she is aware of God's mercy, is to be Christ's "agent," as 2 Corinthians 5 puts it. Ask what the prime ambition or main ambitions of those in your class may be.

4. *AFFECTION.* Don't let the class discussion meander into fuzzy religious generalities, however. Have your people examine the list of very practical ways in which Christians relate to one another in Ephesians 4:17–5:2. Make it clear that Christians are not exempt from getting angry at others, or having greedy inclinations, or being tempted to be dishonest, or feeling bitter. The main thing is how Christians handle these. Christians also must live in community with others and will have to deal with the problems of work, gossip, personal hurts, Christians must be "imitators of God" (Ephesians 5:1).

5. *AMBASSADORS.* Press your class members to relate in their own words what they think it means to be an "ambassador of Christ" (2 Corinthians 5:20). An ambassador, of course, is one who represents his or her government in a foreign country. As Christ's ambassadors, your class must look after His interests in this sometimes hostile society. With the kidnappings and deaths of many ambassadors in recent years, being ambassadors in the secular world is not easy. Remark to your people that it will not be less so with Christ's ambassadors.

TOPIC FOR ADULTS
THE RESULT: NEW PERSONS

Gourmet Adopts a Christian Cadence. A decade ago, Graham Kerr was the wine-toting charismatic "king of the kitchen," a familiar face on television from coast to coast.

The drive of Kerr and his wife, Treena, who produced the show, parlayed the "Galloping Gourmet" TV series, and the best-selling cookbooks that came out of it, into a multimillion-dollar success story with all the trimmings—a mansion on Chesapeake Bay in Maryland, a luxury yacht, and a $52,000 test kitchen. The show was broadcast around the world, and as a result, Kerr was considered to be the highest-paid cook in history.

A Christian conversion in 1975 shifted Kerr's focus from gourmet cooking to the problems of world hunger. He insists that he has only rechanneled the ebullience that made him an international culinary celebrity. The preparation of food is still part of his life. In fact he has written two books *The New Seasoning* and *The Love Feast* that celebrate the joys of the Christian family and represent a search for a Christian approach to good food for family and friends.

Today the Kerrs live in an Oregon religious missionary complex, where they have built an energy-efficient home. Some of their fortune they gave away, saving only enough for their annual income of $12,500.

Why the life-style change? The Kerrs are open about the collapse of their lives. Although seemingly "sitting on top of the world," they had problems—with marriage, with children, with finances. A near-fatal auto accident in 1972 brought an end to the TV series. Treena became addicted to drugs that had been prescribed to ward off emotional collapse. Just as she was about to be admitted to a mental institution for a lengthy stay, she went to a small church where Jesus stepped into her life.

She didn't tell her skeptical husband about the conversion—he first learned of it from a supermarket checker. But as he watched her become free of the drugs and fears that had plagued her, as he watched her light up the lives of their family with love, Graham Kerr, too, asked Jesus to come into his life.

The Kerrs sold their Maryland estate and purchased 600 acres in the Rocky

Mountains of Colorado for a retreat for married couples. Ultimately, though, they sold this venture and settled in Salem, Oregon, where they live in a simple life-style that emphasizes energy and food conservation.

Through Youth With a Mission, for which he has worked in an unsalaried capacity for a number of years, Graham Kerr has developed Project LORD (Long Range Development for the World). It involves buying parcels of land in third-world countries. A piece of land is turned over to a couple to farm, with the expectation that the farm will provide food for the family and a surplus for market as well. After a few years the family buys the property for a small sum. Efforts are being concentrated in Latin America at the present time, but it is hoped that this idea for feeding the world's hungry poor will be taken up and used elsewhere by other organizations. Kerr travels around the world promoting Project LORD, which is supported by people who send "$5 here and $2 there."

Changed Persons Expected. During the Middle Ages, people felt uncomfortable receiving Communion. They sensed that once the body and blood of the loving Jesus Christ was coursing through their veins and there was no change in them, they began to experience terrible guilt. Therefore, many persons deferred taking Communion throughout their lives until they were elderly or dying.

In a way, they had a point. They realized that Jesus Christ calls believers to be new persons. Do we? Do we receive the Bread and Cup, then refuse to share Christ's concern for others? "If anyone is in Christ, he is a new creation."

Saved From the Storm. "Consider God's scheme of salvation as a great harbor. After a wild night we have gone down to the harbor, over whose arms the angry waves have been dashing with boom of thunder and in clouds of spray. Outside, the sea has been tossing and churning; the cloudrack driving hurriedly across the sky; the wind howling like the furies of the old fables. But within those glorious walls, the barks which had put in during the night were riding safely; the sailors resting, or repairing rents in sail and tackle, whilst the waters were unstirred by the storm raging without. Room in it for whole navies of souls to ride at anchor. There is a vessel once manned by seven devils, a pirate ship, but captured by our Emmanuel; and at her stern the name Mary of Magdala. And here one dismasted, and almost shattered . . . and on her stern the words The Dying Thief. And there another . . . now flying a pennon from the masthead, Chief of Sinners and Least of Saints. And all around a forest of masts"—F. B. Meyer, *The Way into the Holiest.*

Questions for Pupils on the Next Lesson. 1. What exactly is the meaning of God's "covenants" with His people? 2. What was the covenant with Moses and the people of the Exodus? 3. Why are marriage vows like a sacred covenant? 4. Why will God never break His covenant with His people? 5. Why do some people resist binding agreements of any kind?

TOPIC FOR YOUTH
THE NEW YOU

Is There a New You? Although 85 percent of normal American teen-agers say they feel happy most of the time, things have been going downhill since the early 1960s. Three Chicago-area researchers surveyed 1,331 adolescents, the majority in the Midwest, during the early 1960s and another group of 1,385 in the late 1970s and in 1980. Those in the first group were more confident and trusting, felt greater affection for their families and mastered "their inner feelings and impulses" better. The '70s teen-agers were less secure, had more problems and more worries about their bodies, described themselves as more easily hurt than the earlier group, and had lower ethical standards. "Over approximately an eighteen-year period," say psychiatrist Daniel Offer and psychologists Eric Ostrov and Kenneth I. Howard, "the self-perceptions of American teen-agers apparently have become decidedly less positive."

Their survey, published by Basic Books in 1981 under the title *The Adolescent: A Psychological Self-Portrait,* also finds that girls feel worse about their bodies than boys and are less open to sexual feelings.

Although the study states most teen-agers are in good shape psychologically— about 20 percent report feeling empty emotionally, are confused most of the time, and would rather die than go on living.

New Persons, New Surroundings. When the sun shines on the multicolored house at 322 N. Church St. in Allentown, Pennsylvania, there reflects off the glowing surface of a six-foot-high gold cross painted on the dwelling's bricks. Each brick is painted a different color. The mortar between the bricks is painted a shiny silver. The same kind of silver paint is applied thickly to the sides and the base of the house, giving it a sculptured effect.

The house belongs to Richard and Gloria Morgan, who live on his disability pension. Morgan's life has been filled with hardships—hardships that were the will of God to test his strength. As a child he was abandoned by his parents, and at fifteen he was jailed for stealing a car. He suffered two serious accidents that left him disabled, and he had drinking problems. His wife, too, was in ill health and was severely depressed several years ago when she lost a custody fight to retain her children by a previous marriage.

But, says Morgan, his life and his attitude have changed since Christmas Day, 1980. Until then, says Morgan, his life lacked something. But it wasn't until Christmas, he says, that he realized what his life lacked was Jesus Christ. At that point, he was inspired to repaint his formerly white brick, three-story row home.

In spite of his disability, he climbs a forty-foot extension ladder to apply coat after coat of paint to the bricks while his wife paints the first twenty-six rows. Eventually, he says, he will cover the whole house with polyurethane so the colors will last. They are scrimping and saving and retrieving cans of paint from garbage cans to finish the project. He chose the colors—powder blue, dark blue, gold, white and scarlet—because they are mentioned frequently in the Bible, he says. The cross is there to remind passersby that Christ is "the way, the truth and the *light,*" Morgan says.

Although we may smile at Richard and Gloria Morgan's way of expressing their new-found faith, we must credit them for recognizing that Jesus Christ means being new persons. We may not paint our houses as the Morgans are doing, but we must reflect the joy of Jesus in our homes and daily surroundings.

Same View as Critic. The "New You" which Jesus Christ brings also means having a sense of humility about yourself. Few have this. One who did was President Ulysses S. Grant. On one occasion, Grant was on the way to a reception. Grant shared an umbrella with a stranger, who said: "I have never seen Grant, and I merely go to satisfy a personal curiosity. Between us, I have always thought that Grant was a very much overrated man." Grant's response was just right: "That's my view also."

Sentence Sermon to Remember: A Christian is God Almighty's gentleman.—Augustus William and Julius Charles Hare, in *Guesses at Truth.*

Questions for Pupils on the Next Lesson. 1. When are some of the times in your life when you were given a second chance? 2. Do you feel you are accepted without any strings attached by any persons? If so, who? Do you also feel that God accepts you in this way? Why or why not? 3. Why do you sometimes have problems with the idea of obeying? 4. Does God always keep His promises? 5. What does the word *Covenant* mean in the Bible?

LESSON IX—OCTOBER 30

GOD'S GRACIOUS COVENANT

Background Scripture: Exodus 19:3–6; Jeremiah 31:31–34; Hebrews 8:6–13
Devotional Reading: Jeremiah 31:31–34

KING JAMES VERSION

EXODUS 19 5 Now therefore, if ye will obey my voice indeed, and keep my covenant, then ye shall be a peculiar treasure unto me above all people: for all the earth *is* mine:

6 And ye shall be unto me a kingdom of priests, and an holy nation. These *are* the words which thou shalt speak unto the children of Israel.

HEBREWS 8 6 But now hath he obtained a more excellent ministry, by how much also he is the mediator of a better covenant, which was established upon better promises.

7 For if that first *covenant* had been faultless, then should no place have been sought for the second.

8 For finding fault with them, he saith, Behold, the days come, saith the Lord, when I will make a new covenant with the house of Israel and with the house of Judah:

9 Not according to the covenant that I made with their fathers in the day when I took them by the hand to lead them out of the land of Egypt; because they continued not in my covenant, and I regarded them not, saith the Lord.

10 For this *is* the covenant that I will make with the house of Israel after those days, saith the Lord; I will put my laws into their mind, and write them in their hearts: and I will be to them a God, and they shall be to me a people:

11 And they shall not teach every man his neighbour, and every man his brother, saying, Know the Lord: for all shall know me, from the least to the greatest.

12 For I will be merciful to their unrighteousness, and their sins and their iniquities will I remember no more.

13 In that he saith, A new *covenant*, he hath made the first old. Now that which decayeth and waxeth old *is* ready to vanish away.

REVISED STANDARD VERSION

EXODUS 19 5 "Now therefore, if you will obey my voice and keep my covenant, you shall be my own possession among all peoples; for all the earth is mine, 6 and you shall be to me a kingdom of priests and a holy nation. These are the words which you shall speak to the children of Israel."

HEBREWS 8 6 But as it is, Christ has obtained a ministry which is as much more excellent than the old as the covenant he mediates is better, since it is enacted on better promises.

7 For if that first covenant had been faultless, there would have been no occasion for a second.

8 For he finds fault with them when he says:
"The days will come, says the Lord,
    when I will establish a new covenant with
        the house of Israel
    and with the house of Judah;

9 not like the covenant that I made with their
        fathers
    on the day when I took them by the hand
    to lead them out of the land of Egypt;
    for they did not continue in my covenant,
    and so I paid no heed to them, says the
        Lord.

10 This is the covenant that I will make with
        the house of Israel
    after those days, says the Lord:
    I will put my laws into their minds,
    and write them on their hearts,
    and I will be their God,
    and they shall be my people.

11 And they shall not teach every one his
        fellow
    or every one his brother, saying, 'Know the
        Lord,'
    for all shall know me,
    from the least of them to the greatest.

12 For I will be merciful toward their in-
        iquities,
    and I will remember their sins no more."

13 In speaking of a new covenant he treats the first as obsolete. And what is becoming obsolete and growing old is ready to vanish away.

KEY VERSE: *I will put my laws into their minds, and write them on their hearts, and I will be their God, and they shall be my people.* Hebrews 8:10 (RSV).

HOME DAILY BIBLE READINGS

Oct. 24. M. *The Covenant With Israel.* Exodus 19:1–6.
Oct. 25. T. *The Conditions of the Covenant.* Exodus 20:13–17.
Oct. 26. W. *The Celebration of the Covenant.* Exodus 24:1–8.
Oct. 27. T. *Life in the Covenant.* Deuteronomy 30:15–20.

Oct. 28.   F.   *The New Covenant Promised.* Jeremiah 31:31–36.
Oct. 29.   S.   *The New Covenant Celebrated.* 1 Corinthians 11:23–27.
Oct. 30.   S.   *The New Covenant Proclaimed.* Hebrews 6:6–13.

BACKGROUND

A covenant is a contract or agreement between two parties. Generally, it refers to a promise made by God and agreed to by men. There are quite a few covenants in the Old Testament, but only one in the New Testament.

The most important Old Testament contract was the one between Moses and God. But there were others which were only agreements made between men. Jacob and Laban made a covenant in which they promised not to harm each other. Jonathan and David made one in which David promised not to harm the descendants of Jonathan. Ahab made a covenant with Ben-hadad, the defeated king of Damascus, in which it was promised that the cities destroyed in war should be restored. These were covenants made between individual men; God had little or no part in them.

Then there were other covenants in which one of the parties was God who promised to confer His favors upon man. God's covenants with Noah was one of these, and so was His agreement with Abraham.

All of these covenants had virtues and good points, and met certain needs at the time they were made. They were good, but not good enough. The Prophet Jeremiah saw this clearly; he saw that even the great Sinai covenant had become, in his time, ineffective as the Israelites broke their words in covenants with the greatest of ease, because they were *external* laws, made not by individuals but by tribes. He prophesied that God would make a new covenant with His people which would be *internal*. This was the covenant of the New Testament—something totally new.

NOTES ON THE PRINTED TEXT

When Moses came down from Sinai, he brought with him a code of laws which, if obeyed by His people, would bring them into the Promised Land and into a close relationship with God. That was a code imposed upon the people by God and that new relationship of the people with God was wholly dependent upon their keeping of the law. Jeremiah came to the conclusion that strict obedience to this imposed law had *not* brought about the union of God and people that God wanted; this first covenant was not faultless or perfect and therefore had become obsolete. The time had come for the Old Covenant to "vanish away."

Now that might lead us to think that God had changed His mind. Not so. God, through Jeremiah, was only finding a better, more effective way in a *new* covenant—the one described at the Last Supper, in which Jesus announced His covenant—one in which and under which the great High Priest (Himself) would function.

Just what was "new" about this Last Supper covenant that was better than any preceding it?

It was new in the sense that it was different; it wiped out and cancelled the legalism of the older covenants. It was a covenant based on love and not law. It was a covenant made in the presence of the Son of God, One they could *see* in their midst. One about to seal it by giving His blood and life: Likewise after supper He took the cup; and when He had given thanks, He gave it to them, saying, "Drink ye all of this; for it is my blood of the New Testament." It was a covenant that wiped out sin in all who believed in Him.

It was new in the sense that it was applied "to the house of Israel and the house of Judah." A thousand years before this, in the days of Rehoboam, the kingdom had been split into two sections, which had not come together again; under the

Jesus covenant, they would be reunited. Some commentators believe that "the Christian community is that Israel and Judah."

However this may be, it is certainly true that close fellowship with God in Christ *does* bring a unity among men that is otherwise impossible. The arms of Christ on His cross were stretched out to reach and hold *all* men, and not a privileged few.

That must have come as a shock to Jews who hated Gentiles, and the Pharisees who kept the law religiously but snubbed their noses at those who did not. All men, wise and unwise, famous or obscure, would know the Lord, under this Christian covenant; in Christ's Kingdom, the doors which had been slammed shut between men were opened—by His key of love.

Greater even than all this, the writer of Hebrews, in the closing verses of this passage, speaks of the new covenant as something "written upon men's hearts and minds." The old Mosaic code had been written on tablets of stone; the new code, or covenant, would be written on the heart. Quite a difference! When we love God in our hearts, we obey Him because we love Him and *want* to obey Him. This would not be an external law which would call for unwilling experience; it would be an inner *desire* to do God's will. Such a covenant, or agreement between God and man, would bring forgiveness on the part of a God who rejoiced to see His children, at last, living with Him as they should.

SUGGESTIONS TO TEACHERS

A group of college students were arguing about religion late one night in a dormitory room. Only one of the boys acknowledged that he took his faith seriously. Two of the others tried to bait him. "How can you take God seriously?" said one with contempt. The Christian quietly replied, "How can I not?" "Aw, c'mon. Give me one proof. Give me one reason why you're so sure any God gives a ———— about you!" objected the other militant nonbeliever. The Christian boy refused to be cowed. After reflecting for a few moments, he answered, "Because He's given me His promise, and I can be sure because of Jesus that He'll never go back on His word."

That college-age Christian expressed beautifully what God's covenant is. "God's given me His promise, and I can be sure because of Jesus that He'll never go back on His word" summarizes your lesson for today.

Familiarize yourself with the material from Exodus, Jeremiah, and Hebrews as you prepare the lesson, and bring out the following facets of God's gracious covenant.

1. *CARRIED ON EAGLE'S WINGS.* The magnificent picture of a great soaring eagle, carrying its young to safety, served as a simile for God's delivering the Israelites from Egypt. The same image applies to what God has done in His great act of deliverance through the Resurrection of Jesus Christ. God has taken action on our behalf. He has worked in history for us. His promise rests on what He has done, not on wispy hopes or speculation.

2. *CONNECTED WITH THE UNIVERSE'S CREATOR.* The biblical writers say plainly that the Lord is not a little local deity but the Creator and Deliverer of the entire universe. How big is the God of your class members? Is He merely regarded as the God of your tribe? Or is He the Ruler of the Cosmos? As Lord of everyone and everything, He must be obeyed.

3. *CALLED AS CHOSEN PRIESTS.* Your lesson should hammer the point that God's people are covenanted with Him in order to serve. Repeatedly, the Bible insists that *everyone* in God's community is called to the priesthood. And a priest, you may remind your class, must intercede between God and the people, meaning, of course, that everyone in your class is called to be a bridge between the Creator and the rest of His creation. Take some time to talk together of what a

priest must do, and how each church member is "called" to the priesthood.

4. *CONTROLLED BY AN INNER LAW.* Jeremiah 31:31 and Hebrews 8:10 speak of the meaning of the solemn new pact established by God in which God's intentions are not engraved on stone tablets but on the heart of each believer. Each Christian is meant to be inner-directed. Every believer lives a godly life not so much because he or she "ought" to but because he or she wants to! The covenanted person lives by more than a rule book! Do the members of your class?

5. *COMPLETED BY JESUS CHRIST.* Throughout the lesson for this Sunday, keep before your people the fact that God's gracious covenant has been spelled out for us through Jesus Christ's life, death on the Cross, Resurrection from the dead, and presence through the Holy Spirit today. "No Christ, no covenant," as far as we Christians are concerned. Jesus completes all human hopes of a permanent bond with God. God has given His word that He intends to continue to stand with us in love!

TOPIC FOR ADULTS
GOD'S GRACIOUS COVENANT

Covenanting God Never Capricious. The helicopter crash on March 2, 1981, that killed Lt. Gen. Ahmad Badawi, chief of staff of the Egyptian army, and more than a dozen other officers including many members of the Egyptian army's general staff, was declared "an act of God" by the Egyptian government. However, according to informed sources in Cairo, what actually caused the crash at the Siwa oasis near the Libyan border in Egypt's western desert was too many boxes of dates that overloaded the helicopter. According to the four crew members who survived the crash, a local official insisted on presenting each of the visiting Egyptian generals with about seventy-five pounds of dates, which together weighed about half a ton. When the pilot complained that the extra load was too much for the helicopter and threatened not to fly with it, he later told investigators, the generals accused him of cowardice. So, the date-filled chopper took off and crashed moments later, killing all the Egyptian generals aboard.

Often, we place the blame for personal tragedy or national misfortune on God. In actuality, however, the pain we suffer is not an "act of God," but the result of our own stupidity or selfishness. Most important, the God who covenants with us in the biblical story which culminates in Jesus Christ never acts capriciously. He relates to us in love!

No Secret Escape Clauses. Sissy Spacek, the actress who starred in *Coal Miner's Daughter, Carrie, Prime Cut, Badlands,* and other films, was married to production designer-director Jack Fisk in 1974. At that time, Sissy put aside $30 in a secret bank account. Her explanation was that thirty dollars is what it cost to file divorce papers in California! Although Sissy and Jack managed to build an enduring marriage, Sissy did not grasp the idea that marriage is a covenant in the same way that our relationship with God is a covenant.

God's covenant with us has no secret escape clauses, He did not hold back His commitment to His people "just in case things don't work out." Neither can Christian marriage have reservations or private arrangements to cushion one or the other in the event that the relationship doesn't turn out the way one desires. Marriage between Christians basically is covenant making.

God Controls. One-time baseball great Joe Garagiola stepped up to the plate when his turn to bat came. Before assuming his stance, however, fervent Roman Catholic Joe took his bat and made the sign of the cross in the dirt in front of homeplate. Catcher Yogi Berra, also a devout Catholic, walked out and erased Garagiola's cross. Turning to the astonished Garagiola, Berra smiled and said, "Let's let God watch this inning."

We do not control God. He controls us. God covenants with us to be faithful to us, and calls us to be faithful to Him. He is not impressed with pious gestures. He wants obedient service!

Questions for Pupils on the Next Lesson. 1. When were some of the times when guilt was a serious problem in your life? How did you handle it? 2. Why do we all have a need to experience authentic love and acceptance? 3. Do you search for some meaning in life beyond yourself? 4. In a world of change, what sense of constancy does God give? 5. Does God deal with us according to our transgressions or according to His steadfast love?

TOPIC FOR YOUTH
ONE PROMISE YOU CAN COUNT ON

No Encouragement Needed. A few years ago, Archbishop Michael Ramsay of the Church of England attended a presentation of the folk-rock musical *Godspell.* The archbishop enjoyed the production so much that at the end he rose to his feet and shouted, "Long live God!"

Malcolm Muggeridge, the sharp-tongued critic, took Ramsay to task for his words. Muggeridge pointed out that Ramsay's comments made as much sense as shouting "Carry on eternity" or "Keep going infinity."

Although we can appreciate the exuberance of the archbishop, we must also recognize the accuracy of Muggeridge's thinking. We don't have to encourage God, or to hope that He has "long life." God does not need to be affirmed. He has given us a promise we can count on. His gracious covenant through Jesus Christ means that He stands by us whether we cheer for Him or not.

Time to Cross the Line. At the army induction center at Fort Dix, New Jersey, there is a box at the door of the room through which recruits must pass before being sworn into the army. The box was for any forbidden articles. The sign states plainly that no questions would be asked but that all knives, drugs, and other possessions not permitted on the army base by military personnel are to be deposited in that box. On the other side of the box is a line. Once past the line, any recruit possessing any forbidden article is subject to arrest. Every inductee finally has to cross the line. Crossing the line means making decisions.

God's gracious covenant means His promise you can count on. However, it also means promise-making by you. You must make up your mind that you will accept the fact that He means to induct you into His service. You must decide you will leave behind your old life. You must give Him your word you will be loyal and obedient to Him. The time comes in your life when you must cross the line!

Every Note God's. Johann Sebastian Bach, the great composer-musician, understood God's promise. Bach counted on the promise of God. He lived by it. His compositions reflect the Covenant of God.

The driving force of his genius was his simple faith. Bach believed that "the aim and final reason of all music should be nothing else but the glory of God and the refreshment of the spirit." As conductor and composer Leonard Bernstein says in his book, *Joy of Music:* "For Bach, all music was religion; writing it was an act of faith; and performing it was an act of worship. Every note was dedicated to God and nothing else." This explains why, at the beginning of every manuscript, Bach scribbled J.J., *Jesu, Juva,* or "Jesus, help me." And at the end he wrote S.D.G., *Soli Deo Gloria,* or "To God alone the glory."

Sentence Sermon to Remember: And this is the promise that he hath promised us, even eternal life.—1 John 2:25.

Questions for Pupils on the Next Lesson. 1. What examples from your own experiences can you give of what love is? 2. Whom do you care about the most? Why? 3. Can God's love be measured? 4. Have you ever had to deal with guilt? 5. What does God do to enable us to handle our guilt?

LESSON X—NOVEMBER 6

GOD'S STEADFAST LOVE

Background Scripture: Psalm 103; Ephesians 1:3–10
Devotional Reading: Psalms 107:1–9

KING JAMES VERSION

PSALMS 103   1 Bless the LORD, O my soul: and all that is within me, *bless* his holy name.

2 Bless the LORD, O my soul, and forget not all his benefits:

3 Who forgiveth all thine iniquities; who healeth all thy diseases;

4 Who redeemeth thy life from destruction; who crowneth thee with lovingkindness and tender mercies;

5 Who satisfieth thy mouth with good *things; so that* thy youth is renewed like the eagle's.

6 The LORD executeth righteousness and judgment for all that are oppressed.

7 He made known his ways unto Moses, his acts unto the children of Israel.

8 The LORD *is* merciful and gracious, slow to anger, and plenteous in mercy.

9 He will not always chide: neither will he keep *his anger* for ever.

10 He hath not dealt with us after our sins; nor rewarded us according to our iniquities.

11 For as the heaven is high above the earth, *so* great is his mercy toward them that fear him.

12 As far as the east is from the west, *so* far hath he removed our transgressions from us.

EPHESIANS 1   5 Having predestinated us unto the adoption of children by Jesus Christ to himself, according to the good pleasure of his will,

6 To the praise of the glory of his grace, wherein he hath made us accepted in the beloved.

7 In whom we have redemption through his blood, the forgiveness of sins, according to the riches of his grace;

8 Wherein he hath abounded toward us in all wisdom and prudence;

9 Having made known unto us the mystery of his will, according to his good pleasure which he hath purposed in himself:

10 That in the dispensation of the fulness of times he might gather together in one all things in Christ, both which are in heaven, and which are on earth; *even* in him:

REVISED STANDARD VERSION

PSALMS 103   1 Bless the LORD, O my soul; and all that is within me, bless his holy name!

2 Bless the LORD, O my soul,
and forget not all his benefits,

3 who forgives all your iniquity,
who heals all your diseases,

4 who redeems your life from the Pit,
who crowns you with steadfast love and mercy,

5 who satisfies you with good as long as you live
so that your youth is renewed like the eagle's.

6 The LORD works vindication
and justice for all who are oppressed.

7 He made known his ways to Moses,
his acts to the people of Israel.

8 The LORD is merciful and gracious,
slow to anger and abounding in steadfast love.

9 He will not always chide,
nor will he keep his anger for ever.

10 He does not deal with us according to our sins,
nor requite us according to our iniquities.

11 For as the heavens are high above the earth,
so great is his steadfast love toward those who fear him;

12 as far as the east is from the west,
so far does he remove our transgressions from us.

EPHESIANS 1   5 He destined us in love to be his sons through Jesus Christ, according to the purpose of his will, 6 to the praise of his glorious grace which he freely bestowed on us in the Beloved. 7 In him we have redemption through his blood, the forgiveness of our trespasses, according to the riches of his grace 8 which he lavished upon us. 9 For he has made known to us in all wisdom and insight the mystery of his will, according to his purpose which he set forth in Christ 10 as a plan for the fulness of time, to unite all things in him, things in heaven and things on earth.

KEY VERSE: The Lord is merciful and gracious, slow to anger and abounding in steadfast love. Psalms 103:8 (RSV).

HOME DAILY BIBLE READINGS

Oct. 31.	M.	*"O Give Thanks to the Lord."* Psalms 107:1–9.
Nov. 1.	T.	*"An Everlasting Love."* Jeremiah 31:2–6.
Nov. 2.	W.	*"They Who Wait for the Lord."* Isaiah 41:21–31.
Nov. 3.	T.	*"Who Can Separate Us?"* Romans 8:31–39.
Nov. 4.	F.	*"Every Spiritual Blessing."* Ephesians 1:3–10.
Nov. 5.	S.	*"Bless the Lord, O My Soul."* Psalms 103:1–14.
Nov. 6.	S.	*"From Everlasting to Everlasting."* Psalms 103:15–22.

BACKGROUND

The Psalms were written as hymns or songs sung in the synagogue or in the home. They were written, or composed, in the long period from the beginning of the Israelite nation to the fourth or third century B.C. David wrote some of them, many of them, but hardly all of them: we call them The Psalms of David; it would be better not to use the word *of,* but the words *to,* or *for* David.

Some Psalms are expressions of praise to God; some are laments of individuals, or protestations of innocence, or penetential prayers, or thanksgiving. All in all, they are the faith of Israel composed to music.

Psalm 103 is an ecstatic shout of praise to God for His mercy and love and forgiveness—qualities that persist and never die, as God watches His children stumble and fall—and rise again in faith and gratitude.

In the passage from Ephesians 1, we find the faith of the old Israelite carried down into the New Testament and linked with the labors and death of Jesus Christ.

NOTES ON THE PRINTED TEXT

Psalm 103 is as much a prayer as it is a song of praise. It reminds us, as we read it, of the ten lepers healed by Jesus in Luke 17. Nine of them, according to the story, failed even to thank Jesus for what He had done for them; only one had the grace to do that. This one was brought back out of a life that for him had been pure hell. Lepers were shunned, isolated, driven out of Jewish society. The one who thanked Him for His healing was not only a leper; he was a despised Samaritan to boot. The sympathy and healing of Jesus overwhelmed him; he fell on his face on the ground, "giving him thanks."

Doubtless, this man had prayed for healing before Jesus came along, hoping against hope that somehow, some time, he would find healing. When it finally happened, he prayed again, this time in gratitude. There is a vast difference between those two prayers. Prayer can be selfish, and often it is with all of us. Most of us are prayers that ask something of God. Heal my sickness, Lord. Give me this, give me that. Give me, give me! Then we get up from our knees, hoping that God has heard us.

But others pray in thankfulness for all that God *has* done for them in the past. The writer of this Psalm, says David Redding, "doesn't have time to ask for anything. He is too busy trying to catch up in thankfulness for yesterday's flood of kindness. Not every prayer tries to get something more out of God."

What do we have to thank God for? First, we should bless God for giving us *forgiveness*—a forgiveness that is as wide and deep as the boundless seas. God's forgiveness has no bounds, no end, no matter how much we sin against Him. Men may be short—very short—in the art of forgiving, but God's forgiving is endless. He forgives *all* our iniquities; only He can do that!

God heals all our diseases, be they physical or spiritual. He gives us redemption and the chance to start again, to turn over a new leaf. He even gives us redemption from death. He wipes out our sins and helps us to sin no more, and our youth is renewed like the eagle's. The eagle molts annually, shedding feathers that are dead and useless, and soars high again as new feathers renew his strength. Just so does God constantly renew us, give us strength to rise and be lifted up again. These are *personal* benefits. "Bless the Lord, O my soul, and forget not all his benefits" (verse 2).

There are other benefits; the Psalmist turns now, in verses 6–12, to praise God for His *national* benefits. The steadfast love of God is revealed in the history of His people, as well as in the individual heart. He has brought Israel out of Egypt. He has forgiven their sins in the wilderness. He has punished them for that, but not as much as they deserved. Oh, yes, God "chided" them in anger, but His anger was and is short-lived in love; He removed their transgressions from them, as far as east is far from the west.

His love speaks to us. Our God does not sit waiting, in a mood of vengeance to punish us for our transgressions. He sits waiting for us to turn back to Him in gratitude for His many mercies and for His forgiving heart.

In Ephesians 1, we find the love and deliverance of God expanding the Old Testament ideas. The Old Testament used the word *deliverance* to describe the deliverance of Israel from bondage in Egypt; in the New Testament Paul uses the word to describe the deliverance of God's people from sin and death. This is a deliverance obtainable through the shed blood of Christ. This is the ultimate, all-inclusive deliverance for all men, few of whom deserve it. The kindness of God flowed down into history from the cross on Calvary.

Here we discover the very *purpose* of God, His secret reason in sending His Son to live among us. "His unchanging plan has always been to adopt us into his own family by sending Jesus Christ to die for us" (Ephesians 1:5, *The Living Bible*). It was also the purpose of God to gather, when the time was ready, all of us together to be one in Christ, forever.

Up to the coming of Christ, this purpose of God was a riddle; men could only guess at what they thought to be God's will. Now this "mystery of his will" is made clear.

So, after all, it did not just happen that Christ came when He did. It was no accident that He died on the cross when He did. It was all planned.

SUGGESTIONS TO TEACHERS

A young and inexperienced pastor was trying to offer guidance to a youthful questioner. The pastor enjoyed discussing abstract theological theories and was speaking hopelessly over the head of the young man in his study. Finally the youth blurted, "Gee, every time I try to pin you down about what you mean, you give me that spiritual smoke screen. What exactly do you mean?"

Some people try to turn the Christian message into a spiritual smoke screen. But not the people who wrote the Scriptures. These persons recounted what they experienced. And they could say of God's steadfast love, "It's like this. . . ."

Your lesson this Sunday is to listen with your class as the Bible says that God's steadfast love may be compared to specific things. Your biblical material will provide so many clues as to what God's faithful caring is like that you will have to be selective. Try some of these similies from the Scripture for today's lesson.

1. *LIKE A SAVING PARDON.* The Bible often pictures divine mercy as a reprieve from death, almost like a man sentenced to go before a firing squad suddenly having his sentence commuted, or a person diagnosed as hopelessly ill unexpectedly being told a miracle-cure is available. Encourage your class to give their own pictures of what a saving pardon is like. Then, of course, point out that God's astonishing mercy is even greater than any of these comparisons.

2. *LIKE A STANDING PROMISE.* God keeps His word. He will not go back on His promise. Behind all of the apparent stern words of His judgment is the assurance that His love is constant and unconditional. Check the words again in Psalm 103 in which God commits Himself to caring for all, particularly the hurting and the oppressed. He forgives. He heals, He provides for our deepest needs. Ask if anyone in the class can relate any incident in which it can be said that God failed to keep His promise.

3. *LIKE A SENSITIVE PARENT.* Note the note of tender, parental concern in Psalm 103. As a good father or mother remembers the needs of offspring, how much more the Lord keeps us in mind! Have your class do some remembering for a few moments by recalling incidents in their own lives in which they were aware that God was remembering them. Through the memory of these occasions, help each person in your class to realize that God is not a vague impersonal power or nasty-spirited despot but The Loving Parent-God.

4. *LIKE A SECRET PLAN.* In Ephesians 1:3–10, Paul tells us that God's master plan or secret blueprint for the human race has been disclosed in Jesus. And that secret plan which we now know is to share His steadfast love with us. What do your class members think that the purpose of the universe may be? Where do they think life is headed? What does the Creator have in mind? Close with the summing up of what God's steadfast love is like—to you!

TOPIC FOR ADULTS
GOD'S STEADFAST LOVE

Faithful Trumpeter. Every day, thousands of watches are set by the trumpet that blares at noon from the top of St. Mary's Church in the old market square in Cracow, Poland. The ceremony is carried over national radio, and the steps of the trumpeter, an off-duty fireman, can be heard as he moves about in the bell tower to sound his instrument from the four points of the compass. Each time he breaks off, abruptly, at the same half-note, because it was precisely on that half-note that a Tatar arrow pierced the throat of a faithful watchman sounding an invasion alarm in the fourteenth century. According to tradition, the watchman could have saved his life by not climbing the tower to sound the trumpet. Out of love and loyalty to his fellow townspeople, however, he steadfastly mounted the steps.

God's steadfast love is like that! He sacrifices for us. In Jesus Christ, God faithfully stands with us whom He loves.

Singing Once Again. Laurens Van der Post in *The Seed and the Sower* tells the story of two brothers in South Africa. The elder brother was a strong, tall, intelligent, athletic student. Sent off to an exclusive boarding school, he soon became well known. He was a popular leader of the students. His brother was six years younger. This boy was not handsome or capable. Furthermore, he was a hunchback. However, he had one gift of a magnificent voice.

Eventually the younger brother joined the older brother at the same school. One day the students ganged up on the younger brother. They teased him, pushed him and tore off his shirt to reveal his hunchback.

The older brother became aware of what was happening. It would have been easy for him to have gone out and faced the mob of cruel, sadistic boys. One word from him would have put a stop to the whole spectacle. He was a leader. He could have acknowledged the hunchback boy as his brother. Instead he remained in the chemistry lab doing his work. He betrayed his brother by what he failed to do.

The younger brother was not seriously injured, but he was never the same again. He kept to himself, he no longer sang. Finally he returned home to the family farm. Meanwhile the older brother joined the army in World War II. One night, lying outdoors gazing into the sky, he began to realize what he had done to his younger brother in their school days. He knew that he would never have peace until he went home and asked his brother for forgiveness. And so he made the incredibly difficult wartime journey from Palestine to South Africa and met his brother. They talked long into the night. He acknowledged that he had betrayed him by what he had not done. They wept together and embraced. The breach between them was healed.

Something else happened that night. As the older brother was falling asleep, he heard the beautiful voice of his younger brother singing once again!

God's master plan for the human race calls for us to give and accept forgiveness to one another. Only then can we and our brothers and sisters sing again!

A Royal Task. Marriage is an area where steadfast love can be experienced. At the wedding of Prince Charles and Lady Diana Spencer at St. Paul's Cathedral, the archbishop of Canterbury, the Rt. Rev. Robert Runcie, pointed out: "Here is the stuff of which fairy tales are made; the Prince and Princess on their wedding day. But fairy tales usually end at this point with the simple phrase 'They lived happily ever after.' This may be because fairy tales regard marriage as an anticlimax after the romance of courtship. This is not the Christian view. Our faith sees the wedding day not as the place of arrival but the place where the adventure really begins. . . .

"Marriage is first of all a new creation for the partners themselves. . . . But any marriage which is turned in upon itself, in which the bride and groom simply gaze obsessively at one another, goes sour after a time. A marriage which really works is one which works for others. . . . If we solved all our economic problems and failed to build loving families, it would profit us nothing, because the family is the place where the future is created good and full of love—or deformed.

"Those who are married live happily ever after the wedding day if they persevere in the real adventure, which is the royal task of creating each other and creating a more loving world. . . . All couples on their wedding day are 'royal couples' and stand for the truth that we help to shape this world and are not just its victims. . . ."

Questions for Pupils on the Next Lesson. 1. Since Jesus Christ is not with us bodily, how are we helped to interpret His teachings? 2. How does the Holy Spirit intercede for us when we seem too weak to pray properly? 3. Do we understand truth only through observation, or is there also a way of grasping truth through inner experience? 4. Are you ever concerned about what happens when you die? 5. How do you find meaning for your living?

TOPIC FOR YOUTH
GOD KEEPS ON LOVING US

No Minor Characters. James Agate, the scholarly writer-critic on the staff of the *London Sunday Times,* once received a letter from the editor of a prestigious English literary magazine inviting him to contribute an article on "The Minor Characters in Dickens." Agate immediately fired off a telegram to the editor: "THERE ARE NO MINOR CHARACTERS IN DICKENS!" He followed this wire with a brilliant essay explaining that even the "extras" in the stories written by Charles Dickens became beautiful and important personalities. Dickens, Agate wrote, had the unique capacity of making apparent lightweights and miscellaneous nonentities into memorable people.

With God, there are "no minor characters," either. His steadfast love reaches out toward each of us. Through His care, He transforms each of us into persons of significance.

Sharing God's Steadfast Love. In the fourth century, St. Ambrose of Milan wrote a book telling clergy how they might grow in Christian love. His advice is as practical today as then for all of us:

"It gives a very great impetus to mutual love if one shows love in return to those who love us and proves that one does not love them less than oneself is loved, especially if one shows it by the proof that a faithful friendship gives. What is so likely to win favour as gratitude? What more natural than to love one who loves us? What so implanted and so impressed on men's feelings as the wish to let another, by whom we want to be loved, know that we love him? Well does the wise man say: 'Loose thy money for thy brother and thy friend,' and again, 'I will not be ashamed to defend a friend, neither will I hide myself from him.' "—St. Ambrose, *The Duties of Clergy*, Book II, Chapter VII.

Experiencing Love Repeatedly. God keeps on loving us. And He wants us to keep on loving each other. This means we must keep on telling each other that we care. Often, however, we are like the old midwestern farmer who never said any caring words to his wife. She often complained that he never told her he loved her. One Sunday after church services, he rose silently from the dinner table and prepared to settle in his easy chair with the paper when she mentioned again that he never said any caring words about how he felt about her. Laying down the newspaper, the old farmer answered, "Now Bessie, when I married you twenty years ago, I told you I loved you. If that ever changes, I will let you know."

Sentence Sermon to Remember: Love is the key to the universe which unlocks all doors.—Anonymous.

Questions for Pupils on the Next Lesson. 1. What are some of the times when you have been aware that God is real in your life? 2. Can you recall episodes in your life when God has apparently kept on helping you? 3. Will God remember us after we die? On what do you base your answer? 4. How does God help us to pray when we cannot or will not?

LESSON XI—NOVEMBER 13

GOD'S INDWELLING SPIRIT

Background Scripture: John 4:24; 14:25, 26; Romans 8:9–17, 26–28
Devotional Reading: Romans 8:1–8

KING JAMES VERSION

JOHN 14 25 These things have I spoken unto you, being *yet* present with you.

26 But the Comforter, *which is* the Holy Ghost, whom the Father will send in my name, he shall teach you all things, and bring all things to your remembrance, whatsoever I have said unto you.

ROMANS 8 9 But ye are not in the flesh, but in the Spirit, if so be that the Spirit of God dwell in you. Now if any man have not the Spirit of Christ, he is none of his.

10 And if Christ *be* in you, the body *is* dead because of sin; but the Spirit *is* life because of righteousness.

11 But if the Spirit of him that raised up Jesus from the dead dwell in you, he that raised up Christ from the dead shall also quicken your mortal bodies by his Spirit that dwelleth in you.

12 Therefore, brethren, we are debtors, not to the flesh, to live after the flesh.

13 For if ye live after the flesh, ye shall die: but if ye through the Spirit do mortify the deeds of the body, ye shall live.

14 For as many as are led by the Spirit of God, they are the sons of God.

15 For ye have not received the spirit of bondage again to fear; but ye have received the Spirit of adoption, whereby we cry, Abba, Father.

16 The Spirit itself beareth witness with our spirit, that we are the children of God:

17 And if children, then heirs; heirs of God, and joint-heirs with Christ, if so be that we suffer with *him*, that we may be also glorified together.

26 Likewise the Spirit also helpeth our infirmities: for we know not what we should pray for as we ought: but the Spirit itself maketh intercession for us with groanings which cannot be uttered.

27 And he that searcheth the hearts knoweth what *is* the mind of the Spirit, because he maketh intercession for the saints according to *the will of* God.

28 And we know that all things work together for good to them that love God, to them who are the called according to *his* purpose.

REVISED STANDARD VERSION

JOHN 14 25 "These things I have spoken to you, while I am still with you. 26 But the Counselor, the Holy Spirit, whom the Father will send in my name, he will teach you all things, and bring to your remembrance all that I have said to you.

ROMANS 8 9 But you are not in the flesh, you are in the Spirit, if in fact the Spirit of God dwells in you. Any one who does not have the Spirit of Christ does not belong to him. 10 But if Christ is in you, although your bodies are dead because of sin, your spirits are alive because of righteousness. 11 If the Spirit of him who raised Jesus from the dead dwells in you, he who raised Christ Jesus from the dead will give life to your mortal bodies also through his Spirit which dwells in you.

12 So then, brethren, we are debtors, not to the flesh, to live according to the flesh—13 for if you live according to the flesh you will die, but if by the Spirit you put to death the deeds of the body you will live. 14 For all who are led by the Spirit of God are sons of God. 15 For you did not receive the spirit of slavery to fall back into fear, but you have received the spirit of sonship. When we cry, "Abba! Father!" 16 it is the Spirit himself bearing witness with our spirit that we are children of God, 17 and if children, then heirs, heirs of God and fellow heirs with Christ, provided we suffer with him in order that we may also be glorified with him.

26 Likewise the Spirit helps us in our weakness; for we do not know how to pray as we ought, but the Spirit himself intercedes for us with sighs too deep for words. 27 And he who searches the hearts of men knows what is the mind of the Spirit, because the Spirit intercedes for the saints according to the will of God.

28 We know that in everything God works for good with those who love him, who are called according to his purpose.

KEY VERSE: But you are not in the flesh, you are in the Spirit, if in fact the Spirit of God dwells in you. Romans 8:9 (RSV).

HOME DAILY BIBLE READINGS

Nov. 7.   M.   *The Teaching of the Spirit.* John 14:15–26.
Nov. 8.   T.   *The Promise of the Spirit.* Acts 1:1–11.

Nov. 9. *W.* *The Power of the Spirit.* John 20:19–23.
Nov. 10. *T.* *The Pouring Out of the Spirit.* Acts 2:14–21.
Nov. 11. *F.* *The Life of the Spirit.* Romans 8:1–8.
Nov. 12. *S.* *The Children of the Spirit.* Romans 8:9–17.
Nov. 13. *S.* *The Intercession of the Spirit.* Romans 8:18–28.

BACKGROUND

In John 14 and Romans 8, we hear the most inspiring Good News that was ever to fall upon the ears of mankind. In John 14, Jesus is speaking to a group of disciples so disconsolate that they were about ready to give up before they started, for they had been told by Jesus Himself that He was about to leave them. Leave them? They cried in their hearts, "What do we do now, without You?" He told them what to do and how to do it.

In Romans 8, Paul is speaking to a whole new band of disciples who were trying to work after Jesus had indeed gone from this earth. At least, these latter day disciples may have sighed, the Twelve worked with Jesus in their midst. We don't have that, so?

Jesus tells them that they are wrong and ignorant of a Presence in their hearts—the Presence of a Holy Spirit.

And just what was and is this Holy Spirit?

NOTES ON THE PRINTED TEXT

The words *Holy Spirit* are confusing or unclear to many of us, but they need not be. To put it in the fewest possible words, the Holy Spirit is the intangible power of God working in the human heart. Like electricity, we cannot *see* it, any more than we can see God, but we can *feel* its presence deep within us.

John 14 has Jesus saying to His disciples, "I will not leave you *comfortless.*" The Revised Standard Version uses the word *Counselor,* which means, literally, a legal helper, an advocate. This makes the Spirit an advisor, helper, encourager, an inspirer speaking in the heart of the believer. That word *believer* is important, as we shall see as we read on: only the faithful can know God in this light.

All through Romans 8, Paul seems to be obsessed by two words which are repeated over and over again. One of those words is *flesh,* and the other is *spirit.* What he is actually doing, with the use of these words, is describing two different kinds of life. All of us live either one way or another.

The way of the flesh is the life of selfish desire, the way of a man who says, "I'll live as I please; it's my life, isn't it?" It is a life dominated by purely human passion, pride, and ambition. This man takes what he wants, by any method. Anything goes. Live as you please; God will forgive you in the end. In the eyes of God, this is pure suicide. And there comes a time in such a life when there is an explosion in the mind and heart when we realize that we have been fools wasting every moment of our lives.

This morning we read in our newspaper a story of thieves breaking into a medical research laboratory to steal several tubes of dangerous radioactive medical isotopes. They were fools and didn't know it. The stuff in those tubes could kill anybody who came in contact with them. It is a pertinent illustration of what happens to anyone who packs his life with sin against God: it can kill him spiritually if not physically.

Then there is the life guided by the Holy Spirit. What a difference such a life is when the mind which was in Christ becomes the mind in man. Christ is his life, his dominating law—a Christ-centered life, Spirit-controlled—the more abundant life. There is no good future for the man who lives in selfishness; there is a glorious future in this life and the life to come when we turn it all over to the Master.

God gave us life, and we are in debt to Him for that. Paul calls us "debtors," and it is a good word to describe us. He also calls us the "adopted sons of God." That is based upon the old Roman law of adoption. An adopted son could and usually did gain all the rights of the natural sons in his new family. He was co-heir with all the other sons of the father's estate.

So, through Christ, all *believing* men became the (adopted) sons of God. Says Dr. William Barclay: "It was Paul's picture that when a man became a Christian, he entered into the very family of God. He did nothing to deserve it; God, the great Father in His amazing love and mercy, has taken the lost, helpless, poverty-stricken, debt-laden sinner and adopted him into His own family, so that the debts are cancelled and the unearned love and glory inherited." The working of the Holy Spirit in the heart of the adopted son is witness—all the witness that is needed—to this. The converted ones have become His own children and co-heirs of the Holy Son, Jesus Christ.

But there is something more. It is evident in the words of Romans 8:28. "And we know that all things work together for good to them that love God. . . ." Notice that this experience *comes only to those who love the God revealed in Jesus Christ.* All things work together only to those who love and trust Him in all things. They may face disasters; disasters have been known to precede blessings; pain and sorrow are often wiped out by the presence of the Spirit in the heart. He who sees God's hand and purpose in *everything* will be at perfect peace.

SUGGESTIONS TO TEACHERS

Any talk about the Holy Spirit will automatically raise some questions and some uneasiness on the part of some in your class. Some of these questions will relate to Who (please note that the Holy Spirit is not a "what" but a "Who"!) the Spirit is and exactly what He (again note that the Holy Spirit is always described with the personal pronoun!) does. Some of the uneasiness comes because certain charismatic groups seem to claim exclusive possession of the Spirit and insist that anyone knowing the Spirit must speak in tongues.

Although the issue of the charismatics may come up, the focus of your lesson is intended to be God's Indwelling Spirit as promised in John and Romans. If you work faithfully with the Scripture passages in today's lesson, and do not let yourself get off on side issues such as glossolalia (speaking in tongues), you will find several important emphases. Some of these describing the person and the work of the Spirit are as follows:

1. *TEACHER.* Notice that Jesus in John 14 states that the "Helper" will teach us. The Helper will also make us remember what Jesus has told us. What a superb description of the Perfect Teacher, as you as a teacher should realize. The Holy Spirit instructs. The Holy Spirit refreshes our memories of Jesus. Let your class reflect for a time on what the Spirit has instructed it about Jesus by recalling why Jesus is so important. Use a chalkboard or piece of newsprint and mark down the memories of Jesus' meaning in the lives of your people. This, you may show your class, is the Holy Spirit teaching today!

2. *LIFE-GIVER.* The Holy Spirit bestows new vitality. He counteracts the destructive powers of human spirits. The Spirit negated the effects of death. He resurrects. The Spirit of Jesus Christ brings life to people on a death-trip, regardless of what form the destruction may be taking. What are the types of destruction which seem to be most powerful and pervasive in our culture? Let your class know that the Spirit is stronger than any of these killers!

3. *ADOPTER.* The Romans' passage offers a touching way of describing the work of the Spirit. The Spirit is God's way of adopting us as His own sons or daughters. Some in your class will probably be familiar with adoption in which parents welcome a baby not their own into their lives because they want that

child. They give the child their own name. They care for the helpless little one. They sacrifice for its well-being. The Holy Spirit in His work of adopting us into God's own family circle brings the same sense of being loved, wanted, and included.

4. *PLEADER.* The Spirit also prays for us. He intercedes on our behalf. He transmits our groans and decodes our moans into forms of praying. The Spirit translates our wordless gasps into prayers when we don't seem to be able to pray! Spend some of your lesson time on discussing the prayer life of your people and the way the Spirit is so deeply part of their praying.

TOPIC FOR ADULTS
GOD'S INDWELLING SPIRIT

Makes Harmony and Gives Hope. A few years ago in Pittsburgh, I attended a Christmas party in a crippled children's hospital. Fred Rogers and his pianist, Johnny Costa, were entertaining the children. One pathetic little boy suffering from cerebral palsy asked to sing a carol. The child's speech was halting and uncertain. When he began to sing "Silent Night," the sound was wavering and halting. The boy not only had difficulty in framing the words for the carol, but shifted key on every note. As he began painfully to meander through "Silent Night," the rendition was so impossibly bad that nearly everyone shuddered and tried to shut out the discordant sounds. Johnny Costa, however, quietly began to provide background music for the little boy's solo. On the portable organ, Costa wove beautiful chords with each note the child sang, and no matter how off-key the line was, brought beauty and harmony into that child's singing. Costa seemed to anticipate where the little boy's next croak would be on the scale and worked the boy's note into one of the loveliest performances of "Silent Night" I have ever heard.

In the same way, the Spirit takes and hears our prayers and perseveres with us. "In everything, God works for good with those who love Him, who are called according to his purpose" (Romans 8:28)—William P. Barker.

Spirit Takes Over. Faith is created when the Spirit takes over and gets control. Spirit becomes the power and inspiration which generates belief. Man is expected to be more than a clod, is expected to say *yes* or *no*. Hans Küng wrote, "I am expected to make an advance, to venture, to take a risk."

After the "leap of faith" (Kierkegaard's expression) has been made, all problems are far from being neatly solved, so that one can repose in green pastures and wait for Utopia. When God calls, He expects some response, and woe to anybody who has absolutely no inkling of what God expects of him.

Belief in God must anticipate attack from atheists, agnostics, and cynics, by logical argument, scientism, public opinion, and even by principalities and powers in high places.

In his book, *Does God Exist?* (Doubleday) Hans Küng wrote: "Belief in God is continually threatened and—under pressure of doubts—must constantly be realized, upheld, lived, regained in a new decision; even in regard to God himself, man remains in insoluable conflict between trust and mistrust, belief and unbelief."

The struggle to remain faithful is what Christian doctrine means by the term *sanctification.*

Spirit a Guide. Evangelist Billy Sunday once gave his Christian experience: "Twenty-two years ago, with the Holy Spirit as my guide, I entered this wonderful temple we call Christianity. I entered at the portice of Genesis, walked down thru the Old Testament art-gallery where the pictures of Noah, Abraham, Moses, Joseph, Isaac, Jacob, and Daniel hang on the wall. I passed into the music-room of Psalms where the Spirit swept the keyboard of nature and brought forth the dirge-like wail of the weeping Prophet Jeremiah to the grand, impassioned strain of Isaiah, until it seemed that every reed and pipe in God's great organ of nature responded to the tuneful harp of David, the sweet singer of Israel.

"I entered the chapel of Ecclesiastes where the voice of the preacher was heard; and into the conservatory of the Song of Solomon where the Rose of Sharon and the Lily of the Valley's sweet-scented spices filled and perfumed my life. I entered the business office of Proverbs, then into the observatory-room of the prophets where I saw telescopes of various sizes, some pointing to far-off events, some to nearby events; but all concentrated upon the Bright and Morning Star which was to rise above the moonlit hills of Judea for our salvation.

"I entered the audience-room of the King of kings and caught a vision of His glory from the stand-point of Matthew, Mark, Luke, and John; passed into the Acts of Apostles where the Holy Spirit was doing His office-work in the formation of the infant Church; then into the correspondence-room where sat John, Paul, Peter, James, and Jude penning the Epistles. I stepped into the throne-room of Revelation and I got a vision of the King sitting upon His throne in all His glory and I cried:

" 'All Hail the power of Jesus' name, Let angels prostrate fall; Bring forth the royal diadem, And crown Him Lord of all.' "

Questions for Pupils on the Next Lesson. 1. Do you find that many adults are searching for meaningful directions for their lives? 2. Why do we sometimes tend toward disillusionment and seek renewal? 3. What do you do when you find yourself pulled in many directions and having difficulty living consistently? 4. What is the "faith story" from your life that you would share if asked? 5. In what group do you feel most accepted?

TOPIC FOR YOUTH
GOD KEEPS ON HELPING US

Spirit Interprets Scripture. Dr. Ogden once met up on board a cruise ship with a critically minded professor. Upon learning that Dr. Ogden was a minister, the professor asked him for a Bible. Turning to several passages he said, "Did you notice this little absurdity?" Totally ignoring the profound fact that the Spirit interprets the Scriptures, and ignoring the way in which the Spirit speaks through the laws of Moses, the social concern of the prophets, the nobility of Jesus' life and teaching, all he could say was, "Did you notice this little absurdity?" Dr. Ogden's well-developed sense of humor saved him from overreacting. He tells how he amusingly pictured God placing His finger on the bald professor's head and saying, "Did you notice this little absurdity?"

From Tearful to Cheerful. A nineteenth-century professor in England named Thomas Spooner was famous for the ways in which he unintentionally interchanged words with the same sounds. The mistakes were often hilariously funny and came to be known as "spoonerisms." One of Dr. Spooner's most famous slips was the time when he solemnly spoke of the "tearful chidings of the Gospel" instead of the "cheerful tidings of the Gospel."

We often want to make the news of Jesus into "tearful chidings." Instead, the Spirit continually informs us that Jesus means cheerful tidings! Through the Spirit, we can rest assured that God continues to keep on helping us!

Multiplier of the "Widow's Mite." Shanti Solomon of New Delhi, India, is one of those rare people who have had a daring dream become a reality within their own lifetime.

In 1956, Mrs. Solomon was traveling in East Asia with an international group of Christian women. She was barred from entering Korea, however, because that nation did not have diplomatic relations with her homeland. Separated from the rest of the team, she stayed on in the Philippines. There she studied the Bible with local women and came to feel the close ties that a shared faith can bring to strangers. The Spirit seemed real to them.

Then an idea came to her: through a fellowship of prayer the same sense of unity might be experienced everywhere by women who could not travel.

Common prayer for peace, community, and the world's needy would break down barriers between people. In addition to praying, each woman would follow the example of the biblical widow who gave her mite and would contribute the smallest coin of her nation's currency as a symbol of reconciliation.

Shanti's dream has been realized in the Fellowship of the Least Coin—a movement that has caught the interest of thousands of women in seventy-eight lands. Their least coins mount up to significant sums of money, allocated yearly to programs that promote ecumenical fellowship, reconciliation, and, says Mrs. Solomon, "anything that will help people know the Good News."

Because Shanti Solomon dared to dream twenty years ago, the Fellowship of the Least Coin has helped to bring help and hope to hundreds of people. Among them are prostitutes in Korea, native Americans in California, aborigines in Australia, foreign workers in Europe, sharecroppers in Mississippi, ravaged women in Bangladesh. The Spirit still nudges and directs us!

Sentence Sermon to Remember: I should as soon attempt to raise flowers if there were no atmosphere or produce fruits if there were neither light nor heat, as to regenerate men if I did not believe there was a Holy Spirit.—Henry Ward Beecher.

Questions for Pupils on the Next Lesson. 1. Do you ever feel any need for guidance in living? If so, where do you go? 2. What are your favorite role-models? Why? 3. How can your church be more loving? What could you do to make it more harmonious? 4. What does it mean to be part of "God's Called-Out People"?

LESSON XII—NOVEMBER 20

GOD'S CALLED-OUT PEOPLE

Background Scripture: Colossians 3:1–17; 4:5, 6; 1 Peter 2:9–17
Devotional Reading: Colossians 3:1–12

KING JAMES VERSION

COLOSSIANS 3 1 If ye then be risen with Christ, seek those things which are above, where Christ sitteth on the right hand of God.

2 Set your affection on things above, not on things on the earth.

3 For ye are dead, and your life is hid with Christ in God.

4 5 Walk in wisdom toward them that are without, redeeming the time.

6 Let your speech *be* alway with grace, seasoned with salt, that ye may know how ye ought to answer every man.

1 PETER 2 9 But ye *are* a chosen generation, a royal priesthood, an holy nation, a peculiar people; that ye should shew forth the praises of him who hath called you out of darkness into his marvellous light:

10 Which in time past *were* not a people, but *are* now the people of God: which had not obtained mercy, but now have obtained mercy.

11 Dearly beloved, I beseech *you* as strangers and pilgrims, abstain from fleshly lusts, which war against the soul:

12 Having your conversation honest among the Gentiles: that, whereas they speak against you as evildoers, they may by *your* good works, which they shall behold, glorify God in the day of visitation.

13 Submit yourselves to every ordinance of man for the Lord's sake: whether it be to the king, as supreme;

14 Or unto governors, as unto them that are sent by him for the punishment of evildoers, and for the praise of them that do well.

15 For so is the will of God, that with well doing ye may put to silence the ignorance of foolish men:

16 As free, and not using *your* liberty for a cloke of maliciousness, but as the servants of God.

17 Honour all *men*. Love the brotherhood. Fear God. Honour the king.

REVISED STANDARD VERSION

COLOSSIANS 3 1 If then you have been raised with Christ, seek the things that are above, where Christ is, seated at the right hand of God. 2 Set your minds on things that are above, not on things that are on earth. 3 For you have died, and your life is hid with Christ in God.

4 5 Conduct yourselves wisely toward outsiders, making the most of the time.

6 Let your speech always be gracious, seasoned with salt, so that you may know how you ought to answer every one.

1 PETER 2 9 But you are a chosen race, a royal priesthood, a holy nation, God's own people, that you may declare the wonderful deeds of him who called you out of darkness into his marvelous light. 10 Once you were no people but now you are God's people; once you had not received mercy but now you have received mercy.

11 Beloved, I beseech you as aliens and exiles to abstain from the passions of the flesh that wage war against your soul. 12 Maintain good conduct among the Gentiles, so that in case they speak against you as wrongdoers, they may see your good deeds and glorify God on the day of visitation.

13 Be subject for the Lord's sake to every human institution, whether it be to the emperor as supreme, 14 or to governors as sent by him to punish those who do wrong and to praise those who do right. 15 For it is God's will that by doing right you should put to silence the ignorance of foolish men. 16 Live as free men, yet without using your freedom as a pretext for evil; but live as servants of God. 17 Honor all men. Love the brotherhood. Fear God. Honor the emperor.

KEY VERSE: *You are a chosen race, a royal priesthood, a holy nation, God's own people, that you may declare the wonderful deeds of him who called you out of darkness into his marvelous light.* 1 Peter 2:9 (RSV).

HOME DAILY BIBLE READINGS

Nov. 14. M. *Christ Is All.* Colossians 3:1–11.
Nov. 15. T. *Put on Love.* Colossians 3:12–17.
Nov. 16. W. *Continue Steadfastly in Prayer.* Colossians 4:2–6.
Nov. 17. T. *A Living Sacrifice.* Romans 12:1–13.
Nov. 18. F. *The Body of Christ.* 1 Corinthians 12:14–27.

Nov. 19. S.   *You Shall Be Holy.* 1 Peter 1:13–15.
Nov. 20. S.   *God's Own People.* 1 Peter 2:1–10.

BACKGROUND

Whenever we see the word *chosen* in the Old Testament, of course we think of the people of the Old Testament as being the chosen people of God. They were indeed that; in their view, God had chosen (elected) them to perform a peculiar task; in Exodus 19:5, 6, God made of the Israelites "a kingdom of priests and an holy nation." But somehow this did not work out as God had planned, and He found it necessary to choose (call out) yet another people who would take up His torch and together form a Church in which men could be built into a Temple of which Christ was the cornerstone. The Old Testament covenant with the Hebrews was based upon the keeping of the Law.

Now, God calls a new people, the Christians in the Church. What was new, or different, about this?

NOTES ON THE PRINTED TEXT

Paul wrote the Christians at Colossae to warn them against the sin of asceticism. An ascetic is a man who leads a life of contemplation, a man who simply sits in isolation from the world. Sitting and thinking is not, however, altogether bad—provided that the man puts his thinking into *action.* The final test of the Christian lies in his behavior—in how he lives.

The new Christian, having been baptized into the new faith, will have a new set of values. The early Christians regarded this baptism as a dying and arising again, which meant that as they were submerged in the waters of baptism, they are buried in death; as they rose from these waters, they were "resurrected" into a new life in Christ; from this point onward, they must be guided by the thought of things that are "above." They will not be so much interested in the *trivial* things of life as they will be in being led by the eternal truths of God in His heaven.

This does not mean, however, that he should shun the earth, and pay no attention at all to what happens on earth. God did not hate the world; He gave His only begotten Son to save it. The Christian must set himself to do God's will in the world, but his standard in doing that must not be the standard of men but the standard of God "above."

This is a call to look upon the world as God looked upon it. He must, like Christ, be an example of righteousness, sacrifice, and devotion to that which is eternal and not temporary.

Just how does he do that?

He does it, first of all, with his *speech,* in what he says. Let his speech be one that tells the Good News. Let it be that positive. And let it be "gracious," gentle, charitable. Let it *never* be derogatory, never be gossip, but a telling of the truth and mercy of God. Let there never be a sneer or a pompous "righteousness" in any of it. Never boast that you are somehow better than those who do not see all things as you see them. Let it be as humble a speech as the speaking of the One who led you out of darkness into the light of God's truth.

Second, "abstain from the passions of the flesh that wage war against your soul" (1 Peter 2:11). Don't go out trying to save the un-Christians if you commit the same sins that they commit; they will not even listen to you if you play the hypocrite. Let yourself appear among the unsaved as one whose character is unblemished. If you have that, if you behave as the priests (followers) of the King, as His newly chosen people, they will listen to you. "They will end up praising God for your good works when Christ returns" (1 Peter 2:12, *The Living Bible*).

Last but hardly least, the Christian will be different when he fears (loves) God and honors the king (the government). "Render unto Caesar the things that are Caesar's, and to God the things that are God's" (Mark 12:17). To understand that statement, we must know that government in New Testament days was *authoritarian,* or a dictatorship by the Romans. The Roman Caesar was an absolute monarch. To disobey him could mean death. Jesus, for instance, was crucified not because He was born a Jew but because He was, in Caesar's mind, a rebel against the State; the charge was *treason.* But still He said, in effect, pay your taxes to Caesar, render unto him his due.

But neither Jesus nor Paul ever told us to obey a corrupt Caesar or king or government. They did require of all Christians that they be *good citizens.* In Paul's view, government was ordained by God; it was an instrument created in the interests of law and order. Without it, we would have anarchy—and who wants that? But if an evil king came to rule, or a corrupt government defied the will and commands of God, they were not approved of God. Pay your taxes, yes, but not to further corruption and oppression.

In our time, we have not dictatorship as a model but *democracy,* and democracy is not subjection but cooperation, and in this form of government every citizen is called upon to take his share in ruling as an *obligation.* Live in it not as slaves but as free men, as the servants of God. To do that, the citizen may often find himself forced to obey God rather than his human governors. It is all summed up in 1 Peter 2:17: "Honor all men (high or low, slave or free). Love the brotherhood (of Christians). Fear God (love, follow *His* laws). Honor the emperor (the elected official, so long as he is a good, God-directed official)."

So God's called-out people are *commanded* to do this.

SUGGESTIONS TO TEACHERS

A woman was filling in an application to join a swimming club. When she came to the part asking her to list other organizations to which she belonged, she found herself putting down the names of her sorority, the professional society, the Little Theater Group, and her Thursday night bowling team. She was almost ready to fold the application and put it in the envelope when she remembered one other organization. Unfolding the form, she added "Grace Baptist Church." The thought surprised the woman. Later, she told her pastor that she was astonished that she had come to look upon her church membership as "just one more organization," and an afterthought at that!

Is the Church merely a P.S. at the end of the list (usually too long a list) of groups and organizations to which you or your people belong? Sadly, some in your class have little sense of being God's called-out people.

Your lesson for this Sunday is intended to help your class members deepen their sense of being called out by God. Remind them for starters that the very word *church* in the New Testament is the Greek word *ekklesia* (the root of our English word *ecclesiastical*) which means "called out" or "called apart." In Greek cities, citizens had the status and the responsibility of being those who would be called out to meet any civic crises or problems. Your people as citizens of God's realm have also been given the standing and the task of being called out.

The Scripture for today offers many practical suggestions of exactly what it means to be part of God's called-out community. In fact, there are so many that it would be a good idea to put them into categories. One way of sorting these suggestions from Scripture would be to list them, "Within the Congregation" and "Toward the Community."

1. *WITHIN THE CONGREGATION.* Begin the lessons by having the class focus on what their identity as Christians is. Significantly, the New Testament does not speak of "joining the church" as if one took out membership in it. Colossians boldly claims that Christians have been "resurrected with Christ." They

have put to death immorality, greed, and hate. As people raised from the dead, they ignore society's distinctions based on religious tradition, or race, or ethnic background, or geography, or economic class. Furthermore, in the list of qualities of the called-out people, Christians worship together. Using the qualities of Christians listed in Colossians as a check-list, how does your church rate?

2. *TOWARD THE COMMUNITY.* Passages in both Colossians and 1 Peter make it clear that the called-out people turn outward toward the world. As a missionary-minded people, they are savvy in using opportunities to show the faith to nonbelievers. Are your people? According to the Scripture passages, God's people speak and act in ways which attract others to Christ. This is particularly true in relating to all authorities. How is your church regarded in your community? What, for example, does the kid who works at the gas station down the street think about your church?

TOPIC FOR ADULTS
GOD'S CALLED-OUT PEOPLE

Friends of God. Harry Golden occasionally talked about his agnostic father who came from an Orthodox Jewish tradition. The father claimed that he could not believe in God. However, the old man attended synagogue services regularly. Once, someone asked the father why he went to synagogue if he didn't know if there was a God. The elder Golden replied, "My friends go to the synagogue to meet God. Me? I go to meet the friends of God."

What better description of God's called-out people! We are the "friends of God."

"No longer do I call you servants, for the servant does not know what his master is doing; but I have called you friends," said Jesus. "You are my friends if you do what I command you" (John 15:15, 14).

Wrong Number, Pleaazze. " 'Do you have a pinion gear for a 1976 Opel?' New phone equipment installed in 1979 caused our church number to be changed. Still three or four times a week, we get calls for an auto parts store that used to have the number. Stunned are those lost mechanics who, expecting a parts house get a worship house. How would you feel if you dialed the church and got a parts house? People wouldn't listen. We answer the phone, 'Highland Church,' yet they go right on with their order.

"A more profound problem are unchecked assumptions. They assume they know what they're going to get when they dial an auto parts number out of the 1977 phone book. Some people miss what the church has to offer because they approach it with out-of-date assumptions. The parts house metaphor really describes the church for some folks. They see the church only as a place with sufficient inventory to supply their emergency repair needs for a crisis cam shaft, a prayer piston ring, or biblical quote brake linings. It never occurs to them that the church is a fellowship of people who by their interaction with each other and God keep their vital life signs tuned up.

"The church is an enterprise that offers not parts, but *participation.* One of the appeals (curses, benefits?) of large congregations is that they often attract families who want the church to be like a big cafeteria—a place where you go occasionally, pick out food you want and leave without ever having to relate socially or in loving service to the other eaters. Wisely, Reformed theology forbids the private celebration of the sacraments. Baptism and the Lord's Supper have meaning only in the context of the people gathered as the church.

" 'Hello, Gospel Life Auto Parts. Yes sir, you may pick up that piston rod at 11:00 A.M. Sunday' "—Ron Guinn, from *Presbyterian Outlook* (512 E. Main St., Richmond, VA 23219), January 12, 1981.

Belonging to a Noble Company. "To suffer for Christ is to share the work of

Christ; to have to sacrifice for the faith is to share the sacrifice of Christ. When Christianity is hard, we can say to ourselves, not only, 'Brothers, we are treading where the saints have trod,' we can say also, 'Brothers, we are treading where the feet of Christ have trod.' There is always a thrill in belonging to a noble company. Eric Linklater in his autobiography tells of his experience in the disastrous March retreat in the First World War. He was with the Black Watch, and they had come out of the battle with one officer, thirty men, and a piper left of the battalion. 'The next day, marching peacefully in the morning light of France along a pleasant road, we encountered the tattered fragments of a battalion of the Foot Guards, and the piper, putting breath into his bag, and playing so that he filled the air like the massed bands of the Highland Division, saluted the tall Coldstreamers, who had a drum or two and some instruments of brass that also made a gallant music. Stiffly we passed each other, swollen of chest, heads tautly to the right, kilts swinging to the answer of the swagger of the Guards, and the Red Hackle in our bonnets, like the monstrance of a bruised but resilient faith. We were bearded and stained with mud. The Guards—the fifty men that were left of a battalion—were button-bright and clean shaved—we were a tatter-demalion crew from the coal mines of Fife and the back streets of Dundee, but we trod quick-stepping to the brawling tune of "Heilan' Laddie," and suddenly I was crying with a fool's delight and the sheer gladness of being in such company.' It is one of life's great thrills to have the sense of belonging to a goodly company and a goodly fellowship."—William Barclay, *The Gospel of Matthew, Vol. I,* Edinburgh: St. Andrews Press, 1956; Philadelphia, The Westminster Press.

Questions for Pupils on the Next Lesson. 1. How does Christian witnessing enrich and illumine a person's life? 2. Is it optional or mandatory for a Christian to tell others about the faith? 3. How does our relationship with Christ affect our relationship with others? 4. What does it mean to be "an agent of reconciliation"? 5. Who are those who seem to be most alienated from the church in your circle of acquaintances?

TOPIC FOR YOUTH
GOD'S SPECIAL PEOPLE

Why Pick Me? St. Francis of Assisi had a compassion toward all others. People came to St. Francis because they sensed his love and his patience with them. One day, one of his fellow monks became irritated at the way other people sought out Francis. The monk remarked sarcastically to Francis, "Why did God pick you?"

Francis smiled and answered quietly, "My brother, He looked for the most unlikely and most unprofitable servant He could find so that His glory, not mine, would show through."

You are also one of God's special people. Although you may wonder what is so special about you and why God should decide to pick you, you should realize He has called you out in order to let His glory shine through you!

No Jolts for Jesus. The Rev. Dwight Wymer of Grand Rapids rigged up an "electric stool" which he claimed was designed to teach kids about "God and God's love." Wymer's device was a stool that shocked children with a 12-volt battery, as a warning to follow God. Wire screens built into the seat are connected by conductors to the battery and a transformer coil. When Wymer pressed a portable push-button also wired to the battery, an electric shock was applied to the child sitting on the stool. After protests from some worried parents and the county prosecutor, Wymer reluctantly stopped using his electric stool to make children obey the Lord.

God Himself does not zap us. He does not sizzle us or jolt us into obeying Him. He loves us to serving. Through Jesus Christ, He gently helps us to grow to be His special people.

Choose Adventure! Pizarro, the adventurer and explorer offered his little band a tremendous choice. The choice was between the known safety of Panama, and the as yet unknown splendor of Peru. He took his sword and he traced a line with it on the sand from east to west: "Friends and comrades!" he said, "on that side are toil, hunger, nakedness, the drenching storm, desertion, and death; on this side, ease and pleasure. There lies Peru with its riches; here, Panama and its poverty. Choose each man what best becomes a brave Castillian. For my part I go south," and he stepped across the line. And thirteen men, whose names are immortal, chose adventure with him.

Likewise, Jesus Christ calls us to step across the line from security to service, from safety to sacrifice with Him. He leads. He summons us to be the special company of His friends and fellow adventurers! Will you choose to follow Him?

Sentence Sermon to Remember: The Christian call is made to both clergy and laymen: it is no more than a recognition of the needs of mankind, and a realization that with Christ we can satisfy those needs.—J. T. Hendricks.

Questions for Pupils on the Next Lesson. 1. How can you share with others in your class to live more meaningful lives? 2. Have you considered ways in which you can be a more positive role-model for your peers? 3. Have you discovered that sharing the joys of a Christ-filled life can be an enriching experience? 4. How does your relationship with Christ affect your relationship with others? 5. What is the most effective way you can let others know that you are a Christian?

LESSON XIII—NOVEMBER 27

GOD'S WITNESSING PEOPLE

Background Scripture: Matthew 5:13–16; 28:18–20; 2 Corinthians 5:18–21;
2 Timothy 4:1–5
Devotional Reading: 2 Timothy 4:1–5

KING JAMES VERSION

MATTHEW 5   13 Ye are the salt of the earth: but if the salt have lost his savour, wherewith shall it be salted? it is thenceforth good for nothing, but to be cast out, and to be trodden under foot of men.

14 Ye are the light of the world. A city that is set on an hill cannot be hid.

15 Neither do men light a candle, and put it under a bushel, but on a candlestick; and it giveth light unto all that are in the house.

16 Let your light so shine before men, that they may see your good works, and glorify your Father which is in heaven.

28   18 And Jesus came and spake unto them, saying, All power is given unto me in heaven and in earth.

19 Go ye therefore, and teach all nations, baptizing them in the name of the Father, and of the Son, and of the Holy Ghost:

20 Teaching them to observe all things whatsoever I have commanded you: and, lo, I am with you alway, *even* unto the end of the world. Amen.

2 CORINTHIANS 5   18 And all things *are* of God, who hath reconciled us to himself by Jesus Christ, and hath given to us the ministry of reconciliation;

19 To wit, that God was in Christ, reconciling the world unto himself, not imputing their trespasses unto them; and hath committed unto us the word of reconciliation.

20 Now then we are ambassadors for Christ, as though God did beseech *you* by us: we pray *you* in Christ's stead, be ye reconciled to God.

21 For he hath made him *to be* sin for us, who knew no sin; that we might be made the righteousness of God in him.

2 TIMOTHY 4   1 I charge *thee* therefore before God, and the Lord Jesus Christ, who shall judge the quick and the dead at his appearing and his kingdom;

2 Preach the word; be instant in season, out of season; reprove, rebuke, exhort with all longsuffering and doctrine.

REVISED STANDARD VERSION

MATTHEW 5   13 "You are the salt of the earth; but if salt has lost its taste, how shall its saltness be restored? It is no longer good for anything except to be thrown out and trodden under foot by men.

14 "You are the light of the world. A city set on a hill cannot be hid. 15 Nor do men light a lamp and put it under a bushel, but on a stand, and it gives light to all in the house. 16 Let your light so shine before men, that they may see your good works and give glory to your Father who is in heaven."

28   18 And Jesus came and said to them, "All authority in heaven and on earth has been given to me. 19 Go therefore and make disciples of all nations, baptizing them in the name of the Father and of the Son and of the Holy Spirit, 20 teaching them to observe all that I have commanded you; and lo, I am with you always, to the close of the age."

2 CORINTHIANS 5   18 All this is from God, who through Christ reconciled us to himself and gave us the ministry of reconciliation; 19 that is, in Christ God was reconciling the world to himself, not counting their trespasses against them, and entrusting to us the message of reconciliation. 20 So we are ambassadors for Christ, God making his appeal through us. We beseech you on behalf of Christ, be reconciled to God. 21 For our sake he made him to be sin who knew no sin, so that in him we might become the righteousness of God.

2 TIMOTHY 4   1 I charge you in the presence of God and of Christ Jesus who is to judge the living and the dead, and by his appearing and his kingdom: 2 preach the word, be urgent in season and out of season, convince, rebuke, and exhort, be unfailing in patience and in teaching.

KEY VERSE: We are ambassadors for Christ, God making his appeal through us.
. . . 2 Corinthians 5:20 (RSV).

HOME DAILY BIBLE READINGS

Nov. 21.   M.   *The Call to Influence.* Matthew 5:13–16.
Nov. 22.   T.   *The Call to Proclaim.* 2 Timothy 4:1–5.
Nov. 23.   W.   *The Call to Make Defense* 1 Peter 3:8–17.

Nov. 24. T. *The Call to Love.* 1 Corinthians 13.
Nov. 25. F. *The Call to Persevere.* Philippians 3:12–16.
Nov. 26. S. *The Call to Reconcile.* 2 Corinthians 5:16–21.
Nov. 27. S. *The Call to Witness.* Matthew 28:16–20.

BACKGROUND

The scriptural material for this last lesson of the quarter, in which we have been dealing with Christian doctrine, is based upon the preaching of Jesus in the famous Sermon on the Mount. In Matthew 4:23, there is a short word of introduction to what Jesus said in that Sermon; He spoke to His disciples, and quite possibly to a crowd of curious people who wanted to hear more from the Man who had been preaching and teaching and healing throughout Galilee. It is probable that on the mount (one of the little hills on the shore of Lake Tiberias) He was addressing most of the first part of His sermon to the disciples. Some scholars believe that this sermon was really a composite of several sermons. But there is no doubt as to what He was doing that day on the mount. He was announcing a new age—a Messianic age. It was as though Jesus came as a new Moses, making known a new law and blessed Good News to the children of Israel.

In the passages from 2 Corinthians and 3 Timothy, Paul enlarges on this theme in speaking of the reconciliation of God's people—and lays down certain "advices" to the disciple-ambassadors of God.

NOTES ON THE PRINTED TEXT

There are two key words in our Scripture for this lesson which must be the main emphasis for the teacher. One is the word *salt.* Ye are the salt of the earth, all ye who are called to follow me. Now salt has two properties or functions. Salt is a *preservative.* It prevents decay. How well the fishermen of Galilee must have known about that. The disciples are the salt of the earth and of the Kingdom. They keep the Word, the truth of God, alive.

Salt also gives "taste." We sprinkle it on our food to bring out a tastiness that is not naturally in that food. Nathaniel Hawthorne said once, "Salt is white and pure—there is something holy in salt." What a freshness was the Coming of Christ into a world shattered by sin and corruption! Says Suzanne de Dietrich: "The truth of believers, bearers of the Covenant of God, *witnesses of His mercy*—is it this which makes the world acceptable to God?" It is. The disciples were and are witnesses to the truth of God.

But be careful, disciple: salt has a way of losing its savor. It can become insipid, and worthless, and worthy of only being trodden under the foot of men. Be careful, ye who witness, lest you let that happen. Be careful, you churches of Christ, lest the churches dilute the message given you by its Founder. There is nothing worse than the church which gives in to the world in preaching politics or a weak morality. That is the road to sudden death.

The true disciple is also "the light of the world." The very light of God is in the hands of the disciple. Don't hide it under a bushel basket! Let it shine out as though it were set on a high hill. This is the light of God's truth, His righteousness, His love. Let that light go out in the disciple's heart, and the world is doomed.

In 2 Corinthians 5, Paul says that we are being "reconciled" to God through Christ. That means "being brought back to God." He does not say that God is reconciled to us, but that we are reconciled to Him. He does not need reconciliation; we do.

A good teacher friend came to us with a problem and a suggestion. He firmly believed in the necessity of accepting Christ as a way to salvation, but he said, "Sometimes I wonder if we should not concentrate on making ourselves acceptable to Him. Am I wrong?" It is a good question; what would you have said to him?

In Paul's second letter to Timothy (a gentle and often a heartrending letter), we see an old veteran writing to a young disciple. Paul's ministry is almost over; he writes from Rome where he is awaiting the sentence of death. Timothy is a young minister in Ephesus; he has much to learn, and Paul is anxious to give the young pastor the benefit of the old veteran's experience in preaching and teaching the Word.

There is urgency to the charge which Paul gives to the young minister whom he calls "his beloved son." It is a charge given "in the presence of God and of Christ Jesus who is to judge the living and the dead." The time will come when we "must *all* appear before the judgment seat of Christ" (2 Corinthians 5:10). He tells Timothy what he must do to deserve the accolade of "well done, good and faithful servant," at that judgment.

The charge is short and sharp. Preach with an urgency, Timothy. Preach as though you were to die tomorrow. (That is a possibility for all of us!) Preach and teach "in season and out of season"—whenever, wherever you can, when it is convenient or not convenient. (True pastors and teachers have no office hours!) Correct your people when they are wrong; encourage them when they are right. Never give up. Be patient. Give them the Good News and leave the rest to God.

In old Scotland, there was a discouraged old minister trying to hold together a congregation that was smaller than small. He preached in the face of discouragement and disinterest. But one night he preached a sermon that struck fire in the heart of a young boy, a boy named David Livingstone, who became a world-famous missionary who threw open the whole great African continent to the messengers of God.

Be patient, teacher, preacher. You never know what miracles your witness may inspire.

SUGGESTIONS TO TEACHERS

John Baillie, beloved Scottish professor, used to say, "The Church must do as a congregation what Jesus Christ would do were He here in the flesh."

You will find it hard to top this saying as a way of summing up what your church is meant to be doing. In addition, you may use Professor Baillie's statement as a synopsis of your teaching for this day.

The background Scripture for this lesson describes God's witnessing people in several arresting ways. The New Testament, by the way, assumes that God's people *will* be witnessing. Jesus Christ commands it! Witnessing is not an option. Try organizing your lesson material around several imperatives in the biblical material for today.

1. *PRESERVE.* Jesus states emphatically that God's people are the salt. Jesus means that as the salt (the main preservative in those days, especially for fish) God's people are intended to be the agent that preserves society from decaying. Destructive forces are at work, threatening to rot and destroy the community in the world. God's people have the heavy burden of witnessing to God's renewal program of the world through the work of Jesus Christ.

2. *PROJECT.* "You are the light of the world," Jesus tells us (Matthew 5:14). Unless we, the Church, be the beacon in the midst of the darkness, projecting the light of Jesus Christ, humanity will be shipwrecked. How is your congregation illuminating the darkness of despair and loneliness, and the other forms of darkness which you can think of in your community?

3. *PROCLAIM.* Concentrate some prime time of this lesson on the Great Commission in Matthew 28:18–20. Have each member of your class share what he or she thinks your congregation should do to carry out that Commission. Insist

on specifics. Prod your class into additional comments by asking whether the mission giving in your church is adequate. It may also be helpful to gather reports from missionaries with whom you and your class are personally familiar.

4. *PACIFY.* Christians are called to witness to God's work of peacemaking through Jesus Christ. As His people, we are summoned to work for peace. Take enough time to consider the way the world spends for arms. Collect some statistics to point up the cost of instruments of destruction. Discuss practical ways in which your denomination and your congregation can more actively work to bring peace.

5. *PERFORM.* Finally, consider the sections in Paul's letter to Timothy (2 Timothy 4:1–5) as a special message to your class for today. Let your class understand that each member, as part of God's witnessing people, is called to perform the tasks of serving by preaching. Remind your class that there is more than the "pulpit" way of preaching; have the class indicate ways whereby each lay person may "preach."

TOPIC FOR ADULTS
GOD'S WITNESSING PEOPLE

A Missionary Church. "In a truly missionary church, the function of church courts, conferences, conventions, or other deliberative bodies is not to get the will of my party voted, nor yet a compromise between my party and your party, but to determine, if we can, the will of Christ.

"This marks the end of all notions that the church should 'speak for its members,' take the position on issues that is most congenial to the majority of its constituency. A missionary church, which knows itself to be sent into the world by Christ, will seek Christ's will. That may well be difficult to determine, but we shall never determine it if we are seeking something else or something less. . . .

". . . Of course a church has services to render to its own members. They have great needs. They are ignorant and must be taught the foundations of faith—Christian education. They are apathetic and must be aroused—preaching. They are bruised and wounded by life and must be healed—pastoral work. They are in each other's way and need organizing—administration. All these ye ought to have done!

"The question is, Where is the priority? Where is most of the time of church members spent when they do what they call 'church work'? Are they out in the world in the work of proclamation, justice, compassion, and peace? Or are they oiling the ecclesiastical machinery? Examine the church budget. How many dollars go to serve the needs of the world, and how many to maintain the institution of the church? Have we gone out into the world in any meaningful way, or are we still hiding in the sanctuary?

"All too often our churches are not transparent. They are terribly opaque, directing attention to their possessions, their achievements, their image, their reputation in the community. So the glory of God cannot shine through them; only the glory they bestow upon themselves. . . ."—Albert Curry Winn, *A Sense of Mission: Guidance from the Gospel of John,* Philadelphia, Westminster Press, 1981.

Modern-Day Missionaries. "Missionaries in the nineteenth century ventured into what were for them uncharted continents, armed only with the confidence that there are no cattle on any of a thousand distant hills that have not been formed by the Creator's hand and that there is no human being in any jungle compound who is not created in the image of the God who has revealed his will in Jesus Christ. Similarly, we as Christian laity must participate in the complex worlds of business, medicine, law, entertainment, and government with the full confidence that there is no economic or political sin for which the Lamb of God is not a worthy sacrifice and that there is no dark or dusty corner of industry or education that falls outside the scope of the Gospel's power.

"And we must carry out this assignment with the zeal and spirit of self-sacrifice that have been typical of much of the 'foreign missions' enterprise. For those who have been willing to follow through on their Christian commitment, no matter what the cost, the goal has never been simply success or personal happiness or 'worldly acclaim.' The goal has been that of obedience itself, in the knowledge that the God who gives the mandate to act obediently is also the one who sent his own son into the world, not to condemn the world, but that the world might be saved through him."—Richard J. Mouw, *Called to Holy Worldliness*, Philadelphia: copyright © 1980 by Fortress Press, used by permission.

What Kind of Christian. "In Korea today there are three types of Christians: those who do nothing but pray fervently; those who are busy with action, without praying; and those who live through prayer and action, and who are in the extreme minority."—Dr. Tai-Young Lee, first woman lawyer in Korea.

Of these three types, which type are you?

Questions for Pupils on the Next Lesson. 1. Will all people everywhere eventually be taught the ways of God? 2. Does God judge the nations of the world today? 3. Will there ever be an era of peace? 4. Is there any hope in the midst of national and world crises these days? 5. How may your church more effectively work for justice, environmental concerns, and peaceful relationships?

TOPIC FOR YOUTH
GOD'S SHARING PEOPLE

"You Outdid Yourself, Lord." "A small elderly lady waited ahead of me in the supermarket with a cart full of groceries, and the line behind was fairly long. Apparently the check-out girl knew her and they chatted, and I heard the elderly lady say, 'Oh, be SURE to look out that window and see the view today, dear!' The girl did, taking a deep breath of joy, and then smiled at the customer who slowly pushed her cart along. Those behind her, including me, had been a little irritable at this delay. I had only two items and when checked out, rushed toward the door to my car, for I had a sixty mile trip ahead of me.

"There she sat on the bench outside the store and she did not look too elderly—she had such contentment on her face. I thought how lovely she was, how much at peace she seemed. As if we were old friends, she moved over, 'Won't you stop a minute, dear, and look over those beautiful treetops to that view? Have you ever seen such shades of blue in the sky, and the ocean looks almost aqua.' I looked—how had I been here so many times and not really looked over those trees? She added, 'You can see Myles Standish monument today—it is so clear the little sail boats look very close, and I can see the lobster boats at work. . . .'

"I sat down beside her. Then I saw the braces on her legs and her gnarled hand on the little pushcart. But I followed her other hand as it motioned to the view, and inside me something ceased 'being in a hurry.' We sat there, quietly. She spoke, not to me, 'You outdid Yourself today, God.'

"I found she did not have a ride home nor had called a taxi, but usually walked that mile or so to her apartment. I insisted on driving her, if she would guide the way.

"We reached her street and her apartment side door. I stopped at the sight of her beautiful window box, overflowing with the most colorful petunias I have ever seen. Beside it was a bird feeder. Neither of us moved, for near the feeder was a gorgeous cardinal and his little mate. My friend, her eyes shining with happiness, said, 'You have outdone Yourself again, God.'

"I drove homeward along the expressway and this time it did not seem monotonous. I realized how wonderful it was to have green trees along the way for coolness, the colors of goldenrod and vetch and Queen Anne's lace for inspiration. And the clouds. Had the air always been so fragrant? And I said it this time—'You have outdone Yourself today, God!' "—Harriett Connor, *Praying Hands*, Winchester, Mass., October 1980.

The Ministry of the Laity Is in the World. "First, we need lay persons who are firmly convinced of the corporate calling of the people of God. They must sense the mandate and be willing to be engaged in the process of being educated to fulfill that mandate effectively. Second, we need lay persons who are willing to explore the difficult questions of how the Gospel relates to various occupations and professions. This is an area in which there is a desperate need to go beyond general talk about 'theology of the laity. . . .' Third, the laity must approach these questions with utter candor and an openness to self-examination. . . ."—Richard J. Mouw, *Called to Holy Worldliness*, Philadelphia: copyright © 1980 by Fortress Press, used by permission.

Sentence Sermon to Remember: The performance of one act for Christ is worth more than a hundred mere statements of what we believe.—Billy Sunday.

Questions for Pupils on the Next Lesson. 1. Will better times for peace and justice in the world ever come, or will it always be the same? 2. Does God hold nations responsible? 3. Is God able to handle cruel dictators and ruthless regimes? 4. Do you feel there is any hope in the midst of the present national and world crises? 5. What can your church do to help bring a better future?

DECEMBER, 1983, JANUARY, FEBRUARY, 1984

STUDIES IN ISAIAH

LESSON I—DECEMBER 4

A NEW DAY FOR GOD'S PEOPLE

Background Scripture: Isaiah 2:1–5; 62; 65:17–25
Devotional Reading: Isaiah 65:17–25

KING JAMES VERSION

ISAIAH 2 2 And it shall come to pass in the last days, *that* the mountain of the LORD's house shall be established in the top of the mountains, and shall be exalted above the hills; and all nations shall flow unto it.

3 And many people shall go and say, Come ye, and let us go up to the mountain of the LORD, to the house of the God of Jacob; and he will teach us of his ways, and we will walk in his paths: for out of Zion shall go forth the law, and the word of the LORD from Jerusalem.

4 And he shall judge among the nations, and shall rebuke many people: and they shall beat their swords into plowshares, and their spears into pruninghooks: nation shall not lift up sword against nation, neither shall they learn war any more.

62 1 For Zion's sake will I not hold my peace, and for Jerusalem's sake I will not rest, until the righteousness thereof go forth as brightness, and the salvation thereof as a lamp *that* burneth.

2 And the Gentiles shall see thy righteousness, and all kings thy glory: and thou shalt be called by a new name, which the mouth of the LORD shall name.

3 Thou shalt also be a crown of glory in the hand of the LORD, and a royal diadem in the hand of thy God.

REVISED STANDARD VERSION

ISAIAH 2 2 It shall come to pass in the latter days
that the mountain of the house of the LORD
shall be established as the highest of the mountains,
and shall be raised above the hills;
and all the nations shall flow to it,
3 and many peoples shall come, and say:
"Come, let us go up to the mountain of the LORD,
to the house of the God of Jacob;
that he may teach us his ways
and that we may walk in his paths."
For out of Zion shall go forth the law,
and the word of the LORD from Jerusalem.
4 He shall judge between the nations,
and shall decide for many peoples;
and they shall beat their swords into plowshares,
and their spears into pruning hooks;
nation shall not lift up sword against nation,
neither shall they learn war any more.

62 1 For Zion's sake I will not keep silent,
and for Jerusalem's sake I will not rest,
until her vindication goes forth as brightness,
and her salvation as a burning torch.
2 The nations shall see your vindication,
and all the kings your glory;
and you shall be called by a new name
which the mouth of the LORD will give,
3 You shall be a crown of beauty in the hand of the LORD,
and a royal diadem in the hand of your God.

KEY VERSE: *And they shall be called The holy people, The redeemed of the Lord.* . . . Isaiah 62:12 (RSV).

93

HOME DAILY BIBLE READINGS

Nov. 28. M. *A World Transformed.* Isaiah 65:17–25.
Nov. 29. T. *A Hope of Fulfillment.* Romans 8:18–25.
Nov. 30. W. *"The Lord Will Comfort Zion."* Isaiah 51:1–12.
Dec. 1. T. *"Your God Reigns."* Isaiah 52:7–12.
Dec. 2. F. *The New Age of Peace.* Micah 4:1–5.
Dec. 3. S. *The New Age of Peace.* Isaiah 2:1–5.
Dec. 4. S. *The New Jerusalem.* Isaiah 62:1–12.

BACKGROUND

Now comes Isaiah for the next thirteen lessons. Isaiah! In the mighty constellation of the prophets, he was the mightiest. He puts all others in eclipse. His least word fell like the blow of a battle-ax; he spoke in poetry so eloquent that it was often lost among the stars.

Most biblical scholars believe that there was not one Isaiah, but three, writing against the historical backgrounds of their times. The man who gave the book his name was an eighth century B.C. prophet. His part of the book extends from chapter 1–39; chapters 40–55 contain the prophecies of what we call Second or Deutero-Isaiah; the Third or Trito-Isaiah prophesied in the remaining 56–66th chapters. Often, in those days, the prophets were divided into what might be called schools, or groups of prophets all proclaiming quite the same message. The Isaiah we study today could well have been the founder of the school.

Born in Jerusalem, this first Isaiah was active as a prophet over a period of about forty years, during the reigns of Jotham, Ahaz, and Hezekiah. It was a time of great trouble. Judah was threatened with extinction. Jotham tried to "do that which was right," and failed. Ahaz, son of Jotham, was a royal disgrace, a mere vassal of Assyria. Hezekiah was a good and great king, and he did much to rebuild a faltering Judah but he came too late. Isaiah preached in the streets, warning him, but the die was cast.

NOTES ON THE PRINTED TEXT

If there is any passage in the Old Testament that seems directed at we who live in the twentieth century, this passage from Isaiah is it! It is a passage dealing with a people frightened at the prospect of destruction. It was written in a day when the Mediterranean world was racked by war. To read Isaiah 1 is to believe that there was no hope for Jerusalem and Judea. Israel was already put under the heel of Assyria—and Isaiah spoke for God when he said that the same fate awaited Jerusalem and Judea.

But Isaiah was no warrior, shouting, "To arms!" He talked of peace and foretold a peace that, with us, seems to pass all understanding. Like Amos and Micah (contemporaries of Isaiah), he was "fed up" with the apostasy and hypocrisy of the Judeans; he railed against the "solemn assemblies" of a people who were only pretending to love and *obey* the God of their fathers. That they would pay dearly for their apostasy, he was certain. But he did not speak in despair; he was convinced that there would come a day when not only Israel and Judea but the whole world, the whole of mankind, would live together in faith, righteousness, and brotherhood.

We may call this wishful thinking; if we do, we are wrong. It is an expression of *the perpetual longing of the human heart for peace.* It is the crying out of God for men to beat their swords into plowshares, their spears into pruning hooks—to call an end to war and to live together like sensible, God-directed men. That would come, prophesied Isaiah. "It shall come to pass in the latter days that the mountain of the house of the Lord shall be established . . . and all nations shall flow to it" (Isaiah 2:2).

Wishful thinking? A dream? No: this is the only way out of the military power that holds our modern world in fear. We put our trust in princes, and the princes betray us. We sign solemn treaties and break them as though they were no more than scraps of paper. We wage war after war, have peace for a while; and then comes another war! We die like sheep at the command of a military officer and find the dying useless. (Remember Vietnam?) In the past, says Nahum Goldmann, the famous Israelite statesman, men died in war for religion's sake, but now.... "Today, we kill for the big banks, the arms manufacturers, and the extension of the power of the state." Sad, but how true!

What Isaiah is saying is that there is a better way than this; it is the way of acknowledging the eternal supremacy of God. It means stopping our lip service to Him and organizing our lives to live under His love and His will. "Isaiah sees the day when the distrust of men will be overcome by trust in God. When misunderstandings are laid out before a judge whose righteousness is absolute, and whose wisdom is infinitely greater than man's, when the councils of the nation are overseen by one who is mighty in goodness; then, as Isaiah says, it is God who settles the issues; as a result of trust in the Great Judge, the suspicions, hatreds, and fears of men are dispelled, and they trust one another."—G. G. Kilpatrick in *The Interpreters Bible*, vol. 5, by permission of Abingdon Press, publishers.

Fantastic? No, this is our last chance, the last best hope of man. We have tried everything else; isn't it time we tried this? If any one of us has a better way, let him stand up and speak!

SUGGESTIONS TO TEACHERS

The Christmas Season may be filled with peace and gifts for most people but is freighted with pain and grief for others. Sadly, the referral rate to counselors, including psychiatrists, psychologists, and clergy, rises sharply during and after the holidays. "I don't have anything to look forward to," lamented one client in a counselor's office three weeks before Christmas.

Christ's people, of course, look foward with joy to the celebration of this season. The reason is that hope has come in the form of the birth of the Messiah, Jesus.

Your lessons for the next four Sundays concentrate on the Messianic hope as described by Isaiah. Many of the passages will be familiar. Listen to them with the ears of a person who has had little if any hope in the world during these weeks. You will discover new depths of understanding the hope that Jesus Christ brings. Start today's lesson by emphasizing the hope that the new day for God's people that Christ brings.

1. *A NEW REIGN.* Isaiah offers the vision of a new reign on earth: God's. No longer is the universe apparently ruled by evil powers. God's promise is given in a new way. Isaiah uses lovely images to tell that an era comes in which persons everywhere will go to a mountain to worship the Lord. Help your people to realize the tremendous historic and global significance of Jesus' Coming.

2. *A NEW HOPE.* Most people have scaled-down expectations for the future compared to those of a generation ago. Some of this is healthy realism. On the other hand, many have lost hope. Allow plenty of time in this lesson to reflect on how Christ means hope, both for here and the hereafter. Quiz your class on whether your people really entertain any hope for a world living in peace and in justice. With God, there is always a future!

3. *A NEW NAME.* List the many "before and after" titles Isaiah offers to describe God's people (no longer "Forsaken" or "Desolate" but now called "My Delight," "Your Land Married" and "Sought Out"). Salvation is coming for God's people. They will be claimed by the Lord as "holy" or special! With what groups do your people in your class identify most closely? How do they describe themselves in their relationship to God? You may even wish to take a poll to find what

name or names tells most about their faith ("Forsaken" or "Sought Out").

4. *A NEW EARTH.* Isaiah's dream in chapter 65 is picked up in 2 Peter 3:13 and Revelation 21:1, where we learn that there will be an end of weeping and despair. The Messiah's Coming means each person can live, not simply exist, during his/her life span. Joy, not gloom, prevails. A harmony pervades the entire order of nature. Are your class members living in this new day, and therefore not hurting or destroying but healing and developing in every way they can?

TOPIC FOR ADULTS
A NEW DAY FOR GOD'S PEOPLE

"Just in Case There Is a God." Martin Bailey, a Christian journalist, writes of his visit to Cuba where he talked with Elio Constantin, the managing editor of Havana's daily newspaper, *Granma:*

"After the usual introductions and pleasantries, we inquired about his news-gathering methods and the newspaper's circulation in Havana and beyond. Before the revolution there were twelve papers in Cuba's capital; now there is just *Granma.* Its 625,000 daily circulation is greater than all the papers combined before the war. Regional editions are printed in the provinces. There is no opposition press. Our conversation became animated as we pressed him on questions of credibility. Did he really assume his reader would believe reports in a controlled press? One of the goals of the revolution was better education; does that not require that people have access to more than one source of news and point of view? More than once our translator became embarrassed at having to relay our pointed questions and expressions of disbelief. The conversation was direct, a virtual debate.

"Eventually there was little more to say. As we rose to leave, Mr. Constantin's mood changed. Constantin walked with us down . . . flights of stairs and out onto the sidewalk. There were warm handshakes all around—considerably more than a polite farewell.

"Elio Constantin then drew us into a little circle. 'I came downstairs to tell you something that I couldn't say upstairs.' (We assumed that his office was bugged.) 'I thought you might be interested in knowing that I was raised in a Roman Catholic home, I went through Roman Catholic parochial schools. In fact, for several years before the revolution, I studied for the priesthood.

" 'But when Fidel came to power I decided to cast my lot with him. I believe in what he proposed to do for the poor, for the uneducated masses. To follow him, of course, I had to renounce my faith. To join the party, you must be an atheist. The revolution has been good for Cuba. I have never been sorry.

" 'But, my good friends, please pray for me—just in case there is a God.'

"There was a wistfulness in his voice and we were deeply moved. Jim Wall found a few Spanish words for a most appropriate reply: Vaýa con Dios: 'Walk with God.' "—Excerpted from "The Church in Castro's Cuba" (August 1981 *A.D.*). Copyright *A.D.* Excerpted and used by permission.

God's people celebrate the joyous news that there not only *is* a God, but that this God has come to us in person! The Messiah has come! A new age has dawned! We have hope!

Our Source of Hope. "Amid all the creak and clatter of our far-flung Christian plans, therefore—the commissions, committees, campaigns, surveys, federations, and budgets—all thoughtful Christians who are interested to avoid the disillusionment which the failure of so much splendid effort would inevitably cause will bear down hard upon the central matter: the achievement of a deeper sense of God's reality. That is the foundation of all our building. If that weakens, the excellence of the superstructure does not matter. That is the dynamic. If that fails, the skillful workmanship of the engine is effort thrown away.

"Now, the sense of God's reality is a different experience from belief that God exists. All men believe that natural beauty exists, but some men feel it vividly, rejoice in it heartily, while others are never moved by it at all. Atheism is not our greatest danger, but a shadowy sense of God's reality. We do not disbelieve that God exists, but we often lack a penetrating and convincing consciousness that we are dealing with him and he with us. This is the inner problem of prayer.

"The troubles of our generation which so urgently demand of us a fresh consciousness of God can help us to the very experience for which they cry. For God is like water—the intense reality of it is never appreciated by one who has not known thirst. So God's unreality to us in part is due to our easy-going way of taking him for granted, with little sense of dire and dreadful need.

"Even now dismal possibilities lie ahead—upheaval, anarchy, violence; and the whole world going on with this military business, using all inventive genius for destructive ends and making a worse hell of it all than the Stone Age a thousand times over. Or, on the other side, what glorious possibilities! What hopes worth praying, toiling, fighting for! If only this world were meant to enshrine a better order; if only creation were moral to the core; if only—God! For if creation is not basally moral, no God at all, and we with unaided human fingers are trying to make an ethical oasis in a spiritual desert, where no oasis was ever meant to be, then we are beaten at the start. Soon or later the desert will heave its burning sands against us and hurl its blistering winds across us, and all that we have dreamed and done will come to naught."—Harry E. Fosdick, "The Sense of God's Reality," copyright 1919 Christian Century Foundation. Reprinted by permission from the November 6, 1919 issue of *The Christian Century*.

New Day for the Guilt-Ridden. It has been more than two years since Kansas City's most elegant hotel became a forty-story memorial to 112 people.

But the 187 injured survivors of the Hyatt Regency Hotel disaster, the rescue workers who dug through the tons of debris, the friends and relatives of those killed or maimed have not forgotten.

"When you see human slaughter of that magnitude, you can't not be moved and still be human," said Don Eisenberg, a director of disaster services for the Red Cross who was at the scene.

When two Hyatt skywalks collapsed on July 17, onto a crowded weekend tea dance, thousands of lives were altered. Those who witnessed the horrors of that evening were experiencing a spectrum of emotions, including anger, insomnia, loss of appetite, supersensitivity to smell and noises, and the inevitable survivor's guilt.

Those who were there mentally arrange, then rearrange, that night, questioning if perhaps they had just done something differently, a wife, husband or best friends might still be alive. John Davis was one of them. He had entered through the revolving doors only fifteen minutes before. Now he is a widower and wears a hip-to-neck metal brace for his broken back. Mr. Davis, looking forward to his vacation, had escorted his wife, Judy, and their two best friends, Larry and Suzanne Watson, to the tea dance. Only he is alive today.

"This was our last chance this summer to go to the tea dance," he said. "I said, 'They may not have them when we get back.'

"Logically, I shouldn't feel any guilt. But it's still there."

Logically, we should not be feeling any guilt. Yet we do! Mere thinking or wishing will not take away the grim affliction of guilt. The new age for the guilt-ridden comes through Jesus Christ. In spite of past horrors and regrets, God brings a new day through Christ's Coming. There is hope for the future!

Questions for Pupils on the Next Lesson. 1. Do you sometimes feel unable to achieve your goals and visions by yourself? 2. Who in your congregation most needs the experience of being comforted, healed, and freed? What is your church doing to bring that experience to these people? 3. Who are the "afflicted" in your community? 4. Where are the greatest needs for justice in our society? 5. What are the responsibilities of the Church in regard to the afflicted?

TOPIC FOR YOUTH
LOOK TO THE FUTURE

Futile Future? Many young persons despair over the future, assuming that there will be a nuclear conflagration soon. Even in the universities, many of the brightest students have no hope in a tomorrow. Professor Harvey Cox of Harvard related recently that he had taken a poll of one of his courses that has about 100 students enrolled.

"I picked the course especially because there were people in it from various parts of the university," he says. "There were undergraduates and divinity students and law students and students from the schools of education and public health and so on. I wanted as much of a cross section as you could get.

"Over 80 percent of the students thought both that there would be a nuclear war and that they would not survive it. And here's a place where people are applying for graduate school, doing their term papers. We think of this as the last bastion of delayed gratification."

In the face of such pessimism, Isaiah announces a new Day. The Messiah comes. God brings hope through Jesus Christ's Coming.

Ultimate End. . . ? After the spiritual vacuum in China, after more than three decades of official atheism, the failure of Communism as a substitute religion and the collapse of Mao as a savior, young Chinese are searching for reasons for hope. A young woman named Pan Xiao, a twenty-three-year-old worker, wrote a letter to the China Youth magazine a couple of years ago in which she asked, "Life, is this the mystery you try to reveal? Is the ultimate end nothing more than a dead body?" The magazine has a circulation of nearly four million, and when Pan Xiao's letter was published, 60,000 young readers wrote in response. No wonder that China's churches find that from one-third to one-half of the revived congregations are made up of young persons!

Do we in the Western World appreciate the meaning of the hope that the Coming of Jesus Christ brings? Do we see that the hope for the future comes because of Him, not because of some ideology or hero or "ism"?

Permanent Hope. A sign hung in a Hollywood jewelry store for several months before a newspaper reporter finally mentioned it in the *Los Angeles Times.* Apparently everyone assumed the sign was no big deal because the write-up never made the front page or a prominent space in the paper. The sign read:

WE RENT WEDDING RINGS.

Many laughed: "What's the use of thinking there is a future for marriage and the family, so why shouldn't they rent rings?"

God's people look to the future. The Coming of Christ brings hope for meaningful personal relationships, including making commitments as Christian husbands and wives.

Sentence Sermon to Remember: Life with Christ is an endless hope; life without Him is a hopeless end.—Anonymous.

Questions for Pupils on the Next Lesson. 1. Do you feel free or do you feel trapped? Why? 2. Do you sometimes wonder if justice will win out? 3. How would you help someone to cope with grief? 3. Who are the afflicted and disadvantaged in your church, and in your community? 4. Why is the Coming of Jesus called the "Gospel" which means "Good News"? Is His Coming Good News to you personally? Why or why not?

LESSON II—DECEMBER 11

GOOD NEWS FOR THE AFFLICTED

Background Scripture: Isaiah 61
Devotional Reading: Isaiah 61:8, 9

KING JAMES VERSION

ISAIAH 61   1 The Spirit of the Lord GOD *is* upon me; because the LORD hath anointed me to preach good tidings unto the meek; he hath sent me to bind up the broken-hearted, to proclaim liberty to the captives, and the opening of the prison to *them that are* bound;

2 To proclaim the acceptable year of the LORD, and the day of vengeance of our God; to comfort all that mourn;

3 To appoint unto them that mourn in Zion, to give unto them beauty for ashes, the oil of joy for mourning, the garment of praise for the spirit of heaviness; that they might be called trees of righteousness, the planting of the LORD, that he might be glorified.

4 And they shall build the old wastes, they shall raise up the former desolations, and they shall repair the waste cities, the desolations of many generations.

5 And strangers shall stand and feed your flocks, and the sons of the alien *shall be* your plowmen and your vinedressers.

6 But ye shall be named the Priests of the LORD: *men* shall call you the Ministers of our God: ye shall eat the riches of the Gentiles, and in their glory shall ye boast yourselves.

7 For your shame *ye shall have* double; and *for* confusion they shall rejoice in their portion: therefore in their land they shall possess the double: everlasting joy shall be unto them.

REVISED STANDARD VERSION

ISAIAH 61   1 The Spirit of the Lord GOD is upon me,
because the LORD has anointed me
to bring good tidings to the afflicted;
he has sent me to bind up the broken-hearted,
to proclaim liberty to the captives,
and the opening of the prison to those who are bound;
2 to proclaim the year of the LORD's favor,
and the day of vengeance of our God;
to comfort all who mourn;
3 to grant to those who mourn in Zion—
to give them a garland instead of ashes,
the oil of gladness instead of mourning, the mantle of praise instead of a faint spirit;
that they may be called oaks of righteousness,
the planting of the LORD, that he may be glorified,
4 They shall build up the ancient ruins,
they shall raise up the former devastations;
they shall repair the ruined cities,
the devastations of many generations.
5 Aliens shall stand and feed your flocks,
foreigners shall be your plowmen and vinedressers;
6 but you shall be called the priests of the LORD,
men shall speak to you as the ministers of our God;
you shall eat the wealth of the nations,
and in their riches you shall glory.
7 Instead of your shame you shall have a double portion,
instead of dishonor you shall rejoice in your lot;
therefore in your land you shall possess a double portion;
yours shall be everlasting joy.

KEY VERSE: . . . the Lord has anointed me to bring good tidings to the afflicted. Isaiah 61:1 (RSV).

HOME DAILY BIBLE READINGS

Dec. 5. M. *A More Splendid Temple.* Haggai 2:1–9.
Dec. 6. T. *"Your Light Has Come."* Isaiah 60:1–7.
Dec. 7. W. *"The City of the Lord."* Isaiah 60:8–14.
Dec. 8. T. *A Land at Peace.* Isaiah 6:15–22.
Dec. 9. F. *"A People . . . the Lord . . . Blessed."* Isaiah 61:8–11.
Dec. 10. S. *Impatient for the New Jerusalem.* Isaiah 62:1–12.
Dec. 11. S. *"Good News to the Humble."* Isaiah 61:1–7.

BACKGROUND

It is a long jump from Isaiah 2 to Isaiah 61, which gives us a story and a prophecy which must have come long years after the first Isaiah had died. Notice that this whole quarter of lessons is made up of many "messages" of the Book of Isaiah; the messages are scattered through the whole Book, but in our lessons they are not in chronological order.

In 539 B.C., Cyrus the Great of Persia conquered the Chaldean army at Babylon, and in Babylon he found thousands of Jewish prisoners previously captured by the Babylonians. Cyrus was perhaps the most merciful king in Old Testament history: he set free some 43,000 of these captive Jews, and sent them back to live again in the blessed land of their fathers.

These released Jews must have marched back home in great exultation. Going home to Jerusalem! What could give them more happiness than this? But when they reached Jerusalem, they found a city of ruins and rubble, and a people in despair, suffering from skepticism and overcome by religious apathy. Had it not been for the prophet who appeared before them to lift them out of all this, they might well have wished that they had never left the land of Cyrus. It was this Isaiah, or prophet of the Isaiah school, who was called of God to tell them that they stood not at a moment when Judah would die but at the beginning of a new and glorious age—a Messianic Age.

NOTES ON THE PRINTED TEXT

God had His man ready for this hour—a man, a prophet upon whom was the Spirit of the Lord God (61:1). In the heart and on the lips of this anointed one was the Good News that Judah longed to hear. He was sent of God, this prophet said, to lift up the suffering and the afflicted (afflicted in heart and spirit and soul), to comfort the brokenhearted (God never leaves such people desolate), to set free the captives (the prisoners of fear, the hopeless); He would open the eyes of the blind (those who had lost sight of Him).

To those who only sat and mourned ("Blessed are they that mourn: for they shall be comforted," said Jesus), to all these would come One who would be called Wonderful, Counsellor. It is not strange that these verses, this hope, from Isaiah, were read in the synagogue at Nazareth, and applied them to Himself (Luke 4:16–19).

Modern Christians should, must, understand that this was and is the work of Christ's Church. The people of His Church are called not *only* to sing the praises of God but to hold out the hand of love for the poor, the suffering, the blind, the captives of sin who live beyond the walls of the Church. The Church is God's servant to all these who mourn in despondency; for them, in His name, the Church can bring beauty and not ashes, joy and not mourning, hope and not heaviness.

Yes, the prophet says, the old Jerusalem will be restored; its people will raise up a new city on its ashes, and other ruined cities will be repaired. God would surely help them to do this, for they were His servants—often called a Servant People. As servants, they had the quality of an old oak tree that seems to die in winter, only to be restored with the coming of spring. They would rise again, as "oaks of righteousness" (verse 3). The Servant People would live on as God's messengers, and as priests, a nation of priests who will enjoy the wealth and privileges denied their predecessors, and as ministers of God within and beyond their own land.

It has happened. There are in our modern world some 14,000,000 Jews scattered all over the world. Only 18 percent of these Jews are living in Palestine; the rest are "dispersed" from pole to pole, still loyal to their faith.

And since the Counsellor and the Prince of Peace preached that sermon in Nazareth, there are more than a billion of His followers keeping His faith. Where ancient Judaism left off, Christ began. This Christ, being raised in a Jewish atmosphere, respected it, and often quoted from it. Like the Jewish people, His people have suffered many a holocaust, opposition and persecution all along the way. Still, like the old oak, it persists in a Servant called the Church.

In any city or town in our country, everything seems to have changed with the march of time. In every community, Main Street has seen many businesses come and go, but one Son of God goes on about His Father's business. Everything seems to disappear but the Church!

SUGGESTIONS TO TEACHERS

North of Stroudsburg, Pennsylvania, on Route 209, stands a large sign blazoned with the words: CLINIC OF HOPE. Bulletin board for a Church? Sign for a retreat center, or camp, or Christian enterprise? No. When one reads the next lines in smaller letters, it is learned that the sign advertises the offices of two chiropractors.

Every Christian group, however, should be a "clinic of hope." Any church that has had any exposure to Isaiah 61 will sense its call to share Good News with the afflicted.

Your lesson this week, continuing the Unit's theme of the Messianic Hope, should spur your class and your church to become more of the clinic of hope which the Lord intends.

1. *ANOINTED WITH SPIRIT.* Your class should be made mindful of the importance of Isaiah 61 for Jesus. As teacher, you may point out how Jesus quoted this section as the basis for inaugurating His public ministry in His first sermon at Nazareth. Bring the Isaiah passage to your class by insisting that your people think about the fact that the Spirit has also anointed them "to bring good tidings to the afflicted . . . to bind up the brokenhearted, to proclaim liberty to the captives . . . to proclaim the year of the Lord's favor . . . to comfort all who mourn." Just as the Spirit was given to Jesus, the Spirit has touched our lives also!

2. *APPOINTED FOR CAPTIVES.* Examine Isaiah 61:1, 2 and ask your class to ponder who the "afflicted," the "brokenhearted," the "captives," "those who are bound," and those who mourn are in your area. Consider the many forms of captivity, such as economic oppression or emotional despair.

3. *ACCLAIMED AS MINISTERS.* Set aside enough of your lesson time to think about some of the ramifications of Isaiah 61:6 ("you shall be called priests of the Lord, men shall speak of you as the ministers of our God"). Is this what the community around you thinks of folks in your church? Is this what people in your class regard themselves as being? Hammer the point that every member of Christ's community of hope is "ordained" through baptism. Every Christian church member is one of God's representatives!

4. *ACKNOWLEDGED IN RIGHTEOUSNESS.* Do not neglect to stress Isaiah's point that the real way to honor God is through justice. Justice, you may inform your class, is love spread around for everyone. The church that is most truly the "clinic of hope" which God calls it to be will be constantly sensitive to justice issues both in its own immediate community and in the wider community. What are key matters which call for justice, as your class sees them?

TOPIC FOR ADULTS
GOOD NEWS FOR THE AFFLICTED

Help for the Homeless. He graduated from the New York University School of Law, where he had crossed Washington Square Park each day and gotten a close look at the city's wayward population. His apartment on West 16th Street provided another vantage point.

Some people can pass the city's vagrants like another piece of scenery on the walk home, but Mr. Hayes has never been able to. "I had to do something," he said. "It became something of an obsession. The Supreme Court talks about insular minorities—racial minorities, illegal aliens—but I can think of no more disenfranchised minority than the homeless."

New York City's tens of thousands of homeless men did not appoint Robert Hayes to represent them, nor did a social service agency knock on his door and ask him to take their case.

As the young lawyer put it, "I'm just an ordinary guy who got mad."

By day, he would tread on soft beige carpeting in the hushed offices of his firm and work on antitrust and securities cases. At night, he would walk the Bowery, talking to his newfound clients, the bedraggled men who check in at the Men's Shelter and are sent to cheap hotels in the area or to the city's large shelter on Wards Island.

Mr. Hayes saw that the homeless remained on the stoops of the neighborhood unless they could find shelter nearby. He also saw that these homeless men needed local, community based shelters rather than the huge, remote buildings proposed at the time by the city officials.

He was twenty-five years old when he first started the case against the city and the state social-services department. Robert Hayes, with the blessing of his law firm, went to church-sponsored Holy Name Center for Homeless Men on the Bowery and gathered his first clients of afflicted, homeless persons. Mr. Hayes began to press the City of New York to provide shelter in the light of the state of New York Constitution. Hayes was concerned for the afflicted the Bible speaks about. Finally, after exhausting efforts on behalf of New York's homeless men, his three years of work on their behalf culminated when city officials signed an agreement with Mr. Hayes that will require New York City to provide clean and safe shelter to any man who asks for it.

What Hope for the Afflicted? Despite progress, there are still more hungry people in the world than ever before—both in absolute numbers and as a percentage of total world population. The rising cost of food has contributed to this situation.

By most estimates, more than 500 million people—roughly one out of every nine—suffer from serious malnutrition today, compared with 100 million to 200 million—one out of every fourteen to twenty-five people—in the 1950s.

Refugee camps are still filled with wide-eyed children with swollen bellies. Millions of malnourished adults in Asia and Africa are still doomed to live and work far below their normal capabilities.

The coexistence of bounty and want is, in short, as stark as it ever was. The reason is that food production has not kept up with rising incomes around the world, and those income gains are not being equitably distributed.

As more countries—particularly the rapidly developing middle-income countries—and wealthier people in those countries gain in purchasing power, they consume more food. This in turn puts pressure on food prices and means that poorer people everywhere have a harder time buying enough to eat.

"There has been significant progress in a few developing countries," John Mellor, head of the International Food Policy Research Institute in Washington, said in a recent interview. "But the gains do mean that the poorest people will be worse off. It's a good development, but it is increasing inequalities."

"The ghost of Malthus," as Shahid J. Burke of the World Bank recently put it "is not buried yet." Christ, for the 500 million afflicted with malnutrition, will be Good News in the form of food. The Bread of Life will be Glad Tidings when He is brought in the form of wheat, rice, and milk powder to the hungry. We who have more than enough to eat must not only share but devise means by which the have-nots of our global family may sustain themselves. We are the ones through whom the Good News of Jesus Christ comes, and we must bring Him in the form of food.

What Do We Know? The late General Omar Bradley said: "Ours is a world of nuclear giants and ethical infants. We know more about war than we know about peace, more about killing than we know about living. We have grasped the mystery of the atom and rejected the Sermon on the Mount."—*Quote*, September 1, 1981.

General Bradley's point should remind us that we Christians must first realize that Christ is Good News for all of us, then share Him with all who are afflicted.

Questions for Pupils on the Next Lesson. 1. How does God reveal Himself? 2. How may people find security and permanence in a "throw away" society? 3. How is God's glory recognized? 4. How do you find affirmation as a person of worth? 5. Does your church offer people a sense of fulfillment in a cause that offers personal and community value?

TOPIC FOR YOUTH
WHEN LIFE GETS TOUGH

Chafe Watch. On racing yachts, there are numerous dangers and problems not encountered in any other sport. The big seagoing sailing boats are sleek and beautiful when their sails are filled with wind. Few realize that these graceful craft are prone to what is known as chafe.

The crew constantly inspects for chafe, one of the biggest problems in long-distance sailing. Sails rub on the rigging and worn spots have to be patched before entire sails tear. Chafe also occurs on the wire halyards that are used to hoist and hold up the sails, and that can spell disaster in a strong wind if they break. We humans find ourselves suffering from a type of chafe from the pressures, stress, and wear of daily life. Life gets tough and threatens to break even the strongest person. There is Good News, however, for everyone afflicted with "chafe" of the mind or spirit. Jesus Christ comes bringing renewed strength. With Him, we have new staying power. No matter how severely we are afflicted with tough storms in life, He stands by us enabling us to cope.

Customized Tombstones. In a computerized society where little opportunity for individuality remains, a Seattle firm offers personalized designs etched into gravestones. A new technique allows almost any picture or design to be applied to a granite marker for a cemetery by using sandblast grains and a special rubberized stencil. Some of the designs, ordered by parents to commemorate young children, are heartrending. One pictures a leaf blowing off the tree of life. Adults often choose occupational symbols: a sewing machine, a policeman's badge, a B-52 in remembrance of a Boeing employee who was loyal to the bitter end. There are also golfers, fishermen, a teen-ager's customized 1965 Mustang complete to the license plate BAD NUZ, and a skier taking off on a jump, above the legend BILL WENT FOR IT. One woman had her stone engraved with four aces over the Christian symbol of the fish.

Christians, however, don't have to seek such pathetic ways of seeking to be remembered. Nor do Christ's people need to worry about finding means of preserving their sense of individuality. For those afflicted with the worry of "Who will remember me?" or "How can I express that I am special?" Jesus Christ is the Good News! He is good tidings for all who are afflicted, including those afflicted with a sense of worry over their personal insignificance.

He Remembered. A group of black youths were bound together in chains in West Africa, being marched toward a slave ship during the horrible days before slavery was outlawed. One young African man stood proudly and walked with immense dignity in spite of the manacles hobbling his feet and cutting his wrists. The others stared in terror and hunched in defeat as a result of the traumas of capture, of the terrible forced march under the cruel lash, and of the prospect of a deadly voyage away from a homeland they would never see again. Pointing to the young black man who stood with his head up and looked undefeated, one of the ship's officers asked, "What about that boy? Why is he standing so proudly?"

"Him?" replied one of the slavers. "He can't forget he's a son of the king!"

We are "sons of the king." We belong to Christ. We will walk with pride. Although we may be afflicted, we must remember that we belong to Him!

Sentence Sermon to Remember: Jesus Christ came into the world to comfort the afflicted—and to afflict the comfortable.—Author Unknown.

Questions for Pupils on the Next Lesson. 1. Do you sometimes feel that no one really cares about you? Do you have friends that feel this way? 2. Are some of your friends confused about the different philosophies of life? 3. Do you realize that you have some limitations? 4. Why is Christ's Coming called "the Good News"? 5. Do you think that being tender and loving is a sign of weakness or of strength?

LESSON III—DECEMBER 18

PREPARING FOR GOD'S COMING

Background Scripture: Isaiah 40,41
Devotional Reading: Isaiah 46:8–13

KING JAMES VERSION

ISAIAH 40 3 The voice of him that crieth in the wilderness, Prepare ye the way of the LORD, make straight in the desert a highway for our God.

4 Every valley shall be exalted, and every mountain and hill shall be made low: and the crooked shall be made straight, and the rough places plain:

5 And the glory of the LORD shall be revealed, and all flesh shall see *it* together: for the mouth of the LORD hath spoken *it.*

6 The voice said, Cry. And he said, What shall I cry? All flesh *is* grass, and all the goodliness thereof *is* as the flower of the field:

7 The grass withereth, the flower fadeth: because the spirit of the LORD bloweth upon it: surely the people *is* grass.

8 The grass withereth, the flower fadeth: but the word of our God shall stand for ever.

9 O Zion, that bringest good tidings, get thee up into the high mountain; O Jerusalem, that bringest good tidings, lift up thy voice with strength; lift *it* up, be not afraid; say unto the cities of Judah, Behold your God!

10 Behold, the Lord GOD will come with strong *hand,* and his arm shall rule for him: behold, his reward *is* with him, and his work before him.

11 He shall feed his flock like a shepherd: he shall gather the lambs with his arm, and carry *them* in his bosom, *and* shall gently lead those that are with young.

REVISED STANDARD VERSION

ISAIAH 40 3 A voice cries:
"In the wilderness prepare the way of the LORD,
make straight in the desert a highway for our God.

4 Every valley shall be lifted up,
and every mountain and hill be made low;
the uneven ground shall become level,
and the rough places a plain.

5 And the glory of the LORD shall be revealed,
and all flesh shall see it together
for the mouth of the LORD has spoken."

6 A voice says, "Cry!"
And I said, "What shall I cry?"
All flesh is grass,
and all its beauty is like the flower of the field.

7 The grass withers, the flower fades,
when the breath of the LORD blows upon it;
surely the people is grass.

8 The grass withers, the flower fades;
but the word of our God will stand for ever.

9 Get you up to a high mountain,
O Zion, herald of good tidings;
lift up your voice with strength,
O Jerusalem, herald of good tidings,
lift it up, fear not;
say to the cities of Judah,
"Behold your God!"

10 Behold, the Lord GOD comes with might,
and his arm rules for him;
behold, his reward is with him,
and his recompense before him.

11 He will feed his flock like a shepherd,
he will gather the lambs in his arms,
he will carry them in his bosom,
and gently lead those that are with young.

KEY VERSE: "... prepare the way of the Lord, make straight in the desert a highway for our God." Isaiah 40:3 (RSV).

HOME DAILY BIBLE READINGS

Dec. 12. M. *In Might.* Isaiah 46:8–13.
Dec. 13. T. *In Deliverance.* Isaiah 41:21–29.
Dec. 14. W. *In Sovereignty.* Isaiah 41:21–29.
Dec. 15. T. *In Affection.* Isaiah 54:1–10.
Dec. 16. F. *In Victory.* Isaiah 54:11–17.
Dec. 17. S. *In Greatness.* Isaiah 40:27–31.
Dec. 18. S. *In Comfort.* Isaiah 40:1–11.

BACKGROUND

The background of this lesson is Babylon—a Babylon once overwhelmingly powerful but now trembling at the thought of being conquered by the rising Cyrus of Persia. All the signs of such an event were clear, and the Jewish captives in Babylon were as much afraid as were the Babylonians themselves. Judah had perished; Jerusalem was a vast ruin.

The scene is the Exile. The "actors" are the exiled Jews, some of whom are inconsolable and despondent, some hoping against hope for freedom and release from captivity. Miles of deadly desert stood between their homeland and Babylon. It was a time in which many hung their harps on the willow trees and sat down to weep when they remembered Zion.

It was time for someone, some prophet, to come and dry their tears. He appears in Isaiah 40.

NOTES ON THE PRINTED TEXT

Over and over again, in the Old Testament, we read that God was a *punishing* God. More than one prophet said just that. The author of Isaiah 40 firmly believed it, but he also believed that the "punishment" of the captives in Babylon was over and finished. He said that the Exile was over, finished; a *loving* God is about to bring release and *redemption* to the disconsolate ones, who had hung their harps on the willows, and bring them back to their homeland. The call of the prophet is really the announcement of God's new and dramatic intervention for the purpose of salvation.

"A voice cries, 'In the wilderness prepare the way of the Lord, make straight in the desert a highway for our God' " (Isaiah 40:3). This, to the prophet, was a voice from a heavenly court, defining his mission. It is pure poetry. It does not mean that the captives were to build a *new* road across the desert between Persia and Jerusalem; it means, rather, that "Forces beyond their knowledge or control—the forces of history, ultimately God Himself, the one supreme factor in the on goings of the universe—are preparing a route along which God will arrive and lead them."—Henry Sloane Coffin. God provides the way back; those who travel it are to "keep it in shape" by following Him down His road. There will be obstacles in that road; not towering mountains or treacherous valleys, but obstacles that were political, moral, psychological, and spiritual.

Go God's way, Israelite and Judean, and you will find it a way in which all obstacles are conquered. Dangerous (moral and political) valleys will be "exalted" (filled up); all rough places will be made level and safe.

The voice bids the prophet to "Cry." Or "shout." Shout *what?* Let him shout that the Cyrus who finally let them go was nothing more than a puppet of God, unconsciously doing His will! Let them see God's hand in Cyrus conquering Babylon. Shout that men are like grass, or like flowers that bloom, wither, and die. Men are like that. They have their little hour on God's stage, and then disappear, and other men come, and God uses them all for His purpose. Men build empires, and the empires fall. Men go to war and many die in war; others come to take their place and find a better way—God's way. Cynics, agnostics, atheists strut for a short time, and then they pass into obscurity. And "the world passeth away, and the lust thereof; but he that doeth the will of God abideth for ever" (1 John 2:17). Do you see it clearly?

"Behold, the Lord God comes with might, and his arm rules for him; behold, his (man's) reward is with him . . ." (Isaiah 40:10). Again, we gave poetry—no, truth expressed in a poetry that stirs the soul. It does *not* suggest that God will come marching at the head of a great army; it means that God's mightiness lies in His love, and that in love He will eventually win the final victory over the evils which beset mankind.

To be honest about it, too few of us really *believe* that. Emile Zola spoke for our disbelievers when he wrote that human affairs were like a railroad train drawn by a locomotive whose driver has been killed, dashing headlong·into midnight: "The train is the world; we are the freight; fate is the track, death is the darkness; God is the engineer—who is dead!" No, Mr. Zola, you are sadly wrong. It is not God who is dead, but men who refuse to put their trust in Him. You are only one of many who have held that God is dead; cynics die and are forgotten, but God marches on.

There is a call to mission in verse 9 of this chapter, a call to "lift up thy (our) voice with strength." Israel and Judah were called to spread the voice of God not only among Jews, but to all the world. That has meaning for the Christian Church: churches that try to keep the Word to themselves and send out no missionaries have a habit of dying quickly.

Now read verse 11, and see God as the prophet saw Him not as a punisher, but as a shepherd. A Good Shepherd, as we saw Him in Jesus of Nazareth, a Shepherd who would never fail to seek and find and bring back His wandering sheep to His fold.

Somehow, it all reminds us of Washington on his knees at Valley Forge. When the war seemed lost, he went down on his knees—and got up to win his war!

SUGGESTIONS TO TEACHERS

Nearly everyone in your class (yourself included!) is caught up in the holiday frenzy. In spite of good intentions, hardly anyone has taken time out to prepare for God's Coming. Today is the day.

Begin by asking what kind of a God are your people expecting? Or, are they expecting God at all? Since this lesson is mostly an opportunity to reflect on the hope brought by Jesus' Coming, use Isaiah 40, 41 to spell out the kind of God who has come to us in this season. An astonishing list of titles is suggested. Here are a few:

1. *COMFORTER.* Ask your class to comment on the time when Jesus Christ has brought comfort in the lives of each of them. The literal meaning of the word *comfort* is "with strength," and your class members should share memories of occasions when the Lord has stood by them "with strength."

2. *COMPARISON.* Isaiah contrasts the Lord to other powers, such as great nations, popular idols, and mighty kings. Let your people draw up their own lists of powers which command respect in our society. Compare the Lord to these; He emerges as the greatest always!

3. *CREATOR.* Our God is the tireless Energizer, the Continuer of all life. Consult Isaiah 41 for new insights on personality traits of the One who comes to us this blessed season.

4. *CHOOSER.* Isaiah 41:9 offers a good antidote to the slushy sentimentality which sometimes tries to pass as religious feelings during the Christmas season. The God who comes to us in the person of Jesus chooses us for service. "You are my servant," He tells us: Remind your class that God came among us as One who serves and selects us to continue the kind of serving Jesus inaugurated.

5. *CONFOUNDER.* The God who comes to us continually surprises us by turning the tables on the wise, rich, and haughty. Furthermore, "When the poor and needy seek water, and there is none . . . I the Lord will answer them, I the God of Israel will not forsake them" (Isaiah 41:17). Have your class contemplate the disturbing claims by the prophet that the Lord is on the side of the oppressed. If this is so, God may be confounding many who think they are safe and comfortable.

6. *CONTENDER.* The Lord challenges those who challenge His rule to state their case against Him (Isaiah 41:21). The Lord will not be trifled with. He insists

on being taken with utmost seriousness. In the light of Isaiah 41, how would it be best to celebrate Christmas?

7. *COUNSELOR.* The Lord who comes among us is unparalleled in wisdom and goodness. All other so-called counselors next to Him are "a delusion" (Isaiah 41:29). Bring examples from your own experience of how Jesus Christ has given you counsel. Close the lesson by reminding your class that He continues to be "Wonderful Counselor" among His many titles.

TOPIC FOR ADULTS
PREPARING FOR GOD'S COMING

"How Much for Hope?" A woman who had to work long hours to support herself and her children earned barely enough to pay the bills. Frequently, however, she bought a ticket in the state lottery. After watching this woman spend another dollar to gamble in this way, a friend asked, "Why do you waste your money on a lottery ticket when you can hardly make ends meet?"

"Yeh, I buy a ticket every day," the woman acknowledged. "But a dollar is not too much to pay for twenty-four hours of hope."

Countless people feel, like this woman, that they live hopeless existences. Many live near you. Probably you have felt this way yourself at times.

The Coming of Jesus Christ brings you hope. Isaiah's message is for this Christmas! Prepare the way for the Coming of our Lord into the lives of your church family members!

Beacon of Hope. When Alexander the Great was leading his armies, a bright light from a high tower burned until a later hour each night. As long as that light shown in the night's darkness, anyone who had a grievance or any soldier who had deserted could enter the camp and appear directly to the emperor.

Jesus Christ as the light of the world is God's beacon. His Coming means that no one is ever denied the privilege of coming directly to the Emperor of the universe.

Can Others Tell? Preparing for God's Coming means radiating the joy Christ brings. In this busy season, do your expression and your mannerisms reflect that you have hope because of Jesus Christ?

A small girl came into the kitchen and noticed that her mother appeared glum. "Mommy," she said "Aren't you happy?"

"Why, certainly I'm happy," replied her mother.

"Well," said the little girl, "you certainly haven't told your face yet!"

Have you prepared for the Coming of the Lord by "telling your face"? Can others tell that God has come by the way you look and talk and act?

Questions for Pupils on the Next Lesson. 1. Why is celebration such a basic ingredient for a full and meaningful life? 2. What may your church do to help others be more at peace with others and with their environment? 3. How exactly does the Coming of Jesus Christ enable you to achieve peace and harmony within your life? 4. Is the ultimate triumph of righteousness a certainty? 5. What are models of attitude and conduct you and others may look to?

TOPIC FOR YOUTH
PREPARE THE WAY

Senseless Life to Senseless Shooting. The world was shocked by the shooting on a sunny Wednesday in St. Peter's Square in Rome on May 13, 1981. A twenty-three-year-old terrorist named Mahmet Ali Agca aimed a 9 mm pistol at Pope John Paul II and wounded him in five places. Fortunately, the Pope survived the assassination attempt, although he was severely injured. Police arrested the would-be killer.

During the interrogation, Mahmet repeated to those questioning him, "My life doesn't have any more sense. Nothing matters to me, nothing. I couldn't care less about life."

Some astute students of human nature point out that there is a connection between a person's outlook and a person's action. A sense that life is hopeless leads to senseless shootings.

Although you or your friends will probably never sink to such mindless violence, how do you view life? Is there hope? Are you preparing the way for the coming of new purpose in your life? Have you prepared to live with the positive outlook that a person may have as a result of Christ's Coming?

Girl Sues for Visits From Father. In a twist in child-custody cases, a Los Angeles girl born out of wedlock four and a half years ago is suing in an attempt to force her father to visit her. The suit was brought against Owen C. Olpin, on behalf of Kimberly Anne Olpin by Kimberly's mother.

She said the visitation idea came about after the child began coming home from school demanding: "Where's my daddy?"

But the state Court of Appeals Justice Robert Kingsley said that even if the court issured an order requiring Olpin to visit his daughter, he was uncertain it would be enforceable.

Attorney James Griffin, arguing on behalf of the girl and her mother, conceded that could be a problem but insisted such an order was a proper first step rather than simply allowing him to "take a walk" out of his daughter's life.

Some feel that God is like a disinterested parent who must be cajoled or forced into showing some concern. Is the Lord like Kimberley Anne's father? Must God be compelled to come to us? Has the Almighty "taken a walk" out of our lives?

Christmas means that God has come to us in love! We live with the joy and hope of remembering the birth at Bethlehem. Prepare to make this season a time of celebrating the Coming of God to us, His children!

From Rock 'n' Roll to Rock of Ages. Little Richard the rock 'n' roll star now is the Rev. Richard Penniman.

With his unprecedented "A Wop Bop Aloo Bop A Wop Bam Boom," Richard camped his way into music history in the '50s and '60s, guiding the course of rock 'n' roll with classics like "Tutti Frutti," "Long Tall Sally," "Good Golly Miss Molly," and "The Girl Can't Help It."

Richard, called "Little" because he was small and skinny as a rail, started his musical career pounding out gospel tunes on a rickety old upright piano. He was washing dishes in a Greyhound bus station and making $15 a week when he heard a Nashville radio station play "Tutti Frutti." His career took off in 1957.

Those were the old days. Today Rev. Richard is working as a minister. Thirty years of worldwide fame, frustrating periods of obscurity which he blames on racism, battles with drugs and a religious experience that he said changed him from being homosexual—Little Richard has traveled full circle. He still wears a wafer-thin mustache. Those large, rolling expressive eyes that entertained hundreds of thousands of screaming teen-agers since 1957 have never dimmed. Expressions like "darlin' " and "God bless you"—all said with inflection—still sugar his talk. Inside, however, says Richard Penniman, Little Richard, now Rev. Penniman, is a new man.

"God brought me from rock 'n' roll to the Rock of Ages," he says. "I'm going to be a part of the new history that won't be burned up in flames, a history with God."

Are you preparing for a new history with God? He wants you to be part of a new world which He brings with Christ's Coming!

Sentence Sermon to Remember: The only decision we have to make is to live with God; He will make the rest.—Anonymous.

Questions for Pupils on the Next Lesson. 1. What are you and your church doing to bring peace in the world for the Prince of Peace? 2. Why are so many people often depressed at Christmastime? 3. What do you think is the real source of inner peace and joy? 4. What Christian celebration experiences mean the most to you and why? 5. What difference has the Coming of Jesus Christ to the world made in your life?

LESSON IV—DECEMBER 25

A REIGN OF RIGHTEOUSNESS

Background Scripture: Isaiah 9:1–7; 11:1–10
Devotional Reading: Isaiah 12:1–6

KING JAMES VERSION

ISAIAH 9 2 The people that walked in darkness have seen a great light: they that dwell in the land of the shadow of death, upon them hath the light shined.

3 Thou hast multiplied the nation, *and* not increased the joy: they joy before thee according to the joy in harvest, *and* as *men* rejoice when they divide the spoil.

4 For thou hast broken the yoke of his burden, and the staff of his shoulder, the rod of his oppressor, as in the day of Midian.

5 For every battle of the warrior *is* with confused noise, and garments rolled in blood; but *this* shall be with burning *and* fuel of fire.

6 For unto us a child is born, unto us a son is given: and the government shall be upon his shoulder: and his name shall be called Wonderful, Counsellor, The mighty God, The everlasting Father, The Prince of Peace.

7 Of the increase of *his* government and peace *there shall be* no end, upon the throne of David, and upon his kingdom, to order it, and to establish it with judgment and with justice from henceforth even for ever. The zeal of the LORD of hosts will perform this.

11 1 And there shall come forth a rod out of the stem of Jesse, and a Branch shall grow out of his roots:

2 And the spirit of the LORD shall rest upon him, the spirit of wisdom and understanding, the spirit of counsel and might, the spirit of knowledge and of the fear of the LORD;

3 And shall make him of quick understanding in the fear of the LORD:

REVISED STANDARD VERSION

ISAIAH 9 2 The people who walked in darkness
have seen a great light;
those who dwelt in a land of deep darkness,
on them has light shined.

3 Thou hast multiplied the nation,
thou hast increased its joy;
they rejoice before thee
as with joy at the harvest,
as men rejoice when they divide the spoil.

4 For the yoke of his burden,
and the staff for his shoulder,
the rod of his oppressor,
thou hast broken as on the day of Midian.

5 For every boot of the tramping warrior in battle tumult
and every garment rolled in blood
will be burned as fuel for the fire.

6 For to us a child is born,
to us a son is given;
and the government will be upon his shoulder,
and his name will be called
"Wonderful Counselor, Mighty God,
Everlasting Father, Prince of Peace."

7 Of the increase of his government and of peace
there will be no end,
upon the throne of David, and over his kingdom,
to establish it, and to uphold it
with justice and with righteousness
from this time forth and for evermore.
The zeal of the LORD of hosts will do this.

11 1 There shall come forth a shoot from the stump of Jesse,
and a branch shall grow out of his roots.

2 And the Spirit of the LORD shall rest upon him,
the spirit of wisdom and understanding,
the spirit of counsel and might,
the spirit of knowledge and the fear of the LORD.

3 And his delight shall be in the fear of the LORD.

KEY VERSE: . . . his name will be called "Wonderful Counselor, Mighty God, Everlasting Father, Prince of Peace." Isaiah 9:6 (RSV).

HOME DAILY BIBLE READINGS

Dec. 19. M. *A Reign of Justice.* Luke 1:46–55.
Dec. 20. T. *A Reign of Deliverance.* Luke 1:67–79.
Dec. 21. W. *A Reign of Joy.* Luke 2:1–7.
Dec. 22. T. *A Reign of Righteousness.* Isaiah 32:1–8.

Dec. 23.   F.   *A Reign of Hope.* Isaiah 12:1–6.
Dec. 24.   S.   *A Reign of Light.* Isaiah 9:2–7.
Dec. 25.   S.   *A Reign of Peace.* Isaiah 11:1–9.

BACKGROUND

Of all the visions and messages of Isaiah, the one described in Isaiah 9 is by far the most well known and the most beautiful. It is a deathless song of faith. We all stand up when we hear its thoughts repeated in Handel's *Messiah.*

The song deals with the Messiah and the Messianic Hope and Age. Verse 1 in chapter 9 gives us the scene and the date when it was written. The words "the land of Zebulun and the land of Naphtali" refer to the war with Tiglath-pileser in 733; that war tore Galilee away from Israel and made it a puppet province of Assyria. The word *calamity* hardly describes the mood of both Israel and Judah. Their future seemed too horrible to contemplate. All was lost!

Not quite. God lifted up a man named Isaiah to promise a future that would be not horrible but glorious.

NOTES ON THE PRINTED TEXT

Leading up to the time of Isaiah, there were just too many kings in Israel and Judah who were inadequate and inefficient and plain bad. The "divine right of kings," under their rule, had become a grim joke; slowly but surely there deepened a darkness in the land as it approached the midnight of the Exile.

Then, suddenly, unexpectedly, like a bolt from the blue, the people caught in that darkness saw "a great light." Like a sudden burst of sunshine after a flood, it filled the hearts of God's people with a hope that was almost dead and offered the promise of a better tomorrow, a tomorrow in which peace and not war would spread over the land and love would fill the hearts of men, for a new king would come who would be called the Prince of Peace. The yoke of the oppressors would fall from their shoulders. "For God will break the chains that bind his people and the whip that scourges them, just as he did when he destroyed the vast host of the Midianites by Gideon's little band. In that glorious day of peace there will no longer be the issuing of battle gear; no more the blood-stained uniforms of war; all such will be burned" (Isaiah 9:4, 5, *The Living Bible*).

Dr. G.G.D. Kilpatrick, writing in *The Interpreter's Bible,* tells us the story of what happened in the city of Mons on the day (November 11, 1918) when the people of that city learned that World War I was over. The German troops marched out of town, and the people burst out into the streets wild with joy and shouting, "Hang out your flags!" The long night of terror was over; peace had come.

But the peace would come to the Jews not by anything the people had done, but at the hands of a Messiah for whose appearance they had prayed so long. "For unto us a child is born . . . and the government shall be upon his shoulder" (verse 6). The Messiah to come was that child. He would be their new king—and king of the world. He would come bearing titles, names, that no king before Him had been worthy to bear: "Wonderful Counselor, the Mighty God, the Everlasting Father, the Prince of Peace." He would establish a new day and age, would rule in righteousness and justice from the throne of David forever.

Now, as we study the words, we may think that the Coming of this Messiah brought these blessings only to Israel, only to restore the old Israeli longing for the restoration of the throne and house of David. Modern Jews still interpret it thus; for them, the Messiah is still to come. But to the Christian, it means something else. The Christian believes that this whole great passage in Isaiah is bound up to faith in Jesus Christ as the Son of God. Whatever the author of Isaiah 9 had in mind, it is still true that every prediction of the prophet has been fulfilled in the person and mission of Jesus Christ. For us, the light of the knowledge of the glory of God in the face of Jesus Christ flashes out, wherever and whatever we are. For Him, we hang out our flags of faith, as did the people of Mons.

The Messianic prophecies of Isaiah 11:1–3 should be studied along with those in Isaiah 9:2–7. When we do that, we find that nowhere in either of these passages is there mention of the word *Messiah,* but the inference is clear. All down their history, up to the time of the Exile, the Jews had hailed every new king that rose to rule over them as the Lord's "anointed"—kings who would inaugurate a new golden age. But when the last of the Davidic kings died in exile, their faith in the coming of a divinely appointed king was transferred to the Messiah. They could not give up the hope that this king should be of the Davidic line, and so they saw, or rather Isaiah saw, that the promised deliverer-king would come "out of the stem (stump) of Jesse" the father of David—but quite different from all their other kings. He would be cut off from the Davidic line as a branch is cut off from the old roots. The old kings had thought too often that they could get along without the help of God, but the One to come would have the Spirit of the Lord upon Him as it had not been on the predecessor kings. He would truly be one coming from God.

He would also be gifted with the wisdom and an understanding which God demands in any leader; he would have the spirit of wise, God-based counsel and might (power), and "the spirit of knowledge and the fear (love) of God"; he would be one ready to live according to God's moral demands. These requirements distinguished the Messiah-king from all others.

Isaiah applied all this to the Hebrews; we who are Christians must apply it to ourselves, and to those who hold places of leadership in our day. Our day has too few who would meet such requirements. Tyrants rule too much of our world; dictators are slaughtering their opponents as a cattleman slaughters his cattle; in them there is no allegiance to God. We see congressmen and senators in high places indulging in corruption; few there are who ask God's advice before they make crucial decisions. A large percentage of modern citizens and voters distrust their governments and stay home on election day. Isaiah's ideal of the good governor means nothing to them. Morally, we do seem to be bankrupt!

Gilbert G. Chesterton has biting words for us; he said, "The Christian ideal has not been tried and found wanting; it has been found difficult, and left untried." If that be true, what should we do about it?

SUGGESTIONS TO TEACHERS

Teaching a lesson on Christmas Day is a rough assignment. You and everyone in your class have been too busy. Possibly for some in your class, it will be the first time in weeks that they have slowed down. Others have been so preoccupied with holiday-making that they have not allowed the Coming of Jesus to have much meaning for them. Therefore, teacher, you have work to do. Although you may not feel psyched up to another lesson, especially with lots of personal plans for this day, and although you may not have much time to prepare this lesson, remember that you have people in your class who need to know what the rule of the newborn Messiah means. With the discipline that any teacher worthy of the title must cultivate, sit yourself down with the Isaiah passages, and get your thoughts together on the significance of God's reign of righteousness through Christ's Coming.

1. *JOY-FILLED DARKNESS.* Isaiah 9:1–5 offers a memorable picture of people living in the gloom of hopelessness and being surprised by a new dawn. Christ is the burst of light upon a dark world. Have those in your class think of various kinds of darkness in which they and people they know have had to walk, such as loneliness, anxiety, grief, depression or regret. Christ's rule means that people in

the deepest kinds of gloom will know joy again. Is your class, your church, your religion basically happy and foward-looking? The reign of righteousness should make it so!

2. *JESSE'S DESCENDANT.* Since this is the celebration of Jesus' birth, have the class reread Isaiah 9:6, 7 and 11:1, 2 for insights on who Jesus as the promised Messiah is. Notice that the emphasis is not on a cute, cuddly baby in the manger but on the spirit-filled Deliverer. The Messiah will be renowned for His wisdom and understanding, according to Isaiah. Encourage the class to relate ways in which Jesus is the Person of insights for people today.

3. *JUST DECISIONS.* Talk of God's judgment on Christmas Day may at first seem like "Scrooge-talk." Don't shy away from Isaiah 11:3–5, however. The new reign of righteousness brought by God's coming to us makes the point that God is *fair.* We may not like the way the Lord calls them, but we must recognize that He balances the interests of all His children so that all are remembered. God brings justice.

4. *JOINT DWELLERS.* The magnificent vision of Isaiah 11:6–10 where all nature dwells harmoniously is the basis for some of the greatest art and music. The new age of God brings a sense of wholeness for every part of Creation. Are you and your people able to live at peace with nature, with other persons, and with yourselves?

TOPIC FOR ADULTS
A REIGN OF RIGHTEOUSNESS

View From Bethlehem. "When the astronaut, Edgar Mitchell, returning from the moon, spied through the window of his capsule his home, a small distant planet, he claims to have had an intense visionary (he called it religious) experience. He saw ... from that perspective that one human race is more important than one hundred and sixty-three nationalities. ... I was thrilled once to hear him tell his tale, but I couldn't help thinking, 'You shouldn't have had to go to the moon to have that vision; it's enough to go to Bethlehem.' For the message of Bethlehem is that all human beings are members of one family, brothers and sisters of the Holy Child."—William Sloane Coffin, Jr.

Following the Footsteps. Shortly after he retired as an engineer with Bell Labs, a New Jersey man set out to fulfill a dream of walking the length of the Appalachian Trail from Georgia to Maine. Recently, Gordon Gamble described some of the highlights of his 187 days on the Appalachian Trail. This 2,106 mile hike through fourteen states was completed when a group of day hikers greeted him with cheers and applause, as he took his last steps on the peak of Mt. Katahdin in Maine. "This," Gamble said, "marked the completion of the first major project of my retirement." In spite of arthritis, his project was the climax of determined purpose, persistent devotion and a support system ably directed by his wife, Dorothea, whereby he was supplied along the trail through scheduled meetings, mailings, and caches.

In one instance, he described being lost during a snow storm. Following a compass course in hopes of picking up the trail, his steps finally led to the trail and a shelter. When another hiker arrived later at the shelter, Gordon asked how he had fared coming over the mountain. "Just like you," he replied. "I followed your footsteps wherever you wandered and got to safety."

Jesus Christ is the One whose Coming has opened the trail to hope for us. Christmas offers us the glorious news that we may follow in His footsteps and know that we will fare safely. Although we may feel alone and uncertain, a Deliverer has come and walks ahead of us in our world. Jesus Christ has been born! He is the Living Way. With Him, we enter the realm of God Himself!

God's Reign of Righteousness in the Office. Several years ago, Ray Kroc was a salesman selling paper cups and milkshake makers. One day, he called on two brothers in San Bernardino, California, named Mac and Dick McDonald who ran a fast-food store. Kroc noticed that the McDonald brothers used several milkshake machines at the same time and sold only hamburgers, shakes, and the best french fries Kroc had ever tasted. Kroc bought the name and the procedures from the two brothers. He built McDonalds into a nation-wide operation in which assembly-line production, immediate take-out service of tasty food, uniformity and image have made him a millionaire. In his autobiography, *Grinding It Out, The Making of McDonald's,* Kroc continually expresses his faith in the capitalistic system as well as his company loyalty. "I speak of faith in McDonald's as if it were a religion," he writes, "I believe in God, family, and McDonald's—and in the office, that order is reversed."

The Coming of Jesus Christ, however, means that the order of God first holds for the office as well as elsewhere. Jesus Christ's birth inaugurates a new era. A reign of righteousness has begun. God claims preeminence in every part of our lives. Because of Jesus Christ, we believe first in the Lord, then in family, business or job and other important commitments.

Has His birth made you establish the proper priorities in life?

Questions for Pupils on the Next Lesson. 1. How does God regard worship which does not lead to just social relationships? 2. What exactly is worship? 3. What do you think that God expects of us? 4. Are adults always responsible for their own moral behavior? 5. What is your reaction to Isaiah's image of God entering a lawsuit against His people?

TOPIC FOR YOUTH
A NEW DAY COMING

Knew a Friend Named Lincoln. In the year 1874 the immigrant ship *Westphalia* landed at Castle Garden in New York City. Among the immigrants was a Serbian lad named Michael. It was then a condition that no alien could be admitted unless he had in his possession a sufficient sum of money to enable him to live for a time, or he must have relatives to whom he was going. When they questioned him, they found he had but five cents in his pocket and all his relatives were across the sea. He was set aside to be returned to the land from which he came. But there was an official there who had been impressed by the boy and resolved to question him further. He took him aside and said to him: "Don't you know anyone in America?" "I know a man who used to live around here, Abraham Lincoln." And then the boy, his eyes shining like stars, told how in his mountain home in Serbia, when the day's work was done, he had read the life of Lincoln, and wanted to grow up in the land he had loved.

The official to whom he told his story had once been an immigrant boy. He had lost a leg on a battlefield, and he was profoundly moved. He told the lad's story to the other officials. They set aside the rules and opened the gates of America to this boy with the shining eyes, the five cents in his pocket, and the knowledge of Abraham Lincoln.

That lad, Michael Pupin, became one of the most famous scientists of his time. It was the unconscious influence of a man long dead that reached out over the years to that humble Balkan home and lifted that lad out of the mire and set his feet on the rock.

Just as knowing Lincoln brought a new day for a poor boy who arrived as a stranger without friends, so knowing Jesus Christ brings a new day for people today. Jesus might have been born twenty centuries before, but understanding the meaning of His Coming ushers men and women into a life of possibilities.

Have you recalled Jesus Christ's real meaning for you? This day of celebrating

His birth, remember that His Coming brings a new day for you and all persons!

New Day: New Changes and Challenges. The Coming of Jesus Christ means a new day has come. As Isaiah announced, the Messiah's arrival brings the new and mighty reign of God. What does the coming of this new day mean to you? Eugene McCarthy's words in an article a few years ago suggest what the day should mean for you and other Christians: "We continue to be the most overtransported, overheated, overcooled, overfed (most of us), overhoused (many of us), overdefended (all of us), and overadvertised people the world has ever known. We need a revolution of moderating expectations, a change of spirit, leading to a sharing of work, of resources, not only with our contemporaries, but with some thought to future generations. We need to confront, and accept a challenge not unlike that which John Adams laid down to the American colonists as a cost to them of the Revolution and of separation from England. Adams said, "We must change our habits, our prejudices, our palates, our taste in dress, furniture, equipage, architecture, etc. . . . But we can live and be happy."—Eugene McCarthy, *Commonweal,* May 8, 1981.

Spending Priorities. We celebrate Jesus' birth as the Coming of the "Prince of Peace," and the dawn of a new day. Yet the world's spending priorities reflect a commitment to the gods of war. The United Nations has been trying to begin a "global negotiation" aimed at shifting billions of dollars from the industrialized world to the developing nations. A perennial theme in the debate—the amount of resources expended on arms—was underlined by Rüdiger von Wechmar, former president of the U.N. General Assembly.

"We are witnessing—almost helplessly—an acceleration of the arms race," he said. "This year, nearly $500 billion are earmarked for sophisticated weapons and military hardware." An increase in official development assistance equivalent to only 5 percent of that figure, he said, would be enough to meet United Nations targets "to help those millions of human beings who still live in want and poverty."

Statistics released two years ago disclosed that the United States spends $499 for each man, woman, and child for the military, but only $341 per person for health. What does it say about us and our country when we spend more on destructive purposes than on healing?

Sentence Sermon to Remember:

> It is Christmas on the highway,
> In the thronging, busy mart;
> But the dearest, truest Christmas
> Is the Christmas of the heart.
> —Author Unknown.

Questions for Pupils on the Next Lesson. 1. Why is sin often defined as rebellion? 2. What do you think worship is? 3. Why is God more concerned about how you show justice than how religious your feelings may be? 4. How do you react to Isaiah's claim that God has a lawsuit against His people? 5. Do you feel accountable to God?

LESSON V—JANUARY 1

GOD'S CASE AGAINST HIS PEOPLE

Background Scripture: Isaiah 1:2–6—3:15
Devotional Reading: Isaiah 3:1–7

KING JAMES VERSION

ISAIAH 1   2 Hear, O heavens, and give ear, O earth: for the LORD hath spoken, I have nourished and brought up children, and they have rebelled against me.

3 The ox knoweth his owner, and the ass his master's crib: *but* Israel doth not know, my people doth not consider.

4 Ah sinful nation, a people laden with iniquity, a seed of evildoers, children that are corrupters: they have forsaken the LORD, they have provoked the Holy One of Israel unto anger, they are gone away backward.

5 Why should ye be stricken any more? ye will revolt more and more: the whole head is sick, and the whole heart faint.

6 From the sole of the foot even unto the head *there is* no soundness in it; *but* wounds, and bruises, and putrifying sores: they have not been closed, neither bound up, neither mollified with ointment.

18 Come now, and let us reason together, saith the LORD: though your sins be as scarlet, they shall be as white as snow; though they be red like crimson, they shall be as wool.

19 If ye be willing and obedient, ye shall eat the good of the land:

20 But if ye refuse and rebel, ye shall be devoured with the sword: for the mouth of the LORD hath spoken *it.*

REVISED STANDARD VERSION

ISAIAH 1   2 Hear, O heavens, and give ear, O earth;
 for the LORD has spoken:
"Sons have I reared and brought up,
 but they have rebelled against me.
3 The ox knows its owner,
 and the ass its master's crib;
but Israel does not know,
 my people does not understand."
4 Ah, sinful nation,
 a people laden with iniquity,
offspring of evildoers,
 sons who deal corruptly!
They have forsaken the LORD,
 they have despised the Holy One of Israel,
they are utterly estranged.
5 Why will you still be smitten,
 that you continue to rebel?
The whole head is sick,
 and the whole heart faint.
6 From the sole of the foot even to the head,
 there is no soundness in it,
but bruises and sores
 and bleeding wounds;
they are not pressed out, or bound up,
 or softened with oil.

18 "Come now, let us reason together says
 the LORD:
though your sins are like scarlet,
 they shall be as white as snow;
though they are red like crimson,
 they shall become like wool.
19 If you are willing and obedient,
 you shall eat the good of the land;
20 But if you refuse and rebel,
 you shall be devoured by the sword;
for the mouth of the LORD has spoken."

KEY VERSE: The Lord has taken his place to contend, he stands to judge his people. Isaiah 3:13 (RSV).

HOME DAILY BIBLE READINGS

Dec. 26.	M.	Judgment on the Unrighteous. Isaiah 1:21–28.
Dec. 27.	T.	Judgment on Reliance on Wealth. Isaiah 2:6–11.
Dec. 28.	W.	Judgment on Idolatry. Isaiah 2:12–22.
Dec. 29.	T.	Judgment on Leaders of Society. Isaiah 3:1–9.
Dec. 30.	F.	Judgment on Exploiters of People. Isaiah 3:10–15.
Dec. 31.	S.	Lament Over the Nation. Isaiah 1:1–9.
Jan. 1.	S.	Futility of Worship Without Righteousness. Isaiah 1:10–17.

BACKGROUND

King Uzziah ruled Judah from (approximately) 809–758 B.C. We are told in Isaiah 6:1 that "In the year that king Uzziah died I saw also the Lord sitting upon a throne, high and lifted up. . . ." After him came Jotham, Ahaz, and Hezekiah, and it was during Hezekiah's reign that "Sennacherib came up against all the fenced cities of Judah and took them" (2 Kings 18:13). Judah was a pile of ruins when the Prophet Isaiah stood to prophesy of the future.

His prophecies were a mixture of condemnation and hope, and those who heard him must have been a bit bewildered by it all. He both scolded and encouraged them. The Judeans didn't particularly *want* to listen to his scoldings, but that made no difference to the prophet. He didn't want to become a popular preacher; he only wanted to make his confused people see what had happened and what was about to happen to them whether they liked it or not. Such preachers are invaluable.

NOTES ON THE PRINTED TEXT

If we could sum up the whole prophecy of Isaiah (which would be more than difficult), we might say that one great theme ran through all his teaching and prophesying: that is that *God is at once a judge and a father.*

Our lesson pictures God as a judge. (The Old Testament is strong in its description of God as a judge and His frightening judgment; the *New* Testament is strong in its conception of God as a Father.) As we read our lesson Scripture, we are led to see the picture of God sitting as a judge, holding court. His witnesses are people both in heaven and on earth—the angels in heaven and the humans on earth. Both of these people know what has happened to Judah, and *why* it has happened. The "accused" in the dock are the Judeans who have committed the worst of sins—they have broken their covenant with God.

The Judge is almost brutal in His indictment. He points in anger and scorn at the miserable Judeans (and perhaps to Israel as a whole); He charges that while He has nourished and brought them up as children, they have insulted Him in rebellion against His will. Even animals do better than that! Donkeys and oxen know their owners and are grateful for their care. But *you*—you have turned your back on your God and gone off like so many prodigal sons "to live as you please." You have despised the Holy One of Israel, and cut yourselves off from Him.

Why? Hadn't they suffered enough, when they did that? Look at what had happened to them: look at their ruined land, their captivity under alien kings. They stood there like a man watching his house burn down. All they have gained in rebellion were wounds and death. Why go on asking for more punishment?

Now forget Judah, and look at *us,* in our little day on earth. Why do we go on as we have been going on, shoving God back into second place and making the world an international house of fear? Think of Vietnam; what good came out of that? Think of a Germany which gave us a Luther and an Einstein, and countless other greats, a nation with tremendous potential—but where is Germany now? How long, O Lord, how long must we go on with this?

But stern as He is, God is something more than an outraged Judge. He is a merciful Father. In this passage from Isaiah, He is a sorrowing Father pleading with His children to turn back and walk with Him again, telling them that as a man soweth, so does he reap. He piles up undeniable accusations; He tells His children that they have brought their tragedy on themselves when they began to listen to the mad advice of kings and completely forgot that He is the sovereign King of all the earth.

God holds out His hand of mercy—like a father forgiving his prodigal son, and welcoming him home again. God is not all indignation and punishment: He is perfect, forgiving love. Come now, He says, let us sit down and reason *together,* about the Fatherhood of God and the brotherhood of man.

Yes, we have all sinned, and come short of the glory of God, but by God's grace we shall have redemption, *if we want it! If* you are willing and obedient—what a tremendous "if" that is, what a *frightening* thing it is! God's mercy and forgiveness are not based upon a reading of our church attendance record. That would be making a mockery of worship. It is based upon a willingness to accept and practice His moral precepts.

Much as He loves us, God cannot save us if we insist upon being an unrepentant people. His terms are these: consider, accept, obey, and receive forgiveness or perish.

SUGGESTIONS TO TEACHERS

Although New Year's Day may not appeal to you and to some in your class as the ideal time for a Sunday-School lesson, the calendar calls you to work! Instead of moaning about the problems of the day, however, mull over the possibilities. A New Year—a new beginning. A fresh look at everything. In the light of God's gift of 1984, develop your lesson for this first day of January.

You will continue to take your teaching material from Isaiah. Today's lesson comes from the prophet's claim that God addresses His people in the form of a lawsuit. Let your imagination play with this notion. Think of the Lord bringing charges against *us!* Isaiah insists that God's indictment against Israel has the following points. Be sure to examine these to see if they do not also apply to us.

1. *REBELLION.* The Lord complains that the ox knows its owner and the ass its master, but God's people refuse to recognize their Owner-Ruler. Here is the root cause of God's case against us. We have "forsaken the Lord . . . despised the Holy One of Israel . . . are utterly estranged" (Isaiah 1:4). Can your class come up with a better definition of sin than this? Note also that Isaiah suggests that forsaking the Lord not only brings an estrangement from Him, but produces a sick society. Have your class comment on what each thinks to be the symptoms of the sickness in the society in these times. Ask if the cause for such societal illness is any different today than in Isaiah's time.

2. *"RELIGION."* Surprisingly, there was a lot of "religion" in Isaiah's time, as now. But God cared nothing for it. Study carefully the section in Isaiah 1:11–17. Elaborate ceremony and expensive offerings are empty when there is not concern for justice. In fact, the Lord groans that He is weary of such piety. When His people pollute their praying with evil doing, worship is a sham. Prod your class to consider what it means for the Church to seek justice, correct oppression, defend the fatherless and plead the widow today.

3. *REFINING.* Isaiah states that God puts His people through a refining process in which the impurities are smelted away. Ask your class members if they agree with Isaiah. Isaiah also claims that the impurities removed in the refining are superstitions, reliance on wealth and arms, and a haughty attitude. Are these prevalent in our society?

4. *RECKONING.* Isaiah's list of woes against his contemporaries may sound grim. Remind your class, however, that the Lord's case against His people means that they are called to accountability. When God's people refuse to live responsibly, privation, oppression, national drift and disasters follow. Do you and your class see any connection between the ills of our society and God's displeasure with our behavior?

TOPIC FOR ADULTS
GOD'S CASE AGAINST HIS PEOPLE

One at a Time. "Shortly after World War II, I met and became friends with a young German theological student, Reinhard Neubauer. Upon getting to know him as a warm, caring person, I asked him the haunting question: 'Reinhard, with persons like you and your family, Christians like you, millions like you, how could Hitler happen?' 'I am afraid it's quite simple,' replied Reinhard. 'You see, it all happened one day at a time, one speech at a time, one law at a time.'"—John R. Bodo, *Monday Morning*, August 1981.

What Remains. To believe that God is Lord of history and that His sovereign will is being expressed through events is to find freedom even amid the most coercive of situations. And being given freedom, we do not remain helpless. Faith restores to us the initiative. We are placed in a position to act.

There are few more inspiring incidents in history than that of Augustine's response to the news that Rome had fallen. One day in the year A.D. 410 a boat appeared off the coast of Africa at Hippo. Swiftly a messenger disembarked and burst into a room where Augustine sat with some of his priests. The man shouted, "Rome is fallen! Alaric and his Goths have sacked the city." All were thrown into consternation, until presently one of the priests turned to the old bishop for guidance. Augustine told him, "What we see today is the doom which falls upon an empire that has betrayed its sons." Fearfully the priest asked, "But if the earthly dominion passes away, what remains?" "The city of God remains," replied Augustine quietly, "and the church of God remains through which it is brought within the passing world."

God's Case Today. For over thirty years, wise and far-seeing people have been warning us about the futility of any war fought with nuclear weapons and about the dangers involved in their cultivation. Some of the first voices to be raised were those of great scientists. Every president, from Dwight Eisenhower to Jimmy Carter, has tried to remind us that there could be no such thing as victory in a war fought with such weapons.

Looking back over the history of these warnings, one has the impression that the sense of urgency has been lost. One senses, even on the part of those who today most acutely perceive the problem, a certain discouragement, resignation, perhaps even despair, when it comes to raising the subject again. The danger is so obvious. So much has already been said. What is to be gained by reiteration? Look at the record. Over all these years, competition in the development of nuclear weaponry has proceeded relentlessly, without the faintest regard for all these warning voices. We have gone on piling weapon upon weapon, missile upon missile, new levels of destructiveness upon old ones. We have done this helplessly, almost involuntarily: like the victims of some sort of hypnotism, like lemmings heading for the sea, like the children of Hamlin marching blindly along behind their Pied Piper. The result is that we have created, we and the Soviets together, devices and their means of delivery with levels of redundancy so grotesque as to defy rational understanding.

How have we got ourselves into this dangerous mess? We ought not confuse the question by blaming it all on our Soviet adversaries. They have made their mistakes, and I should be the last to deny it. But we Americans have taken the lead in the development of nuclear arms. We first produced and tested the atomic bomb; we were the first to raise the level of destruction with the hydrogen bomb; we introduced the multiple warhead; we have declined every proposal for the renunciation of the principle of "first use." We alone, God help us, have used the weapon in anger against others—against tens of thousands of helpless noncombatants. We had our reasons but, in the face of this record, let us not lose ourselves in self-righteousness and forget our own complicity in creating today's situation.

What brought this to pass? It is primarily the independent momentum of the weapons race itself—the compulsions that arise when the great powers compete in building major armaments.

As a diplomatic historian, I have seen this same phenomenon in the relations among great European powers as much as a century ago. Conceived initially as a means to an end, this competition has become the end itself. It has taken possession of our imagination and behavior, detaching itself from the political differences that initially inspired it, and now leads both parties, invariably and inexorably, to the war they no longer know how to avoid.

Questions for Pupils on the Next Lesson. 1. What is the symbolism of "God's vineyard"? 2. What kind of "harvest" does the Lord expect of us? 3. How do you think God judges His Church in these times? 4. Do our human actions always have moral consequences? 5. Do we as Christians have to be concerned about social issues? Why or why not?

TOPIC FOR YOUTH
ACCOUNTABLE TO GOD

Our Stake in a World of Hungry People. "World hunger is an enemy of all of us, and it will take all of us working in unison to overcome it, or even to limit it.

"Hunger's impact on humanity in the 1980s is already catastrophic. Whatever social ill we examine, crime or any other aberration, we are likely to find hunger at its root. Both personal and national rebellions are born of hunger. Leaders over the ages have recognized this.

"It was the ancient Roman Seneca who said: 'A hungry people is unreasonable, unjust, and unmerciful.'

"It was Albert Einstein who said: 'An empty stomach is not a good political adviser.'

"It was Woodrow Wilson who said: 'No one can worship God or love his neighbor on an empty stomach.'

"It was Adlai Stevenson who said: 'A hungry man is not a free man.'

"And it was Jimmy Carter who said: 'We cannot have a peaceful and prosperous world if a large part of the world's people are at or near the edge of hunger. The United States has a stake in helping to solve this problem . . . we must look for ways to tap the talents and commitment of the American nation in an effective international effort.'

"We all know that this problem must be solved; this war against imminent world famine must be won. We have no acceptable alternative."—Hugh O. Labounty, president, Case Polytechnic University.

Accountable for Present. When the famous novel, *Gone With the Wind,* was first sent in for publication, the proposed title was "Tomorrow Is Another Day." The author, Margaret Mitchell, was thinking of the temptation of the central character Scarlett O'Hara to refuse to address the present situation and turn away from involvement by fantasizing about the future. Sometimes, we are surprised at the way Scarlett O'Hara streaks come out in our words and thoughts and acts. God calls us to accountability each day. Although we are tempted to evade responsibility for the present by dreaming of tomorrow, the Lord summons us to be obedient.

Accountable in the Garbage Can. Americans throw away 15 percent of their food at a cost of $11 billion a year. The General Accounting Office revealed this figure after a six year study of the garbage of residents of Tucson, Arizona. Researchers at the University of Arizona found also that Americans waste more food when it's scarce than when it's plentiful. The research showed that when people turned to unfamiliar cuts of beef as they did in the beef shortage in 1973, they threw away more than they normally would have because they did not know how to prepare it.

If we are accountable to God, what does this study about our waste of food suggest?

Sentence Sermon to Remember: No sound ought to be heard in the Church but the healing voice of Christian charity.—Edmund Burke.

Questions for Pupils on the Next Lesson. 1. How is Israel "God's Vineyard"? 2. Does God expect a "harvest" or "fruits" from His people today? If so, what? 3. Do you accept responsibility for all your actions, or do you find yourself blaming others? 4. What do you think your potential is for serving others? 5. What do you think God is expecting of you in the next five years?

LESSON VI—JANUARY 8

SONG OF THE VINEYARD

Background Scripture: Isaiah 5
Devotional Reading: Isaiah 24:1–13

KING JAMES VERSION

ISAIAH 5 1 Now will I sing to my well-beloved a song of my beloved touching his vineyard. My wellbeloved hath a vineyard in a very fruitful hill:

2 And he fenced it, and gathered out the stones thereof, and planted it with the choicest vine, and built a tower in the midst of it, and also made a winepress therein: and he looked that it should bring forth grapes, and it brought forth wild grapes.

3 And now, O inhabitants of Jerusalem, and men of Judah, judge, I pray you, betwixt me and my vineyard.

4 What could have been done more to my vineyard, that I have not done in it? wherefore, when I looked that it should bring forth grapes, brought it forth wild grapes?

5 And now go to; I will tell you what I will do to my vineyard: I will take away the hedge thereof, and it shall be eaten up; *and* break down the wall thereof, and it shall be trodden down:

6 And I will lay it waste: it shall not be pruned, nor digged; but there shall come up briers and thorns: I will also command the clouds that they rain no rain upon it.

7 For the vineyard of the LORD of hosts *is* the house of Israel, and the men of Judah his pleasant plant: and he looked for judgment, but behold oppression; for righteousness, but behold a cry.

REVISED STANDARD VERSION

ISAIAH 5 1 Let me sing for my beloved a love song concerning his vineyard:
My beloved had a vineyard
  on a very fertile hill.

2 He digged it and cleared it of stones,
  and planted it with choice vines;
he built a watchtower in the midst of it,
  and hewed out a wine vat in it;
and he looked for it to yield grapes
  but it yielded wild grapes.

3 And now, O inhabitants of Jerusalem and
  men of Judah,
judge, I pray you, between me
  and my vineyard.

4 What more was there to do for my vineyard,
  that I have not done in it?
When I looked for it to yield grapes,
  why did it yield wild grapes?

5 And now I will tell you
  what I will do to my vineyard.
I will remove its hedge,
  and it shall be devoured;
I will break down its wall,
  and it shall be trampled down.

6 I will make it a waste;
  it shall not be pruned or hoed,
  and briers and thorns shall grow up;
I will also command the clouds
  that they rain no rain upon it.

7 For the vineyard of the LORD of hosts
  is the house of Israel,
and the men of Judah
  are his pleasant planting;
and he looked for justice,
  but behold, bloodshed;
for righteousness,
  but behold, a cry!

KEY VERSE: Yet I planted you a choice vine, wholly of pure seed. How then have you turned degenerate and become a wild vine? Jeremiah 2:21 (RSV).

HOME DAILY BIBLE READINGS

Jan. 2. M. *Parable Against a Nation.* Matthew 21:33–46.
Jan. 3. T. *Lament Over Evil Doers.* Isaiah 5:8–17.
Jan. 4. W. *Lament Over Evil Doers.* Isaiah 5:18–23.
Jan. 5. T. *"His Hand Is Stretched Out Still."* Isaiah 5:24–30.
Jan. 6. F. *Parable Against Abimelech.* Judges 9:7–16.
Jan. 7. S. *Parable Against David.* 2 Samuel 12:1–7.
Jan. 8. S. *Parable Against a Nation.* Isaiah 5:1–7.

BACKGROUND

Up to this point, in our study of the prophecies and messages of Isaiah, we have been dealing primarily with the national life and history of Judah. Now we are to

123

deal with something deeply *personal*. In the first line of Isaiah 5, God is pictured as a singer of a song that is both bitter and inspiring. God says, "Now will I sing to my wellbeloved, . . . touching (concerning) his vineyard."

It may be that this song was a song to be sung at the time of harvest—a festival song. But as we read its words, we find them rather bitter, at least at the beginning. It has to do with sour grapes (a parable), and it calls to mind the words of the Prophet Jeremiah (31:30): "Every man that eateth the sour grape, his teeth shall be set on edge." Isaiah's song is a song of unpleasant taste.

NOTES ON THE PRINTED TEXT

The song starts out on a good note, a congratulatory note. God's beloved—the people of Judah—has set up a vineyard "on a very fertile hill." Good! Any sensible farmer or wine-grower would do that. The land was cleared of stones, plowed carefully, surrounded by a fence to keep the marauders out; the master of the vineyard set up a watchtower to warn him of the marauders, and built a good winepress. So far, so good. But after all this, he made a fatal mistake. Having done all this, he just sat down and waited for the grapes to grow.

We knew a man once, who did that. He planted a "war garden," back in the days of World War II. That was good patriotism. But having put in his seed, he paid no more attention to his little garden. He got no vegetables out of it—only weeds. His philosophy was, "If I go to all the trouble of planting it, I'll let nature do the rest of it."

Through the prophet, God asks this foolish—and lazy—grape grower if he realizes what he has done: "What more could I have done for you? Why did *my* vineyard give me wild (sour) grapes instead of sweet?" God had done all He could do: He had given this man good soil and rain to give life to good grapes. Notice that God says the vineyard is *His*, not the man's. It was the Creator who made the land, not man; men are only the temporary tenants on the land. When God puts this tenant in charge of the soil, He *expects him to take good care of it*, to do whatever has to be done to make it produce good grapes and not sour ones. A good garden demands constant care.

So does the good life, the life with God, the life under God. The ruler of this world—and it is God's world, not ours—calls for constant effort, constant reliance on Him, after He has planted within us the seeds of salvation and union with Him. The awareness of Him involved in conversion is only the *start* of a new life; after conversion there must be a constant labor of mind and spirit, or it all "dies on the vine."

Now what will God do about this miserable vineyard uncared for by its "master"? Verses 3–6 tell us what He will do. Phrased in the typically Hebrew fear of the punishment of God, God is described as One who will inflict ruin upon these children of His in Judah who have given Him wild grapes instead of sweet ones, injustice and unrighteousness and even bloodshed. He will tear down their fences. (Those little fences of men who spend their lives fencing themselves *in* and God *out!*). He will let the vines grow wild, let His vineyard (Judah and Israel) become wasteland, trampled down by cattle and sheep, unpruned, overgrown by briars and thorns.

Worst of all, He will no longer send His gentle rain from heaven to give life to all on earth. Can anyone imagine what would happen to us all if there were no rain? If He gave us everything else, and withheld His rain, what would become of us?

We in Christ's Church have a way of smiling and playing down the youth of our time who "sow their wild grapes" in unchristian living. Oh, well, they say, youth will grow out of that and mature into good men, somehow, sometime. When we do that, we overlook the brutal fact that too many grown men go on and on sowing their wild grapes. Too many of us are just too busy in an effort to "make it," to grow rich, to win the high places no matter how. They wait too long, and do not see the folly of their ways until the angel of death knocks on their doors. Too late! Only yesterday we read in our morning newspaper of a man who died and left his estate to the devil. What the courts will do about that, nobody knows. All we know is that this man didn't take very good care of his life's vineyard; he didn't even bother to sow good seeds. May God have mercy upon him— and upon us.

May we repeat something here that we may have said before, in these lessons? Namely, that perhaps the only thing we will be asked about our lives at the promised judgment of God will be, "What did you *make* of your life?"

SUGGESTIONS TO TEACHERS

In a cartoon, a tall, angular gent with a goatee and wearing a striped top hat is always Uncle Sam. Everyone knows that Uncle Sam stands for the United States of America. A bear represents Russia. Cartoons also depict France as a woman in flowing gown, and Britain as a lion or a John Bull attired in a vest emblazoned with the Union Jack. Cartoons are shorthand ways of communicating a point.

Likewise, a parable is a brief story illustrating a truth. Like cartoons, parables in the Bible often had standard figures. The vineyard was such a well-known parable-figure that no one needed to explain that it referred to Israel.

Start your lesson on Isaiah's Song of the Vineyard by reminding your class that like a cartoon figure, mention of the vineyard in Isaiah would get instant recognition.

1. *PARABLE AS PROPHECY.* Go into the details of what biblical writers meant by Israel being God's vineyard. Although few of us are familiar with tending grape vines, you can quickly show your class how carefully God cultivates His vineyard, Israel, and how He expected good results. In spite of His effort and attention, however, the vineyard does not produce. The Lord's work was in vain. The vineyard has turned out to be useless. With the Bible story in mind, ask your class what God expects of us, His people, now. How productive has the Church, as part of God's vineyard, been in our times?

2. *PROPHECY AS PREACHING.* After discussing the expectation and the explanation of the vineyard story, Isaiah continues with a message of excoriation and extermination. His "sermons" list the problems of the community. Isaiah enumerates at least six. They include greed (people conniving to cheat others or scheming to take over land, thereby depriving poor farmers of their livelihood), leisure (wealthy folk lolling in drunken indolence), haughtiness ("wise" persons sneering at the Lord and His requirements), inverted values (people insisting on calling evil good), pride (moral leaders permitting injustice, accepting bribes and depriving the innocent of their rights). How up to date is Isaiah's list? Would your class add to the list, or remove any of Isaiah's points? What do those in your class think of Isaiah's conclusion, namely that disobedient people will perish? Could this happen to our country? To our Church? To your congregation?

TOPIC FOR ADULTS
SONG OF THE VINEYARD

We Must Speak. "If it (the Christian faith) were merely knowledge and wisdom it could be taught; if it were simply a religious way of life, people could be initiated into it; if it were a program, it could be put into effect by a concentrated effort. The Gospel is, however, in essence an event to be declared.

"The Christian faith says something has happened, something has been done, which is of supreme significance and importance for all men in every generation, for all time.

"God had become man. That man has borne the burden of human sin. He has conquered death. He is the Eternal Contemporary, seeking man to enlist him in His service. He is the Ruler above all rulers, the King above all kings, the Lord above all lords. He sheds abroad His love in the hearts of men. Of Him, the Spirit of God is constantly speaking in the secrecy of each man's soul, saying to each man, 'He is your Saviour, accept Him. He is your Lord, serve Him. He is your Brother, love Him. He is your Judge, fear Him.'

"We must speak because these events must be proclaimed. Every man has the right to know them. So that we who know, have also the obligation to share...."—D. T. Niles and others, *Why We Must Speak*, World Council of Churches, Department of Studies in Evangelism, Geneva, 1963.

Stick My Neck Out. The Christian Community as God's "vineyard" today must recognize that God holds it responsible to bring forth a harvest of justice. This is not easy. One pastor describes his experiences: "In my last pastorate in Idaho, I served in a community which, for a time, was strangled by legalized gambling interests. Slot machines were to be found in almost every public place. The local tax structure came to depend upon a cut or tax from such machines to operate the community. The local Elks lodge owned and operated a golf course without charge to its 3,000 members because of slot machine revenue. The American Legion sponsored a whole string of youth activities with revenue received from slot machines in its club house. Meanwhile, men lost their pay checks, women their grocery money. Merchants were frantic because of their difficulty in collecting bills. Some of us were determined to fight this evil monster. We were opposed by the local paper and by advertisements printed by the City Council threatening to triple taxes if slot machines went. Some of us tried to get fifty leading citizens, church members, businessmen, and community leaders to sign a simple statement that they opposed legalized gambling. After two weeks of effort, calling on every responsible community leader, we got just eight names. People were afraid— afraid because of the threat of physical violence and economic reprisal. No public school teacher would support us because one school board member was part owner of a gambling hall. No member of the faculty of the local state teachers' college would support us because a member of the Board of Regents had financial interest in eating places where slot machines were in operation. Finally, we got two leading physicians, the manager of the telephone company whose boss was in another state, and three courageous owners of local businesses who took a terrific financial beating for a time, and two wealthy retired men. Many others would slip us money. Many pats on the back were given. But over and over we heard, 'I can't stick out my neck on this thing.' "—Douglas Vance.

Motto of Your Church? A well-known church leader recalls traveling to a conference of Christians in Ann Arbor, Michigan. After registering at the University of Michigan Union, he passed one of the large churches in the area near the campus. Adjacent to the entrance of the church parking lot was a prominent sign which read: RESTRICTED AREA: CHURCH OFFICIALS AND CHURCH BUSINESS ONLY. This, the church leader contends, could be the motto of many American Christian churches today. Does his criticism apply to yours?

Questions for Pupils on the Next Lesson. 1. What was the political and religious situation in Judah in the eighth century B.C. when Isaiah had his vision and call? 2. What was the symbolism of Isaiah's vision? 3. What was Isaiah's mission after his call? 4. Have you ever had a sense of God's nearness and a feeling that God has plans for you? 5. Do you think that there is a greater or lesser sense of transcendence in the lives of most adults?

TOPIC FOR YOUTH
WHAT GOD EXPECTS

Found Out Yet? The Church is God's specially-prepared instrument to reach out to others. God expects each congregation and each Christian to be part of His "vineyard" and to produce significant results because of his care. Sometimes, however, as churches, we are like the old Vermont couple who were asked about the new neighbors. "How do you like the folks that came to live down the road last year?"

"Ain't found out yet," came the reply of the old timers. "They don't neighbor none."

God expects you and your congregation to "neighbor" a lot!

Unfinished Church Building. When the Cathedral of St. John the Divine in New York City was having financial trouble because of a stand that the bishop had taken, he simply said that, if they could not finish the Cathedral, its unfinished state would stand as a memorial to a time when the diocese preferred an unfinished church to compromise with great Christian, social principles.

Do you and your church leaders have this sense of carrying out what God expects—even at the cost of sacrificing cherished plans?

Major Task. "The major task of the church as the peacemaking community is not 'to bind up the wounds of a bleeding world,' though it may need to continue to do that simply because there are still so many open wounds. The major task of the church is rather to be the embodiment of a creation that will make it unnecessary for people to leave one another bleeding in the first place. This can be called 'salvation' or 'liberation' or 'reconciliation' or any one of a number of similar words. It will involve ministering to the whole person and the whole society, since piecemeal approaches will no longer do. . . ."—Robert McAfee Brown, *Making Peace in the Global Village,* Westminster, Philadelphia, 1981.

Sentence Sermon to Remember: God likes help when helping people.—Irish proverb.

Questions for Pupils on the Next Lesson. 1. What was happening in Isaiah's nation when he had his religious experience in the Temple? 2. Have you ever had any occasion when you have felt God was particularly real in your life? 3. What does it mean to be "called" by God? 4. Have you looked for a vision and call from God to help you in your search for a sense of purpose in life? 5. Does God's call always mean that the person must serve others?

LESSON VII—JANUARY 15

VISION AND MISSION

Background Scripture: Isaiah 6
Devotional Reading: Isaiah 30:15–18

KING JAMES VERSION

ISAIAH 6 1 In the year that king Uzziah died I saw also the Lord sitting upon a throne, high and lifted up, and his train filled the temple.

2 Above it stood the seraphims: each one had six wings; with twain he covered his face, and with twain he covered his feet, and with twain he did fly.

3 And one cried unto another, and said, Holy, holy, holy, *is* the LORD of hosts: the whole earth *is* full of his glory.

4 And the posts of the door moved at the voice of him that cried, and the house was filled with smoke.

5 Then said I, Woe *is* me! for I am undone; because I *am* a man of unclean lips, and I dwell in the midst of a people of unclean lips: for mine eyes have seen the King, the LORD of hosts.

6 Then flew one of the seraphims unto me, having a live coal in his hand, *which* he had taken with the tongs from off the altar:

7 And he laid *it* upon my mouth, and said, Lo, this hath touched thy lips; and thine iniquity is taken away, and thy sin purged.

8 Also I heard the voice of the Lord, saying, Whom shall I send, and who will go for us? Then said I, Here *am* I; send me.

REVISED STANDARD VERSION

ISAIAH 6 1 In the year that King Uzziah died I saw the Lord sitting upon a throne, high and lifted up; and his train filled the temple.

2 Above him stood the seraphim; each had six wings: with two he covered his face, and with two he covered his feet, and with two he flew.

3 And one called to another and said:

"Holy, holy, holy is the LORD of hosts;
  the whole earth is full of his glory."

4 And the foundations of the thresholds shook at the voice of him who called, and the house was filled with smoke. 5 And I said: "Woe is me! For I am lost; for I am a man of unclean lips, and I dwell in the midst of a people of unclean lips; for my eyes have seen the King, the LORD of hosts!"

6 Then flew one of the seraphim to me, having in his hand a burning coal which he had taken with tongs from the altar.

7 And he touched my mouth, and said: "Behold, this has touched your lips; your guilt is taken away, and your sin forgiven."

8 And I heard the voice of the Lord saying, "Whom shall I send, and who will go for us?" Then I said, "Here I am! Send me."

KEY VERSE: *I heard the voice of the Lord saying, "Whom shall I send, and who will go for us?" Then I said, "Here am I! Send me." Isaiah 6:8 (*RSV*).*

HOME DAILY BIBLE READINGS

Jan. 9. M. *The King of the Universe.* Psalms 47:1–9.
Jan. 10. T. *The King of the World.* Psalms 93:1–5.
Jan. 11. W. *The Head of the Heavenly Council.* Jeremiah 23:18–22.
Jan. 12. T. *The Sinfulness of the Nation.* Isaiah 1:4–9.
Jan. 13. F. *A Prayer for Forgiveness.* Amos 7:1–6.
Jan. 14. S. *The Insensitivity of the People.* Matthew 13:10–15.
Jan. 15. S. *The Call of a Messenger.* Isaiah 6:1–13.

BACKGROUND

Uzziah was crowned king of Judah when he was only eleven years old; he must have had good tutors and advisers, for on the whole he was a very good king during his reign (786–746 B.C.). But he died of leprosy, which was to his people a sign that their king was not altogether good, and they were right about that. For one thing, Uzziah interfered as head of the state with the functions of the religious leaders (*see* 2 Chronicles 26:16–19) and otherwise violated the Priestly Code. Guilty as charged or not, his death from leprosy sent the people of Judah into an emotional frenzy and a mood of total chaos. The great king was dead; how could they possibly get along without him? What could they do now?

NOTES ON THE PRINTED TEXT

Isaiah had great respect for Uzziah as a wise ruler and a righteous man; now, like the people of Judah, he had his doubts. His king, after all, was a great sinner punished by God. Disillusionment passed into panic, into morale-destroying fear. Surely, Judah might and probably would perish without such a king as Uzziah on the throne, and there seemed to be no such man available.

It was a grim moment for the young Isaiah; he was almost ready to give up. But it is always darkest just before the dawn—and when he least expected it, a dawn broke upon him. He had a vision and he heard a voice. It is often held by some interpreters that this vision came to Isaiah in the Temple at Jerusalem, but actually the biblical record does not tell us where he was at the moment of the vision, but that is not important. The record does tell us that the vision is concerned with God in His heavenly court, where He was surrounded by a choir of angels singing "Holy, Holy, Holy, is the Lord of hosts; the whole earth is full of his glory" (verse 3). Hovering above them were mythical "seraphim"—mythical creatures believed to be half animal and half human, winged creatures serving as attendants of the heavenly King.

With the earth shaking under his feet, there stood Isaiah. He stood there still conscious of the tragedy that had come to Uzziah and Uzziah's people. What must he have been thinking? How small he must have felt, how insignificant. And how *unworthy*. How unworthy are we all, if and when we stand before our Christ! No matter how much we like to think well of ourselves, we feel like insignificant dwarfs, when compared with Him.

That was the first reaction of Isaiah. "Woe is me! . . . because I am a man of unclean lips. . . ." He felt unclean, dirty; he had an overwhelming sense of guilt.

That wasn't weakness in the prophet; it was *courage*. Is there any man on earth who at one time or another has not spoken evil with dirty lips, any man who has not struggled with a sense of guilt? So many of us, as we grow older and wiser, lie awake nights bemoaning the sins we have committed in the past. That can become an obsession, a remorse that can almost drive us out of our minds. It is unnecessary, for, in the first place, we cannot change the past; and in the second place, God cannot do much for or with a man who is unwilling to admit his shortcomings and his offenses against God.

We do not need to give way to this remorse for God offers us forgiveness that comes with confession. In his vision, Isaiah was approached by one of the seraphims, who (symbolically) touched his lips with a live coal. Symbolic, yes, but it was also the answer of God's mercy to a confessed sinner. It was the touch of the fire of God's cleansing. Isaiah does not say that there was any pain, any burning, in this incident of the application of the coal; there was only—*forgiveness!*

Now the climax. The prophet once more hears the voice of God. God speaks to him of the unclean lips and lives of his fellowmen in Judah. There are so many of them, such a great need of forgiveness and salvation, such need for messengers to carry the word of His forgiveness among the men of earth. Almost to Himself, it seems, God asks, "Who shall I send? Who will be willing to go?" But Isaiah hears it, and he cries, "Send *me*." Unlike Moses and Jeremiah, who hesitated in accepting God's call, Isaiah is anxious and ready to go, ready to hear and obey the call of God.

He was a volunteer; God did not order him to go, for God knew well that an army of volunteers is far better than an army of draftees. He still calls. He calls laymen as well as ministers. He calls for Christian teachers, doctors, clerks and businessmen, laborers and executives. These are called, as well as clergymen. "It is possible for a man facing the opportunity of some honest labor or great profession and ready to give his life to it, to hear, as Isaiah did, a summons, and to answer as he did, 'Here am I, send me' "—G.G.D. Kilpatrick, in *The Interpreter's Bible.*

How does the call come? First comes the awareness of being unclean, then the removal of guilt, then a willingness to serve the Lord, then the call and the commission. That's the way it works. That does it!

SUGGESTIONS TO TEACHERS

What are the marks of a genuine conversion? How do you know whether a "call from God" is authentic? After all, there are fakes in religion as in art. Sometimes phony reproductions in art circles have fooled even the experts, and counterfeit piety is just as hard to detect.

Isaiah's call offers you and your class an excellent opportunity to talk about the real versus the spurious "call." Throughout this lesson, however, remind your class that each Christian has received a "call" through Jesus Christ. The key question becomes: "What are you doing about God's call to you?"

1. *MAJESTY.* Isaiah's call came during a period of national crisis when King Uzziah had died. Isaiah was worshiping in the Temple. His experience of the presence of the Lord was, of course, distinctly personal, but it essentially reflected a sense of awe. One clue about how authentic a "call" or "conversion" may be is here. Phony religion plays up God as merely a Good Ole Buddy. Real faith recognizes the majesty of the Lord.

2. *MINUTENESS.* Isaiah senses his own unworthiness when he realizes he stands before the Eternal. Here is another mark of a genuine religious experience. Like all honest men and women writing of their encounter with the Lord, Isaiah acknowledged his guilt and smallness. Note that there is no morbid harping on his misery, nor is there undue emphasis on emotions. How does Isaiah's conversion account compare with the call or conversion of each person in your class in this regard?

3. *MERCY.* Isaiah and all others in the biblical tradition down to our own times was overwhelmed with divine mercy. From a sense of being unclean, Isaiah passed to an awareness of God's love. He knew how his lips had spoken lies and talked against the Lord; he also learned that his guilt was burned away by God's forgiveness. (Note the significant imagery of his lips being touched by coals from the altar, symbolizing the purifying fire of God's goodness.) Unless there is supreme stress on the love of the Lord, any report of a "call" or "conversion" is suspect. Have your class members personally appreciated the mercy of Christ in their lives?

4. *MISSION.* "Here am I. Send me!" Isaiah responds (6:8). Part of any real call of God has to do with mission. If a person has been encountered by the Lord, he or she is immediately called to report for duty! And that duty means serving in ways and places that will not be always fun or simple. Isaiah learned this. Jesus died for this fact. Do your class members appreciate that a real "call" means being sent to sacrifice?

5. *MESSAGE.* Isaiah's message which God commanded him to speak to his contemporaries was a terrible assignment: to tell of coming misery for the nation because of its disobedience. However, the message also included the promise of a remnant ("a holy seed" in the stump) of God's people who would be spared to continue God's mission. Have your people share what they consider God is asking the Church to say in these times. What exactly is the vision of mission which the Lord has for those He calls today?

TOPIC FOR ADULTS
VISION AND MISSION

Second Conversion. Each of us must be converted to the transcendent God who encounters us in Jesus Christ. However, we must also have what might be called a "second conversion" in which we understand God sends us into the world in His name to share His love. Thomas Merton, the Trappist monk, describes these two conversions as they happened to him. In Corpus Christi Church on Broadway, in New York City, Merton the worldly agnostic was turned toward God, the Lord of all. Like Isaiah, Merton experienced a vision of the transcendent One. He became a Trappist monk and settled in Kentucky at the Gethsemane monastic community. His "call" to mission, however, did not come until nearly ten years later. You notice that something extraordinary has come to Thomas Merton. You can turn to it in his diary, *Conjectures of a Guilty Bystander,* and see what it was. One day he had to go into the neighboring town to see a doctor. It is a lovely drive through beautiful country where they distil gin and train racehorses. There, in the town with hundreds of Americans milling around, it happened.

"In Louisville, at the corner of Fourth Avenue and Walnut Street, in the center of the shopping district, I was suddenly overwhelmed with the realization that I loved all these people, that they were mine and I theirs. . . . It was like waking from a dream of separateness. . . . This sense of liberation from an illusory difference was such a relief and joy to me that I almost laughed out loud. . . . To think that such a commonplace realization should suddenly seem like news that one holds the winning ticket in a cosmic sweepstake."—Thomas Merton, *Conjectures of a Guilty Bystander,* Burns and Oates, 1968.

No Solitary Religion. Every vision of the Lord means joining both with others of God's community and also serving others. John Wesley understood this well and repeatedly emphasized it to his societies and associates. "Sir, you wish to serve God and go to heaven? Remember that you cannot serve Him alone. You must therefore find companions or make them: the Bible knows nothing of solitary religion."—John Wesley's *Journal,* I.

Do you understand this aspect of the vision and mission you have received from God?

The Cost of Discipleship in Cuba. Cuban Christians are learning that Christ's call means receiving both a vision and a mission. They can also help other Christians to understand that taking Jesus Christ seriously means serving and paying the cost of being a prophet. Although the Cuban Constitution under Castro upholds religious freedom, churches are prohibited from evangelizing publicly, and Cubans who openly profess belief in God are barred from membership in the Communist Party. Theoretically, party officials say, religious tests cannot be applied for job promotion, but Christians say that as a practical matter the prevailing attitude is that "a Christian cannot be boss." "If you are a Christian, you sacrifice your career in government," said one official. "It's a choice." Christians are also subjected to more subtle pressure. Meetings of Communist youth are regularly scheduled during churchgoing hours on Sunday morning, for instance, and young men are expected to serve in the militia on the same day.

The challenge faces Emilio Rodriguez, a civil engineer who will leave soon for Cambodia on a church-related project to build irrigation systems. He is a staunch Presbyterian who says that, "Everyone should know I'm a Christian," and he voices support for the medical, educational, and social goals of the revolution. At the same time, he believes that his Christianity will restrict his career.

"I don't want a promotion if I have to renounce my faith," he said. "Whatever I lose being a Christian I lose gladly."

Questions for Pupils on the Next Lesson. 1. What are some of the things or causes that many people turn to in order to try to find some sense of security? 2. What are some of the forms of idol worship that you see in these times? 3. Is God still fulfilling His purposes in history? 4. What are some of the ideologies which compete with the Christian Gospel in our culture? 5. Why did Isaiah warn his people against relying on political alliances?

TOPIC FOR YOUTH
GOD'S MISSION FOR ME

Your Mission to Tell Others. "Our failure to speak out is often a sign of giving in; likewise, our failure to put our foot down is often a sign of giving up.

"When we should speak out against evil, our silent assent is as self-damaging, as destructive, and as cowardly as verbal consent.

"A timid, halfhearted witness is not a witness, but a mere apology for luke-warm-ness.

"When Christ commanded us to be lights of the world, He had in mind brilliant beacons, not spiritual lightning bugs.

"Often a criminal goes free because a witness fears to testify; likewise many remain enslaved by sin because we who should witness for Christ are afraid to share our testimony. We proudly sing, 'We've a Story to Tell to the Nations' and then neglect to share the Good News with our next-door neighbor."—William A. Ward, *Quote,* September 5, 1971.

Love's Dress. "Some of us may be surprised to learn that love is work and has tremendous tasks to perform. We are more likely to think of love as always wearing party clothes and playing glamorously in perpetual sunsets and moonlight. What a surprise to discover that love does some of its most serious work in stained and torn bluejeans in the heat of the day. . . ."—Reuel L. Howe, *The Creative Years.*

Listening for God's Voice. "The world that you want to transform in a just manner will not be transformed because you yourselves are not transformed. And so long as you refuse to change yourselves, the world will not change. But the world can change if you change.

"How do you change? By listening to God; because, as the sun is always shining, so God is constantly speaking. How do you listen to God?

"The best time is in the morning, before all distractions and activities intervene. How can you listen to God, you ask me?

"This is the answer; you write. Write, so that you may better hear the Word that is in you and keep His instructions."—Pere Alphonse Gratry 1805–1872.

Sentence Sermon to Remember: Conversion is, in great part, a recognition of the world's need.—Joseph Haines.

Questions for Pupils on the Next Lesson. 1. What do you place your greatest trust in? Why? 2. What are the main idols in the lives of your peers? 3. Why do you sometimes feel insecure? 4. Where do you feel most accepted? 5. What are the ideologies which seem most attractive for youth in these days?

LESSON VIII—JANUARY 22

TURN TO THE LORD

Background Scripture: Isaiah 30, 31
Devotional Reading: Psalms 107:1–9

KING JAMES VERSION

ISAIAH 31 1 Woe to them that go down to Egypt for help; and stay on horses, and trust in chariots, because *they are* many; and in horsemen, because they are very strong; but they look not unto the Holy One of Israel, neither seek the LORD!

2 Yet he also *is* wise, and will bring evil, and will not call back his words: but will arise against the house of the evildoers, and against the help of them that work iniquity.

3 Now the Egyptians *are* men, and not God; and their horses flesh, and not spirit. When the LORD shall stretch out his hand, both he that helpeth shall fall, and he that is holpen shall fall down, and they all shall fail together.

4 For thus hath the LORD spoken unto me, Like as the lion and the young lion roaring on his prey, when a multitude of shepherds is called forth against him, *he* will not be afraid of their voice, nor abase himself for the noise of them: so shall the LORD of hosts come down to fight for mount Zion, and for the hill thereof.

5 As birds flying, so will the LORD of hosts defend Jerusalem; defending also he will deliver *it; and* passing over he will preserve *it.*

6 Turn ye unto *him from* whom the children of Israel have deeply revolted.

7 For in that day every man shall cast away his idols of silver, and his idols of gold, which your own hands have made unto you *for* a sin.

REVISED STANDARD VERSION

ISAIAH 31 1 Woe to those who go down to Egypt for help
and rely on horses,
who trust in chariots because they are many
and in horsemen because they are very strong,
but do not look to the Holy One of Israel
or consult the LORD!

2 And yet he is wise and brings disaster,
he does not call back his words,
but will arise against the house of the evildoers,
and against the helpers of those who work iniquity.

3 The Egyptians are men, and not God;
and their horses are flesh, and not spirit.
When the LORD stretches out his hand,
the helper will stumble, and he who is helped will fall,
and they will all perish together.

4 For thus the LORD said to me,
As a lion or a young lion growls over his prey,
and when a band of shepherds is called forth against him
is not terrified by their shouting
or daunted at their noise,
so the LORD of hosts will come down
to fight upon Mount Zion and upon its hill.

5 Like birds hovering, so the LORD of hosts
will protect Jerusalem;
he will protect and deliver it,
he will spare and rescue it.

6 Turn to him from whom you have deeply revolted, O people of Israel. 7 For in that day every one shall cast away his idols of silver and his idols of gold, which your hands have sinfully made for you.

KEY VERSE: "In returning and rest you shall be saved; in quietness and in trust shall be your strength." Isaiah 30:15 (RSV).

HOME DAILY BIBLE READINGS

Jan.	16.	M.	*The Holy Purpose of God.* Isaiah 10:5–15.
Jan.	17.	T.	*A Covenant With Death.* Isaiah 28:14–22.
Jan.	18.	W.	*Learn From the Farmer.* Isaiah 28:23–29.
Jan.	19.	T.	*A Rebellious People.* Isaiah 30:1–7.
Jan.	20.	F.	*The Suicide of Rejecting Faith.* Isaiah 30:12–17.
Jan.	21.	S.	*The Compassionate God.* Isaiah 30:18–26.
Jan.	22.	S.	*No Substitute for Faith in God.* Isaiah 31:1–7.

133

BACKGROUND

Geographically and politically, both Israel and Judah are caught in a trap not of their own making during the days of Isaiah. In our lesson for today, we find Assyria and Egypt in a desperate conflict for power, which raged for more than five hundred years, with poor little Judah and Israel caught right in the middle. Enslaved under the Assyrians, Palestine rebelled and King Sennacherib invaded Palestine to put down the rebellion. The Judean kings usually formed alliances with Egypt when they stopped paying tribute to the Assyrians, and that, Isaiah said, was the worst thing they could have done.

Isaiah was right in telling them that, but there were many who disagreed with him. What else could they do but to secure the aid of powerful Egypt? It was a question of national security. Isaiah didn't think it was a very sensible security, and he suggested something else.

NOTES ON THE PRINTED TEXT

If we had been alive when Judah sought help from Egypt, we would quite probably have done just what Judah did; we would have demonstrated our belief in "any port in a storm." To the average man, it seemed common sense to protect the nation at any cost. When a supposedly righteous nation is threatened by an unrighteous one, that nation would fight back in order to save itself. We call it National Security.

But Isaiah disagreed. He was probably hooted in the streets for taking a stand against any alliance with pagan Egypt, but the prophet held his ground. He called Judah's attention to the fact that God's people had made a covenant with Him in which they promised that they would put their trust in Him. Now they were planning to put their trust in *Egypt!* Egypt had a multitude of chariots— terrifying chariots, with spinning knives on their wheel hubs. Right now, Judah could use the help of those monstrosities. Right now, they had a plan of their own, a military plan, with which they could destroy Assyria. God's plan could wait. They would put their trust and their hopes in Pharaoh of Egypt not in the Holy One of Israel.

Isaiah told them that they were fools. These Egyptians were men and not God. They could be beaten in war with Assyria: where would Judah be, then? The best laid plans of mice and men, said Bobby Burns, "Gang aft a-gley"—go wrong. God's plans never go wrong. In the end, God wins.

Judah wouldn't listen to that. Neither do we! What ghastly blunders have we made in putting our trust in chariots, cannon, and bayonets. In two short days of battle at Shiloh in our Civil War, three thousand men were killed. If only wiser heads had prevailed and if we had had fewer hot-heads on both sides, the whole tragic Civil War could have been prevented before the war began. We lost some 50,000 men dead in Vietnam in a war that should never have been.

We, too, put our trust in alliances in the name of National Security. Once we hated Communist China; today we are planning cooperation with China! Today we in our Christian United States are selling deadly arms to both Israel and Saudi Arabia! Where will it all end?

Isaiah has a word of warning about the end: "When the Lord stretches out his hand, the helper will stumble, and he who is helped will fall, and they will all perish together" (Isaiah 31:3). Read it and weep!

In verses 4–6, Isaiah gives us the suggestion of God in the images of a roaring lion and a gentle bird. He does this by way of illustrating both the severe judgment and the hovering of God of love over His people. The idea of God as a lion may be difficult for us to accept, until we understand that our God is a God of righteous anger, and that divine anger is something man needs as he fights the battle of life. God is occasionally angry with us, but it is the anger of a Father to a wayward child. "Paradoxically," says one commentator, "there is such a thing as the merciless judgment of love." The prophet is only saying that God is to come as an enraged lion to the defense of Jerusalem—a lion unafraid of "when a band of shepherds is called forth against him." Lions hunting food in the Jordan Valley were a serious problem; the shepherds often tried to frighten off the lions by making a great noise. God will not be frightened at the presence of a noisy enemy! He will fight on to deliver Jerusalem from the roaring enemies of His people.

The image of God as a bird hovering over His children is easier to understand. Many a mother bird, when an intruder threatens her brood in the nest, will thrash around in the brush, pretending that she has a broken wing and hoping that she will distract the intruder from the young ones. If such a mother bird will do that for her children, will not God stand between His people and their enemies?

Summing it all up, Isaiah here is telling us that God's plan is better than any man-made plan, that God is active in history, and that the final disposition of men and nations is God's, and not ours. Charles Wesley summed it up in his glorious hymn:

> O spread thy covering wings around,
>   Till all our wanderings cease,
> And at our Father's loved abode,
>   Our souls arrive in peace.
>
> All my trust on thee is stayed,
>   All my help from thee I bring,
> Cover my defenseless head
>   With the shadow of thy wing.

SUGGESTIONS TO TEACHERS

"Why bother with all this ancient history? What do I care about hearing about the Assyrians 2,700 years ago? None of this stuff has any relevance to me."

These words by a bright young professional woman, college educated and intellectually alert, echo the thinking of a lot of persons who look briefly at the Bible and turn away. You perhaps have some in your Sunday-School class who feel this way. As you continue to prepare lessons from Isaiah, you should remember that you are not dealing merely with facts from the distant past. You are recounting God's story for the coming week. You may teach with the confidence that the Scriptures are as up to date as tomorrow morning's newspaper!

1. *FAULTY RELIANCE.* Israel depended upon clever diplomacy instead of God's guidance. Isaiah took the unpopular stand of denouncing Israel's alliance with Egypt. "Playing the power game of aligning yourself with the superpowers will only get you crushed in the end," Isaiah in effect said. He accused his people of selling out their faith and buying protection which would prove useless. Use this lesson to think for a while about policies in the Church and in the nation which do not square with our faith. What does it mean to forget faulty alliances with worldly powers and live by faith and obedience to the Lord?

2. *FOOLISH REFUSAL.* Isaiah learned that the life of a prophet is lonely and harsh. His own people refused to hear the instructions of the Lord and cried out for religious leaders who would tell them pleasant, smooth messages. Isaiah told them that these leaders merely prophesied illusions. Don't people today still want smooth-talking prophets? Are there not religious leaders who prophesy illusions in our times? Use this period in the lesson to discuss the dangers of blindly following the personality cults of many of our smiling electronic church preachers.

3. *FULSOME RENEWAL.* Reread the promise of security for those who return and wait for the Lord. This will be a good occasion to bring up the need for personal devotional life—something very few Christians practice. Isaiah as a seasoned veteran of the prayer-campaign can instruct you and your class on the need for learning to "rest" in the Lord. As Isaiah promises, the Lord graciously heals and renews those who turn to Him. God gives "a song in the night" (30:29), and assures those who trust Him that "the Egyptians are men, not God, and their horses are flesh, and not spirit" (31:3). Faithful praying and trusting enables faint-hearted believers to see God and the world with greater clarity!

TOPIC FOR ADULTS
TURN TO THE LORD

He Took a Wrong Turn. "Recently a trucker missed his exit from the interstate, so he laughed and said, 'I'll take the next exit, cross over and come back.' He took the next exit, thought he was crossing over, only to learn that he had made a wrong turn and was now on another Interstate. He was getting farther away from where he needed to go and didn't know how to get off and get on the right road. Everyone who drives can smile and relate to his predicament because we have all made wrong turns. Some wrong turns can be humorous, some irritating.

"Wasted time and wasted fuel are usually the only loss, but some wrong turns can be fatal. Take the case of the four-wheeler which made a wrong turn and entered an expressway on an exit ramp. He speeded up, assuming all was well. But he was going in the wrong direction. He crashed head-on into an oncoming car, resulting in the death of several people in both cars. He was unaware that he had made a wrong turn . . . unaware that he was going in the wrong direction . . . unconcerned right up to the moment of his death.

"This vividly illustrates another fatal wrong turn . . . the one all-important wrong turn on the highway of life. Our first parents took a wrong turn from the path of obedience to God, bringing the fatal disease of sin into their lives and into the whole human race. Men have been turning from God's way ever since. The Bible says: 'All we like sheep have gone astray; we have *turned* every one to his own way' (Isaiah 53:6).

"Making this wrong turn puts a man on the highway which Jesus describes as: '. . . broad is the way, that leadeth to destruction, and many there be which go in thereat' (Matthew 7:13). The wisest man in the world, seeing people relying on their judgment that they were on the right way, said: 'There is a way which seemeth right unto a man, but the end thereof are the ways of death' (Proverbs 14:12). That's a sobering statement, but think how merciful and gracious God is to let us know what lies at the end of the road of our wrong choices.

"But there is a way to get off the wrong road. Look for the signs. God wants you to get off the broad freeway to Hell and get on the narrow road to Heaven. Take that exit sign that says: '*Turn* you at my reproof: behold, I will pour out my spirit unto you . . .' (Proverbs 1:23). God's reproof of your sin is nothing less than His conviction of the evil in your heart. You can get off at that exit if you will respond to God's conviction, and *turn* to Him.

"There's the exit marked: 'Repent, and *turn* yourselves from all your transgressions; so iniquity shall not be your ruin' (Ezekiel 18:30). God says to the man who takes that exit: 'I have no pleasure in the death of him that dieth, saith the Lord God: wherefore *turn* yourselves and live ye' (Ezekiel 18:32)."—L. Latimer Brooker, in the *Highway Evangelist,* Route 25/Trip 2.

You Can't Defend Your Faith With Violence. "Neither the murder of Abraham Lincoln nor that of Martin Luther King stopped what those leaders believed in.

"Those who thought they could destroy what Jesus represented by crucifying Him were also deluded. The Crucifixion was followed by the Resurrection, and the gates of hell have not been able to prevail against the church of Christ, in spite of heresy and persecution. Christ remains Lord.

"If the truth can't be destroyed by destroying its champion, the corollary is also valid, namely, that violence and assassination and war can't defend the truth.

"That's why Jesus refused to accede to the wishes of some of His followers who wanted Him to lead a military confrontation against the opposition. He maintained that if His Kingdom were of this world, His followers would fight. But the Kingdom was not of this world. If we have any respect at all for Christ and His views, it's incumbent upon us to trust His way of peace rather than Caesar's way of war and violence as a means of safeguarding the faith. Jesus was willing to die for the truth but not to kill for it. There's an eternal difference between dying for truth and killing for it.

"Those who advocate the proliferation of nuclear weapons as a way of salvation against atheistic ideology are deceiving themselves. We may be able to defend ourselves as a political, economic, and social body against invasion, but we have no military defense against internal indifference, or moral and spiritual apathy.

"We're not going to become more humane, more loving, more religious, righteous, and God-fearing no matter how many atheists we kill. If we're not sincerely committed to the Kingdom of God in the first place, if the Kingdom and its life mean zero to us, how can we, through violence, defend what we don't possess? If we're committed to the truth, we can believe hell can't destroy it, even though we let ourselves be crucified for what we believe.

"We have little faith in God if we fear He and His cause will fail if we don't come to His rescue with the sword. We need His support; He doesn't need ours."—Rev. Joseph Mohr. Reprinted with permission from *The Morning Call Weekender,* Allentown, PA; Saturday, April 4, 1981.

Time to Turn to the Lord. "To the man of our time, so conscious of all the pressures upon him, Michel Quoist says: 'God is waiting for you here at this very moment, at this very place and nowhere else.'

"At the end of the day he recommends a quiet review of what we have done— in the light of what God says to us through the Gospels and through the circumstances of our lives. And this review, he says, 'should lead spontaneously to prayer: a four-dimensional prayer of praise, thanksgiving, penance, and petition.' And Quoist the sociologist is insistent that our prayer should be no individualistic pietism; rather it ought to be concerned with society and with changing its structures.

"To give time regularly to God is, Michel Quoist reiterates, vital. It is an indispensable sign of our love for God, just as a husband not only works for his wife, but also gives her time, day by day.

"Don't say: 'I haven't time to pray, but that doesn't make any difference, I offer my work up and that's a prayer.' Love demands that you stop for a while. If you love, you must find the time to love. To pray means to stop for a while; it means to give some of your time to God, each day, each week. Nor, without regular praying, shall we see and serve the Lord in the circumstances of our life, 'for in order to see Him and understand what He says, you have to look for Him and listen to Him in those brief daily encounters which prayer makes possible'"— Michel Quoist, *The Christian Response.*

Questions for Pupils on the Next Lesson. 1. Do you sometimes feel inadequate in facing life's problems? 2. How does your church reach out to those with handicaps to which they must adjust? 3. How do you handle those worries over what the future holds for you? 4. Is forgiveness a once-and-done-with matter, or is mercy continually needed in your life? 5. Where are the best opportunities for you to express gladness and joy?

TOPIC FOR YOUTH
LEARNING TO TRUST

Trade-Offs. We are told that our security comes from more powerful armaments. Therefore, we are spending larger amounts than ever on national security. Isaiah and the biblical writers challenge the claim that we will find our security in anything but the Lord. In the face of mounting military budgets, consider the following trade-offs that could be made:

Two B-1 bombers = $400 million = the cost of rebuilding Cleveland's water-supply system.

Two nuclear-powered aircraft carriers = $5.8 billion = the cost of converting 77 oil-using power plants to coal, saving 350,000 barrels of oil per day.

Three Army AH-64 helicopters = $29 million = the cost of training 200 engineers to design and produce trolleys in the U.S.

Forty-six Army heavy (XM-1) tanks = $120 million = 500 top quality city buses.

Ten B-1 bombers = $2 billion = the cost of dredging six Gulf Coast and Atlantic coast harbors to handle 150,000 ton cargo ships.

Trusting in the Lord has practical and economic considerations!

Hard to Trust. Learning to trust is hard. Young people, especially, feel insecure. Sometimes youth trust inadequate sources of security. As a young vaudeville performer, W. C. Fields felt this way. Tragically, he never outgrew these feelings. Facing near-starvation at times during his poverty-stricken boyhood, he worried that he would never be secure. Consequently, he began opening bank accounts under fictitious names wherever he happened to be. Sometimes the deposits were small. More often, however, Fields plunked down big sums in various cities all over the country, sometimes as much as $50,000. The accounts were usually listed under a silly sounding name, such as Sneed Hearn, Aristotle Hoop, Ludovic Fishpond, Figley E. Whitesides, Dr. Otis Guelpe, or Cholmondley Farmpton-Blythe, because Fields imagined that the secrecy offered him greater security. Having these bank accounts in many cities made Fields less anxious, but he never learned to trust or to feel secure throughout his life. Tragically, when Fields died in 1946, only forty-eight of these accounts could be located, and another 700 or so totalling over $1,300,000 are considered lost forever.

The pathetic man apparently never learned that the Lord is a person's only true source of security, and that this same gracious God may be trusted.

Commandments, Please. An Atlanta, Georgia, service station carries the following message on its marquee: "God did not call them the Ten Suggestions."

For our own good, the Lord delineated our responsibilities to one another in the form of Commandments. When we turn to Him, we learn to trust His plans and orders for our benefit. We know that God had our well-being in mind when he gave us those Commandments. We gratefully must accept them not as suggestions but as orders to be obeyed.

Sentence Sermon to Remember: Don't try to hold God's hand; let Him hold yours. Let Him do the holding, and you the trusting. —Hammer William Webb-Peploe.

Questions for Pupils on the Next Lesson. 1. What are the occasions in which you feel most discouraged and fearful? 2. How are most of your friends trying to find true happiness? 3. Do you ever wish you could change your ways of living but seem to be unable to do so? 4. Does your faith in God make you glad and joyful? Why or why not?

LESSON IX—JANUARY 29

A DAY OF JOY AND GLADNESS

Background Scripture: Isaiah 35
Devotional Reading: Isaiah 26:7–11

KING JAMES VERSION

ISAIAH 35 1 The wilderness and solitary place shall be glad for them; and the desert shall rejoice, and blossom as the rose.

2 It shall blossom abundantly, and rejoice even with joy and singing: the glory of Lebanon shall be given unto it, the excellency of Carmel and Sharon, they shall see the glory of the LORD, *and* the excellency of our God.

3 Strengthen ye the weak hands, and confirm the feeble knees.

4 Say to them *that are* of a fearful heart, Be strong, fear not: behold, your God will come *with* vengeance, *even* God *with* a recompence; he will come and save you.

5 Then the eyes of the blind shall be opened, and the ears of the deaf shall be unstopped.

6 Then shall the lame *man* leap as an hart, and the tongue of the dumb sing: for in the wilderness shall waters break out, and streams in the desert.

8 And an highway shall be there, and a way, and it shall be called The way of holiness; the unclean shall not pass over it; but it *shall be* for those: the wayfaring men, though fools, shall not err *therein.*

9 No lion shall be there, nor *any* ravenous beast shall go up thereon, it shall not be found there; but the redeemed shall walk *there:*

10 And the ransomed of the LORD shall return, and come to Zion with songs and everlasting joy upon their heads: they shall obtain joy and gladness, and sorrow and sighing shall flee away.

REVISED STANDARD VERSION

ISAIAH 35 1 The wilderness and the dry
land shall be glad,
the desert shall rejoice and blossom;
like the crocus 2 it shall blossom abundantly,
and rejoice with joy and singing.
The glory of Lebanon shall be given to it,
the majesty of Carmel and Sharon.
They shall see the glory of the LORD,
the majesty of our God.

3 Strengthen the weak hands,
and make firm the feeble knees.
4 Say to those who are of a fearful heart,
"Be strong, fear not!
Behold, your God
will come with vengeance,
with the recompense of God.
He will come and save you."

5 Then the eyes of the blind shall be opened,
and the ears of the deaf unstopped;
6 then shall the lame man leap like a hart,
and the tongue of the dumb sing for joy,
For waters shall break forth in the wilderness,
and streams in the desert:

8 And a highway shall be there,
and it shall be called the Holy Way;
the unclean shall not pass over it,
and fools shall not err therein.
9 No lion shall be there,
nor shall any ravenous beast come up on it;
they shall not be found there,
but the redeemed shall walk there.
10 And the ransomed of the LORD shall return,
and come to Zion with singing,
everlasting joy shall be upon their heads;
they shall obtain joy and gladness,
and sorrow and sighing shall flee away.

KEY VERSE: And the ransomed of the Lord shall return, and come to Zion with singing. Isaiah 35:10 (RSV).

HOME DAILY BIBLE READINGS

Jan. 23. M. *Praise for Final Victory.* Isaiah 26:1–6.
Jan. 24. T. *Prayer for a Sorrowing People.* Isaiah 26:7–19.
Jan. 25. W. *"No Kingdom There."* Isaiah 34:1–12.
Jan. 26. T. *"For Violence Done to Your Brother."* Obadiah 10:18.
Jan. 27. F. *"To You Also the Cup Shall Pass."* Lamentations 4:18–22.
Jan. 28. S. *"Remember, O Lord. . . . the Edomites."* Psalm 137.
Jan. 29. S. *A Glad Restoration.* Isaiah 35:1–10.

BACKGROUND

The immediate background for this lesson is to be found in Isaiah 34. Read it, if you can! It is filled with a horror that is repulsive, particularly as it pictures a God engaged in bloody vengeance. "The sword of the Lord is filled with blood" (Isaiah 34:6).

God, in this grim chapter, has summoned all the nations to be judged. In a great fury, His sword descends upon one of the nations that has been wicked and anxious to destroy His Chosen People. He seems to single out Edom as His main target, for Edom has most consistently inflicted wrongs upon Zion. It is a day of wholesale slaughter. Amazingly, Isaiah seems to approve of it; at least, he does not condemn it.

NOTES ON THE PRINTED TEXT

However that may be, whatever Isaiah prophesied about Edom, he makes a sudden turn in chapter 35 from destruction to delivery—the delivery of his people from such a fate. Isaiah 35 is a chapter full of joy and gladness, a poem singing of a happiness and a prosperity for *Israel*, in sharp contrast with what He causes to happen to Edom. The exiles in Babylon must have sung it in a joy and a faith that passes human understanding.

Isaiah pictures Israel as pilgrims walking a long road back from Babylonia to their own Jerusalem. The road back! That was a desert road, a hot, treacherous, barren road, but as the ex-exiles travel down it, in their joy they see a desert that shall blossom like a rose, a land as fertile as the blessed lands of Carmel and Sharon. Let the timid and the weak take heart and have courage, as they walk this road, for God has delivered them from their enemies in Edom; they will walk in perfect safety. The blind will be able to see, the lame to walk uprightly, the deaf to hear. The desert will abound with streams and springs—all in what was once a land of thirst and sudden death. It will be a holy road for faithful pilgrims, a road upon which the unrighteous and the ungodly will not be permitted to travel. It will be God's road, unmolested by the usual wild beasts. This road they shall travel, as they go up to Zion. It was promised of God—and that promise was fulfilled.

So what does this mean to we Christians living in A.D. 1984?

It means that the Christian, like all others on this earth, is a pilgrim walking a long road from birth to physical death. The road of life is dangerous in more ways than one; all sorts of accidents can befall the traveler. But on the whole it is not so rough a road as it was before Christ came. To the Jew, there was always the hope of a Messiah who should come; to the Christian, the Messiah *has* come. When John the Baptist awaited death in prison, he asked whether Jesus Christ was really the Messiah; he was told to look around him and behold what this Messiah had already *done:* "The blind receive their sight, and the lame walk, the lepers are cleansed, and the deaf hear, the dead are raised up, and the poor have the gospel preached to them" (Matthew 11:5). In Him, what was a dream has become a reality.

The joy that possessed the Jewish exiles on their way home should possess us, for the road down which we walk through life is not a desert road, but a road of hope fulfilled in Jesus of Nazareth. Yes, there are still some dangers to be faced in our time. We walk through a world that is not yet a road of peace; we walk with many fears surrounding us. But if we see our Christ as the promised Redeemer of men, then "Every common bush is afire with God." The way is opened to us; "This is the way, walk ye in it" (Isaiah 30:21).

Mankind, taken as a whole, is an aggregation of plodders; in the eternal hunt for peace and the good life, we try first one road and then another, and another, and often take the low road instead of the high road, stumbling along, hoping somehow to find the *right* road. This futile walking must have been in the mind of John Oxenham when he wrote:

> See There! God's signpost, standing at the ways
>   Which every man of his free will must go—
> Up the steep hill, or down the winding ways,
>   One or the other, every man must go.
>
> He forces no man, each must choose his way,
>   And as he chooses, so the end will be;
> One went in front to point the Perfect Way,
>   Who follows fears not what the end will be.
>   POEM BY JOHN OXENHAM, 1852–1941.

Our world is not yet the world that God wants it to be but, provided we walk His road, His way, it can be.

SUGGESTIONS TO TEACHERS

What keeps you going when you're ready to quit? (Yes, Sunday-School teachers, like all of God's saints, are sometimes tempted to quit!) What encourages you to continue another week to struggle with teaching a class, or persisting in your Christian duty for another day, when you feel like giving up? Obviously, as you know, the answer is having some vision of the future, some glimmer of hope for tomorrow.

The people in the biblical story knew times of despair. Isaiah saw that his contemporaries faced such bleak times that most were ready to quit. After all, when the world's mightiest power is ready to crush your country and deport you, you wonder whether it's worth it to keep on as God's person. Isaiah did not blink in the face of the terrors confronting his people. However, he retained his sanity and poise, knowing that the Lord prevails. A day of joy and gladness always follows with the Lord. Our God is the Lord of the Resurrection!

1. *DESERT'S REJOICING.* Isaiah assures his countrymen that because of the Lord's caring faithfulness "The wilderness and the dry land shall be glad, the desert shall rejoice and blossom" (35:1). God brings new growth! Let your class tell about the times when life seemed to be a barren desert for them and the Lord brought a new season of rejoicing and blooms. Point out that because of our knowledge of God's mighty acts, culminating in Christ's Resurrection, we may plod on across the "wilderness and the dry land" times. What have been the worst "desert experiences" of those in your class?

2. *DESPAIRING'S RESTORATION.* Isaiah describes the blind, the deaf, the lame, the dumb receiving healing and a new vitality. Certainly you as a teacher have felt discouraged enough to want to give up, but have been surprised by the way the Lord has restored you. You may wish to share experiences from your own life or tell of others you know who have been given new strength by the ever-caring Lord.

3. *DELIVERER'S ROUTE.* Isaiah tells about the highway of the Lord, a "Holy Way" (35:8). The faithful people of God shall travel this and discover safety and security. Bring up to your class the title which Jesus applied to himself: "the Way" (John 14:6). In the Greek, the word for *the way* means "the road." Jesus Christ is our highway back to God. Discuss the meaning of traveling this road.

4. *DEPORTED'S RETURN.* Although Isaiah has previously predicted a time of exile for his people, he also promises a return to Jerusalem. He assures his hearers that they will eventually be ransomed and brought back with singing, joy, and

gladness. This offers you and your class a good chance to talk together of what motivates you as God's people in these times to persevere in serving Him in spite of rough days. You should reassure your people that God holds out hope for the future for His people today as well as in Isaiah's era.

TOPIC FOR ADULTS
A DAY OF JOY AND GLADNESS

Celebrate Your Ministry! ". . . Ministry grounded in the love of God is, above all, sheer celebration of the God-given capacity to receive, share, and express the love of God for me and the other.

". . . the capacity to care is a liberating gift of God, and God's caring for us and for the others goes far beyond any benevolent feelings we can generate on our own. Even our failures in caring—and we will fail!—are embraced in the exquisite care of a God, whose forgiving love greets us even in our failure. If that is true, as the biblical word insists, there is nothing for it but to find specific ways to celebrate God's love for us and for the others by risking our own acts of caring. . . .

". . . We are free to risk failure, because our failures are not God's last word about us or about those we serve. But, more importantly, we are free to succeed in expressing God's caring, without the oppressive weight of supposing that we have done anything heroic or spectacular. Where God's ministry succeeds through us, we have done nothing more than celebrate with another human the one love by which each of us lives and sustains hope. Perhaps it is true that only on the basis of such spiritual lightheartedness are we free to minister seriously, in God's name, to any human being. The appropriate prayer, then, on undertaking any task of ministry, goes something like this: 'You know me, Lord, what my gifts and skills are, what I can and cannot do. Show me myself in this other. Each of us is beyond help unless you minister to each of us equally. Let your love happen between us, through our fragmentary means of relating. Forgive us and keep us both in your care. Amen.' Having said that, expect miracles, remembering that the greatest miracle of which the Bible speaks is God's will to be faithful to us through and beyond our failures or even our tragedies. And every penultimate indication of human healing in response to ministry is a God-given sign of the wholeness for which God intends us. To undertake ministry on these grounds is an exercise not only in faith and love but also in hope—hope for oneself, for the other, and for the entire human experiment. It is designed to be the most liberating, authentically serious, and joyous calling on earth."—"Theology and Ministry in the Hebrew Scriptures" by James A. Wharton; from *A Biblical Basis for Ministry*, edited by Earl E. Shelt and Ronald Sunderland. Westminster Press, 1981.

The Devil's Beatitudes. Blessed are they who are too tired and busy to assemble with the Church on Sunday: for they are my best workers.

Blessed are they who are bored with the minister's mannerisms and mistakes: for they get nothing out of the sermon.

Blessed is the Church Member who expects to be invited to his own church: for he is important to me.

Blessed are they who do not meet with the church on Sunday: for they cause the world to say, "The Church is failing."

Blessed are they who are easily offended: for they get angry and quit.

Blessed are they who do not give to carry on God's work and mission: for they are my helpers.

Blessed are the trouble-makers: for they shall be called the children of the devil.

Blessed is he who professes to love God but hates his brother: for he will be with me forever.

Blessed is he who has not time to pray: for he shall be easy prey for me.

New Symphony Uncovered. The music world was elated with news that a symphony composed by Wolfgang Amadeus Mozart had been found in February, 1981. It was known that the symphony existed, but it was believed lost. The symphony, a three-movement work in F major, KV 19 A, was discovered by the Bavarian State Library in a bundle of manuscripts offered for sale by an unidentified private person. The library did not disclose the price but indicated it might have cost about $300,000. The symphony was composed by Mozart in 1765 when he was nine years old.

Christians know the same kind of joy and gladness over the Coming of Jesus Christ that Mozart lovers feel over the uncovering of a newly-discovered symphony. As Isaiah sang happily of how "the ransomed of the Lord shall return and come with singing," God's people in our times rejoice that new beauty and harmony has been orchestrated into human life by the new day of Jesus Christ's reign!

Questions for Pupils on the Next Lesson. 1. What do some persons do in order to try to get some sense of hope and importance and success in life? 2. Why must we trust in people and powers beyond ourselves? 3. Do you sometimes struggle with feelings of unimportance and insignificance in the face of changing times? 4. What are the most destructive forces rampant in our world in these times? 5. How may we find protection from these destructive powers?

TOPIC FOR YOUTH
JOY UNLIMITED

Joy Through Easy Technology? ". . . In the first twenty years of an American kid's life, he or she will see something approaching 1 million television commercials at the rate of about a thousand a week. This makes the TV commercial the most voluminous information source in the education of youth. These commercials are about products only in the sense that the story of Jonah is about the anatomy of whales.

"A commercial teaches a child three interesting things. The first is that all problems are resolvable. The second is that all problems are resolvable fast. And the third is that all problems are resolvable fast through the agency of some technology. It may be a drug. It may be a detergent. It may be an airplane or some piece of machinery, like an automobile or computer. The essential message is that the problems that beset people—whether it is lack of self-confidence or boredom or even money problems—are entirely solvable if only we will allow ourselves to be ministered to by a technology. . . . Commercials teach these important themes through parables. Repeatedly, the parable is structured in the same way. The problem is stated; then, in eight to ten seconds, the middle part comes, which is the resolution of the problem—through a painkiller or an ointment or a flight to Hawaii or a new car. Then there's a moral. The moral is nailed down at the end, where we are shown what happens if a person follows this advice. And the actor, of course, is usually ecstatic. One has simply got to wonder what the effects are on a young adult who has seen a million of these little vignettes. One has to ask, 'What is being taught?' "—Neil Postman, NYU, from a copyrighted interview in *U.S. News & World Report*, January 19, 1981.

Feather-Duster Religion. A noted piano teacher patiently worked with a timid but promising pupil for a long time. Finally, one day, the teacher said, "You seem to play the piano with a feather duster. You never strike down deep to the music that is potential in the instrument." Frequently, we allow our expression of the faith to be the same way. We tentatively plink a few hesitant notes but never bring forth the great melodious chords of joy which knowing God's goodness can produce. The Christian faith should never produce feather-duster followers. Rather, knowing the meaning of Jesus Christ means joy unlimited!

God's presence in our lives means joy without limits. We trust our lives and the lives of others to His keeping. We cheerfully can "let go" of our control or attempted control over others. We do not have to be like the mother of a new freshman at S.M.U. who once wrote to Dr. Willis Tate, the President of the University. In her long letter, the woman asked Tate to make certain that her son would be given a roommate who did not smoke, swear, tell smutty stories, drink, carouse, and who went to church regularly, retired by ten every night, and had good study habits. The anxious mother also demanded that Dr. Tate tell some university official to ask her son each week if he went to chapel and said his prayers. Furthermore, she insisted the boy be placed in a dormitory farthest from all bars, and on a floor where all the boys were Christians. The solicitous mother concluded her letter by stating that she was so concerned about her boy because "this is the first time he has been away from home, except for the three years he spent in the Marines."

It is not hard to imagine how little joy this worry-filled woman had!

Have you experienced the joyous release from anxieties which the Lord's glad day brings?

Sentence Sermon to Remember: If you have no joy in your religion, there's a leak in your Christianity somewhere.—Billy Sunday.

Questions for Pupils on the Next Lesson. 1. Do you sometimes long for a genuine sense of belonging? 2. What are the times in your life when you seem to be overwhelmed by circumstances? 3. Why does everyone want to love and be loved? 4. Is there any person who does not know loneliness? 5. Do events in history ever have any meaning?

LESSON X—FEBRUARY 5

I AM THE LORD

Background Scripture: Isaiah 43; 45
Devotional Reading: Exodus 19:1–6

KING JAMES VERSION

ISAIAH 43 1 But now thus saith the LORD that created thee, O Jacob, and he that formed thee, O Israel, Fear not: for I have redeemed thee, I have called *thee* by thy name; thou *art* mine.

2 When thou passest through the waters, I *will be* with thee; and through the rivers, they shall not overflow thee: when thou walkest through the fire, thou shalt not be burned; neither shall the flame kindle upon thee.

3 For I *am* the LORD thy God, the Holy One of Israel, thy Saviour: I gave Egypt *for* thy ransom, Ethiopia and Seba for thee.

4 Since thou wast precious in my sight, thou hast been honourable, and I have loved thee: therefore will I give men for thee, and people for thy life.

5 Fear not: for I *am* with thee: I will bring thy seed from the east, and gather thee from the west;

6 I will say to the north, Give up; and to the south, Keep not back: bring my sons from far, and my daughters from the ends of the earth;

7 *Even* every one that is called by my name: for I have created him for my glory, I have formed him; yea, I have made him.

REVISED STANDARD VERSION

ISAIAH 43 1 But now thus says the LORD,
he who created you, O Jacob,
he who formed you, O Israel:
"Fear not, for I have redeemed you;
I have called you by name, you are mine.

2 When you pass through the waters I will
be with you;
and through the rivers, they shall not
overwhelm you;
when you walk through fire you shall not
be burned,
and the flame shall not consume you.

3 For I am the LORD your God,
the Holy One of Israel, your Savior.
I give Egypt as your ransom,
Ethiopia and Seba in exchange for you.

4 Because you are precious in my eyes,
and honored, and I love you,
I give men in return for you,
peoples in exchange for your life.

5 Fear not, for I am with you;
I will bring your offspring from the east,
and from the west I will gather you;

6 I will say to the north, Give up,
and to the south, Do not withhold;
bring my sons from afar
and my daughters from the end of the
earth,

7 every one who is called by my name,
whom I created for my glory,
whom I formed and made."

KEY VERSE: "Turn to me and be saved, all the ends of the earth! For I am God, and there is no other." Isaiah 45:22 (RSV).

HOME DAILY BIBLE READINGS

Jan. 30. M. *Thanksgiving for God's Care.* Psalms 65:1–12.
Jan. 31. T. *Fear Not; Trust God.* Isaiah 41:8–16.
Feb. 1. W. *The New Exodus.* Isaiah 43:14–28.
Feb. 2. T. *God's Amazing Choice.* Isaiah 45:1–8.
Feb. 3. F. *Who Dares Deny God's Choice.* Isaiah 45:9–13.
Feb. 4. S. *God's Invitation to All People.* Isaiah 45:14–25.
Feb. 5. S. *God, Your Deliverer.* Isaiah 43:1–7.

BACKGROUND

The background of this lesson is clearly the story of the Exodus; Isaiah 43:2 sets the premise: "When thou passeth through the waters, I will be with thee." But the foreground is the coming conquest of Egypt by the Persian Cambyses, in 525 B.C. The prophet sees this conquest as a "ransom" paid for the deliverance of Israel, and it was a stiff price: ("I [the Lord] gave Egypt for thy ransom, Ethiopia and Seba for thee").

Two words leap up out of all our lesson Scripture: one is *fear*, and the other is *love*. In the whole picture, it is easy for us to understand what he means by fear, for fear plagued the children of Israel all the way from the Red Sea to the Promised Land, and even after they were settled in the Land. But *love?* There seemed to be a shortage of love during the Exile. Who loved whom, then, and *why?* It appears, in our Scripture lesson, that all the love was on God's side. Why was this? *Because* God's purpose for Israel was built on His love for her.

NOTES ON THE PRINTED TEXT

God, through His prophet, has three main points of emphasis in Isaiah 43:1–7. Point 1 is this: "I am the Lord thy God." There are no other gods, insofar as Israel is concerned, who have done for Israel what He has done. As long ago as 1546, John Heywood wrote, "God is no botcher." He makes no mistakes; that is a priority of man. God knew exactly what He was doing when He brought His people out of Egypt.

This one true God had *created* them; "I have redeemed thee, I have called thee by thy name; thou art *mine*" (verse 1). Having created them, did they think He could desert them? He had brought them through great waters in the past, He would bring them through great dangers in the future. This act of Creation was not just one act, performed at a certain time; it was a *continuing* act; it goes on and on, as His people go on and on. To desert them would be for God to admit that He had failed with them—*and God never fails, is never defeated.*

This is one point on which both Old and New Testaments agree. In Psalms 138:8, the author sings: He will "not forsake the work of thy (His own) hands," and in Philippians 1:6 Paul writes, "I am sure that he who began a good work in you will bring it to completion."

Point 2: In this God of Israel there is an astounding grace or benevolence. The word *grace*, as it is used in the Scriptures, refers to someone doing a favor for someone else; in this chapter of Isaiah, we see God doing a favor for Israel that Israel, at this particular moment in their history, did not deserve. But no matter how unworthy of His grace she might be, God never admitted defeat by abandoning them. Why? Because "I have *loved* thee!" The Revised Standard Bible puts it in slightly different words: "You are precious in my eyes, and honored, and I love you" (verse 4). In today's newspaper, we read of a man who pushed a child out of the path of an automobile—and almost lost his life in doing it. Asked why he did it, the man said, "Because I love him." It was not his son!

So it is with God; there may be little in us for Him to love us, but love us He does, no matter what.

At the time this was written, God's people were scattered (dispersed) across the world. This is called the *Diaspora*, and it is a word still used by the Jews in our world. There are something over 14,999,999 Jews in today's world, scattered from Chicago to China. They are not yet gathered together from the ends of the world, as Isaiah predicts in verses 5–7. But there is a movement called Zionism which is working to bring back the Jews from north, south, east, and west to Jerusalem. Not all modern Jews want this; there are only 18 percent of the world's Jews in Palestine. Some prominent Jews want not a Jewish state of Palestine, but a center of the Jewish faith. Will it work out as Isaiah predicted, or not? However it works out, the Jews are still great witnesses for their God in an almost Godless world.

Of what use is this passage from Isaiah to modern Christians and the Christian Church? We Christians believe that God created the Church; in doing that He had a divine purpose, just as He had a purpose for the Jews. But His Church is not yet perfect; it, too, is scattered. We have better than 280 Christian denominations competing with each other, often denying any unity whatever nor wanting it. The Church has its share of failures in working out God's promise; being constituted of human beings, mistakes are inevitable. But God is not through yet with the Church.

What our Church needs is what Israel needed: a unity of faith. Not Church *union*, but *unity* among Christians. Someone has said of the Church that, "The world is just too strong for a divided Church." Like it or not, there is real truth in that. We need not all worship under one roof, not be a mammoth single Church in all the world, but we do need a unity of faith and fellowship between all of us. We need, too, more of a sense of the grace and presence of God in churches named for His Son.

So, when next we rise together to sing in the grand old hymn:

> Through many dangers, toils and snares,
> I have already come;
> 'Tis grace hath brought me safe thus far,
> And grace will lead me home.

Let's sing it and *mean* it, and *practice* it!

SUGGESTIONS TO TEACHERS

"Life is a gigantic lottery," intoned a famous actor, "and I happened to draw the right numbers at the right times." Is this the way the world is run? Is human existence merely a throw of the dice, a matter of luck? Or, is Isaiah right? God is in control, the prophet insists. The Lord's deeds reveal His sovereignty.

Your lesson for this Sunday presents Isaiah's (and the Bible's) claim as opposed to the "mere chance" viewpoint. It would be helpful to get this lesson underway by asking how many in your class think that life is actually nothing but a matter of chance or accident. Also, it would launch your lesson discussion to air the claims that life is merely a lottery. Keep in mind, however, that the main thrust of your lesson is based on Isaiah 43 and 45, and shouts God's Word that "I am the Lord!"

1. *CLAIMS.* The Lord makes claims on the lives of His people. He accompanies them. He protects them when they pass "through the deep waters" (43:2). He regards His people as "precious in my eyes"(43:4). Repeatedly, God tells His people that because He claims them they need not fear. This section of Isaiah offers you and your class to bring some of the fears plaguing people out in the open. What are the anxieties besetting those in your class? What are the times of passing through the deep waters which threaten to overwhelm those in your class?

2. *CREATES.* The Lord created and continues to create. "I am doing a new thing," He announces (43:19). Is God doing any new things in these times? Does your class think that God is still creating? If so, what? If not, why not?

3. *CALLS.* God works through human agents. Sometimes, as in the case of Cyrus, ruler of the Persians in the sixth century B.C., God uses humans who may not worship Him. The Lord is sovereign, however, He calls whomever He pleases to accomplish His purposes. Ask your class to comment on ways God may be active in human history in our era. Is it possible He is using even governments or leaders we may not like to carry out His plans?

4. *CONCLUDES.* The Lord patiently continues to call His people back to His service. He intends to conclude what He began at Creation. He endures Israel's indifference, according to Isaiah, but warns that the rebellion of His people is like the clay arguing with the potter (45:9ff). In spite of the way God's people continue to second-guess God, however, the Lord insists that He knows what He is about. He did not create chaos! In the end, He will see to it that His plans prevail.

"Turn to me and be saved, all the ends of the earth!" (45:22) for at the end "every knee shall bow, every tongue shall swear" allegiance to the Almighty! (45:23). Do your people sense this claim? If so, what are they doing about it?

TOPIC FOR ADULTS
I AM THE LORD

Emotional Scars in Victims and Rescuers. After the disaster at the Kansas City Hyatt in July, 1981, in which the skyways collapsed, killing over 100 persons, both the victims and their rescuers were left with emotional scars.

Some survivors can outline the collapse almost moment by moment. But many could not or would not. People talked about different parts of what they remembered about that night, and blocked out parts they said they didn't remember—a defense mechanism. A high percentage say they don't remember hearing any noise, and some report not seeing anything at all, such as blood or dismembered bodies. It's almost impossible that they didn't see anything.

Sgt. Jim Treece, a news media relations officer with the Kansas City Police Department, spent the night trudging back and forth between the Hyatt lobby, a temporary morgue set up in a store-room, the care center established on the front lawn, and a roped-off area where reporters gathered across the street. And he, too, was an observer of the most grisly details.

"I remember thinking, 'My God, it's never going to stop.' It was always, 'Here comes another black bag' containing a body. I must have asked that question a million times that night: 'Is this the last one?' The trouble with policemen is they have this macho image. But they're humans, they're affected like everyone else. We'll never forget; it's like a bad dream. It's something you remember."

Many of those touched by the disaster experienced anger but were unsure where to direct it. It's the kicking-the-dog routine, getting angry at something not directly related to the situation. Situations that never bothered them before made them very angry later.

Experienced counselors pointed out that those affected so deeply by the Hyatt disaster needed a sense that life still has purpose, and that people may have a feeling of importance. This, of course, comes from realizing that God is still to be trusted, in spite of terrible events and horrible memories. The Lord is still the Lord! In Isaiah's words, "For I am God, and there is no other" (45:22).

Just Happened That It Happened? Pete Rose, baseball's "Charley Hustle" whose grand-slam home-runs and hard-charge base stealing have made him a sports superstar, had his share of antics out of the stadium. His marriage to Karolyn went through severe strains. Karolyn Rose reports, "We separated three times, and came back together twice. But the last time, well, it was too much to take. Pete didn't seem to have any conscience about being with other women. It got so embarrassing for me, and for the children, that I couldn't accept it any longer."

Pete Rose, however, shrugs. He says: "Karolyn was a good wife, a tremendous mother, and brought my kids up great while I was on the road. She's one of my biggest supporters. She knows baseball, and she's the one who takes my little boy to his baseball games and my daughter to her volleyball games—I guess that's the job mothers get stuck with in the suburbs. The divorce wasn't her fault, but divorce is sort of a common thing these days, and it just happened that it happened to me."

Divorce, however, does not just happen to happen to someone. Although it may be tragically frequent in our society, it is not an occurrence which simply takes place as a sort of accidental happening. Divorces, like most other disastrous events in our lives, happen because we let them happen. And they happen when we "live in the fast lane at home as well as in the ballpark," as Karolyn Rose puts it. Or, in the terms of the Bible, destructive things take place when we forget that God is supreme. Until and unless every married person responds to the plea of the Lord, "Turn to me and be saved . . . for there is no other" (Isaiah 45:22), no married relationship can flourish.

Doggone Shame. An author named Colin Cherry had three successive editions of a book published by the M.I.T. Press of Boston. In the first edition, Dr. Cherry dedicated the book: "To my dog, Pym." In the second edition, Dr. Cherry wrote the following inscription: "To all those human beings who have inquired so kindly after my dog Pym." When the third edition was prepared, the author had the following words placed in the inscription page: "To the memory of my dog Pym." Curiously, Cherry's book carries the title *On Human Condition.*

All this suggests that Professor Cherry has focused most of his affection on his dear departed dog. Now there is nothing wrong with caring for canines. But when a pup pushes aside people in a person's priorities, it's more than a case of life going to the dogs or being a doggone shame. There's a theological aspect, too! Life is meant to be lived with an awareness of the Lord as well as with pets and persons. Pym might have been a special pal, but the Eternal God is still Lord of life!

Questions for Pupils on the Next Lesson. 1. Who is the "Servant of the Lord" referred to in Isaiah 42–53? 2. How did Jesus carry out the role of being the Servant mentioned in Isaiah? 3. Do you sometimes struggle with the role you will play in society? 4. What gives you your greatest fulfillment and why? 5. How do you respond to the conflicting pressures of good and evil?

TOPIC FOR YOUTH
NO OTHER GOD

Captain Disaster. Brian Heise seemed to have an exceptional streak of bad things happen to him during the summer of 1981. Heise's apartment was flooded. His car had a flat tire and was later stolen. He was wounded when he accidentally sat on a bayonet. Part of his ceiling fell, killing four valuable breeder canaries. The Associated Press chronicled Brian Heise's bizarre string of unfortunate events. Someone nicknamed him "Captain Disaster." Heise, a thirty-year-old law student in Provo, Utah got telephone calls from many people, including a radio station in Sydney, Australia. Several letters and callers told Heise that his misfortunes were due to the stars. "And a guy in Las Vegas, Nevada, called and wanted to do my biorhythms and my horoscope," Heise said. "He says I've got to be in one of the biggest biorhythmic pits of all times."

Although Heise does not personally attribute his Captain Disaster summer to astrology or biorhythms, he has been surprised at how many apparently believe that life is controlled by these.

Christians affirm that there is no other God. Only the Lord runs this universe. Christian people do not fret that mysterious malignant powers control human lives, but affirm that the Lord God Almighty which Isaiah describes still sustains and directs all that is!

Hair Count. Isaiah insists that God is sole Lord. Jesus lived this and taught it. No other God but He! There, don't fret. Jesus stated that the Lord even knows how many hairs you have on your head (Matthew 10:30). If God knows this, He can be trusted to know all your needs. Even the hairs of your head are numbered. How incredible? How absurd it sounds! Max Factor of Hollywood once employed a girl to count the hairs on a woman's head. It was a tedious job, but the tally showed that on her head there were 135,168 hairs. On a man's beard there were 60,000 hairs; on a mustache, 7,000.

If God knows the count of every hair on every head, there can be no other to take His place! He is The Lord!

A Teacher Named Failure. Sometimes, we think that failure means the end of life. Perhaps we forget that God is able to transform our failures into new possibilities. As Thomas Watson, Sr. (of IBM) once said, "It is a common mistake to think of failure as an enemy of success. Failure is a teacher—a harsh one, but the best. Pull your failures to pieces looking for the reason, then put them to work for you."

There is no other God. Failure is not supreme or final. Only the Lord is! As Isaiah and countless others testify, our God allows us to put our failures to work for Him!

Sentence Sermon to Remember: Every man's life is a plan of God.—Horace Bushnell.

Questions for Pupils on the Next Lesson. 1. In what ways was Jesus a Servant? 2. Why do people prefer to be served rather than to serve? 3. What gives you your greatest sense of satisfaction and fulfillment in life? 4. Who are some of the persons whose service to others has impressed you? 5. What does it mean "to suffer for others"?

LESSON XI—FEBRUARY 12

THE SERVANT OF THE LORD

Background Scripture: Isaiah 42:1–4; 49:1–6; 50:4–11; 52:13–53:12
Devotional Reading: Isaiah 50:4–11

KING JAMES VERSION

ISAIAH 42 1 Behold my servant, whom I uphold; mine elect, *in whom* my soul delighteth; I have put my Spirit upon him: he shall bring forth judgment to the Gentiles.

2 He shall not cry, nor lift up, nor cause his voice to be heard in the street.

3 A bruised reed shall he not break, and the smoking flax shall he not quench: he shall bring forth judgment unto truth.

4 He shall not fail nor be discouraged, till he have set judgment in the earth: and the isles shall wait for his law.

49 5 And now, saith the LORD that formed me from the womb *to be* his servant, to bring Jacob again to him, Though Israel be not gathered, yet shall I be glorious in the eyes of the LORD, and my God shall be my strength.

6 And he said, It is a light thing that thou shouldest be my servant to raise up the tribes of Jacob, and to restore the preserved of Israel: I will also give thee for a light to the Gentiles, that thou mayest be my salvation unto the end of the earth.

53 4 Surely he hath borne our griefs, and carried our sorrows: yet we did esteem him stricken, smitten of God, and afflicted.

5 But he *was* wounded for our transgressions, *he was* bruised for our iniquities: the chastisement of our peace *was* upon him; and with his stripes we are healed.

6 All we like sheep have gone astray; we have turned every one to his own way; and the LORD hath laid on him the iniquity of us all.

REVISED STANDARD VERSION

ISAIAH 42 1 Behold my servant, whom I uphold,
my chosen, in whom my soul delights;
I have put my Spirit upon him,
he will bring forth justice to the nations.

2 He will not cry or lift up his voice,
or make it heard in the street;

3 a bruised reed he will not break,
and a dimly burning wick he will not quench;
he will faithfully bring forth justice.

4 He will not fail or be discouraged
till he has established justice in the earth;
and the coastlands wait for his law.

49 5 And now the LORD says,
who formed me from the womb to be his servant,
to bring Jacob back to him,
and that Israel might be gathered to him,
for I am honored in the eyes of the LORD,
and my God has become my strength—

6 he says:
"It is too light a thing that you should be my servant
to raise up the tribes of Jacob
and to restore the preserved of Israel;
I will give you as a light to the nations,
that my salvation may reach to the end of the earth."

53 4 Surely he has borne our griefs
and carried our sorrows;
yet we esteemed him stricken,
smitten by God, and afflicted.

5 But he was wounded for our transgressions,
he was bruised for our iniquities;
upon him was the chastisement that made us whole,
and with his stripes we are healed.

6 All we like sheep have gone astray;
we have turned every one to his own way;
and the LORD has laid on him
the iniquity of us all.

KEY VERSE: *Behold my servant, whom I uphold, my chosen, in whom my soul delights.* . . . Isaiah 42:1 (RSV).

HOME DAILY BIBLE READINGS

Feb. 6. M. *In the Synagogue at Nazareth.* Luke 4:16–30.
Feb. 7. T. *The Good News of Jesus.* Acts 8:26–29.
Feb. 8. W. *Justice to the Nations.* Isaiah 42:1–9.
Feb. 9. T. *Light to the Nations.* Isaiah 49:1–13.

Feb. 10. F₁ *Set Like a Flint.* Isaiah 50:4–11.
Feb. 11. S. *A Man of Sorrows.* Isaiah 53:1–6.
Feb. 12. S. *An Offering for Sin.* Isaiah 53:7–12.

BACKGROUND

Of all the dramatic and beautiful ideas set forth in The Book of the Prophet Isaiah, the idea or concept of the Suffering Servant is probably the most significant and the most debated. There has been an endless war over this Servant; he has been *thought* to be, at different times, Jeremiah, Isaiah, Israel, the faithful remnant of Israel, the ideal people of God, and, more important to the Christian, the Messiah of the New Testament in whom the prophecies of Isaiah are fulfilled. There have been arguments about when it was written, by whom, and for what purpose.

What we call "The Servant Passages" in Isaiah are found in five chapters: 42:1–4, 49:1–6, 50:4–9, 52:13–53:12. There are difficulties to be faced in these passages, but they still remain rich in beauty and expression, far-reaching in teaching, and definitely bound to the New Testament. They are all *evangelical;* the prophet who gave them to us is the prime evangelist of the Old Testament who leads us straight and gently into the New Testament.

Keep one thing straight about Isaiah's Old Testament Servant; he was and remains a *Suffering* Servant. That is basic.

NOTES ON THE PRINTED TEXT

Just what is a servant? Mr. Webster, in his famous dictionary, calls a servant, among other things, "one who exerts himself for the benefit of another." That describes the servantship of Christ, from the Sermon on the Mount to the Crucifixion.

This Servant is chosen, or "elected," of God, who has "put my Spirit upon him" (42:1). Under that Spirit, He will "bring forth justice to the nations" (verse 1), not to Jews only, but to the Gentiles of the *world* as well. And just how does He do that? He does it quietly. He does not stand in a temple and shout loud enough to be heard in the street. The approach to the heathen Gentiles is low-key. Good! Congregations tire quickly of a shouting preacher; the nonchurched don't listen at all!

To the nonchurched, as to the heathen Gentiles of the day, He speaks quietly with a still small voice. He looks upon the heathen as a people resembling a bruised reed (which He will not break) or a flickering wick (which He will not quench). He acts as the modern sensible missionary works: He does not roar and storm against them; He speaks softly, not belligerently. He also speaks with the certainty of a servant who knows that he cannot fail in his service to "others," and who cannot be discouraged. He never sits and moans over His lack of quick success: He never "sings the blues." He never gives up because He has lost one convert, one "member"; He goes on and converts another.

In chapter 49:5, 6, God lays another burden upon the shoulders of the Suffering Servant: He tells the Servant plainly that it will not be enough for Him to bring Jacob (Israel) back to Him; that is "too light a thing"; God wants more than the preservation of Israel. He wants every nation to hear the Word of salvation. Israel did not like such a task or assignment from God; Israel wanted God to take care of *them,* restore *them* to the old glory. ("Us first; then the others, if you have time!")

We once knew a churchman who despised foreign missions. "Giving them money is useless," he said. "Let the heathen stew in their own juice." Then one sad day, his only son was murdered by a Chinese terrorist. The juice in the pot had boiled over, and he didn't like that at all. But he went right on not believing in missions to the "heathen." Well—do we do that, too?

Israel was called to be God's servant, but Israel didn't want to be a Suffering Servant just to win a few Gentiles!

This Suffering Servant is aptly and beautifully described in Isaiah 53. The suffering isn't easily understood, especially by those who are afraid of suffering, who refuse to suffer for someone else! God had brought suffering upon Israel, and Israel resented that. Israel was ordered of God to spread His Word among the nations, and Israel refused. God called her to be a Suffering Servant and Israel rejected the command. There was nothing "attractive" in suffering. But there was much that was attractive in the Coming of One who made suffering the prelude to peace and salvation. He stood out as One willing and ready to face rejection and persecution and pain in order that the people of God should find their right place in the world and to offer them the only sure way to peace and redemption. He was rejected; the people wanted nothing to do with Him. He was a Man of Sorrows—but hadn't we had enough of sorrow? He was acquainted with their grief. They had had enough of grief! They ignored Him as He passed by.

But they found it impossible to hide their guilt in ignoring the Servant. He was guilty of none of their sins—but He insisted upon taking a punishment that should have been inflicted upon them. He took responsibility for their sins! He was wounded and bruised for *their* sins, not His, in order that they might be saved. Like innocent men dying in battle for the blunders and wickedness of guilty men, this Servant made the supreme sacrifice of His own life for *others*. Like lost sheep, they thought they could get along without their shepherd, and that was their fatal mistake.

The world still does not accept Him or His sacrifice; too many of the world think of Him as a dreamer whose dream has not yet come true. But the world cannot deny that His way is better than ours. That is *our* fatal mistake.

However we may choose to interpret the concept of the Servant in Isaiah 53, we must admit that by "the mysterious moving of God's Spirit the finger of this unknown and at the time unheeded prophet of the Exile points directly to Christ."—William Neil. Without His suffering, we would be little less than an immense flock of stained, stupid, guilty sheep.

SUGGESTIONS TO TEACHERS

This lesson brings your class face to face with the mystery of serving by suffering for others. It is not an easy lesson. After all, who wants to hurt for the sake of someone else? Maybe for loved ones, such as children or spouse. But not for the mean, the cruel, or the stranger, the outsider.

This section of Isaiah is one of the most sublime sections of Scripture. It deeply influenced Jesus. In the Cross, we see the suffering love toward the unlovable in its purest form. Isaiah writes of the Lord's "servant" suffering for others. Who is this "servant"? Is it Israel? A remnant of God's people returning after the Exile in Babylon? Is it Jesus? Or, can it be us, the Christian community today? Without getting into lengthy arguments here, why not assume it may be all of these? The servant of the Lord, regardless of his identity, carries out many functions.

1. *INTENSIFIES.* The servant of the Lord has an awareness of God. He has a sense of call. In fact, the true servant of God feels called from the time he or she was in the womb. Do those in your class have this kind of sense of belonging to the Lord? The closer one is to God the more that person intensifies his service.

2. *ILLUMINES.* Isaiah states that the servant is a "light for the nations" (49:6). What does this suggest for your class, for your congregation, for Christ's Church? How may God's people be such a beacon in the darkness in these times?

3. *INTERCEPTS.* Allot plenty of time to give a thorough review of the pas-

sages in Isaiah dealing with the way God's servant must suffer for others. The servant is the object of hate and anger. He takes it. Try to help your class to plumb the mystery of vicarious suffering. Accepting the hurts of others by offering yourself for others brings healing! Be sure to keep holding up Christ's death on the Cross as the supreme example of how a servant of God intercepts the loathing and shame others have.

4. *IDENTIFIES.* It is extremely important to note that the servant of the Lord identifies with the transgressors of God's rule. The servant never pulls back in disgust or with superiority. Only by standing with sinners can the servant bring release and hope. Talk with your class how Christians are sometimes tempted to want to withdraw from the world, or to set up an exclusive group of the superreligious.

5. *INTERCEDES.* Above all, the servant of the Lord continually intercedes with God on behalf of others. Here is an opening for a good discussion on intercessory prayer. Are you as teacher interceding for those in your class? Are those in your class learning to bring the needs of others to the Lord?

TOPIC FOR ADULTS
THE SERVANT OF THE LORD

In 1639, the Pope sent 10,000 up the mountain passes into the Piedmont to massacre the Protestant Waldensi. There was no time for those Protestants to prepare to organize any resistance. In the pass, into the Waldensi area of mountains in northern Italy, there winds a narrow path where only two men can march abreast. Six of the strongest of the Waldensi volunteered to hold that pass. They said farewell to their families. They marched down and held that pass against the onslaught, giving precious time to their families and friends to escape. The six were finally killed. Their sacrifice saved the Waldensian Community. This is the sacrificial love of serving others, even as the Lord has first served us.

Showing Servanthood. Jesus lived among us as a Servant. He never promoted himself, but lived for others. Sometimes, it takes an everyday experience to show us what His kind of serving means.

A college girl told me that she had little respect for her mother's taste. The girl also admitted that she sometimes felt annoyed at her mother's shiny nose and red hands. Embarrassed by her mother's appearance, the girl tried to avoid being seen with her mother whenever possible. One Sunday, the daughter reluctantly consented to attend worship at church with her mother. The girl, conscious of the latest fashions and fanciest grooming, privately grimaced when her mother put on the only coat she owned, an out-of-date, faded tweed. The mother's hands looked particularly rough and raw that morning.

Shortly after they sat down at church, an impeccably dressed woman swept into the pew in front of them. She was attired in an expensive mink, a costly tailored dress, and diamond earrings. Her hair was elegantly done in the latest style. Everything about the woman seemed to be in perfect taste. The girl took it all in. Glancing at her mother, the daughter was startled to notice that her mother was also noticing the fashion plate in front of them. The girl suddenly realized that her mother also appreciated the tailoring and grooming and jewelry. Her mother's Saturday night do-it-yourself hairdo, the red hands, and the ten-year-old baggy coat were not because her mother did not know or appreciate fine taste. The daughter in that instant became aware that her mother was sacrificing to provide for her by working hours of overtime at a menial job. She saw her mother in a different light. The mother's old tweed coat and beefy hands were evidence of love. The daughter understood how her mother cared so much that she would serve her daughter by giving up her looks and wardrobe!

The Cross is like that. In that sacrifice, we see Servanthood at its fullest! Furthermore, we know that we must live as Christ lived—the life of a servant.

No Safe Conduct Passes. Bishop Lloyd Wicke of the United Methodist Church was approached by a group of clergy wanting to take an active part in a civil rights campaign during the 1960s. Wicke affirmed their sense of social concern. However, they added that they had come to him as bishop not so much for permission as for guarantees that they would not have to face financial reprisals in their home parishes. Wicke reminded them that the Gospel is not ever "a safe conduct pass." They were called to be Christ's Church—the Servant of the Lord! And that usually entails sacrifices.

Questions for Pupils on the Next Lesson. 1. Are there any conditions attached to God's offer of mercy? 2. Is there any genuine satisfaction anywhere in this world? 3. Why do some people seem to think that God is withdrawn from people? 4. Have you ever experienced guilt and brokenness in your relationships with others? 5. How can people who feel locked into the past find that God opens a future?

TOPIC FOR YOUTH
YOUR STAND-IN

Changes for the Lean Years. "The whole church is beginning to think in a relatively unfocused way about responsible changes of life-style. The question is not are we going to change but toward what ends, by what means, for whose benefit? We have entered a new era in which neither church nor society can put the humpty-dumpty of rapid growth back together again. Conservative politics may promise a return to affluence, but the American and international future will still be shaped by conditions of scarcity and inequality. In such circumstances, how can churches witness to the just and sustainable community?

"The church is called to move beyond ordinary survival behavior to hold service of other persons and sectors in society—all the more so in the lean years. Beyond what we have to do under pressure of inflation, we ought to, and want to change in the direction of justice, stewardship, and community. . . . To move corporately in this direction is to affirm a life-style of human solidarity over against a preoccupation with our own survival. Solidarity living embraces three interrelated social values: sufficiency as the norm of justice, sustainable enterprise that exhibits stewardship of precarious resources, and abundant living in a sharing community where quality of being and doing is far more important than quantity of having. . . . Life-style changes must be assessed carefully to discern how they serve all three ends—justice, stewardship, and community—by consistent means." —Dieter T. Hessel, "Congregational Life-Style Changes for the Lean Years," edited by Dieter T. Hessel, 1981, The United Presbyterian Program Agency.

Serving By Listening. The average family spends only fourteen minutes a day talking to their children, twelve of which involve parents telling them what to do and what not to do, according to a recent report of the Pennsylvania Department of Education. Many children complain that their parents don't have time for them, while parents say their children don't want to be with them.

Listening is a form of serving. By listening, you can be a stand-in for the Lord for others. Listening is caring. It means making space for the other. This calls for sacrifice by you. Will you be a servant of the Lord by prompting an atmosphere of listening in your home?

How to Be Immortal. The great thinker Karl Jaspers, after a lifetime of pondering the weightiest truths of human thought, stated, "We are mortal when we are without love, and we are immortal when we love."

Those who realize that as Christ came to serve and sacrifice for others, we are called to live as servants. When we respond to His servanthood by suffering with and for others, we realize that He blesses us with a sense of immortality!

Sentence Sermon to Remember: What we have done for ourselves alone dies with us. What we have done for others and the world remains and is immortal.—Albert Pine.

Questions for Pupils on the Next Lesson. 1. Why do so many youth feel powerless in our society? 2. Where do you think you can find genuine satisfaction in life? 3. Where do you turn for good advice most often? 4. Who do you find is dependable in life? 5. How does God help us when we feel guilty and broken over our poor relationships with others?

LESSON XII—FEBRUARY 19

COME TO THE FEAST

Background Scripture: Isaiah 55
Devotional Reading: Isaiah 56:1–8

KING JAMES VERSION

ISAIAH 55 1 Ho, every one that thirsteth, come ye to the waters, and he that hath no money; come ye, buy, and eat; yea, come, buy wine and milk without money and without price.

2 Wherefore do ye spend money for *that which is* not bread? and your labour for *that which* satisfieth not? hearken diligently unto me, and eat ye *that which is* good, and let your soul delight itself in fatness.

3 Incline your ear, and come unto me: hear, and your soul shall live; and I will make an everlasting covenant with you, *even* the sure mercies of David.

6 Seek ye the LORD while he may be found, call ye upon him while he is near:

7 Let the wicked forsake his way, and the unrighteous man his thoughts: and let him return unto the LORD, and he will have mercy upon him; and to our God, for he will abundantly pardon.

8 For my thoughts *are* not your thoughts, neither *are* your ways my ways, saith the LORD.

9 For *as* the heavens are higher than the earth, so are my ways higher than your ways, and my thoughts than your thoughts.

10 For as the rain cometh down, and the snow from heaven, and returneth not thither, but watereth the earth, and maketh it bring forth and bud, that it may give seed to the sower, and bread to the eater:

11 So shall my word be that goeth forth out of my mouth: it shall not return unto me void, but it shall accomplish that which I please, and it shall prosper *in the thing* whereto I sent it.

REVISED STANDARD VERSION

ISAIAH 55 1 "Ho, every one who thirsts,
come to the waters;
and he who has no money,
come, buy and eat!
Come, buy wine and milk
without money and without price.

2 Why do you spend your money for that
which is not bread,
and your labor for that which does not
satisfy?
Hearken diligently to me, and eat what is
good,
and delight yourselves in fatness.

3 Incline your ear, and come to me;
hear, that your soul may live;
and I will make with you an everlasting
covenant,
my steadfast, sure love for David.

6 "Seek the LORD while he may be found,
call upon him while he is near;

7 let the wicked forsake his way,
and the unrighteous man his thoughts;
let him return to the LORD, that he may
have mercy on him,
and to our God, for he will abundantly
pardon.

8 For my thoughts are not your thoughts,
neither are your ways my ways, says the
LORD.

9 For as the heavens are higher than the
earth,
so are my ways higher than your ways
and my thoughts than your thoughts.

10 "For as the rain and the snow come down
from heaven,
and return not thither but water the
earth,
making it bring forth and sprout,
giving seed to the sower and bread to the
eater,

11 so shall my word be that goes forth from
my mouth;
it shall not return to me empty,
but it shall accomplish that which I purpose,
and prosper in the thing for which I sent
it."

KEY VERSE: *"Seek the Lord while he may be found, call upon him while he is near. Isaiah 55:6 (RSV).*

157

HOME DAILY BIBLE READINGS

Feb. 13. M. *God's Unfailing Love.* Isaiah 54:1–10.
Feb. 14. T. *The Lord Reigns.* Psalms 93:1–5.
Feb. 15. W. *Praise to the King and Judge.* Psalms 98:1–9.
Feb. 16. T. *The Heavenly Banquet.* John 6:32–41.
Feb. 17. F. *"Hold Fast to My Covenant."* Isaiah 56:1–8.
Feb. 18. S. *Invitation to the Covenant.* Isaiah 55:1–5.
Feb. 19. S. *Invitation to Repentance.* Isaiah 55:6–13.

BACKGROUND

Isaiah 55 is the closing chapter of what we call "Second Isaiah"; the whole chapter is one glorious song. "This is a chapter of great beauty, so exquisite that its opening words have sung their way down the centuries and found place in Christian liturgies and in Christian lectionaries. Yet for all its beauty of words it is withal a solemn and earnest chapter."—Robert W. Rogers in *The Abingdon Bible Commentary.*

The scene is laid in Babylon, where the Israelites still moan in captivity; the time is the period just before the Persian conquest of the Babylonian empire in 539 B.C. Read Psalm 137, and learn what the condition of the Hebrew captives was at this time.

The Prophet Jeremiah wrote them to accept their captivity as best they could—as a national punishment. Let them "adjust" to the ways of the Babylonians, pray for peace and do what they could to earn a living until God set them free. In God's good time, they would be liberated. The liberation is described as a great (Messianic) banquet. The Messiah (or Prince) will invite them to this banquet, where they will rejoice and be glad again. Who, according to Isaiah, will be invited to such a banquet? "Ho, every one that thirsteth . . ." shall be invited. This would mean the Gentiles as well as the Jews, but the author of this chapter is concerned only with the Jewish guests.

NOTES ON THE PRINTED TEXT

The Jews had taken the suggestion of Jeremiah a bit too seriously—or ignorantly. Many of them had become merchants selling their goods to the Babylonians; they became, in time, *rich* merchants (they may be *our* world's most capable merchants!). They gained wealth and power—but there were no Jewish temples in Babylon; the old religious fire had almost flickered out, not only among the wealthy but among the poorer and the weaker. (Where have we heard of the lust for money destroying faith in God in modern times?)

God raised Isaiah to make them see the foolishness, the fatality, of all this. *The Living Bible* tells of it in burning words: "Say there! Is anyone thirsty? Come (to the banquet) and drink—even if you have no money." That was "right on target," for there never was a time when men did not thirst for that "something," that water, that would make them better than they were. Even the best of us, at times, find life without God unsatisfactory and a hopeless "grind." Come to the Messiah's table, and drink waters that will make you never thirsty again. It will cost no money, the grace of God is *free!*

Why do we spend money for something that is not "bread" (unsatisfactory)? "He who has no money is invited and only he who is poor in spirit (and longs for the bread of life) is likely to come."—Robert Rogers.

"Incline your ear," you who need what God has to give. Attune your ear to the Infinite; then your *soul* may live! Without a soul, we are not living at all.

Now in every speech, in every sermon, every prophecy, there are always lines that "speak out" loudly. Lincoln's "of the people, by the people and for the people" stands out like fire on a mountain. President Kennedy's ". . . not what your country can do for you, but what you can do for your country" still rings bells in our hearts. And in Isaiah 55, there are several lines or high spots worth memorizing. For instance:

"Seek the Lord while He may be found." That is, see Him while you are still alive and are able to find Him. God is not lost, but we who live selfishly and without Him *are* lost.

"Let the wicked forsake his way." Come in repentance, or not at all.

"For He will abundantly pardon." God's mercy and pardon are infinite, everlasting. It is as wide and deep as the sea and it comes immediately upon confession of our sins.

"For my thoughts are not your thoughts, neither are your ways my ways, saith the Lord." Our ways are ways planned by ourselves. Men who plan their own ways are apt to become victims of a human routine that leaves God out, and our preoccupation with our own interests is God's greatest obstacle, and they are sure to make of us "a mass of indifferent nobodies." God's thoughts and ways must become *our* thoughts and ways if we are to be lifted out of our greatest sin: *apathy!*

"The rain and snow . . . water the earth . . . maketh it bring forth and sprout. . . ." Just so does God's Water produce fruits of the heart and the soul. A farmer would "bring forth" nothing but weeds without God's rain. God's energy in the mind of man is the energy that changes man from nothing into something—something God had in mind for us. His Word is the seed of the more abundant life.

All through our comments on this lesson, we have kept thinking of Jesus' parable of the sower, in Luke 8. Explaining that parable, Luke says that "The seed is the Word of God." Yes! God *is* the divine Sower of history. He plants His seed in our hearts and hands, and He calls upon us to nurture that seed, to see to it that we who say we love and follow Him go about the business of sowing His seed in the lives of others. If we fail in that, we will have only a world full of weeds.

As we write this, the newspaper on our desk shrieks at us with the news that Anwar Sadat has been murdered. Sadat, in his crusade for peace, once quoted Isaiah 2:4. Read it and weep. He died at the hands of men who were more weeds then men. And ponder this: *are* we at least somewhat responsible for this most terrifying event of our times in our failure, in our hesitancy, and apathy to send more missionaries to a land ruled by Godless terrorists?

SUGGESTIONS TO TEACHERS

A sixteen-year-old boy withdrew the seventy-eight dollars he had in his savings account and hitchhiked to San Francisco without telling his parents he was leaving. A week later, he sent his distraught family a postcard with the following message: "I don't deserve to be part of the family. I feel I've failed you, and there's no point in hanging around home anymore. Don't bother trying to contact me. I hope to get in touch with you sometime later if I can get my life together."

That youth's pathetic note is the attitude many people hold toward God. They think they cannot possibly be welcomed to His presence. Some of these people may be in your class.

Your lesson this Sunday comes from the 55th chapter of Isaiah—one of the highpoints in Scripture. Here, Isaiah extends the Lord's welcome to *everyone.*

1. *PROVIDING.* Appropriately, this lesson is called "Come to the Feast." Isaiah 55 portrays God inviting those who are parched from loneliness of separation from the Lord to come to Him, the Living Waters, and those who are famished from trying to exist too long apart from Him to come to Him for the nourishment they crave. The welcoming, big-spending God extends a free offer of mercy for all! Your class discussion should revolve around the meaning of "amazing grace" in our lives. As Christians, we should realize that through Jesus Christ, we have unconditional acceptance and mercy by God!

2. *PLEADING.* Continue your study in Isaiah 55 by pointing out the way God implores His people to seek Him, to return to Him. The cry of Isaiah 55 is acted out in the life of Jesus. Through our Savior, we see and hear the pleading God in action. Remind your people that our God is not pouting, waiting for us to take the first step to return to Him. He has taken the initiative.

3. *PURPOSEFUL.* Move your lesson into an examination of the way God makes clear that His purposes will not be thwarted. "My word shall not return to me empty," He states (55:10). Ask your class members if they think that God is sometimes stymied. Is the Lord ever helpless? Emphasize that our Lord is able!

4. *PEACEFUL.* The closing verses (55:12, 13) provide a stirring vision of an era of harmony everywhere. "You shall go out in joy, and be led forth in peace," God promises. In God's Feast, such joy and peace prevail. Within the Church, we are meant to show forth that joy and peace. Is this the hallmark of your congregation?

TOPIC FOR ADULTS
COME TO THE FEAST

Sacredness of a Meal. Anthropologists point out that in most cultures, to eat a meal with someone or in some place, is to forge permanent ties with that person or place. Where or with whom one eats, a person is somehow committed. That, for example, is why in India a Brahman will never eat in the house of a low-caste harijan; it would tie him there.

Isaiah deliberately uses the picture of the Lord deliberately choosing to eat with His people. God means to forge permanent ties with humans. He is committed to persons. God means to be tied to His people. And He wants us to respond to His gracious invitation!

News From Home. There is a newsstand in Times Square in New York City that sells only home-town papers. More than 350 newspapers from other towns in America are available, and strangers who are homesick will buy the papers to read about what is happening at home. An observer says that they oftentimes act a little furtively, as if they do not want the city people to think they are hicks and lonely.

Homesickness is one of the most terrifying experiences in the world. Most of us suffer it at one time or another, and when it is with us, we are in a desperate situation. The truth is that we are always somewhat homesick and we are forever seeking news from home. To this human situation, the Christian faith comes with some Good News. "Welcome home to the family table," says the Lord. Isaiah 55 is like a special edition printed expressly to headline God's Good News for *you.* Come to the Feast!

Who Is Lost? If we think God is absent or lost, we merely delude ourselves. The little boy who becomes separated from his father in a big department store may think it's his father who is lost, and he will cry to a clerk, "My daddy is lost." God is not like a human father who can get lost. He can't get lost in His own cosmos. He knows His way around. It's we who get lost. God, however, has sought us out. In the person of Jesus, He has found us. Our reunion is likened to a joyous feast in the Bible. He will not allow us to remain lost, but persists in welcoming us home.

Questions for Pupils on the Next Lesson. 1. Does worship make any difference in the quality of your life? Why or why not? 2. What separates people from God? 3. Why does true worship always eventually lead to a concern for the oppressed and afflicted? 4. Does Sunday worship in your church encourage you to serve others? 5. Does God intend us to find fulfillment in life apart from being in community with others?

TOPIC FOR YOUTH
A NEW KIND OF SATISFACTION

Interest in Individuals. Julia Ward Howe, the great reformer and writer, once asked Senator Charles Sumner if she could introduce him to the famous actor, Edwin Booth. Senator Sumner haughtily declined, muttering, "I have outlived my interest in individuals." Julia Ward Howe often recalled Sumner's refusal, and later remarked, "Fortunately, God Almighty has never gotten that far."

She could have added that the Lord God Almighty never will get that far! He assures each of us that He is intensely interested in us individually. He gives us the rich satisfaction of knowing that we are loved *regardless!* And He impels each of us to have the satisfying interest in others as persons!

A New Kind of Satisfaction. Drunk one time too often, he lay fully clothed in the bathtub, the muzzle of a 12-gauge shotgun in his mouth aimed at the brain. His thumb rested against the trigger, ready to push and end it all. But first he thought he should pray. Getting out of the tub, kneeling and talking to God indeed did put an end to the drunk, while signaling the birth of a renewed man of God who would serve his Lord in politics and beyond.

The man's name is The Hon. Harold E. Hughes, esteemed political leader and Christian statesman. From that time when he knelt beside the bathtub, Hughes had a meteoric rise from truck driver to commerce commissioner to governor of Iowa to senator to a 1972 presidential candidate whose campaign was gaining momentum until he realized he would rather be right with God than president. Although he had to battle alcoholism, he discovered that Christ's grace brought him peace and purpose which neither the bottle nor the ballot ever could.

Have you experienced this new kind of satisfaction in your life?

Never Alone. The first question God asked humanity was directed toward Adam, "Where are you?" From that day on, the story repeats itself monotonously: People stray like sheep from the Good Shepherd.

Meister Eckhart, the mystic, said in his sermon, "The Kingdom of God is at hand, God is nearer to me than I am to myself. My being depends on God's intimate presence. So, too, he is near to a stick or a stone but they do not know it. . . . For that reason a person may be more blessed than a stick, in that he recognizes and knows how near he is. And the more he knows it, the more blessed he is; the less he knows it, the less his blessing."

In joy and sorrow, God's presence can make all the difference in the world. We can be assured that we're not alone at any time.

Sentence Sermon to Remember: Be ye all of one mind, having compassion one of another.—1 Peter 3:8.

Questions for Pupils on the Next Lesson. 1. How can people overcome their tendency to be self-centered? 2. Is worship primarily what God does or what you do? 3. Why does genuine worship inevitably lead to a concern for the hurting? 4. Do the worship services in your church sensitize you to the needs of others and impel you to serve them? Why or why not? 5. What is it that puts a barrier between humans and God?

LESSON XIII—FEBRUARY 26

THE SERVICE GOD SEEKS

Background Scripture: Isaiah 58; 59
Devotional Reading: Isaiah 59:9–15

KING JAMES VERSION

ISAIAH 58 5 Is it such a fast that I have chosen? a day for a man to afflict his soul? *is it* to bow down his head as a bulrush, and to spread sackcloth and ashes *under him?* wilt thou call this a fast, and an acceptable day to the LORD?

6 *Is* not this the fast that I have chosen? to loose the bands of wickedness, to undo the heavy burdens, and to let the oppressed go free, and that ye break every yoke?

7 *Is it* not to deal thy bread to the hungry, and that thou bring the poor that are cast out to thy house? when thou seest the naked, that thou cover him; and that thou hide not thyself from thine own flesh?

8 Then shall thy light break forth as the morning, and thine health shall spring forth speedily: and thy righteousness shall go before thee; the glory of the LORD shall be thy rereward.

9 Then shalt thou call, and the LORD shall answer; thou shalt cry, and he shall say, Here I am. If thou take away from the midst of thee the yoke, the putting forth of the finger, and speaking vanity;

10 And *if* thou draw out thy soul to the hungry, and satisfy the afflicted soul; then shall thy light rise in obscurity, and thy darkness *be* as the noonday:

11 And the LORD shall guide thee continually, and satisfy thy soul in drought, and make fat thy bones: and thou shalt be like a watered garden, and like a spring of water, whose waters fail not.

REVISED STANDARD VERSION

ISAIAH 58 5 "Is such the fast that I choose,
a day for a man to humble himself?
Is it to bow down his head like a rush,
and to spread sackcloth and ashes under him?
Will you call this a fast,
and a day acceptable to the LORD?

6 "Is not this the fast that I choose:
to loose the bonds of wickedness,
to undo the thongs of the yoke,
to let the oppressed go free,
and to break every yoke?

7 Is it not to share your bread with the hungry,
and bring the homeless poor into your house;
when you see the naked, to cover him,
and not to hide yourself from your own flesh?

8 Then shall your light break forth like the dawn,
and your healing shall spring up speedily;
your righteousness shall go before you,
the glory of the LORD shall be your rear guard.

9 Then you shall call, and the LORD will answer;
you shall cry, and he will say, Here I am.

"If you take away from the midst of you the yoke,
the pointing of the finger, and speaking wickedness,

10 if you pour yourself out for the hungry
and satisfy the desire of the afflicted,
then shall your light rise in the darkness
and your gloom be as the noonday.

11 And the LORD will guide you continually,
and satisfy your desire with good things,
and make your bones strong;
and you shall be like a watered garden,
like a spring of water,
whose waters fail not."

KEY VERSE: *He has showed you, O man, what is good; and what does the Lord require of you but to do justice, and to love kindness, and to walk humbly with your God?* Micah 6:8 (RSV).

HOME DAILY BIBLE READINGS

Feb. 20. M. *Who Can Be God's Guest?* Psalms 15:1–5.
Feb. 21. T. *God, the King of Glory.* Psalms 24:1–10.
Feb. 22. W. *Condemnation of Corrupt Leaders.* Isaiah 57:9–58:2.
Feb. 23. T. *Crimes of Corrupt Leaders.* Isaiah 57:3–13.
Feb. 24. F. *God's Promise to the Contrite.* Isaiah 57:14–21.

Feb. 25.   S.   *"Is Such the Fast . . . I Choose?"* Isaiah 58:1–5.
Feb. 26.   S.   *"If You Take Away . . . the Yoke."* Isaiah 58:6–14.

BACKGROUND

The Jewish people, all through their long history, have had and still have two great institutions of religious observance; one was the observance of Feasts; these were celebrations of great happenings in the past. The other was a series of Fasts, which were occasions of abstinence from food, a rigor undertaken to evoke the favor of God, to ward off evil, to chasen the soul, or to discipline oneself in times of stress. During fasting, no work was done, sackcloth and ashes were often used, and garments were rent. Most notable among the Fasts was the one on the Day of Atonement, when all Jews were required to fast, the Fast of Tebeth, commemorating the fall of Jerusalem, the Fast of Tammuz observing the breach of Jerusalem's walls, and the Fast of Ab, in July, memorializing the fall of the city and the destruction of the Temple.

In Isaiah 58, we have a prophet speaking out about fasts and fasting. He speaks to a people who have just returned to Jerusalem at the end of the Exile. During the Exile, these people were denied the privilege of worship in their temple for the simple reason that there were no temples in Babylon. But they clung to the institution of the Fast, in believing that by fasting they could find favor with God as His faithful worshipers. Indeed, they *systematized* it. This expression of their faith kept them alive during these terrible years.

The prophet honored them for that, but he saw certain flaws in the system, certain failures to make Fasts what God insisted they must be. Some of their fasing was nothing more than pure hypocrisy.

NOTES ON THE PRINTED TEXT

Through the mouth of His prophet, God asks the restored people of Jerusalem, "These fasts you are celebrating piously—are they the kind of fast that I want? Do you really think that I will honor your fasting while you go on fighting among yourselves at the same time and oppressing the poor in your midst?" The people put on sackcloth and ashes; they "bowed like reeds in the wind," in total lack of repentance and honest humility. They murmured words of praise to God, while they indulged in their own pleasure (attended to their business) and oppressed the laborers who made their fortunes for them. It was an external formality—and it made them a selfish, self-concerned people lost in strife and contention while the poor cried in the streets for bread—and got no bread. Did they really think that they could catch the eye of God and gain favor with Him in such a performance?

In Shakespeare's *Hamlet,* we read this: "My words fly up, my thoughts remain below / Words without thoughts never to heaven go." That was what the prophet was saying—that the man who prays solemnly in church on Sunday and on Monday treats the poor and the weak like so much dirt will *not* be doing the will of God, nor is he "acceptable" to God. He is a disgrace to the Kingdom.

No, such "fasting" is not God's way. God *demands* that we hold out our hands to help those who need help, that we even share our food with them. It is not enough to send a poor family a turkey on Thanksgiving Day; He wants us to invite the poor into our homes and to share at our tables! "Clothe those who are cold and don't hide from relatives who need your help" (Isaiah 58:7, *The Living Bible*).

One Sunday morning, the pastor of our church startled his congregation before he began to preach a sermon on feasting and fasting. He said to them, "Now bow your heads and count from one to ten, *slowly.*" They counted to ten; then he said, "While you were doing that, twenty children died somewhere in the world from starvation." You could have heard a pin drop as he stood silent and let that sink in. It sank, deeply. There was a collection for the relief of the poor—people as far away as Bangladesh and India. An organization called Fish was organized to visit the sick, drive people with no money to the hospital and take food to families who had no food. The congregation "adopted" families of refugees from Viet Nam.

That's it! We in the Church are called not to hide ourselves away from a rat-race, an exhausting world for an hour or so once a week, but to *reach out* from the Church to those who need our substance as well as our prayers. Prayer without action never gets beyond the roof.

Do this, said God through the mouth of the prophet, and you will gain a spiritual prosperity that is priceless. Do this, and you will walk in a light that will drive away every darkness that the world can put upon you. Do this, and when you cry out to God, He will reply, "Here I am." Do this, and you be like a watered garden, whose waters "fail not."

If Israel would do this, God promised, they would be restored in their Jerusalem. He also promises to do the same thing for those of us who worship Him in spirit and in truth as we stumble through our darknesses to a position of high honor in His eyes.

SUGGESTIONS TO TEACHERS

Should a Christian pray or should he be busy in social action? For years, we have argued back and forth. The partisans of personal piety have accused those working for justice of neglecting their prayers. And the Christian activists have replied that their efforts are a form of prayer, and snap at the praying folk for neglecting the oppressed. Which is it: prayer or social action? Faith or works?

Isaiah and of course the rest of the Scriptures make it clear that it is not one or the other but both. Isaiah offers helpful insights to your class, especially in an era such as ours where the old fight between those wanting the Church to address only social justice concerns and those wanting the Church to talk only about devotional matters.

1. *THE PIETY THAT SERVES.* Isaiah has a refreshing balance. He is a person who relies on prayer and has a deep personal sense of God's reality. However, the prophet insists that fasting and other religious forms are futile unless there is an accompanying humility and commitment to serve. Isaiah does not pull any punches. In the face of the oppression, violence, and greed which marked his society, God's people must "loose the bonds of wickedness . . . undo the thongs of the yoke, to let the oppressed go free" (58:6). What does it mean today to "share your bread with the hungry and bring the homeless poor into your house" (58:7)? How can Christians in our time find a balance between a genuine devotional life and an authentic life of serving others?

2. *THE PRESENCE THAT SAVES.* To those who are *doing* justice, and not merely feeling sorry for the hurting, God gives a sense of His presence. Real Christian service means experiencing the darkness of loneliness, rejection, and persecution. However, in the midst of this gloom, the Lord brings refreshment. You should warn your class that God's people will be forced to endure a lot of pain and darkness. But add that God's saints are never abandoned.

3. *THE PARTING THAT SEPARATES.* Do not blink at Isaiah's blunt words about those who let themselves become alienated from the Lord. Christians must always take seriously the power and tenaciousness of evil. Isaiah, who knew the human situation better than most, stated that falsehood, injustice, violence, desolation, powerlessness, and destruction flourish when people refuse to pray to and work for the Lord. God is determined to have all people respect and obey Him! Encourage your class to serve God both in praying and in promoting justice.

TOPIC FOR ADULTS
THE SERVICE GOD SEEKS

True Worship. True worship means a concern for the oppressed and afflicted. It is more than warm feelings. The service God seeks is not ceremony in the church but sacrifice in the world.

Once, after the Battle of Adrianople in the fourth century, Ambrose the Bishop of Milan heard that many captives had been sold into slavery. Ambrose immediately spent all of his personal funds to buy freedom for as many as possible. When these funds gave out, he insisted that the treasury of his church be emptied to provide for these suffering unfortunate victims. He even had the sacred communion ware melted down and the precious metal cast into coins in order to rescue others. Critics sourly accused Bishop Ambrose of being sacriligious. Ambrose replied that those for whom the Lord's blood had been poured out were more precious than the vessels that contained the sacred reminders of that blood.

Serving Others Through Praying. Morton Kelsey points out that the service God seeks includes a concern for those we do not like and who may not like us. Kelsey advocates praying for them in specific ways: "I find that praying for the people whom I dislike and the ones who dislike me has both a practical and metaphysical effect. In my journal, I keep a list of people for whom I pray. I have listed there those who are particularly important to me, those who are sick, those who have asked for prayer, and those who might be called enemies.

"The best method of praying in a general way for other people is to pray the Lord's Prayer for them. If John is the one I am praying for, I say: 'John's Father who are in heaven, Hallowed be thy name in John. Thy kingdom come in John. Thy will be done in John, on earth just as if he were with you in heaven. Give him his daily bread, all that he needs to sustain and enrich his life. Forgive John and help him to forgive others. Do not put John to the test as he is weak like the rest of us, and please deliver John from the Evil One. Let John's joy be in your kingdom and power and glory forever and ever.' While I am praying in this way I visualize John and imagine the Risen Christ with him.

"Praying like this for the enemy has several practical effects. If I am asking God to take care of several people and to pour his blessings upon them, this impedes me from saying or doing anything unkind to them. Such negative action would be at odds with what I am asking God to do and would make me a sheer hypocrite. It would put me in the position of saying, 'Lord, you take care of John, while I'll fix him here below.' "—Morton Kelsey, CARING, Paulist Press, 1981.

Vision of Universal Realities. In *Le Milieu Divin,* Teilhard de Chardin prophesied:

"A tremendous spiritual power is slumbering in the depths of our multitude, which will manifest itself only when we have learned to break down the barriers of our egoism and, by a fundamental recasting of our outlook, raise ourselves up to the habitual and practical vision of universal realities.

"If we wish to be men and women of prayer, we have the responsibility of keeping our eyes open to the ends of the earth and of being alert to realities of practical politics. We saw how Isaiah, a man of prayer, was concerned with social justice; he was equally concerned with the blessing of peace—peace between the warring great powers of his day, Egypt and Assyria, and peace for the small Jewish people caught up between them: 'The Lord of hosts will bless them: a blessing be upon Egypt my people, upon Assyria the work of my hands, and upon Israel my possession' (*see* Isaiah 19:25)."

Questions for Pupils on the Next Lesson. 1. What does Mark mean by the "Kingdom of God"? 2. What was Jesus' authority? 3. What kind of persons did Jesus call to be disciples? 4. What does it mean "to repent"? 5. Do you think that with God there is a possibility of new beginnings for every person or only for certain religious folks?

TOPIC FOR YOUTH
LEND A HAND

What About the One-Fifth at the Bottom? How inequitably our wealth is distributed! One percent of Americans control 34 percent of our wealth. Twenty percent at the bottom scramble for only 5 percent of the total of our country's assets. And when the country grows richer the top 2 percent get nearly half the extra riches.

In the Sermon on the Mount, Jesus tells us that we have no business having even two coats as long as another man has none. Jesus tells us to lend and even give freely. Jesus tells us to take no thought for the morrow concerning material things and that heaven is the only place where a Christian is supposed to lay up treasure.

How to Serve God. "Tremendously, we need God! For tasks inward and outward, personal and international, against sins deep-seated, inveterate, and malign, we need God. Let the need, like thirst, make its own satisfaction real! Let the beatitude on those athirst and hungry be fulfilled! For until a man comes to God in such a mood there is no possibility of reality in prayer.

"The great social needs and the projected social crusades of our days, which so depend on faith in God, may well themselves create the atmosphere in which we find God. It is a grievous misinterpretation to suppose that God's reality dawned on men, like the Old Testament prophets, in mystical aloofness from the social needs and social movements of their time.

"No pathway into the consciousness of God's reality has been trodden by nobler men than this road of social devotion and sacrifice. God's greatest souls have often started like Elijah, determined that at whatever cost he would denounce and defeat the tyranny of Ahab, and they have ended like Elijah, on the mountainside, listening to the still small voice of God. They have started like Dante with a passion to save Italy from chaos, and they have ended like Dante, standing with Beatrice before the Great White Throne. They have started like Lincoln, vowing that if ever he had a chance to hit slavery, he would hit it hard, and they have ended like Lincoln, saying, 'Many times I have been driven to my knees by the overwhelming conviction that I had nowhere else to go.' "—Harry Emerson Fosdick, "The Sense of God's Reality," *The Christian Century Reader,* N. Y. Association Press, 1962.

Church Woman's Crusade. Someone is killed in a drunk-driving accident in the U. S. every twenty-three minutes, an annual toll of more than 26,000. Yet a drunk driver is rarely arrested, and the possibility of stiff punishment is remote.

Some New York church people have done more than feel outraged that drunk drivers are given mere wrist slaps in court. Led by Doris Aiken, a committed Christian, and originally funded by a contribution of $50 from her church, a group called Remove Intoxicated Drivers (RID) was formed in 1978. Says she: "Last year each drunk driver in New York paid, on the average, a $12 fine, while those who killed a deer out of season had to pay $1,500."

Doris Aiken and RID persevered. Finally, in 1981 New York's legislature passed a bill providing a minimum $350 fine for a first drunk-driving offense ($250 even for those who bargain down to the lesser charge of "driving while ability is impaired").

Doris Aiken and her fellow church members understood that the service which

God seeks is not only in the sanctuary but also in society. Working for justice and walking with God go hand in hand!

Sentence Sermon to Remember: To labor is to pray.—Motto of the Benedictine Order.

Questions for Pupils on the Next Lesson. 1. Do you think that people can change? 2. Do you ever sense you are called by Christ to serve others? 3. Why is it so hard to put opportunities for service ahead of personal interests? 4. What is the difference between having authority and being authoritarian? Which was Jesus?

MARCH, APRIL, MAY 1984

THE GOSPEL OF MARK

LESSON I—MARCH 4

JESUS BEGINS HIS MINISTRY

Background Scripture: Mark 1
Devotional Reading: Luke 3:7–17

KING JAMES VERSION

MARK 1 14 Now after that John was put in prison, Jesus came into Galilee, preaching the gospel of the kingdom of God,

15 And saying, The time is fulfilled, and the kingdom of God is at hand: repent ye, and believe the gospel.

16 Now as he walked by the sea of Galilee, he saw Simon and Andrew his brother casting a net into the sea: for they were fishers.

17 And Jesus said unto them, Come ye after me, and I will make you to become fishers of men.

18 And straightway they forsook their nets and followed him.

19 And when he had gone a little further thence, he saw James the *son* of Zebedee, and John his brother, who also were in the ship mending their nets.

20 And straightway he called them: and they left their father Zebedee in the ship with the hired servants, and went after him.

21 And they went into Caperna-um; and straightway on the sabbath day he entered into the synagogue, and taught.

22 And they were astonished at his doctrine: for he taught them as one that had authority, and not as the scribes.

23 And there was in their synagogue a man with an unclean spirit; and he cried out,

24 Saying, Let *us* alone; what have we to do with thee, thou Jesus of Nazareth? art thou come to destroy us? I know thee who thou art, the Holy One of God.

25 And Jesus rebuked him, saying, Hold thy peace, and come out of him.

26 And when the unclean spirit had torn him, and cried with a loud voice, he came out of him.

27 And they were all amazed, insomuch that they questioned among themselves, saying, What thing is this? what new doctrine *is* this? for with authority commandeth he even the unclean spirits, and they do obey him.

28 And immediately his fame spread abroad throughout all the region round about Galilee.

REVISED STANDARD VERSION

MARK 1 14 Now after John was arrested, Jesus came into Galilee, preaching the gospel of God, 15 and saying, "The time is fulfilled, and the kingdom of God is at hand; repent, and believe in the gospel."

16 And passing along by the Sea of Galilee, he saw Simon and Andrew the brother of Simon casting a net in the sea; for they were fishermen. 17 And Jesus said to them, "Follow me and I will make you become fishers of men." 18 And immediately they left their nets and followed him. 19 And going on a little farther, he saw James the son of Zebedee and John his brother, who were in their boat mending the nets. 20 And immediately he called them; and they left their father Zebedee in the boat with the hired servants, and followed him.

21 And they went into Caperna-um; and immediately on the sabbath he entered the synagogue and taught. 22 And they were astonished at his teaching, for he taught them as one who had authority, and not as the scribes. 23 And immediately there was in their synagogue a man with an unclean spirit; 24 and he cried out, "What have you to do with us, Jesus of Nazareth? Have you come to destroy us? I know who you are, the Holy One of God." 25 But Jesus rebuked him, saying, "Be silent, and come out of him!" 26 And the unclean spirit, convulsing him and crying with a loud voice, came out of him. 27 And they were all amazed, so that they questioned among themselves, saying, "What is this? A new teaching! With authority he commands even the unclean spirits, and they obey him." 28 And at once his fame spread everywhere throughout all the surrounding region of Galilee.

KEY VERSE: *"The time is fulfilled, and the kingdom of God is at hand; repent and believe in the gospel."* Mark 1:15 (RSV).

HOME DAILY BIBLE READINGS

Feb. 27. M. *Get ready for the Lord.* Mark 1:1–8.
Feb. 28. T. *John's Forecast.* Luke 3:7–14.
Feb. 29. W. *Jesus' Baptism and Temptation.* Mark 1:9–13.
Mar. 1.   T. *The Right Time Has Come.* Mark 1:14–20.
Mar. 2.   F. *A Man With an Evil Spirit.* Mark 1:21–28.
Mar. 3.   S. *Jesus Heals Many People.* Mark 1:29–34.
Mar. 4.   S. *Ministering in New Places.* Mark 1:35–39.

BACKGROUND

In the Book of Malachi, we learn that God had announced, through the prophet(s), that He would send a Messiah to earth, and that this Messiah would be preceded by a messenger who would prepare the way for His coming. Now, hundreds of years later, a man named Mark writes the first account of the works of Jesus Christ, who to him was the promised Messiah. His story begins with the words, "The beginning of the gospel of Jesus Christ, the Son of God" (Mark 1:1).

Just who was this Mark, and what did he write, and why did he write it?

He was the son of Mary (a property owner and a friend of Christians—Acts 12:12), a cousin of Barnabas and the companion of Peter. The great historian Papas, about A.D. 135, reported that "Mark, who had been the interpreter of Peter, wrote down accurately, so far as he remembered them, the things said and done by the Lord, but not however in order." This was about A.D. 65. This is the oldest and in many ways the most reliable of the Gospels, for Mark was a stickler for facts, not for unfounded tales. He wrote to explain the gospel of Jesus to the Gentiles, to convince them that Jesus was the Messiah, and to help Christians know what it means, what it takes, to follow Him. We may say that Matthew and Luke wrote to tell us what Jesus said, and Mark writes to tell us what He did.

So Mark starts out not with the birth or the boyhood of Jesus, but with the beginning of the ministry of Jesus.

NOTES ON THE PRINTED TEXT

What Isaiah and Malachi had prophesied about a forerunner of the Messiah was fulfilled in the appearance of John the Baptist who came out of a desert crying, "Prepare ye the way of the Lord. . . ." People flocked to hear the Baptist preach; he brought something new to their ears and he blazed like a torch in proclaiming it. Such preachers always get big audiences. The Baptist delivered his message; he was in Herod's prison for preaching as he did when Jesus appeared on the scene preaching the Kingdom of God. Jesus' message closely resembled that of the Baptist: "Repent, and believe. . . ."

So He was finally with us! With us not as a human monarch come to dominate the world but as a humble preacher and teacher talking of a kingdom that was not man's but God's. As a traveling teacher, He had to have help, He had to establish Himself "as the one who should come," He had to set up a preaching and teaching program.

First, He needed helpers; He could not have succeeded without them. So He picked out His disciples carefully. On this first day of His ministry, He picked four: Simon (Peter) and Andrew his brother; James and John *his* brother. They were fishermen. They lived in huts, never went to school or college, had no prominent positions in their communities. Jesus knew all that when He made them disciples—He also knew that they were humble men and men of courage. There wasn't one "well-off" man among the disciples. So it is today; the most effective disciples of Jesus seem to be men who came off poor farms, out of lowly homes, and even out of jails! He deliberately covets the humble, seldom the wealthy. Men who cast nets as fishermen made good casting God's nets for leaders in His Kingdom.

Second, Jesus made good use of existing institutions. He went, this first day, into the synagogue of Capernaum. That took courage on His part, for He had something to say to Jews who put their trust in traditional creeds, customs, and theology. Mark does not record all of that sermon, but it must have been almost terrifying to any loyal Jew. He called for a complete break with the past—their past. He taught them "as one that had authority, and not as the scribes." He preached and taught something dangerously new: the *Good* News of God. With authority—God's authority. When the poor Baptist, languishing in Herod's jail, sent two of his friends to ask of Jesus, "Art thou he that should come, or do we look for another?" (Matthew 11:3), he got a quick answer: at the hands of this Jesus, the blind could see, the lame could walk, the lepers were cleansed, the deaf could hear, and the dead were raised up. This came long after this sermon in Capernaum, but it made it perfectly clear that the Christ spoke with the authority of God, for only God could work such miracles.

To prove His claim of such authority, Jesus wrought the first miracle recorded by Mark. He healed a man with an unclean spirit—a man with a mental sickness or neurosis. In the world of Jesus' day, unclean spirits or demons were the terrorists of the time. Men and women were haunted by fear, worry, anxiety, insecurity. So is *our* world! It has all these unclean spirits, plus a lack of reliance on God.

Jesus healed that man; that is one of the best-supported facts of His ministry. Strange, then, wasn't it that the Jews *resented* that healing? Even the healed one protested: "Let us alone; what have we to do with thee, thou Jesus of Nazareth?"

We still hear that cry from people who hear Him speak but refuse to accept what He spoke and did. Leave us alone! If we want to go to war, leave us alone; we will worship You when it is all over. If we want to cheat a little in business, let us alone. If we want to make millions of dollars while millions of children die of starvation, let us alone.

What we are really doing, when we say this, is demonstrating that Jesus was concerned with and interested in the whole of human life and not only with part of it. The world is His parish; His heart bleeds for all who suffer, whatever their creed, color, or condition. He is like that because He sees the whole world not as man's world, but as His Father's.

Recently we talked with a local politician about the corruption of governments and governed all over our world, and what we should do about it. He said to us, smoothly and piously, "The church ought to stick to religion, and leave politics to the politicians!" Jesus never did that; He spoke to every part of human life and activity. He was killed on the charge of treason. He didn't let anybody alone. The Romans who crucified Him on that cross were saying, "Let us alone, let our kingdom alone. . . ." They just didn't want anything to do with the Godly Kingdom. He died for that.

There wasn't just one crucifixion; we crucify Him every day, under the prodding of those filled with unclean spirits. We might do well, as we teach this lesson today, to have our students make a list of the unclean within us—if we have room enough on our blackboard.

SUGGESTIONS TO TEACHERS

Mark's picture of Jesus crackles with action. To Mark, Jesus is the strong Son of God, the mighty worker who goes about doing good. His shirt-sleeves approach will make your teaching delightfully down-to-earth.

Mark leaps immediately into telling of a Jesus who ministers to human need, and you should do the same. The first chapter of Mark, the basis for your lesson today, packs important details about the start of Jesus' ministry.

1. *FORERUNNER'S CLAIM.* Open your lesson by looking at the person and the place of John the Baptist in the story of Jesus. Remind your class that John the Baptist made a powerful impact, and, although great prophet in the Old Testament tradition he was, insisted that Jesus was the One to follow. As Mark states in his opening words, Jesus is the "Good News." You may find it helpful to have your class members relate why Jesus is "Good News" to them.

2. *FORTY DAYS' CONDITIONING.* Examine with your class the account of Jesus' baptism, call, and temptations in the desert. Move the discussion from being merely an academic exercise about Jesus' experiences. Encourage each in your class to share something of his or her "faith story." Remind those in your class that they, too, are "called" and have been conditioned through "desert" experiences. Sometimes, Christians do not see that the Lord has been working through these times of testing. As Jesus found His call confirmed and clarified in the desert, so your class members will also find their calls confirmed and clarified through their temptation experiences.

3. *FULFILLMENT'S COMING.* Jesus burst into Galilee announcing that God's Kingdom is at hand! Take enough time with your lesson to discuss what the Kingdom is and how it is coming. Your class should be helped to understand that the Kingdom is the rule and the realm of God. Through Jesus, God has staked out His claim on the entire universe, including everything in this life and world and era, as His own. There is both an "already" and a "not yet" aspect to the Kingdom's coming. Remind the class that the petition, "Thy Kingdom come," means a commitment to help bring His rule to pass! Be sure to consider the healings in Mark 1, remembering that these are evidence of Jesus' authority and the Kingdom's coming.

4. *FISHERMEN'S CALLING.* Take a close look at Jesus' first followers. As teacher, hold up the account in Mark of Jesus calling the earliest disciples as a mirror. Let your class see how similar these fishermen are to those in your class. Suggest to your class that Jesus selects common garden variety folks like Peter, Andrew, James, and John, not the intelligentsia or powerful people, to be with Him in ministry.

5. *FAME'S COST.* Look at Jesus' busy life and His need to rise early to have time to pray. He could not endure the exhausting pace without a disciplined prayer life. It would be instructive to your class to consider ways in which your people may have a regular time for praying. A life of service is impossible without such spiritual refreshment.

6. *FAMILY CARE.* Take some time to look at the compassion Jesus showed toward all. Point out the way He even regarded lepers, loathesome and unlovable objects to everyone, as brothers and sisters. Remind your class members that Mark paints a portrait of God in action in showing Jesus literally touching and healing a leper. The Lord means to touch each of us with new life!

TOPIC FOR ADULTS
JESUS BEGINS HIS MINISTRY

New Inscription. G. K. Chesterton once wrote that whereas a poet in the Middle Ages inscribed, "Abandon Hope All Ye Who Enter Here" over the gates of Hell, modern writers inscribe that phrase over the gates of this world. Jesus' ministry, however, rewrites all the inscriptions and all human experiences. His coming means that we may now inscribe over the gates of the world a call to abandon hopelessness and all the pleasures of pessimism. *Jesus ministers to every person's need!*

Leaving the Nets and the Boats. "Discipleship is the synoptic gospels' way of describing what it means to be a Christian. . . . But discipleship confined to the small world of personal morality is not an experience of the drawing near of the kingdom. . . . To stress the site of one's call to discipleship with the abandoned flea-market trivia of beer cans, theater tickets, and a stack of old *Playboy* magazines is hardly the equivalent of the sturdy artifacts of nets, boats, and a father's business. Not until our devotion to the projects the nets and boats represent has been interrupted has the call to discipleship been truly heard. . . . The key to the symbolic meaning of abandoned nets, boats, and parents is the realization that the 'world' exercises a tyranny over us mostly at work and after that in families. If ever God is to break the world's domination of us and displace it with his own reign, it must be in connection with work and family. . . . But neither work per se nor family itself is incompatible with discipleship; Jesus did not demand ascetic withdrawal from them. . . . It is a central conviction of the Protestant adventure that work and family can and must be vehicles of discipleship. The subsequent use Jesus makes of Peter's home and of the boat symbolize that. But the place of work and family within the context of discipleship unfolds only after the positive content of discipleship takes effect. That positive content is given in the command, 'Follow me'. . . . Everything depends on Jesus really being there for one to follow. The essence of discipleship is actually keeping company with Jesus. Being with Jesus, tapping the well-spring of his awesome and graceful presence, sharing the adventure of his mission—this is what makes the risk of abandoning nets, boats, and parents inviting. He is what makes discipleship worthwhile."—Neill Q. Hamilton, *Recovery of the Protestant Adventure.* Copyright © 1981 by The Seabury Press. Used by permission.

Call to Sacrifice. Giuseppe Garibaldi, the great Italian patriot who eventually won independence for his nation, experienced defeats and disappointments but inspired his countrymen to follow him in the struggle. After the siege of Rome in 1849, he issued a ringing challenge to Italians: "Soldiers, all our efforts against superior forces have been unavailing. I have nothing to offer you but hunger and thirst, hardship and death; but I call on all who love their country to join with me." Thousands responded. Eventually, Italy became free.

Jesus' call carries the same note of challenge. The earliest disciples heard His invitation to leave boats and nets and follow Him through sacrifice and hardship. All who love God and desire a new world continue to find that Jesus is the most compelling leader of all. His ministry in our time demands we follow Him through "hunger and thirst, hardship and death," but with the confidence that He will prevail!

Questions for Pupils on the Next Lesson. 1. Why did Jesus' associations with outcasts often provoke hostility? 2. Why are you not always willing to take an unpopular stand? 3. What are some of the occasions in Jesus' life when He broke with religious tradition? 4. Why do people feel threatened by opinions different from their own? 5. How does your congregation handle conflict?

TOPIC FOR YOUTH
READY TO FOLLOW

Christ or Nothing. Jesus Christ still calls men and women to follow Him. He surprises people who have no intention of following Him. He persists in His ministry to those who don't know Him.

Malcolm Muggeridge is a witty and whimsical English writer. For many years, he edited *Punch,* the English humor magazine noted for its sarcastic barbs. Muggeridge's stinging comments made him a controversial but widely respected figure in England. He frequently appeared on television and radio, and irreverently attacked nearly everything sacred. He had no use for religion in any form. Once, in fact, Muggeridge snapped, "I never wanted a God, or feared a God, or felt any necessity to invent one." However, Muggeridge the man who never wanted God found himself driven to the conclusion that God wanted him. Like the Hound of Heaven, the Lord padded after Muggeridge. One day they met. Muggeridge the cynical became a Christian. Recently, he declared passionately to a packed assembly of students in Edinburgh, "As far as I am concerned, it is Christ or it is nothing!"

Have you discovered that this must also be the case in your life? Are you aware that Jesus calls you? Are you ready to follow?

Success or Service? "We have the paradox of those who affirm the absolute authority of the Bible, yet at the same time are cozily conformed to the radical materialism of present-day culture. A self-centered kind of Christian life and testimony—'After I was saved and began giving to Christian work, God blessed me in a new way and prospered me so that now I'm enjoying the good things of life (better car, larger house, costlier vacations) more than even before'—confuses what the world calls 'success' with the biblical pattern of life and service. So a dismaying number of us have slipped into a false sense of entitlement to material luxuries and a more and more elaborate lifestyle"—"Heeding the Whole Counsel of God," by Frank E. Gaebelein (October 2, 1981), copyright 1981 by *Christianity Today* and used by permission.

Ray of Hope. Jesus' coming transforms all things. He turns darkness to light. In A.D. 633, the northern part of what is now England was a pagan kingdom. The Dark Ages had settled on the land. One evening, King Oswald and his nobles took refuge in a manor hall from a winter storm. A large fire burned brightly while snow and hail beat upon the walls outside. Although the men enjoyed shelter for their bodies, their spirits were tempest-tossed. Finally a missionary named Aiden stood up and spoke to them of Jesus, the Light of the world. After some debate, one nobleman commented on the murky mystery of man's life. He compared it to a sparrow warming itself in the hall, which would soon fly off into the cold and dark forever. Then he declared, "In the missionary's teaching there is a ray of hope. As this new doctrine brings something more of certainty, it deserves to be received." King Oswald and his nobles committed themselves to follow Jesus Christ. The light of the Gospel spread throughout Northumbria, transforming the realm from a dismal backwater to a center of Christianity and affecting the entire continent.

When you follow Jesus, you will discover that He continues to bring light to dark places and situations. He continues to transform lives and lands.

Sentence Sermon to Remember: We may be doing Jesus an injustice in stressing the fact that He so frequently said, "Go. . . !" His first word to His disciples was not, "Go" but "Come."—Anonymous.

Questions for Pupils on the Next Lesson. 1. Why are you sometimes reluctant to associate with people who are different? 2. What are some of the traditions you are questioning? 3. Why did Jesus sometimes break with religious traditions? 4. Why did His association with outcasts provoke such hostility? 5. What social injustices are most obvious in your community?

LESSON II—MARCH 11

JESUS ENCOUNTERS HOSTILITY

Background Scripture: Mark 2:1–3:6
Devotional Reading: Mark 2:1–12

KING JAMES VERSION

MARK 2 15 And it came to pass, that, as Jesus sat at meat in his house, many publicans and sinners sat also together with Jesus and his disciples; for there were many, and they followed him.

16 And when the scribes and Pharisees saw him eat with publicans and sinners, they said unto his disciples, How is it that he eateth and drinketh with publicans and sinners?

17 When Jesus heard *it*, he saith unto them, They that are whole have no need of the physician, but they that are sick: I came not to call the righteous, but sinners to repentance.

23 And it came to pass, that he went through the corn fields on the sabbath day; and his disciples began, as they went, to pluck the ears of corn.

24 And the Pharisees said until him, Behold, why do they on the sabbath day that which is not lawful?

25 And he said unto them, Have ye never read what David did, when he had need, and was ahungered, he, and they that were with him?

26 How he went into the house of God in the days of Abiathar the high priest, and did eat the shewbread, which is not lawful to eat but for the priests, and gave also to them which were with him?

27 And he said unto them, The sabbath was made for man, and not man for the sabbath:

28 Therefore the Son of man is Lord also of the sabbath.

3 1 And he entered again into the synagogue; and there was a man there which had a withered hand.

2 And they watched him, whether he would heal him on the sabbath day; that they might accuse him.

3 And he saith unto the man which had the withered hand, Stand forth.

4 And he said unto them, Is it lawful to do good on the sabbath days, or to do evil? to save life, or to kill? But they held their peace.

5 And when he had looked round about on them with anger, being grieved for the hardness of their hearts, he saith unto the man, Stretch forth thine hand. And he stretched *it* out: and his hand was restored whole as the other.

6 And the Pharisees went forth, and straightway took counsel with the Herodians against him, how they might destroy him.

REVISED STANDARD VERSION

MARK 2 15 And as he sat at table in his house, many tax collectors and sinners were sitting with Jesus and his disciples; for there were many who followed him. 16 And the scribes of the Pharisees, when they saw that he was eating with sinners and tax collectors, said to his disciples, "Why does he eat with tax collectors, and sinners?" 17 And when Jesus heard it, he said to them, "Those who are well have no need of a physician, but those who are sick; I came not to call the righteous, but sinners."

23 One sabbath he was going through the grainfields; and as they made their way his disciples began to pluck heads of grain. 24 And the Pharisees said to him, "Look, why are they doing what is not lawful on the sabbath?" 25 And he said to them, "Have you never read what David did, when he was in need and was hungry, he and those who were with him: 26 how he entered the house of God, when Abiathar was high priest, and ate the bread of the Presence, which it is not lawful for any but the priests to eat, and also gave it to those who were with him?" 27 And he said to them, "The sabbath was made for man, not man for the sabbath; 28 so the Son of man is lord even of the sabbath."

31 Again he entered the synagogue, and a man was there who had a withered hand. 2 And they watched him, to see whether he would heal him on the sabbath, so that they might accuse him. 3 And he said to the man who had the withered hand, "Come here." 4 And he said to them, "Is it lawful on the sabbath to do good or to do harm, to save life or to kill?" But they were silent. 5 And he looked around at them with anger, grieved at their hardness of heart, and said to the man, "Stretch out your hand." He stretched it out, and his hand was restored. 6 The Pharisees went out, and immediately held counsel with the Herodians against him, how to destroy him.

KEY VERSE: ". . . I came not to call the righteous, but sinners." Mark 2:17 (RSV).

HOME DAILY BIBLE READINGS

Mar. 5. M. *Jesus Claims His Authority.* Mark 2:1–12.
Mar. 6. T. *Finding New Meanings in Tradition.* Mark 2:18–22.
Mar. 7. W. *Lord of the Sabbath.* Mark 2:23–28.
Mar. 8. T. *Healing on the Sabbath.* Mark 3:1–6.
Mar. 9. F. *Many Heard About Jesus.* Mark 3:7–12.
Mar. 10. S. *Jesus Gathers His Twelve.* Mark 3:13–19.
Mar. 11. S. *Jesus Reveals His Purpose.* Matthew 9:9–13.

BACKGROUND

To the Jews, the Jewish Law was the very word of God. They read of that Law in the first five books in the Old Testament, but that was not enough. They felt that they had to enlarge on it and *make it cover everything.* First they drew up a summary of the Law, in a book (in English) of almost 800 pages. Even that was not enough. They proceeded to write long commentaries on the Mishna, called Talmuds. In the Jerusalem Talmud, there are twelve *volumes;* in the Babylonian Talmud there are sixty volumes.

The Jew was to govern his whole life in obedience to *all* the laws. Two bodies of scholars were appointed to explain and enact these thousands of laws: the scribes who told them what the laws meant, and the Pharisees who saw to it that the laws—every one of them!—were obeyed.

Highly important among these laws were those defining work and the Sabbath. Thirty-nine different kinds of work were covered; the section on the Sabbath, in the Mishna, has twenty-four chapters. The orthodox Jew was expected to understand and obey. That was quite an assignment! It was with this unbelievable mass of rules and regulations that Jesus collided, not once but often.

Here at the very start of His ministry, He came into collision with certain scribes and Pharisees, who were already suspicious and afraid of what such a radical preacher might say about their precious Law.

NOTES ON THE PRINTED TEXT

Almost before He could get started on His mission, Jesus ran into a trouble that followed His footsteps from Nazareth to Calvary. The lesson today deals with tax collectors, men eating corn, and a man with a withered hand.

If there was any individual or group of individuals that were despised and hated in Jewish society, the tax collectors had high priority. Tax collectors gathered taxes under the guidance of the Romans; they were called robbers, thieves, bandits, ruffians, and murderers. Nobody loved them. (Stand up, all ye who love your tax collectors, *now!*) But Jesus Christ loved them—not for what they were, but for what they might be. "As he passed by," one day in the marketplace, He saw a man named Matthew "sitting at the receipt (place) of custom (taxes)" and He challenged Matthew to follow Him. Immediately, the despised collector followed. That was bad enough; even worse was the fact that Matthew invited the Messiah to dine with him in his house along with a number of other publicans (tax collectors). That raised a howl that could have been heard around the world. How *dared* He sit down to eat with such human scum? The very self-righteous Pharisees asked Him that, and His reply left them speechless: "I came not to call the righteous, but sinners to repentance." He came also as a Physician of the soul—and it was the sinners who most needed His healing.

Doctors do not spend much of their time on people who are in good health; they are trained to help the sick, and they go where the sick are. The Great Physician Christ can do little or nothing with people who boast that they have no need of Him, but He can work miracles with those who are sinners and admit it and who long for the healing that He holds in His hands.

Another furor was created when Jesus, walking through a grain field with His disciples, allowed them to pluck ears of corn and eat them. This was done on a Sabbath day, and the minute they did that, the Pharisees shouted in protest. They were breaking the Law; they were *working* on the Sabbath day! The Law said a lot about working; work was classified under thirty-nine different heads and four of these heads were—reaping, winnowing, threshing, and preparing a meal. As the Pharisees saw it, the disciples were breaking all four of these regulations.

Foolish? Yes, to us. And to Jesus. Jesus made it look ridiculous. He cited the example of David, who with his starving men ate the shewbread in the tabernacle. Shewbread was to be eaten only by the priests. David put need before the Law; so did the Master. The Sabbath, He said, was made for man and man was not made for the Sabbath. The Sabbath was to be a day of rejoicing, not a day of exhausting rules and regulations that robbed it of its meaning.

Long ago, we had a saintly grandfather-preacher who refused to ride a train on Sunday, for that made other men work. His good wife never cooked a meal on Sunday. But before they died, they changed all that. Grandfather actually *flew* to preach far from home on the Sabbath. He saved men, doing that. He put the need of men before trains and planes.

Conflict No. 3: Jesus healed a man with a withered hand, on one Sabbath day and in the synagogue! Shame, cried the Pharisees. Against the Law. Under the Law, one was allowed to ease another's pain, but not to *cure* him. That would have been "work."

Jesus knocked that one into the proverbial cocked hat. What should we do, save life or kill? Was it lawful to do good on the Sabbath day, or to do evil? That stopped them: "They held their peace." They said nothing, because there was nothing they could say. They muttered among themselves and talked of destroying this unorthodox man from Nazareth. They had run out of arguments, so they turned to violence.

It all counts up to this: Jesus was more interested in people than He was in rules calculated to keep an institution alive. It was not that He was breaking or ignoring the Law; it was simply that He had found something better. "The man who is really obeying the commandment of God is not he who rigidly observes legalistic rules and regulations but he whose one desire is to bring help to his fellow men. In effect Jesus was saying, 'It is not rules and regulations you ought to love, but men and women. Nothing takes priority over human need.' "—William Barclay in *And He Had Compassion,* Judson Press.

SUGGESTIONS TO TEACHERS

A young executive-type reluctantly agreed to join a neighborhood Bible study group for six weeks. After attending two sessions on the Gospel of Mark and carefully reading the scriptural material, he exclaimed, "Why didn't someone tell me that Jesus was not a bland Mister Nice Guy? He's dynamite! I had it all wrong; I'd been raised on the 'gentle Jesus meek and mild' stuff. I'd assumed He never had enemies anymore than the Easter bunny would have."

The executive's discovery is not surprising. Many in your class have also been led to picture Jesus in dull pastel shades. This lesson will dispel these notions. Jesus, your teaching today should make clear, often provoked hostility.

1. *BLASPHEMER OR BLESSING?* Jesus healed. He associated with outcasts. He broke the taboos such as Sabbath observance to help people. Examine the account of His healing the paralytic in Mark 2. Note the reaction of others, especially the "religious" folk. Point out to your class that people inevitably regard Jesus either as the greatest blasphemer or the greatest blessing they know. Which conclusion do your class members reach, and why? Also take some time to reflect on the interest Jesus had in the paralytic, and in those paralyzed with guilt or

greed or fear or other crippling causes. As God's great blessing, Jesus still releases persons helpless from any paralyzing feelings or habits.

2. *BLUNDERER OR BEFRIENDER?* Mark's Gospel account paints sharply contrasting choices about Jesus. The authorities and some of Jesus' advisers are shocked at the company He keeps. After all, associating with tax collectors was hardly the best way to win friends and influence people! Remind your people that Jesus insists on standing with those who realize they need His help. He doesn't care about being prudent or politic. In choosing to befriend Levi, Jesus makes it clear that He also means to befriend any who "need a physician," regardless of the consequences. Do your class members realize that Jesus has paid a terrible price for His willingness to associate with people like Levi—and them?

3. *SOUSE OR CELEBRATOR?* Does your class realize that Jesus was even accused of carousing with undesirables? "Birds of a feather . . ." people murmured. Your class should recognize that Jesus brings a joyous new era. His coming means celebration. Take a few minutes in this lesson to think together whether your lives and your worship reflect that joy.

4. *LAWBREAKER OR LIBERATOR?* Have your class come to grips with Mark 2:23, describing Jesus facing accusations of breaking the Sabbath requirements. Take note of the way Jesus insisted that human need takes precedence over all traditions, customs, and rules. You must also make sure that your students understand that just as Jesus encountered hostility for His stand, so His people— your class included—must be prepared to receive criticism and hostility. Whenever anyone puts persons ahead of policies, he will conflict. Spend some lesson time on how Christians deal with conflict.

5. *SINNER OR SAVIOR?* Jesus was denounced for healing the man with the withered hand on the Sabbath (Mark 3:1–6). The point should be made with your class that Christians must not expect applause and awards for doing good. To the contrary, being Christ's person means supporting minority groups, associating with persons who are different, and working to correct injustices. And this almost always means enduring pain and opposition. Close with the reminder that accepting such a cross is what the faith is all about.

TOPIC FOR ADULTS
JESUS ENCOUNTERS HOSTILITY

Known by the Name. Bishop Bernard Weil of Chicago knew personally what it was to take unpopular stands for the sake of the Christian Gospel. One time, he heard about a meeting in a working-class neighborhood in which there were strong racist feelings. Although the meeting had been advertised as a rally for patriotism and community, the Bishop suspected that it would promote white supremacy. Bishop Weil feared that the rabble-rousers sponsoring the meeting would arouse the already strong sentiments against blacks and Jews in the community. Against the advice of some who told him to try to ignore the problem or to "stick to religion," Bishop Weil calmly walked into the hall and encountered hostile stares. After a couple of emotionally-charged racist harangues, Bishop Weil rose to his feet and asked to speak. Boos and shouts erupted. The churchman slowly began to walk to the front of the hall. Suddenly a woman leaped up and angrily confronted him. Her face was contorted with rage. Her words were a string of obscenities. Her voice rose to a piercing shriek. "You . . . nigger lover, you! Siding with the niggers and the Jews! God damn you!" By this time her voice had reached an inhuman crescendo: "YOU JEW BASTARD!" Bishop Weil stood silently, unable to proceed around her. She paused momentarily, cleared her throat, and with a mighty explosive sound from her mouth spat at him. The load of saliva caught him squarely on the cheek. Suddenly a silence gripped the entire audience. Weil did not flinch. The woman stood transfixed, her mouth hanging open in perplexity. The tension became oppressive, as everyone watched the saliva roll down the Bishop's face onto his collar. Weil slowly turned the other cheek and waited. The woman seemed frozen. Quietly, Weil moved his head to face her with a patient smile, and said, "Jew bastard? Yes. That's what they called my Lord." Turning quietly, he walked up the aisle and out of the hall. The crowd silently dispersed.

Stood Up for Christ. William Carey, the father of the modern missionary movement, began his career as an illiterate cobbler in Northamptonshire, England. Converted when he was twenty-one, Carey tacked a map of the world over his cobbler's bench and began to teach himself to read and write. He also began to preach. He began to realize that the New Testament stated that the Good News of Jesus Christ was to be taken to all persons everywhere. In the late 1700s, however, no one from the English churches felt compelled to travel overseas to share the faith. When Carey stated his conviction that the Lord called him and others to go as missionaries, he was harshly rebuked by church authorities.

"Young man, sit down," commanded the church leader presiding at the meeting in which Carey first publicly proposed sending missionaries. "When God intends to convert the heathen, He will do it without your help or mine."

In spite of this sharp put-down, and in spite of deeply entrenched opposition by the powerful East India Company merchants, churchmen, and government bureaucrats, William Carey eventually succeeded in reaching India in 1793. His efforts awakened interest in the overseas mission of the church and stimulated the founding of many missionary societies in the late eighteenth and early nineteenth centuries in nearly every denomination in the United States and Britain.

Christians, as Carey knew, frequently encounter hostility as Jesus did.

Hostility From Convictions. The great mathematician and inventor Charles Proteus Steinmetz was a rather small, physically misshapen immigrant. He became one of the greatest scientists of our time. While he was still comparatively young and unknown, Steinmetz developed the theory of alternating current and wrote a paper on his theory. He requested permission to read this paper before a national scientific society. He was finally granted about one hour's time and a small room for this purpose. As Steinmetz presented his paper, one by one the scientists left the room, until only a handful were left to hear the entire paper. Steinmetz was "talking over their heads" and they couldn't follow him. Some of the hostile scientists derided Steinmetz because they felt threatened by his theories or did not want to have to change their cherished opinions. Others privately scorned him because he was a hunchback and spoke with an accent. Charles Steinmetz silently accepted the criticisms and the ostracism because he knew eventually his theories would be proven correct.

Likewise, Jesus endured opposition. He knew that ultimately His truth would triumph.

Questions for Pupils on the Next Lesson. 1. Why do you think Jesus told those present to keep silent about many of His miracles? 2. Did Jesus use His power to awe or to entertain? 3. How do you react when confronted with crisis situations? 4. How did Jesus exercise His power in the face of death? 5. How was Jesus' power operated in your life?

TOPIC FOR YOUTH
PUTTING PEOPLE FIRST

People Ahead of Regulations. One time, during the construction of a great cathedral, the wife of a stonemason came each day with his lunch and sat for a while with her sewing watching him work. The bishop of the cathedral got to know both the mason and his wife and paused each day to exchange greetings and small talk with them. The craftsman and his devoted wife became well known to the churchman and other workers. One day, the wife did not appear. When the bishop inquired about her, the stonemason said that she was seriously ill, but was continuing to keep the cathedral's bishop and all the workers in her prayers. A few days later, when the bishop passed through the construction area, the mason stopped him and, with stumbling words, whispered that his wife was dying and wished to be laid to rest in the cathedral. The bishop shook his head and explained that the cathedral was hallowed ground and not for the wives of simple stonemasons. Several weeks passed, and the bishop happened to encounter the mason one day. The bishop offered his sympathy to the grieving mason, and asked politely where he had buried his wife. "There," replied the workman pointing to a freshly-set stone. He then disclosed that he had mixed her ashes with the mortar so that she could be interred in the holy place on which her husband had so lovingly labored. The bishop humbly bowed his head. "You are very rare and precious to God," he whispered to the craftsman.

Boatman's Insight. Far inland up the Yangtsi River in China, in the city of Wuhu, Christian doctors and nurses founded a hospital. At the top of the simple red brick building, they installed a cross. To the surprise and sometimes the consternation of the inhabitants of the area, they welcomed and treated any person who came for help. The local people at first resisted the Christians, but gradually grew aware that the medical staff at the Wuhu hospital put people first. Slowly, the local people also began to understand that these nurses and doctors put people first because of their religion which used a cross as its symbol. An old Chinese boatman summed it up best. Pointing to the top of the hospital where the cross stood, he said, "That stands for a God with kindness in His hands."

Putting Persons First. "Dear Folks, thank you for everything, but I am going to Chicago to try and start some kind of new life.

"You asked me why I gave you so much trouble, and the answer is easy for me to give you, but I was wondering if you will understand.

"Remember when I was about six or seven and I used to want you to just sit and listen to me? I remember all the nice things you gave me for Christmas and my birthday and I was really happy with those things for about a week—at the time I got the things, but the rest of the time during the year I really didn't want presents. I just wanted all the time for you to listen to me like I was somebody who felt things. But you said you were busy.

"Mom, you are a wonderful cook, and you had everything so clean and you were tired so much from doing all those things that made you busy; but you know something, Mom? I would have liked crackers and peanut butter just as well if you had only sat down with me for a while during the day and said to me: 'Tell me all about it so I can maybe help you understand!'

"I think that all the kids who are doing so many things that grown-ups are tearing out their hair worrying about are really looking for somebody that will have time to listen a few minutes and who really and truly will treat them as they would a grown-up who might be useful to them, you know—polite to them. If you folks had ever said to me: 'Pardon me' when you interrupted me, I'd have dropped dead!

"If anybody asks you where I am, tell them I've gone looking for somebody with time because I've got a lot of things I want to talk about. Love to all, Your Son."

Sentence Sermon to Remember: A true Christian's faith may be tested best not by the number of friends he makes, but by the number of enemies he makes for the sake of his faith.—J. L. Wolliamson.

Questions for Pupils on the Next Lesson. 1. Why did Jesus sometimes use His power to work what we call miracles? 2. What are the times when you are most afraid? 3. Exactly how does Jesus Christ bring peace to a person who is troubled and scared? 4. Why do so many young people take seriously the reports of the supernatural? 5. When have you been most aware of God's power at work in your life?

LESSON III—MARCH 18

JESUS USES HIS POWER

Background Scripture: Mark 4:35–5:43
Devotional Reading: Mark 4:10–20

KING JAMES VERSION

MARK 4 37 And there arose a great storm of wind, and the waves beat into the ship, so that it was now full.

38 And he was in the hinder part of the ship, asleep on a pillow: and they awake him, and say unto him, Master, carest thou not that we perish?

39 And he arose, and rebuked the wind, and said unto the sea, Peace, be still. And the wind ceased, and there was a great calm.

40 And he said unto them, Why are ye so fearful? how is it that ye have no faith?

41 And they feared exceedingly, and said one to another, What manner of man is this, that even the wind and the sea obey him?

5 35 While he yet spake, there came from the ruler of the synagogue's *house certain* which said, Thy daughter is dead: why troublest thou the Master any further?

36 As soon as Jesus heard the word that was spoken, he saith unto the ruler of the synagogue, Be not afraid, only believe.

37 And he suffered no man to follow him, save Peter, and James, and John the brother of James.

38 And he cometh to the house of the ruler of the synagogue, and seeth the tumult, and them that wept and wailed greatly.

39 And when he was come in, he saith unto them, Why make ye this ado, and weep? the damsel is not dead, but sleepeth.

40 And they laughed him to scorn. But when he had put them all out, he taketh the father and the mother of the damsel, and them that were with him, and entereth in where the damsel was lying.

41 And he took the damsel by the hand, and said unto her, Talitha cumi; which is, being interpreted, Damsel, I say unto thee, arise.

42 And straightway the damsel arose, and walked; for she was *of the age* of twelve years. And they were astonished with a great astonishment.

43 And he charged them straitly that no man should know it; and commanded that something should be given her to eat.

REVISED STANDARD VERSION

MARK 4 37 And a great storm of wind arose, and the waves beat into the boat, so that the boat was already filling. 38 But he was in the stern, asleep on the cushion; and they woke him and said to him, "Teacher, do you not care if we perish?" 39 And he awoke and rebuked the wind, and said to the sea, "Peace! Be still!" And the wind ceased, and there was a great calm. 40 He said to them, "Why are you afraid? Have you no faith?" 41 And they were filled with awe, and said to one another, "Who then is this, that even wind and sea obey him?"

5 35 While he was still speaking, there came from the ruler's house some who said, "Your daughter is dead. Why trouble the Teacher any further?" 36 But ignoring what they said, Jesus said to the ruler of the synagogue, "Do not fear, only believe." 37 And he allowed no one to follow him except Peter and James and John the brother of James. 38 When they came to the house of the ruler of the synagogue, he saw a tumult, and people weeping and wailing loudly. 39 And when he had entered, he said to them, "Why do you make a tumult and weep? The child is not dead but sleeping." 40 And they laughed at him. But he put them all outside, and took the child's father and mother and those who were with him, and went in where the child was. 41 Taking her by the hand he said to her, "Talitha cumi"; which means, "Little girl, I say to you, arise." 42 And immediately the girl got up and walked (she was twelve years of age), and they were immediately overcome with amazement. 43 And he strictly charged them that no one should know this, and told them to give her something to eat.

KEY VERSE: Be not afraid, only believe. Mark 5:36.

HOME DAILY BIBLE READINGS

Mar. 12. M. *Jesus Teaches With Parables.* Mark 4:10–20.
Mar. 13. T. *Jesus Calms the Storm.* Mark 4:35–41.
Mar. 14. W. *Power Against Evil Spirits.* Mark 5:1–13.
Mar. 15. T. *Witnessing the Miracle.* Mark 5:14–20.

Mar. 16. F. *Jesus Walks on the Water.* Mark 6:45–52.
Mar. 17. S. *Woman Who Touched Jesus' Cloak.* Mark 5:25–34.
Mar. 18. S. *Jairus's Daughter.* Mark 5:35–43.

BACKGROUND

Do you find it hard, at times, to understand exactly what and who Jesus was? If so, you are one of a great company. Even the disciples found it difficult more than once. If so, this lesson is intended to dispel your doubts and stop your wondering.

It deals with two demonstrations of the power of Jesus to dispel doubt and fear. One demonstration came in a little boat tossing in a storm on Lake Galilee; the other deals with a far more terrible storm—the bitter wind of death raging in the home of a man who was not a disciple. This man was Jairus a ruler of the synagogue. In the house of Jairus, his twelve-year-old daughter lay dead.

Both situations were terrifying. What could be worse than a tiny boat about to sink and a house in which despair had become a panic over the presence of death? Yet Jesus conquered both, and brought peace to those who were terrified.

Just how did He do that?

NOTES ON THE PRINTED TEXT

Those who have seen the Galilean lake will never forget it. It is a gem of a lake, serene and placid most of the time but, surrounded as it is by hills, it is at times dangerous and even deadly. Sudden storms had a habit of bursting out from those hills, even when the sky was blue. Jesus and His disciples were caught in such a storm. The disciples panicked; they screamed in fear to Jesus: "Master, carest thou not that we perish?" Jesus rebuked them gently: "Peace. . . . Why are you afraid? Have you no faith?" (Mark 4:38–40). And suddenly, there was peace in the boat.

This story has been interpreted in two different ways. Some scholars have interpreted it as simply symbolic. The boat in the story, they hold, is a symbol of the Church, which was suffering under persecution when this was written, particularly the Church in Rome. The storm was the storm of hostility to the Church. The sea (lake) was, to the Jews, the abiding place of evil, full of demons—the source of the hostility. Other Christian scholars take the story literally; they believe that Jesus had power over the forces of nature, and verse 41 seems to verify their belief: "What manner of man is this, that even the wind and the sea obey him?"

Take it any way you wish—but there is still convincing evidence that Jesus conquered the fear and the hesitancy to believe in His power in the minds of the terrified disciples. Here they were with Him, when the storm broke. He sat there in the stern of the boat, so unafraid that He *slept!* If Jesus was with them, why should they panic in fear at *anything?* If Christ was with them, who and what could be against them or destroy them?

If Christ be with *us,* who can stand against us? In a way, we still have storms of hostility beating against our little boats, storms from many different directions. We live in fear of a nuclear holocaust that could destroy *all* of us, we fear a depression that could leave us penniless in old age, we bemoan the loss of members in the Church, we consume tons of aspirin in an effort to wash away our anxiety—and all the time, Jesus is in our "boat"! We should take time out from our worries and read what old Isaiah had to say about all this: "When you pass through the waters, I will be with you . . . I love *you.* . . ." Or we might read once more that, "He whose mind is stayed on thee will be at perfect peace."

The basic truth and teaching of the story stands out like a fire on a mountaintop: Jesus has conquered the frenzies of millions of hearts all down the centuries and given them—peace.

In another chapter in Mark, we have the story of the healing of the daughter of Jairus. Jairus was a Jew; as president of the synagogue elders, he was (supposedly) a member of the opposition to Jesus. But he must have had, deep inside, a respect and admiration for the Nazarene for when his little daughter was dying he turned to Jesus for help. Unfortunately, the girl died before Jesus could reach her. It was "all over," or so they thought. The Teacher, said the friends of Jairus, might have been able to heal her but He could not raise her from the dead.

When Jesus arrived, He found a bedlam in the house of Jairus. In compliance with Jewish custom, a loud wailing began immediately after one died. Weeping and wailing and gnashing of teeth! They screamed; they beat their breasts; they tore their hair; they rent their garments. This was the voice of despair out of control.

Jesus put them out of the house. Then, with the father and the mother at His side, He took the hand of the girl and said to her, "Talitha cumi," which meant, "Daughter, arise." She rose, and walked. Notice the calm serenity of Jesus: what a contrast that was, compared with the hopelessness of the mourners! His was the voice of hope, of faith, of belief in the power of God to do the impossible.

Conqueror of the storms that beset us, Conqueror of faithlessness, Conqueror of *death*, Giver of peace in every situation—this was and is Jesus Christ. Why do we collapse in the presence of death? He can give us perfect peace in face of the worst that can happen to us. Said Jesus to Jairus, *"Only believe."*

The peace that comes from Christ is worth striving for. Says a British psychiatrist, "With peace in his heart, a man can face the most terrifying experiences. But without peace in his soul, he cannot manage even as simple a task as writing a letter." Think about that!

SUGGESTIONS TO TEACHERS

Today's lesson is on authority. Or, more specifically, it is on Jesus' authority. Even His enemies recognized that He had authority. Mark and the New Testament Christians insist that Jesus is *the* authority in life for them and for everyone. However, Mark does not speculate much about Jesus' authority; he recounts what Jesus did. Mark shows that Jesus shows His authority by His mighty acts. Mark emphasizes the doing, not the speaking, about Jesus' authority.

The lesson today examines several of these mighty acts. Significantly, Mark does not portray Jesus acting as a dramatic showman. There are no magic-show flourishes, no incantations. There is power and authority, all right, but Jesus uses these to demonstrate that the new realm of God has begun.

Since some in your class will be perplexed about Jesus' miracles, it is important to put these in the perspective of being demonstrations of His authority and not flashy tricks to "wow" the crowds. Look closely at the four examples of Jesus' power in the Scripture for today.

1. *AUTHORITY OVER DESTRUCTIVE ELEMENTS.* Have your class look at the account of Jesus calming the storm, and, incidentally, also calming the panic-stricken fishermen (Mark 4:35–41). It may be useful to remind your class that the theme of Jesus controlling the wind and waves frequently appears in crude drawings on the walls of the catacombs. Apparently this story in Mark had deep personal meaning for people facing terrifying storms in their lives in the early days of the Church. Develop your lesson around the way Jesus still has power to bring calm and hope in the midst of chaos and destruction.

2. *AUTHORITY OVER DEMONIC FORCES.* Next, have your class examine the report of Jesus calming the wild man raging among the tombs (the "Garasene Demoniac" in Mark 5:1). Jesus calms the storms within as well as without. His authority extends over "demons," the strange, destructive urges loose within us and around us. The account of the Garasene Demoniac has so many sidelights

that you may be tempted to spend a great portion of the lesson time discussing Jesus' extraordinary authority over the legions of ruinous powers tearing at the wild man—and at us.

3. *AUTHORITY OVER DISEASE AND ILLNESS.* The story of Jesus curing the woman with the hemorrhage opens up the subject of Jesus' health and healing. You might find it instructive to enlist the help of a physician from your church in this lesson to comment on the importance of attitude in a patient, and the place of prayer in healing. Remember that the word *salvation* means "wholeness." A whole person is one who is constantly receiving healing on every level— physical, mental, emotional, and spiritual. Jesus' authority extends over our bodies and minds.

4. *AUTHORITY OVER DEATH AND EXTINCTION.* Finally, direct your class to scrutinize the verses describing Jesus raising the recently-deceased daughter of Jairus, the synagogue president, to life. Mark tells us this mighty act of Jesus to emphasize that Jesus has authority over the grave. The final and greatest power is not death. Jesus insists that *His* power is mightiest of all! Let your class members express their own personal anxieties and experiences with death and dying, but hold up the glorious promise that Jesus uses His power to bring a resurrection to each of us!

TOPIC FOR ADULTS
JESUS USES HIS POWER

Power Vibrations. Hold two tuning forks side by side. Strike one of them. It emits a hum. Soon the other tuning fork also begins to give off a hum. How? The second tuning fork begins to vibrate with the sound frequency of the first.

This is what happens to people who have been close to Christ. They begin to resonate with His caring. His power is transmitted to others. The tone of His life affects those who turn to Him. He empowers people in our times to live amazing lives, to bring healing and new life to those around them.

God Came in Person. God did not send a committee. He came in person. The power of Jesus demonstrates God's concern and control.

Most of us spend so much time working in committees that we lose sight of the authority of Jesus. No matter how august the group nor how important the task, a committee is still a committee, and every amateur commitologist can define such a group:

A group of people who, individually, can do nothing, but collectively can meet and decide that nothing can be done.

A group which succeeds in getting something done when, and only when, it consists of three members, one of whom happens to be sick and another absent.

A collection of the unfit chosen from the unwilling by the incompetent to do the unnecessary.

In refreshing contrast to the ineptitude of so many committees, Jesus worked authoritatively, using His power wisely and well. God still operates the universe without our advice or consent. He does not need our motions of approval. Through the spirit, Jesus continues to show His power.

Putting Together the World. A school psychologist was giving an intelligence test to a group of eight-year-olds. He took a map of the world from a magazine, tore it into tiny pieces, and handed the fragments to one of the boys.

The lad pondered the pieces intently for a few minutes, then quickly assembled the map without a flaw.

"Wonderful!" exclaimed the psychologist. "How did you do it so fast and so well?"

"Well," replied the boy, "there was a big picture of a man on the other side. If you get that man straightened out, the world will come out all right."

Questions for Pupils on the Next Lesson. 1. Why are losses and gains so important to adults in our society? 2. Why does self-denial not come easily to us? 3. Have you ever made any commitments which have called for real sacrifice? 4. Exactly what does it mean to "minister to others"? 5. If Jesus asked you personally who you thought He was, how would you answer?

TOPIC FOR YOUTH
HELP WHEN YOU NEED IT

Out of Control. About twenty years ago in Burlington, Iowa, a Civil Air Patrol plane went out of control when the pilot twirled the propeller to start the engine. In those days, a pilot had to stand in front of the plane to "crank" it up by spinning the propeller by hand. It was possible for the plane to take off on its own once the engine began to gain speed. And that's exactly what happened.

The plane circled low over Burlington (population about 34,000 then) for an hour. Fire trucks and police cars dashed throughout the city to warn citizens of possible danger. School children were not permitted to leave the buildings. Students at the college evacuated the campus.

After circling the city for an hour, the plane climbed to 12,000 feet, headed west and eventually crashed in a field in Illinois when it ran out of gas. The plane had been airborne for two hours without a pilot.

Our lives may apparently go on for some time without any direction. We may feel we need no one at the controls; we may tell ourselves we need no pilot to guide our lives. In short, we may try to go along as if God does not matter. Eventually, however, we will find ourselves in deep difficulty. Without piloting, our plans and our careers end disastrously.

Jesus Christ is the only one who gives direction and help in your lives. He has the power to bring direction and help in these times!

Jesus the Center of the Universe. "That the particular in the person of Jesus Christ is the universal—that what stands at the center of his message is at the center of the universe. The only way to the universal is through the particular, and you can't stop at the particular, because you know it to be the way of access to the universal. . . . For a Christian that particularity is the life, death, and resurrection of Jesus, but it's not Jesusolatry; it's a window, and you look through it, not at it. That's why it's clear glass, not stained glass."—Jaroslav Pelikan. Reprinted by permission from CONTEXT (March 15, 1981) of Claretian Publication, 221 W. Madison, Chicago, IL 60606.

Love and Power. Jesus loved others. Jesus also used His power. Both love and power are shown in His life.

In the life of Christ's Church, we must keep both love and power in mind. The words of Reinhold Niebuhr, the theologian, apply always: "Love without power simply surrenders the world to power without love. How to make power express love, and love humanize power, is the distinctive task of the church of Christ for the next hundred years." When we use our power to express love and our love to humanize power, we will truly bring help where it is needed—even as Jesus Christ has brought us help when we needed it!

Sentence Sermon to Remember: To whatever side you turn, you are forced to acknowledge your own ignorance and the boundless power of the Creator.—Voltaire.

Questions for Pupils on the Next Lesson. 1. In twenty words or less, how would you summarize what Jesus means to you? 2. When was the last time you had to stand up for your beliefs as a Christian? 3. What are the most difficult challenges facing you at this time in your life? 4. Why do you sometimes have difficulty in seeing the benefits of holding to religious values? 5. Have you ever made any sacrifices for your Christian beliefs?

LESSON IV—MARCH 25

JESUS CALLS PERSONS TO MINISTER

Background Scripture: Mark 8:27–9:50
Devotional Reading: Mark 9:33–41

KING JAMES VERSION

MARK 8 27 And Jesus went out, and his disciples, into the towns of Caesarea Philippi: and by the way he asked his disciples, saying unto them, Whom do men say that I am?

28 And they answered, John the Baptist: but some *say*, Elias; and others, One of the prophets.

29 And he saith unto them, But whom say ye that I am? And Peter answereth and saith unto him, Thou art the Christ.

30 And he charged them that they should tell no man of him.

31 And he began to teach them, that the Son of man must suffer many things, and be rejected of the elders, and *of* the chief priests, and scribes, and be killed, and after three days rise again.

32 And he spake that saying openly. And Peter took him, and began to rebuke him.

33 But when he had turned about and looked on his disciples, he rebuked Peter, saying, Get thee behind me, Satan: for thou savourest not the things that be of God, but the things that be of men.

34 And when he had called the people *unto him* with his disciples also, he said unto them, Whosoever will come after me, let him deny himself, and take up his cross, and follow me.

35 For whosoever will save his life shall lose it; but whosoever shall lose his life for my sake and the gospel's, the same shall save it.

36 For what shall it profit a man, if he shall gain the whole world, and lose his own soul?

37 Or what shall a man give in exchange for his soul?

38 Whosoever therefore shall be ashamed of me and of my words in this adulterous and sinful generation; of him also shall the Son of man be ashamed, when he cometh in the glory of his Father with the holy angels.

REVISED STANDARD VERSION

MARK 8 27 And Jesus went on with his disciples, to the villages of Caesarea Philippi; and on the way he asked his disciples, "Who do men say that I am?" 28 And they told him, "John the Baptist; and others say, Elijah; and others one of the prophets." 29 And he asked them, "But who do you say that I am?" Peter answered him, "You are the Christ." 30 And he charged them to tell no one about him.

31 And he began to teach them that the Son of man must suffer many things, and be rejected by the elders and the chief priests and the scribes, and be killed, and after three days rise again. 32 And he said this plainly. And Peter took him, and began to rebuke him. 33 But turning and seeing his disciples, he rebuked Peter, and said, "Get behind me, Satan! For you are not on the side of God, but of men."

34 And he called to him the multitude with his disciples, and said to them, "If any man would come after me, let him deny himself and take up his cross and follow me. 35 For whoever would save his life will lose it; and whoever loses his life for my sake and the gospel's will save it. 36 For what does it profit a man, to gain the whole world and forfeit his life? 37 For what can a man give in return for his life? 38 For whoever is ashamed of me and of my words in this adulterous and sinful generation, of him will the Son of man also be ashamed, when he comes in the glory of his Father with the holy angels."

KEY VERSE: *"If any man would come after me, let him deny himself and take up his cross and follow me.* Mark 8:34 (RSV).

HOME DAILY BIBLE READINGS

Mar. 19. M. *Peter's Declaration About Jesus.* Mark 8:27–31.
Mar. 20. T. *Jesus' Transfiguration.* Mark 9:2–8.
Mar. 21. W. *Prophecies About Elijah.* Mark 9:9–13.
Mar. 22. T. *Jesus Shows His Disciples How to Minister.* Mark 9:17–27.
Mar. 23. F. *Passion Foretold and True Greatness.* Mark 9:30–41.
Mar. 24. S. *Consistent Christian Lifestyle.* Mark 9:42–50.
Mar. 25. S. *Jesus Calls for Disciples.* Mark 8:34–9:1.

BACKGROUND

Up to this point, in the book bearing his name, Mark has concentrated on the works of Jesus, His theology and teaching. Now there is a sharp turn from all this to an emphasis upon His disciples who were chosen to carry on after He had gone. The disciples hadn't thought very much about that, but they did from this point on. It was a turning point, too, in the life and work of Jesus, for, with the confession of one of those disciples, He knew that they would carry on after He had left them.

Now they were about to start down a long, long road that led from Galilee to Calvary. It was a road running through a country alien to the Galilean fishermen, a road full of pitfalls. Jesus calls them together to make clear certain things they must know before they started down the road—know about Him, and know about what was about to happen to *them* as they moved out into strange territory.

NOTES ON THE PRINTED TEXT

Jesus did not lay down, in perfect order, any "rules for the road"; at this point He simply made clear certain basic truths on which the disciples must start their work. The first truth was that they must know, beyond the shadow of a doubt, exactly who He was. Up to now, they had no clear view of Him. Neither did the world, into which they were to move, have any clear picture. When He asked them who other men said He was, He got the usual answer: some men thought one thing, some another. Some said He was a prophet—you know, like Elijah. Or like John the Baptist. Or just merely a man who went about doing good. Then He asked His followers who *they* thought He was. Peter, impulsive, dynamic Peter who had not been with Him at His Baptism or on temptation's mount—Peter cried out, "Thou art the Christ!"

That was a long, long leap on Peter's part. Jesus Himself had never told Peter that He was the Messiah, *but Peter knew* it; he had a faith in this Messiah born out of long wonder and striving in his mind. The long leap! It is that for *all of us.* The affirmation that He was the Christ is an act of faith, not of intellectual striving. It was a turning point in Peter's life; it was the prelude to *his* crucifixion and it was a vital moment in the life of Jesus. From then on, He knew that He could build His Kingdom on just such a confession of faith.

But He had a warning for the disciples; He cautioned them to "tell no man" about this. They were not quite ready for that, and neither were the Jews or the Romans or the Greeks. *Their* conversion would take a long, long time. The Kingdom was not to be built in a day or in a thousand days.

Before the world or any part of it was won, Jesus said, He must suffer and *die!* That was like dropping a bomb in their midst. The Messiah suffer? The Son of man be rejected, murdered? A man acquainted with grief, a man of sorrows, *despised?* Why should He as Messiah suffer all that? Even Peter couldn't make himself believe it; he "rebuked" Jesus—and Jesus told him flatly that Satan was speaking through the lips of the Fisherman. Only believe, Peter—and the door will be opened. The cross He must carry was to be the key that would open the way to the Kingdom. That is proven in much history. Even the prophets who speak for God go down to death at the hands of desperate men who are afraid of them and so turn their backs and kill the prophets.

While they were pondering that, Jesus gave them still another truth hard to accept. They, too, as His messengers, must take the road to the cross as they preach His Good News. "Whoever will come after me, let him deny himself, and take up his cross, and follow Me" (*see* verse 34). It wouldn't be easy. Their preaching would be no picnic; it could and would bring death upon them, just as it brought death to their Master. Christianity was and still is no rest camp but headquarters for a battle.

He warned His disciples that he who would save his life in shameful cowardice will *lose* his life. He will stumble blindly to the end of that life as though he were ashamed of Jesus. But he who is willing to lay down his life for Christ's sake will save his life. One may gain the whole world, but he will lose his soul—and there is nothing more precious than his soul. Throw away your life in a selfish hunt for human prosperity and Jesus will be ashamed of *you* on Judgment Day. "No cross, no crown."

Charles H. Spurgeon, one of the greatest preachers of all time, put it in a nutshell when he said, "There are no crown-wearers in heaven who were not crossbearers here below."

SUGGESTIONS TO TEACHERS

As every person who has served in the armed forces knows, you are shipped off immediately after being inducted for several weeks of basic training or boot camp. You are quickly changed from raw recruit to military person by an intensive training and toughening-up program.

Jesus calls persons to minister, or drafts them into His service. He also puts them through a cram course on discipleship.

As teacher, your task in this lesson is to make clear that each person realizes that he or she has been inducted into the service of Jesus Christ, and therefore is expected to undergo rigorous discipline. Begin by remembering that you as teacher have been ordered to report for duty! Using today's Scripture as a "military manual" for new draftees into Christ's cause, lay out the basics.

1. *SACRIFICE.* The ultimate question in every person's life is Jesus', "Who do you say that I am?" (*see* Mark 8:24–30). Peter gives the answer which each person in your class must eventually make: "You are the Christ, the Son of the Living God." Jesus continues, however, to instruct by stating that He will take up a cross and sacrifice His life for others. He calls those who are with Him to lives of sacrifice. Discuss the implications of cross-bearing in a Christian's life in these days. What sacrifices have your people felt called to make (if any)? Just as a person inducted into the service of his/her country must be prepared to give up much, even life itself if necessary, so a man or woman called by Jesus Christ should be ready to forsake personal security, comfort, plans, and freedom out of obedience to Christ's orders.

2. *SUPPLICATION.* Point your class to the Transfiguration account, in which Jesus led three leaders from the disciples' group on a prayer-retreat on the mountain. Help your students to grow in comprehending who Jesus is, just as Peter, James, and John grew into a deeper understanding of Jesus. However, take plenty of time to delve into the story of healing the epileptic boy after the disciples had their mountaintop experience. Particularly take note of the crucial importance of prayer for others. This should offer you an opportunity to talk over the problems and the place of praying in the life of a Christian.

3. *SERVICE.* The lesson must also consider Mark 9:33–41, the question of who is greatest. Jesus' words should be repeated many times daily to each follower: "If any one would be first, he must be last of all and servant of all." Remind the class that the word *ministry* is really the word for being a servant. And each Christian is summoned to be a partner of Christ in ministry or serving! Take some lesson time to reflect together on the place and the means of ministry that each person in the class is called to undertake.

4. *SAVOR.* Christians are the "salt" bringing the savor of God's own harmony and peace to the world. Mark 9:49, 50 describes the distinctive role Christ's peo-

ple must carry out in God's scheme of things. Apart from us as the salt (the preservative agent in those days), society quickly spoils and rots!

TOPIC FOR ADULTS
JESUS CALLS PERSONS TO MINISTER

"One of Doctor Schweitzer's most important concepts is that of the Fellowship of Those Who Bear the Mark of Pain. I and my men have found this Fellowship wherever we have gone. Who are its members? Doctor Schweitzer believes the members are those who have learned by experience what physical pain and bodily anguish mean. These people, all over the world, are united by a secret bond. He who has been delivered from pain must not think he is now free, at liberty to continue his life and forget his sickness. He is a man whose eyes are opened. He now has a duty to help others in their battles with pain and anguish. He must help to bring to others the deliverance which he himself knows."—Thomas A. Dooley, M.D., *The Edge of Tomorrow.*

Ministry to Your Own Family. Every person is called to minister to others. One form of ministry we frequently forget is ministering to our own family. Our "parishes" include our own homes.

A recent study disclosed that if both Mom and Dad attend church regularly, 72 percent of their children remain faithful. It also showed that:

If only Dad attends regularly, 55 percent remain faithful.

If only Mom attends regularly, 15 percent remain faithful.

If neither attend regularly, only 6 percent remain faithful.

Your ministry by being an example to your own child is more important than all the efforts of church and Sunday school. If you are serious about your faith, you will minister by demonstrating it to your family. Attending worship with your family means Christ's ministry will continue for another generation.

Outcome of the Journey. "One thing that brought me back to the church was asking simply: What are the alternatives to the church? Where are the communities that sanction the pursuit of meaning and truth as a legitimate enterprise? that have material and personal resources to assist in this search? that renew and inspire? that provide a setting where children are nurtured? where social issues can be debated? There are a number of institutions that deal with one or several of these questions, but historically the church has demonstrated its ability to energize all of these activities.

"I foresee an emerging membership in Christian churches of those for whom theological interpretations are undergoing important transformations. These are persons who recognize the ultimate emptiness of individualism, who seek membership in a community united by a common symbolic paradigm. They are those who want roots that can be celebrated collectively, they are those who have not given up the search for ultimate Truth, but who in all likelihood have concluded that truth is embodied only in community and is expressed and made available to individuals in the collectively and celebrated rites, acts, and service of the community."—Donald E. Miller, *The Case for Liberal Christianity,* Harper & Row, 1981.

Questions for Pupils on the Next Lesson. 1. Do you feel pressures from society to make self-satisfaction one of your highest priorities? 2. How does the world around us measure personal worth? 3. What persons have you met who have lived lives of humble and sacrificial service to others? 4. Why is jealousy such a common experience in our society? 5. What is your yardstick for a great person?

TOPIC FOR YOUTH
CHOOSING THE BEST WAY

Clear Orders. In the early part of the nineteenth century, the church in England was debating the missionary enterprise. A minister was talking to the duke of Wellington, who was a great Christian as well as a great general. The minister asked the duke whether he believed the church should send missionaries abroad, and Wellington responded by asking, "What are your orders?" The minister hesitated a moment, being puzzled by the question, and finally replied, "I'm not sure what you have in mind, sir. Do you mean, 'Go ye into all the world and preach the gospel'?" "What!" cried the man who had defeated Napoleon at Waterloo, "These are your orders and you debate doing them?" To a man whose first reaction was to obey, to debate when the order was clear was treason.

Pitcher's Ministry. Gary Lavelle, relief pitcher for the San Francisco Giants, has pitched in an All-Star Game. He has also won respect for his witness as a Christian. Lavelle is humble about his ministry. Others, however, praise him for his quiet example and words.

For instance, Rob Andrews, an infielder on the Giants squad in the late 1970s recalls that he had been traded from Baltimore and Houston with a reputation as a hothead. He had many personal problems when he came to the Giants. He found his locker next to Gary Lavelle. "I saw Gary Lavelle go through hard times that would have killed me," Andrews recalls. "But he was always calm. He never preached to me but one day I asked him, 'Gary, what is it?' He said it was Christ." Today, Rob Andrews is a youth pastor and teacher in Concord, California.

Or John Montefusco, who played with Lavelle before being traded to Atlanta, recalls, "When I was pitching for the Giants, I hated to come out of a game, but I always felt better when Gary Lavelle came in for me. You could see he had competitive spirit. He may hold back his feelings, and maybe that's not healthy, but he is one of the finest people I've ever met in baseball. These are good people. They are my friends. I think the press took a few things and blew it all out of proportion to make those guys look bad."

Lavelle says he has tried to avoid the "religious fanatic" label by not preaching to people unless they ask him about his faith. He is disturbed that what seems like a positive to him, a stable life, an even disposition, could be described as a potential detriment for a team.

"It seems so natural to me to carry my faith with me into the locker room," Lavelle says. "I'm not asking for things, but I believe my relationship to Christ makes me a better husband, father, ballplayer. To see it turned around the way it has been—it makes me wonder."

Choosing the Right Way Means Discipline. "Where the disciplines of life have faded, gone also are the exciting dreams and the grand hopes.

"The disciplined life meets failure with determination and confidence. He simply puts his purpose back on the drawing board. He regroups his energies for another try.

"The disciplined life is able to look discouragement in the face, and move beyond it.

"The disciplined man has this advantage, among others, over the undisciplined—he is able to begin the longest journey when he needs to. And this is a great advantage.

"The disciplined man determines a goal, then sets out to reach that goal. He is not easily sidetracked or discouraged. His disciplined pursuit keeps him to his task. His gain is not only in reaching a goal, but in conquering himself.

"The disciplined person does not necessarily have more talent or more ability than the undisciplined, but he is able to apply what he has longer, and hence receives greater return and accomplishment."—C. Neil Strait, *Quote* Magazine.

Sentence Sermon to Remember: A Christian man is the most free lord of all, and subject to none; A Christian man is the most dutiful of all, and subject to everyone.—Martin Luther.

Questions for Pupils on the Next Lesson. 1. Why does our society seem to want to measure personal worth in terms of power, possessions, and prestige? 2. Why do we often interpret humility as weakness? 3. Are you making your choice of career in the light of how you can serve others? 4. Why is it so hard to be unselfish? 5. What are your standards for a "great person"?

LESSON V—APRIL 1

THE WAY OF THE SERVANT

Background Scripture: Mark 10
Devotional Reading: Mark 10:23–31

KING JAMES VERSION

MARK 10 32 And they were in the way going up to Jerusalem; and Jesus went before them: and they were amazed; and as they followed, they were afraid. And he took again the twelve, and began to tell them what things should happen unto him,

33 *Saying,* Behold, we go up to Jerusalem; and the Son of man shall be delivered unto the chief priests, and unto the scribes; and they shall condemn him to death, and shall deliver him to the Gentiles:

34 And they shall mock him, and shall scourge him, and shall spit upon him, and shall kill him; and the third day he shall rise again.

35 And James and John, the sons of Zebedee, come unto him, saying, Master, we would that thou shouldest do for us whatsoever we shall desire.

36 And he said unto them, What would ye that I should do for you?

37 They said unto him, Grant unto us that we may sit, one on thy right hand, and the other on thy left hand, in thy glory.

38 But Jesus said unto them, Ye know not what ye ask: can ye drink of the cup that I drink of? and be baptized with the baptism that I am baptized with?

39 And they said unto him, We can. And Jesus said unto them, Ye shall indeed drink of the cup that I drink of; and with the baptism that I am baptized withal shall ye be baptized:

40 But to sit on my right hand and on my left hand is not mine to give; but *it shall be given to them* for whom it is prepared.

41 And when the ten heard *it,* they began to be much displeased with James and John.

42 But Jesus called them *to him,* and said unto them, Ye know that they which are accounted to rule over the Gentiles exercise lordship over them; and their great ones exercise authority upon them.

43 But so shall it not be among you: but whosoever will be great among you, shall be your minister:

44 And whosoever of you will be the chiefest, shall be servant of all.

45 For even the Son of man came not to be ministered unto, but to minister, and to give his life a ransom for many.

REVISED STANDARD VERSION

MARK 10 32 And they were on the road, going up to Jerusalem, and Jesus was walking ahead of them; and they were amazed, and those who followed were afraid. And taking the twelve again, he began to tell them what was to happen to him, 33 saying, "Behold, we are going up to Jerusalem; and the Son of man will be delivered to the chief priests and the scribes, and they will condemn him to death, and deliver him to the Gentiles; 34 and they will mock him, and spit upon him, and scourge him, and kill him; and after three days he will rise."

35 And James and John, the sons of Zebedee, came forward to him, and said to him, "Teacher, we want you to do for us whatever we ask of you." 36 And he said to them, "What do you want me to do for you?" 37 And they said to him, "Grant us to sit, one at your right hand and one at your left, in your glory." 38 But Jesus said to them, "You do not know what you are asking. Are you able to drink the cup that I drink, or to be baptized with the baptism with which I am baptized?" 39 And they said to him, "We are able." And Jesus said to them, "The cup that I drink you will drink; and with the baptism with which I am baptized, you will be baptized; 40 but to sit at my right hand or at my left is not mine to grant, but it is for those for whom it has been prepared." 41 And when the ten heard it, they began to be indignant at James and John. 42 And Jesus called them to him and said to them, "You know that those who are supposed to rule over the Gentiles lord it over them, and their great men exercise authority over them. 43 But it shall not be so among you; but whoever would be great among you must be your servant, 44 and whoever would be first among you must be slave of all. 45 For the Son of man also came not to be served but to serve, and to give his life as a ransom for many."

KEY VERSE: *"For the Son of man also came not to be served but to serve, and to give his life as a ransom for many."* Mark 10:45 (RSV).

HOME DAILY BIBLE READINGS

Mar. 26. *M.* *The Sacredness of Marriage.* Mark 10:1–12.
Mar. 27. *T.* *Blessing the Children.* Mark 10:13–16.
Mar. 28. *W.* *The Rich and the Kingdom.* March 10:17–31.
Mar. 29. *T.* *Passion Told the Third Time.* Mark 10:32–34.
Mar. 30. *F.* *Making Blind Bartimaeus See.* Mark 10:46–52.
Mar. 31. *S.* *A Mother's Request.* Matthew 20:20–24.
Apr. 1. *S.* *Greatness Comes in Serving.* Mark 10:35–45.

BACKGROUND

Jesus and His disciples were on their way to Jerusalem. Judging from what Mark tells us about that walk, it was a far-from-pleasant one. The Twelve were "afraid." Afraid of what?

They had been a long time with Jesus. They had seen Him give bread to that five thousand; they had seen Him work miracles of healing. They had heard Him confound the Pharisees; they had heard Him preach, had seen Him love. And now, they were on "the last lap," the last long mile, moving toward Jerusalem where death awaited the One they called Master.

Perhaps, it was not so much fear as it was an uncertainty as to what would happen to *them* after it was all over. They were concerned with the Kingdom He had promised them. But—what *sort* of Kingdom? Who would rule it, and how? All twelve of them may have been wondering about that (Do not many of *us* wonder about it, at times?), but two of them, driven by ambition—and ignorance—had the audacity to ask Him to give them seats of high place in the Kingdom—like two petty politicians asking for good appointments from the man for whom they had voted!

NOTES ON THE PRINTED TEXT

The two were James and John, whose mother was Salome. Matthew, in his version of the story, says that it was Salome who made this brash request. If, as many think, this Salome was the sister of the mother of Jesus, then it would seem that either she or her sons were asking for preeminence in the Kingdom because they were "members of the family." Whoever asked it got a devastating answer.

It seems strange that such a question could be asked at all at such a moment. Jesus had just told them, once again, of the manner in which He should die—and rise again—in Jerusalem. That should have stunned them and silenced them; it should have made them weep. But no—they were concerned only with what was to happen to *them*.

Jesus denies their request on two grounds. One was that it was not within His power to grant them such a favor; only God the Father could do that. The other was that they must be *baptized* into the Kingdom. He was speaking here not of a formal baptism with water, but of a baptism that would become real only when they had completed their ministry. It was a baptism of fire and suffering, a baptism in suffering and death and in becoming the servants (slaves) of all mankind and of God.

To be baptized, in the usual sense, meant to be *submerged* in water; in this water, the baptized one was purified and led to a new life. But such baptisms were far different from the one Jesus demanded. The baptism He spoke of meant that they must be immersed in unselfish, all-out service to men—submerged in hatred and pain and death. That was the price of entrance to the Kingdom. To their credit, let it be said that the disciples accepted that challenge, even though they did not fully understand it at the time. Most of them died violent deaths in the service of their Christ.

In our own times, we have an example of Christ's meaning in the words of

Winston Churchill, who at the outbreak of World War II told his people that in resisting the onslaught of wicked Nazism, he could offer them only "blood, sweat, toil, and tears." A baptism of fire! That was what Jesus was offering James and John: if they could pass through the toil and tears and martyrdom of *service* to their God, then they would have in their hands the keys to the Kingdom. It could come no other way. The route to heaven is the road to the cross.

We have said that the Twelve accepted the challenge of Jesus; that is true, but there was still some murmuring among the other ten of the disciples. They were indignant, mad at James and John for asking such a question. When they did that, they were thinking of leadership in terms of the old rule of government by kings—kings like the detestable Caligula and Nero. That was "Gentile law," or the way the Gentiles did it. The kings and emperors of the day did as they pleased, and they did it to all of their subjects; they ruled by a ridiculous "divine right of kings"; they murdered their opposition. Jesus rejected that. He saw nothing divine in any of it; against this rule of tyrant kings, He established a new brand of king ruling under the law of the Gospel, of love, of *service.* "Whosoever would be first among you," He told the ten, "must be the slave of all" (verse 44). The great among us are not those who have been given any special privilege or position among men; they are those who earn their greatness in service.

Jesus went one step further: He reminded the twelve that He Himself exemplified the suffering servant, and He had come not to be ministered unto, but to minister to others, to give His life as a ransom for many. He laid down His life to "ransom" us, to bring us back to God. The cross on Calvary was the price paid for our salvation.

Do you long to "play Hamlet," to have the part of a star, a highly successful man among men? Jesus never longed for anything like that; neither did the disciples who laid down their lives in love, not only for God but for mankind.

SUGGESTIONS TO TEACHERS

A church member whose daughter was part of the church junior-high fellowship was called and asked to help prepare a snack-supper for the group on a certain Sunday night. The parent reacted as if it would be an impossible imposition. The caller politely persisted. The mother of the junior-high student replied, "You mean you are asking me to come up to the church and do a *servant's* work?"

Exactly. That's what Christian discipleship is all about. Jesus served. He gave His life for others. His words should be emblazoned on the walls of every Christian's home: "The Son of Man came not to be served but to serve, and to give His life as a ransom for many." Likewise, as your lesson must make abundantly clear, every Christian must realize that he or she is not seeking to be served but to serve!

The lesson material for today comes from Mark 10. Here are a series of descriptions of realms in which Jesus means for us to be serving. Mark them carefully:

1. *MARRIAGE/SPOUSE.* With the climbing of the national divorce rate and the erosion of traditional sexual values in our society, the Church has done little except view with alarm. Today's lesson offers positive help. Christians are called to live as *servants*—and this includes the area of marriage and sex. Humbly giving one's self to the other, or seeking to serve rather than be served, is the practical application of Jesus' words to us in these days. Christians who are husbands or wives will not think in terms of "self-fulfillment."

2. *CHILDREN/FAMILY.* Mark 10 provides good insights on how Christians who are living in families must also willingly undertake the way of the servant. Everyone in your class already knows that the family is in serious trouble. In fact, some of the families represented in your class undoubtedly have had or currently

have problems. Let your class take off on the suggestion that servanthood as a Christian applies particularly to persons who are parents or children, or living under the same roof with others.

3. *POSSESSIONS/PROPERTY.* Every person in your class owns many things. Although each will at first think he/she has relatively little, especially compared to Greek shipping tycoons and Arab oil princes, remind them that they actually possess much. Possessions, including money, are not evil in themselves. It's what they can do. Or, rather, what the owner will do with them. In the case of Christians, Jesus insists that we use what we have to serve others. Do your class members have this notion of servanthood in regard to their checkbooks?

4. *RECOGNITION/AUTHORITY.* Don't let the lesson go too far without devoting a hefty slice of time on Mark 10:35–45. Remind your class that the real authority of a Christian lies in his or her servanthood! Discuss ways in which even Church people sometimes try to lord it over each other.

5. *UNFORTUNATE/UNWASHED.* Jesus constantly encountered suffering persons. Often, like the blind beggar in Mark 10:46, they were unpleasant and difficult. Jesus consistently served—even the blind beggars. If we are truly Christ's, we can do no less! Talk about the "blind beggars" whom your congregation should be serving in your community.

TOPIC FOR ADULTS
NOT TO BE SERVED BUT TO SERVE

The Way of the Servant. A new student at Union Seminary in New York arrived in a taxi. Noticing a white-haired man in shirtsleeves standing by the door of the dormitory, the student asked rather arrogantly, "Hey, mister, do you work here?" Hearing that the man did, the new arrival commanded, "Then you may take my bags up to room 309." The older man silently picked up two heavy suitcases and trudged up the three flights of stairs to the door of 309. The student followed, holding only his raincoat and a light briefcase. When the door was opened, the new student casually flipped the person who'd carried the baggage a small coin. The gentleman with the white hair politely thanked the young fellow, but declined the tip. The following day, the newly-arrived student joined the rest of the seminary community in the opening communion service. He was horrified to see that the man he had assumed was the porter was wearing a pulpit robe and presiding at worship. When he whispered to a neighbor, the young student learned that the white-haired man was the president of the Seminary, the illustrious Dr. Henry Sloane Coffin. Rushing up to President Coffin afterward, the student began to stammer apologies for so brusquely commanding Dr. Coffin to carry his bags. The great scholar-pastor-teacher allowed himself a small smile, and gently answered, "The Son of Man came not to be served but to serve. We must do likewise." It was the most important lesson that young ministerial student learned during his three years at Union.

Servants as Lights. Alasdair Crotsch was Chief of the MacLeods in the first half of the sixteenth century and lived at Dunvegan, Isle of Skye.

Once he was visiting at Holyrood House in Edinburgh. A Lowland noble sneered at him, "You have no such hall, no such table, and no such candlesticks in Skye." Alasdair replied, "Sir, if you and the King come to Dunvegan, I will show you a nobler hall, a finer table, and more precious candlesticks than you have here."

The king arrived with his fleet the following year. Alasdair pointed to the flat-topped hill, Realaval Mor, or MacLeod's Table, and led the way to the top where hundreds of sturdy clansmen were gathered on the summit, each holding a flaming torch of pine.

"Here are my candlesticks, your majesty's faithful servants. I ask you to partake of the banquet which is spread on my table by the light of my torches which my sconces hold."

We are "Christ's candlesticks." As servants of the One who came saying, "I am the Light of the world," we are to be bringers of light, or sharers of His light. This means not seeking to be served but to serve!

Four Weeks out of Four. For a Christian, marriage is a test of whether he or she truly tries to live a life of being one who serves. Married persons who find their marriages vital know that neither can seek to be served. Each must seek to serve. Unfortunately, however, Hollywood instead of the New Testament often seems to provide our examples and guidelines in marriage. One Hollywood actor is taken seriously by many when he speaks about his marriage in terms of demanding to have others please him. "I don't believe in marriage," he says. "I think it's a custom brought about by women who then proceed to live off men and destroy them. . . . I have given my wife a new plan for our marriage. . . . I have told her we will spend roughly one week out of four together. If she doesn't like it, that's the end of our marriage. . . . I will go off with women when I like, and she can do what she wants. That's the way it has to be, or it's all over."

Questions for Pupils on the Next Lesson. 1. Why did Jesus drive the money-changers and sellers of animals out of the Temple? 2. Why did the chief priests want to destroy Jesus? 3. What are the chief evils in our society and its institutions? 4. Is anger ever justified? 5. When has your faith required personal risks on your part?

TOPIC FOR YOUTH
THE WAY TO GREATNESS

Silly Greatness. Our idea of greatness is strutting and shouting in a mighty way so that others will take notice. Of course, this is exactly the opposite of Jesus' idea of greatness. Nevertheless, we are more like the chief of the Macneils, the Scottish clan head who pompously ruled a tiny domain on the island of Barra off the western coast of Scotland. His island was small, and its satellite islands—among them Mingulay, Vatersay, Eriskay—were little more than rocks, but he was *the* Macneil, the sort of man that was once called mighty. In the evenings after dinner, the Macneil would go out onto the battlements of his seabound Kisimul Castle, wipe his lips, sound a trumpet, and shout into the Atlantic winds, "Hear, O ye people! And listen, O ye nations! The Macneil of Barra has eaten! The princes of the earth may now dine!"

We smile at the Macneil's pretensions. His "greatness" seems silly. However, any ideas of greatness apart from Jesus' way of servanthood are just as silly. Whenever we try to measure greatness in terms of power, possessions, or prestige, we are acting as preposterously as the "mighty" Macneil.

Greatness in a Duke. One of the greatest castles in England is Arundel. One of the first families of British aristocracy owns the castle, the Norfolk family. The duke of Norfolk stands first among the dukes.

Once a certain duke of Norfolk happened to be at the railway station near his castle. A little Irish girl was trying to persuade a porter to carry her heavy bag to the castle. She offered him a shilling, which was all the money she had. The porter contemptuously refused. The duke then stepped forward, shabby as he usually was in appearance. He offered to carry her bag to the castle, took it and walked beside her along the road to the castle, talking pleasantly to her.

At the end of the journey, he gratefully accepted the shilling she offered him, never allowing her to know who he was. It was only the next day when she met her employer, that the little Irish girl knew that the premier duke of Britain, the duke of Norfolk, had carried her bag from the station and that she had tipped him a shilling!

The greatest person is not always dressed like a fashion plate. A truly fine person is always a thoughtful person. He or she is thoughtful of others. The duke of Norfolk in the story was too fine a man to embarrass the little girl who had come from Ireland to take a job in his household service, to tell her who he was. He let her think he was just a kind of handyman ready to earn a few cents if he could.

A person with marks of greatness of character never worries about his position, his rank, his place, his name. The porter at the little railway station of Arundel wrapped himself in his little authority. The duke to whom the top rank belonged forgot about it. A much greater man than any duke said, "He that would be greatest among you must be the servant of all." No act of service can be so small, so humble, that it can be beneath a real person's dignity.

Serving Others Instead of Saving Himself. Major John Foote was a chaplain in the Royal Hamilton Light Infantry in World War II. On August 18, 1942, Major Foote went ashore with his troops in the great commando raid on Dieppe. The losses were staggering. Due to many causes, a large number of Canadians were unable to be evacuated from the town and had to be left behind. Foote had personally carried and pushed into boats thirty blinded or wounded Canadian soldiers. Finally the order was given to withdraw. Foote was safely on board a small boat which would have taken him to a larger craft and ultimately back to England. Foote, however, remembered that there were two thousand wounded Canadians still on the streets and docks of Dieppe. He knew they would be captured, perhaps tortured and shot, perhaps left in prison camps for what would be a long war. He knew that they would need all the encouragement and comfort to face the future that anyone could give—and that he was the only padre at Dieppe. Without hesitating, John Foote jumped over the side of his boat and waded ashore. He deliberately went back to be with men without hope, and spent three long, miserable years in Nazi prison camps.

Sentence Sermon to Remember: Doctrine divides but Service unites.—Nathan Soderblom.

Questions for Pupils on the Next Lesson. 1. Why did Jesus throw the money-changers and animal sellers out of the temple area? 2. Why do you sometimes face hostility when you try to help others? 3. When have you ever spoken out against prejudice or mistreatment of others? 4. Is it wrong to feel anger? 5. What makes you most upset in life? Why?

LESSON VI—APRIL 8

CONFRONTATION IN JERUSALEM

Background Scripture: Mark 11:1–12:44
Devotional Reading: Mark 12:28–34

KING JAMES VERSION

MARK 11 8 And many spread their garments in the way; and others cut down branches off the trees, and strewed *them* in the way.

9 And they that went before, and they that followed, cried, saying, Hosanna; Blessed *is* he that cometh in the name of the Lord:

10 Blessed *be* the kingdom of our father David, that cometh in the name of the Lord: Hosanna in the highest.

15 And they come to Jerusalem: and Jesus went into the temple, and began to cast out them that sold and bought in the temple, and overthrew the tables of the money changers, and the seats of them that sold doves;

16 And would not suffer that any man should carry *any* vessel through the temple.

17 And he taught, saying unto them, Is it not written, My house shall be called of all nations the house of prayer? but ye have made it a den of thieves.

18 And the scribes and chief priests heard *it,* and sought how they might destroy him: for they feared him, because all the people was astonished at his doctrine.

19 And when even was come, he went out of the city.

27 And they come again to Jerusalem: and as he was walking in the temple, there come to him the chief priests, and the scribes, and the elders,

28 And say unto him, By what authority doest thou these things? and who gave thee this authority to do these things?

29 And Jesus answered and said unto them, I will also ask of you one question, and answer me, and I will tell you by what authority I do these things.

30 The baptism of John, was *it* from heaven, or of men? answer me.

31 And they reasoned with themselves, saying, If we shall say, From heaven; he will say, Why then did ye not believe him?

32 But if we shall say, Of men; they feared the people: for all *men* counted John, that he was a prophet indeed.

33 And they answered and said unto Jesus, We cannot tell. And Jesus answering saith unto them, Neither do I tell you by what authority I do these things.

REVISED STANDARD VERSION

MARK 11 8 And many spread their garments on the road, and others spread leafy branches which they had cut from the fields.

9 And those who went before and those who followed cried out, "Hosanna! Blessed is he who comes in the name of the Lord! 10 Blessed is the kingdom of our father David that is coming! Hosanna in the highest!"

15 And they came to Jerusalem. And he entered the temple and began to drive out those who sold and those who bought in the temple, and he overturned the tables of the moneychangers and the seats of those who sold pigeons; 16 and he would not allow any one to carry anything through the temple. 17 And he taught, and said to them, "Is it not written, 'My house shall be called a house of prayer for all the nations'? But you have made it a den of robbers." 18 And the chief priests and the scribes heard it and sought a way to destroy him; for they feared him, because all the multitude was astonished at his teaching. 19 And when evening came they went out of the city.

27 And they came again to Jerusalem. And as he was walking in the temple, the chief priests and the scribes and the elders came to him, 28 and they said to him, "By what authority are you doing these things, or who gave you this authority to do them?" 29 Jesus said to them, "I will ask you a question; answer me, and I will tell you by what authority I do these things. 30 Was the baptism of John from heaven or from men? Answer me." 31 And they argued with one another, "If we say, 'From heaven,' he will say, 'Why then did you not believe him?' 32 But shall we say, 'From men'?"—they were afraid of the people, for all held that John was a real prophet. 33 So they answered Jesus, "We do not know." And Jesus said to them, "Neither will I tell you by what authority I do these things."

KEY VERSE: " 'The very stone which the builders rejected has become the head of the corner.' " Mark 12:10 (RSV).

HOME DAILY BIBLE READINGS

Apr. 2. *M.* *Entry Into Jerusalem.* Mark 11:1–11.
Apr. 3. *T.* *Cleansing the Temple.* Mark 11:15–19.
Apr. 4. *W.* *Questioning Jesus' Authority.* Mark 11:27–33.
Apr. 5. *T.* *Parable of the Vineyard.* Mark 12:1–12.
Apr. 6. *F.* *Paying Taxes.* Mark 12:13–17.
Apr. 7. *S.* *Questions About the Resurrection.* Mark 12:18–27.
Apr. 8. *S.* *The Great Commandment.* Mark 12:28–34.

BACKGROUND

Long, long ago (250 B.C.), before Jesus came, the Prophet Zechariah predicted this: "Rejoice greatly, O daughter of Zion; shout, O daughter of Jerusalem: behold, thy king cometh unto thee: he is just, and having salvation; lowly, and riding upon an ass, and upon a colt the foal of an ass" (Zechariah 9:9). Now we see Jesus Christ riding into Jerusalem on a donkey—an unbroken colt.

Jesus planned that entrance carefully. He entered David's city during the celebration of Passover; the city was jammed with thousands of people come to celebrate this day of days, and to worship in the Temple. Many of them had heard of Jesus and respected Him; others despised Him, and some others were already planning His death. It was a dangerous thing for Him to do, but this Christ was never a man to run from danger. His courage was magnificent.

And His purpose was clear. He came to demonstrate to the people that He was the Messiah promised by Zechariah. He came as a King. He came riding an ass, just as earthly kings rode when they came in peace. Jesus came into the city claiming to be a King of peace. That was a contradiction of the belief that the Messiah would come as a smashing, warlike conqueror who would restore Israel to her past glory by way of all-out war.

NOTES ON THE PRINTED TEXT

He rode into a cheering crowd. Palms were thrown at His feet; they even threw their garments for Him to walk upon. And they shouted, "Hosanna!" That word is often interpreted to mean *praise*—and that is wrong. It is a transliteration of a Hebrew word which means, "Save, we beseech thee." It is a word used in 2 Samuel 14:4 and 2 Kings 6:26: "Help, O king," It was *not* a word of praise, but a cry to God to save His people now that the Messiah had come. The picture of the people throwing palm branches and their garments has an Old Testament background.

Once within the gates of Jerusalem, Jesus went at once to the Temple, entering the Temple precincts by way of the Court of the Gentiles. This court was filled with pilgrims who gathered there to pay a Temple tax of one half a shekel a year and to purchase sacrificial doves. Those doves could be bought more cheaply outside the Temple area; the merchants *inside* charged an exorbitant price. This court was meant to be a place of prayer, but it had become a den of thieves—of profiteers and money-changers.

For once in His life, Jesus flew into a rage; He kicked over the money-changers' tables and drove them from the court. Nowhere else in His ministry did He become so infuriated. But it is worth remembering that He went just so far—and then stopped. His rage died quickly.

What made Him so mad? He resented the exploitation of the poor; He protested the desecration of (God's) Temple. This Temple, He cried, was intended to be a place of prayer *for all nations;* it had become a headquarters for racketeers—and He could not tolerate that.

Think on all this. How often do we find the modern Church desecrated by people who use it to make money! Today we have a host of false prophets and preaching cultists—"preachers" who live as millionnaires reaping fortunes at the expense of many who can ill afford to pay. That is the desecration which Jesus *hates*.

All this happened during the first day in Jerusalem. That night, He went out to Bethany to rest—in the home of Mary and Martha and Lazarus.

The second day, He went back to the Temple where He met a delegation (self-appointed) of chief priests, scribes, and elders who were waiting for Him. You could call them a miniature mob who came in fear and anger at one who had dared to question their authority in all matters religious. (They knew all about the money-changers; in fact, some of them might have been sharing the profiteers' profit.) They had to stop this man at any cost.

They asked Jesus just who He thought He was, to do such things, to teach such things, in their Temple area. By what authority did He presume to do all this? (Aye, there was the rub—He had questioned *their* authority!) *They* were in charge here. Just where did He get *His* authority?

It was a tricky question and a trap. If He said He was doing it on His own personal authority, they could have Him arrested. If He claimed any authority from God, they could arrest Him for blasphemy. Either way, they thought they had Him at last.

Not quite. Jesus answered their question with a question of His own, and put *them* in a trap. If they answered His question, He said, He would answer theirs. The question: "Was the baptism of John the Baptist from heaven, or from men?" Was John the possessor of divine authority, or only of an authority bestowed by men?

They cringed. If they said that John's baptism—and authority—were divinely bestowed, Jesus might ask them why they opposed it. If they said that John's work was only a human work, humanly inspired, they were in trouble, for John had become a martyr loved by the people. They couldn't risk offending the people! It was a question they couldn't answer at all. So they mumbled, helplessly, "We do not know." With one final blow, Jesus left them speechless: "Neither will I tell you by what authority I do these things." End of the argument!

Involved in all this are jealousy, fear, and a refusal to face the truth about Jesus Christ. These men were looking at truth in the face of the Christ, and refused to admit it. It is a common sin, now as then.

SUGGESTIONS TO TEACHERS

"Why do you take the opinions and instructions of Jesus so seriously all the time? After all, he has been dead for 1,900 years. Why not listen to other teachers and leaders also?" The questioner was a highly intelligent, articulate graduate student demanding an answer from the person sitting next to her on a cross-continent flight who had disclosed by a comment that she was a Christian.

Ask yourself the woman's question: Why do you take Jesus' opinions and instructions so seriously? Why should you? Why should your class?

Your lesson this Sunday will find you and your class struggling with this question. Jesus, you will quickly discover, makes claims on you and your class. Although the setting in Scripture is the confrontation in Jerusalem, you will find that Jesus also confronts you where you are! Examine His claims.

1. *CLAIMS WITH CLEANSING.* Throughout the eleventh and twelfth chapters of Mark, the authoritative claims of Christ are pitted against the authoritarian claims of the Temple. Jesus' cleansing the Temple was not merely an angry outburst. It was a carefully thought-out demonstration of His authority. It was a coolly-planned tactic within the overall strategy of confronting the world with His claims. Talk with your class about the meaning of His announcing that the Temple was to be a "house of prayer for all the nations."

2. *CLAIMS IN CONFRONTATION.* Call attention to Jesus' staunch courage in the face of fierce opposition. Although Jesus recognized that Temple authorities wanted to destroy Him (and eventually would), He persisted with His claims. Jesus confronted the entrenched evil these leaders represented. Your lesson must devote time on how Christian disciples must persist in their mission even though it involves personal risks. The evils in society and its institutions are deep and vicious. Jesus, however, gives us His authority to persevere in ministry.

3. *CLAIMS AS CORNERSTONE.* Your class will be edified by the parable of the vineyard which Jesus told (March 12:1–12). Jesus left no doubts in the minds of His hearers about who He claimed to be. He is also the "cornerstone" of all our belief-systems and, indeed, of all our living. It would be profitable to take a hard look at the way your people use their money or form their opinions, for instance, in the light of Jesus' claims. Is He truly the cornerstone for your ideas on leisure, on sex, on possessions, on the handicapped, on refugees, on weapon stockpiling, etc.?

4. *CLAIMS FROM QUESTIONS.* Your class will enjoy talking about the way Jesus handled the trick questions put to Him (Mark 12:13–27). Remind your folks, however, that Jesus is doing more than demonstrating His skills of thinking on His feet and avoiding being trapped. He is stating His claims of authority over Temple and Caesar, over tradition and Scripture. Jesus maintains that He must take precedence over everyone and everything!

5. *CLAIMS REGARDING COFFERS.* The delightful little vignette of the widow's mite (Mark 12:41–44) provides a final illustration of Jesus' claim of being the authority. He deliberately sets Himself against popular opinion which said the bigger the gift, the better the person. Pitting yourself against the awesome authority of popular opinion takes exceptional courage! Ask your class to give examples where Jesus' claims mean Christians must flout the authority of what others may think.

TOPIC FOR ADULTS
CONFRONTING ENTRENCHED EVIL

Ministry on Molokai. Joseph de Veuster grew up in Belgium. When his brother was prevented from serving as a missionary because of illness, the young man volunteered to take his brother's place. Taking the name Father Damien after being ordained a priest in 1864, he arrived in Honolulu in the Hawaiian Islands. He was not intending to remain long in Hawaii, but to travel on to serve elsewhere. During his stopover in Hawaii, he noticed the wretched condition of those suffering from leprosy. The authorities, Father Damien learned, deported all those suffering from the dreaded disease to the island of Molokai and left them practically without help. Father Damien saw that neither the leaders of the islands nor the church people would associate with these lepers. Cancelling his plans to serve as a missionary in another area, Father Damien moved to Molokai in 1873. He dressed the sores of the lepers. He washed their bodies. He built their huts. He made their coffins and buried their dead (over 1,600 of them in the first six years he spent on Molokai). Some said, "There was not a pot or a pan on Molokai that Damien had not washed." He also preached the Gospel, beginning each message with the loving words, "My brethren."

One day, he could not feel any sensation of pain in his feet. He knew that this was the first sign of leprosy. Instead of opening his chapel services with the phrase, "My brethren," there came the time when he quietly said, "We lepers."

Father Damien only served sixteen years on Molokai before dying of leprosy at the age of forty-nine. He confronted the entrenched evil of destructive disease and indifferent bureaucracy by sacrificing his life. However, Damien's "failure" won a victory for the care of victims of leprosy everywhere and spurred compassion toward those afflicted by the terrible disease.

Confronting Entrenched Evil of Armaments. The Club of Rome in its third report outlines eight major areas where disaster looms ahead if mankind pursues his present policies.

Leading the list is the arms race which is depriving mankind of enormous financial and human resources as "almost half the world's scientific and technological manpower devote their skills to military research and development." Military expenditures are almost three hundred thousand million dollars a year, and by the mid 1980s the world's nuclear reactors will have produced about a million pounds of plutonium, enough to manufacture fifty thousand bombs. The Club of Rome gave a solemn warning on the situation when they said:

"The problem is not to shift from a war to a peace economy, but from a war to a peace mentality." Whether mankind is able to achieve this will largely determine its chances of surviving the twentieth century.

More Than Laws. Some think that all we have to do in confronting entrenched evil is to pass some more laws. Although there is, of course, the need for laws, merely adding to the legal code will not remove evil. In fact, we already have more than enough laws.

Some of these parts of our legal system are in the category of "crazy laws," but they are nevertheless on the books. For instance, there is a Danville, Pennsylvania, statute which says that "all fire hydrants must be checked one hour before all fires." And, in Cold Springs, Pennsylvania, "liquor may not be sold to a married man except with the written consent from his wife."

In Marengo, Iowa, the law says that not more than twenty-seven persons shall participate in a baseball game.

In Muskogee, Oklahoma, an old city ordinance states no visiting baseball teams shall be allowed to hit a ball over the fence or out of the park.

A Portsmouth, Ohio, law ranks baseball players with "vagrants, thieves, and other suspicious characters."

According to state law in Maine, fishermen must take off their hats to game wardens.

It is illegal to fish on a Chicago breakwater in pajamas.

In the District of Columbia, it is illegal to catch fish while on horseback.

To catch a whale in the inland waters of Oklahoma is against the law.

In Albany, New York, you cannot play golf in the street.

It is against the law of Florida to hunt or kill a deer while in swimming.

In Tennessee, you can't shoot any game other than whales from a moving car.

Hunting with a rifle is permitted in Norfolk County, Virginia, as long as the hunter is fifteen feet off the ground.

New York City says you can't shoot rabbits from the rear of the Third Avenue streetcar—when the car is in motion.

McPherson, Kansas, law forbids small boys to play marbles, "lest they acquire a taste for gambling."

And Homer, Illinois, law forbids anyone but a police officer to carry a sling shot.

Admittedly, these rules on the statute books are silly and unenforceable. However, they all were passed at one time to combat what was considered to be entrenched evil. Laws are necessary in our imperfect society, but needed more are courageous and conscientious citizens!

Questions for Pupils on the Next Lesson. 1. What did Jesus mean at the Last Supper when He spoke of "my blood of the covenant, which is poured out for many"? 2. Why was Jesus so sorrowful in the Garden of Gethsemane? 3. Are

Christians ever susceptible to moral failures? 4. Why do we shrink from experiences that involve pain and rejection? 5. What bold but rash commitments have you made to God?

TOPIC FOR YOUTH
STAND UP AND BE COUNTED

The Best Things in the Worst of Times. A plaque stands in the chapel of Stainton Herold in the English Midlands. In this church, the neighbors have met to worship for more than three hundred years and to this day there stands this dedicatory inscription:

"In the year 1653, when all things sacred were throughout ye nation either demolisht or profaned, Sir Robert Shirely, Baronet, founded this church: whose singular praise it is to have done the best things in the worst times, and hoped them in the most calamitous."

Where Does Your Money Go? Christians must stand up and be counted when it comes to the use of money. Recent statistics show that we spend enormous sums for our pleasure or comfort. Look at the following list, then ask yourself if your spending reflects your faith.

Roller skates $140 million; barbells/weights $200 million; Casio watches $20 million; sports medicine $2 billion; tennis $340 million; hair transplants $10 million; swimming $1 billion; dance/exercise programs $40 billion; clothes $5 billion; skiing $570 million; golf $480 million; baseball $160 million; shoes $1 billion; health clubs $3 billion; electronic gadgetry $600 million; cosmetic surgery $1 billion; diet pills $200 million; diet drinks $6 billion; bottled water $2 billion; vitamins $2 billion; health foods $3 billion; diet/exercise books $50 million estimate; bikes $1 billion; stationary exercise bikes $400 million.

Whom to Blame? An unusual twist developed in a murder trial in Danbury, Connecticut a couple of years ago. Arne Cheyenne Johnson, nineteen, was on trial for the stabbing death of Alan Bono. Johnson's lawyer, Martin Minnella, tried to prove that Johnson was "possessed" by the devil when he attacked and killed Bono in an argument over a girl friend. Minnella's defense was to subpoena several priests to try to "prove" that the devil made Johnson do it, literally. The state prosecutor maintained that the case was a "routine murder, insofar as a homicide can be classified as routine."

We have to accept responsibility. We cannot blame another, whether the devil or God, the president or parents, or anyone. Further, we have to be willing to stand up and be counted when we encounter evil.

Sentence Sermon to Remember: If Shakespeare should come into this room, we would all rise; but if Jesus should come in, we would all kneel.—Charles Lamb.

Questions for Pupils on the Next Lesson. 1. Why do you think that Judas betrayed Jesus and Peter denied Jesus? 2. What did Jesus mean when He spoke of the "blood of the new covenant" at the Last Supper? 3. Why did Jesus pray to have the cup of suffering removed from Him when He was in the Garden of Gethsemane? 4. Why is it so hard to establish priorities? 5. What Christian symbols mean the most to you and why?

LESSON VII—APRIL 15

IN THE SHADOW OF THE CROSS

Background Scripture: Mark 14
Devotional Reading: Mark 14:3–9

KING JAMES VERSION

MARK 14 22 And as they did eat, Jesus took bread, and blessed, and brake *it*, and gave to them, and said, Take, eat; this is my body.

23 And he took the cup, and when he had given thanks, he gave *it* to them: and they all drank of it.

24 And he said unto them, This is my blood of the new testament, which is shed for many.

25 Verily I say unto you, I will drink no more of the fruit of the vine, until that day that I drink it new in the kingdom of God.

26 And when they had sung an hymn, they went out into the mount of Olives.

27 And Jesus saith unto them, All ye shall be offended because of me this night: for it is written, I will smite the shepherd, and the sheep shall be scattered.

28 But after that I am risen, I will go before you into Galilee.

29 But Peter said unto him, Although all shall be offended, yet *will* not I.

30 And Jesus saith unto him, Verily I say unto thee, That this day, *even* in this night, before the cock crow twice, thou shalt deny me thrice.

31 But he spake the more vehemently, If I should die with thee, I will not deny thee in any wise. Likewise also said they all.

32 And they came to a place which was named Gethsemane: and he saith to his disciples, Sit ye here, while I shall pray.

33 And he taketh with him Peter and James and John, and began to be sore amazed, and to be very heavy;

34 And saith unto them, My soul is exceeding sorrowful unto death: tarry ye here, and watch.

35 And he went forward a little, and fell on the ground, and prayed that, if it were possible, the hour might pass from him.

36 And he said, Abba, Father, all things *are* possible unto thee; take away this cup from me: nevertheless, not what I will, but what thou wilt.

REVISED STANDARD VERSION

MARK 14 22 And as they were eating, he took bread, and blessed, and broke it, and gave it to them, and said, "Take; this is my body." 23 And he took a cup, and when he had given thanks he gave it to them, and they all drank of it. 24 And he said to them, "This is my blood of the covenant, which is poured out for many. 25 Truly, I say to you, I shall not drink again of the fruit of the vine until that day when I drink it new in the kingdom of God."

26 And when they had sung a hymn, they went out to the Mount of Olives. 27 And Jesus said to them, "You will all fall away; for it is written, 'I will strike the shepherd, and the sheep will be scattered.' 28 But after I am raised up, I will go before you to Galilee." 29 Peter said to him, "Even though they all fall away, I will not." 30 And Jesus said to him, "Truly I say to you, this very night, before the cock crows twice, you will deny me three times." 31 But he said vehemently, "If I must die with you, I will not deny you." And they all said the same.

32 And they went to a place which was called Gethsemane; and he said to his disciples, "Sit here, while I pray." 33 And he took with him Peter and James and John, and began to be greatly distressed and troubled. 34 And he said to them, "My soul is very sorrowful, even to death; remain here, and watch." 35 And going a little farther, he fell on the ground and prayed that, if it were possible, the hour might pass from him. 36 And he said, "Abba, Father, all things are possible to thee; remove this cup from me; yet not what I will, but what thou wilt."

KEY VERSE: "... *remove this cup from me; yet not what I will, but what thou wilt.*" Mark 14:36 (RSV).

HOME DAILY BIBLE READINGS

Apr. 9. M. *The Plot Against Jesus.* Mark 14:1, 2, 10, 11.
Apr. 10. T. *Anointing for Burial.* Mark 14:3–9.
Apr. 11. W. *The Last Supper.* Mark 14:17–31.
Apr. 12. T. *Praying at Gethsemane.* Mark 14:32–42.
Apr. 13. F. *The Arrest of Jesus.* Mark 14:43–52.

Apr. 14. S. On Trial. Mark:14:53–65.
Apr. 15. S. Peter Denies Jesus. Mark 14:66–72.

BACKGROUND

When Jesus and His disciples entered Jerusalem, they walked in the shadow of the cross. The timing was perfect; Jesus chose this moment, this day, for His final supper with the disciples who must have seen some connection of this supper with the historic Passover Feast in Egypt (*see* Exodus 12:11–14). That first Passover meal was to be remembered "by an ordinance for ever," a Feast that would never let them forget their deliverance from Egypt. They did not forget; they celebrate Passover to this day.

But while Jesus allied this first Passover supper in Egypt with His Last Supper in the upper room, He gave this, His Supper, an entirely different meaning. He gave them a new Covenant.

NOTES ON THE PRINTED TEXT

In the old covenant, Moses sprinkled blood upon the people by way of binding them in allegiance with God. This was a covenant based upon strict obedience to God. Break that law or any part of it, Moses warned, and you cut yourself off from God. Jesus put it otherwise; fellowship with God, He said, depended upon the blood that He would shed on Calvary. It was blood shed in love and not in obedience. He took the bread of the feast and told the disciples that this bread was His body; He gave them wine to drink and said that it was *His* blood. "Do ye this in remembrance of me."

Some call all this "symbolic." Others take it literally—just as a Catholic priest and some Protestant ministers claim that when a communicant of today eats the bread and drinks the wine, he is actually eating Christ's body and drinking His blood. Be that as it may, we can and must accept the explanation of Jesus Himself that just as the communion bread was broken, so was His body to be broken; just as the wine was poured out, so was His blood to be poured out on the cross. This we must do in remembrance of Him.

Jesus knew well that it would take some time for the disciples to understand and accept that. After the Supper, they all went out to the Mount of Olives. Something was said there that Mark does not mention. It must have hurt Him, for from His lips came a mild rebuke to a band of men overwhelmed and confused by the rapidly unfolding events. Men seldom speak wisely or understand well under pressure, and these men had more than they could bear this night.

Jesus quoted from Zechariah (13:7): the shepherd would be smitten; the sheep would be scattered, would run for cover, desert Him. He was right; the disciples in Gethsemane *slept* while He suffered agony.

They couldn't understand it. Peter refused to accept it. "Me, desert you? Never! Even if the rest of them leave you, I never will!" Peter was a man often torn apart by emotion, fickle, mercurial, too hasty in speech. Not betray the Lord? Oh, yes, you will, said Jesus. Before the cock crows twice before tomorrow morning, you will deny me three times. That is exactly what Peter did (Mark 14:72). And he wept even as he did it.

They walked on to the beautiful and fateful garden of Gethsemane. Why Gethsemane? It is likely that Jesus had been in this garden before this time; it may have been the property of some friend. Actually, Jesus had no other place to go; His enemies were looking for Him in Jerusalem (where there were no gardens). He led the way to this garden late at night, hoping to spend His last hours on earth with that little company of men who had been for so long fellow-workers in His ministry. All of them were there, save Judas. But Judas would soon appear.

He asked them to sit with Him while He prayed. They didn't sit; they fell asleep. Only Peter, James, and John, the most faithful, were near Him as He began His prayer. He said to them, "My soul is exceedingly sorrowful unto death; tarry ye here, and watch" (verse 34). The death watch! In other words, He was crushed, almost fallen helpless, almost giving up. In this moment of near despair and defeat, He begged His Father that the cup of bitterness that He was about to drink (death on the cross) might pass from Him, that He might somehow escape that fate.

Yes, even our Lord had this moment of despondency. For once (and, who knows, perhaps at other times), His flesh was weak, His mission seemed a failure, and His God seemed so far, far away! But it was only for a moment; He recovered quickly and prayed that not His will but the will of the Father might be done. Mark it well: Jesus did not *want* to die; He was no man with a deluded longing for martyrdom. He knew what a horrible thing crucifixion was. But now that this one flickering moment of doubt was dispelled, He knew that it was within the purpose of His Father that He should die, and He was ready for it.

When Pope John XXIII was told that he was about to die, he said, "My bags are all packed for that journey." Ready for death, because death is within the plan of God for every man!

> All those who journey, soon or late,
> Must pass within the garden gate;
> Must kneel alone in darkness there,
> And battle with some fierce despair.
> God pity those who cannot say:
> "Not mine but thine"; who only pray:
> "Let this cup pass," and cannot see
> The purpose of Gethsemane.
>   —Ella Wheeler Wilcox

Jesus was ready when Judas came with the soldiers to arrest Him. He did not cringe or run; He looked at them face to face, completely, gloriously unafraid.

SUGGESTIONS TO TEACHERS

Your material from Mark 14 for today's lesson covers the last days of Jesus before His death on the Cross. It's a long chapter. It's packed with events, each of which could be the subject of an entire lesson. Don't feel frustrated if you don't get through every portion of Mark 14. Fix your attention on Jesus and His willingness to lay down His life for others. Keep in mind that throughout the plots and pressures, Jesus was constantly in control of every situation. He went unswervingly to the Cross!

Here are the highlights of those final days in the shadow of the Cross:

1. *INTRIGUE OF THE AUTHORITIES.* Bring out the irony that those engineering Jesus' arrest were the religious leaders. Why is it that sometimes we in the Church seem to stand in the way of or to be unable to see God's plans? Often, religious groups are not as responsive as one would expect when it comes to matters of justice. And almost always, good reasons are given. Whenever the church wittingly or unwittingly acts as a party to human hurts, however, it puts it in the category of conspirators of the Crucifixion!

2. *INSIGHT OF THE WOMAN.* The lovely story of the woman anointing Jesus (Mark 14:3-9) is more than an account of extravagant generosity. Jesus commended her for being the one person who seemed to grasp that He would soon be put to death: "she has anointed my body beforehand for burying" (14:8). In your lesson, discuss the meaning of Jesus' sacrifice on the Cross for us.

3. *INFAMY OF JUDAS.* This part of the lesson can easily gobble up all your

lesson period, so guard against rambling psychological analyses of Judas's motives. It's not too profitable to delve that much into, "What went wrong with Judas?" as much as, "How do *we* keep from betraying Jesus?"

4. *INSTITUTION OF THE COMMUNION.* Every Christian church will be sharing the bread and the cup this week. Whether called Holy Communion, the Eucharist, the Lord's Supper, or other titles, Christians regard this sacrament as "God's Word made visible." Trace the origins to the upper room scene in Mark. Discuss the meaning of the meal to Jesus' followers today in your congregation. Why is this sacrament of such paramount importance to the life of Christians?

5. *INCIDENTS IN THE GARDEN.* Budget enough lesson time to allow your students to reflect on the agonizing prayer of Jesus (". . . remove this cup from me") and the sleepy indifference of Peter, James, and John. You should help the class to understand the temptation Jesus endured in Gethsemane. Also point up the parallels between the disciples in the garden that night and us. Are we faithful in carrying out Jesus' requests to us?

6. *INQUIRY AT THE PRIEST'S HOUSE.* The episodes relating to Jesus' arrest and the hearing in the high priest's house need discussing. Call attention to the majestic calm of Jesus throughout the uproar. Jesus always remains in command!

7. *INSINCERITY OF PETER.* Give your class free rein to talk about Peter's denials in the courtyard of the high priest's house. Every person present will recognize that Peter's story is his or her own. In spite of tears of remorse, however, the Good News is that Jesus Christ died for such persons as Peter and us in order to grant us new beginnings with God!

TOPIC FOR ADULTS
IN THE SHADOW OF THE CROSS

Summary of Goodness. "All good which could be thought or desired is to be found in Jesus Christ alone. For He was humbled to exalt us, He became a slave to free us, He became poor to enrich us, He was sold to redeem us, made captive for our deliverance, condemned for our absolution; He was made a curse for our blessing, an offering for sin for our righteousness, He was marred that we might be restored, He died for our life. So that by Him harshness is softened, anger appeased, darkness made light, injustice justified, weakness made strong, dejection consoled, sin prevented, scorn despised, fear made sure, debt canceled, toil made light, sadness rejoiced, misfortune made blessed, difficulty eased, disorder ordered, division united, ignominy made noble, rebellion quelled, threats threatened, ambushes uncovered, assaults assailed, effort weakened, combat combatted, war warred against, vengeance avenged, torment tormented, damnation damned, ruin ruined, hell held prisoner, death done to death and immortality made immortal. . . ."—John Calvin, preface to French Bible, 1539.

Don't You Understand? The power of self-denying love is described in the reminiscences of the famous *Life* photographer Carl Mydans.

He tells the story of a young Korean who saved the lives of some of our soldiers in the Korean War. The young Korean who guided them to safety was critically wounded. As he lay dying, an old Korean man knelt beside him. The G.I.'s thought the old one was an interpreter and asked him to get the wounded youngster's name. "He saved our lives," said the captain. But the old man did not ask the hurt boy's name, just held his hand. The wounded Korean died on the operating table. "The captain sat motionless for a moment and then lowered his face to the old man. 'He saved us, that boy,' he said intensely. 'He died for us.' And he jabbed his finger at the corporal and himself. The old man just nodded. 'Look at me!' the captain roared into the old man's face. Rising from the cot and grabbing the Korean by the arms, he yelled: 'Don't you understand? Don't you know what I'm saying? He's dead. And now his family will never know what happened to him—how he died.' Gently the old man moved his arms free. Then looking into the captain's face, he said slowly: 'I understand. I know who he is. I have known him for seventeen years. He was my son.' "

This is something like what the Cross says about God.—Carl Mydans, "The Gook" in *More Than Meets the Eye*, Harper & Brothers, 1959.

Shadowy Cross. A group of church officers were planning Holy Week services for their congregation. They were concerned that so many in their church seemed to be indifferent to the significance of the events leading up to the crucifixion of Jesus Christ. As they were discussing the meaning of the special Thursday night Maundy Thursday service, one of the officers, attempting to make the worship have the right liturgy, made an unintentional slip of the tongue and asked, "Is this appropriate to the lethargy?"

In the shadow of the Cross this year, is the reaction you and others have merely one of lethargy? Or, remembering that *liturgy* literally means "work of the people," are you responding to the Cross by together as God's people working as Christ's?

Questions for Pupils on the Next Lesson. 1. What is the significance of the curtain of the Temple being torn from top to bottom when Jesus was crucified? 2. How do you interpret Jesus' words on the Cross, "My God, why hast Thou forsaken me?" 3. How does Easter give us promise that God can even cope with our deaths? 4. Were any of Jesus' followers expecting the Resurrection? 5. How would you explain the meaning of the Resurrection story to someone who had never heard it before?

TOPIC FOR YOUTH
FIRST THINGS FIRST

"Throw Your Cap Over The Wall!" "President John F. Kennedy used to mention how his grandfather liked to tell him of his boyhood days in Ireland. Grandfather Fitzgerald used to walk home from school with a group of youngsters each day. The boys would sometimes taunt each other to climb over the stone walls along the lanes of the countryside. Young Fitzgerald said that he and the other boys would sometimes hesitate to dare the hazardous climbs. However, they devised a way to make them resolve to ascend the steep walls. Fitzgerald reports that he would toss his cap over the wall. That done, there was no hesitation. The lads knew that he would undertake the most perilous climb in order to retrieve his cap.

"There comes a time in Christian discipleship when one must 'throw his cap over the wall,' so to speak. Although taking Jesus Christ seriously may appear to be terribly risky in a specific situation, a person must make an act of resolve and follow through.

"Notoriously the religious orders are nowadays short of vocations, nor has permitting lipstick and the wearing of mini-skirts served to reverse the trend. On the other hand, the Missionaries of Charity are multiplying at a fantastic rate: their Calcutta house is bursting at the seams and each year three or four new enterprises are started in India and elsewhere. As the whole history of Christianity shows, when everything is asked for, everything—and more—is accorded: when little, then nothing. Curious when this is so obvious that today the contrary proposition should seem to be more acceptable."—Malcolm Muggeridge, *Catholic Herald*, May 16, 1969.

First Things First. St. Kilda lies some 110 miles west of the Scottish mainland and is maintained by the National Trust as a nature reserve.

Legend has it that the first owners of the island, the MacLeods, won it in a boat race against the MacDonalds.

The story goes that at the last moment Coll MacLeod, seeing that the Mac-

Donalds were winning, cut off his left hand and hurled it onto the shore of the island, thus winning it for the MacLeods.

This kind of commitment and sacrifice to win a small island is the type of commitment and sacrifice which we must be prepared to make to win the world for its Lord. It must be a "first things first," regardless of the cost, form of loyalty to Christ. After all, in the events leading up to the Cross, and in His sacrifice on that Cross, He has shown His commitment and sacrifice for us!

Sentence Sermon to Remember: Through this sign thou shalt conquer.—Constantine the Great, on beholding the sign of the cross in the sky.

Questions for Pupils on the Next Lesson. 1. Has Easter for you ever been more than the message that Jesus was reported to have been raised from death? 2. Does God ever go back on His word? On what do you base your answer? 3. Why does death make us feel uneasy and frightened? 4. What does the Resurrection of Jesus have to do with our fears of death? 5. How would you explain Easter to a non-Christian foreign exchange student who knew almost nothing about the New Testament story?

LESSON VIII—APRIL 22

CRUCIFIED AND RAISED FROM DEATH

Background Scripture: Mark 15:1–16:20
Devotional Reading: Mark 15:6–15

KING JAMES VERSION

MARK 15 31 Likewise also the chief priests mocking said among themselves with the scribes, He saved others; himself he cannot save.

32 Let Christ the King of Israel descend now from the cross, that we may see and believe. And they that were crucified with him reviled him.

33 And when the sixth hour was come, there was darkness over the whole land until the ninth hour.

34 And at the ninth hour Jesus cried with a loud voice, saying Eloi, Eloi, lama sa-bachtha-ni? which is, being interpreted, My God, my God, why hast thou forsaken me?

35 And some of them that stood by, when they heard *it*, said, Behold, he calleth Elias.

36 And one ran and filled a spunge full of vinegar, and put *it* on a reed, and gave him to drink, saying, Let alone; let us see whether Elias will come to take him down.

37 And Jesus cried with a loud voice, and gave up the ghost.

38 And the vail of the temple was rent in twain from the top to the bottom.

39 And when the centurion, which stood over against him, saw that he so cried out, and gave up the ghost, he said, Truly this man was the Son of God.

16 1 And when the sabbath was past, Mary Magdalene, and Mary the *mother* of James, and Salome, had bought sweet spices, that they might come and anoint him.

2 And very early in the morning, the first *day* of the week, they came unto the sepulchre at the rising of the sun.

3 And they said among themselves, Who shall roll us away the stone from the door of the sepulchre?

4 And when they looked, they saw that the stone was rolled away: for it was very great.

5 And entering into the sepulchre, they saw a young man sitting on the right side, clothed in a long white garment; and they were affrighted.

6 And he saith unto them, Be not affrighted: ye seek Jesus of Nazareth, which was crucified: he is risen; he is not here: behold the place where they laid him.

7 But go your way, tell his disciples and Peter that he goeth before you into Galilee: there shall ye see him, as he said unto you.

REVISED STANDARD VERSION

MARK 15 31 So also the chief priests mocked him to one another with the scribes, saying, "He saved others; he cannot save himself. 32 Let the Christ, the King of Israel, come down now from the cross, that we may see and believe." Those who were crucified with him also reviled him.

33 And when the sixth hour had come, there was darkness over the whole land until the ninth hour. 34 And at the ninth hour Jesus cried with a loud voice, "Eloi, Eloi, lama sabachthani?" which means, "My God, my God, why hast thou forsaken me?" 35 And some of the bystanders hearing it said, "Behold, he is calling Elijah." 36 And one ran and, filling a sponge full of vinegar, put it on a reed and gave it to him to drink, saying, "Wait, let us see whether Elijah will come to take him down." 37 And Jesus uttered a loud cry, and breathed his last. 38 And the curtain of the temple was torn in two, from top to bottom. 39 And when the centurion, who stood facing him, saw that he thus breathed his last, he said, "Truly this man was the Son of God!"

16 1 And when the sabbath was past, Mary Magdalene, and Mary the mother of James, and Salome, bought spices, so that they might go and anoint him. 2 And very early on the first day of the week they went to the tomb when the sun had risen. 3 And they were saying to one another, "Who will roll away the stone for us from the door of the tomb?" 4 And looking up, they saw that the stone was rolled back; for it was very large. 5 And entering the tomb, they saw a young man sitting on the right side, dressed in a white robe; and they were amazed. 6 And he said to them, "Do not be amazed; you seek Jesus of Nazareth, who was crucified. He has risen, he is not here; see the place where they laid him. 7 But go tell his disciples and Peter that he is going before you to Galilee; there you will see him, as he told you."

KEY VERSE: "... *you seek Jesus of Nazareth, who was crucified. He has risen.*" Mark 16:6 (RSV).

HOME DAILY BIBLE READINGS

Apr. 16. M. *Jesus Before Pilate.* Mark 15:1–5.
Apr. 17. T. *Sentenced to Death.* Mark 15:6–15.
Apr. 18. W. *Made Fun of Jesus.* Mark 15:16–20.
Apr. 19. T. *Jesus Is Crucified.* Mark 15:21–32.
Apr. 20. F. *The Death of Jesus.* Mark 15:33–41.
Apr. 21. S. *The Burial of Jesus.* Mark 15:42–47.
Apr. 22. S. *The First Easter.* Mark 16:1–15.

BACKGROUND

What and who put Jesus on the cross? And *why?* The answer is not hard to find. Caiaphas put him there, Caiaphas the high priest of all priests, infuriated because Jesus had threatened their authority. Pilate put him there—a cynical and cowardly Pilate who was told by Caiaphas that this criminal Nazarene had plotted to found a Kingdom. That would be treason to a Roman; for any one to claim that he was a king proved that he was no friend of Caesar—and Pilate feared the wrath of Caesar. And a shouting mob, whipped into a frenzy, shouted in Pilate's courtyard for His death. In this mob, there surely were the money-changers of the Temple court, who were convinced that Jesus was ruining their business!

These, certainly brought about Christ's *physical* death. But Jesus could have prevented that by just running and hiding. This He refused to do. He put Himself up on that cross. Why? To prove to His enemies the limitless love of a God who through the sacrifice of the Son all men might be saved (redeemed). God was saying, "I love *you* with a love that will bear any suffering, even crucifixion, for your redemption."

Only one man, a centurian, grasped that truth as Jesus hung dying.

NOTES ON THE PRINTED TEXT

In order to see clearly the drama of the cross, we might be able to really understand what happened on Calvary *through the eyes of those who watched it.* Who came to watch the Christ die, and why did they come?

There were, first of all, the chief priests and scribes who had helped put him on that cross. At last, they were rid of the Nazarene; He was dying. While He died, they mocked Him. They sneered: this "mighty one" had saved others, but He couldn't save Himself from this vengeful death. They rejoiced that they would see no more of Him. They were fools. We do not crucify a faith or a truth, when we crucify a man. They were to hear of Him again walking by the Galilean lake.

There was a mob of people who also mocked Him, a mob whipped into a frenzy. The rabble-rousers among the priests and the Pharisees had done a good job in enflaming the minds of those who did not have the faintest idea of what was happening. They were, in miniature, much like the mobs in Iran who we saw on TV, screaming, fanatical men of demented minds out of control.

Here and there, in the crowd, were others who came out of curiosity—men who *like* to see another man hung or electrocuted. Casual men. Bystanders, at least one bystander, made a suggestion that perhaps this One on the cross was asking Elijah to help Him! They mocked. Even the two thieves crucified with Him mocked. The mind of man descends easily and often to its lowest depth.

There was the centurian, a tough Roman soldier, in charge of the execution. He did not mock. Never before had this soldier seen a man die like this one. He was convinced that this was indeed the Son of God. Convinced men are the hope of the Church of Christ.

And there were women there: the mother of Jesus and His mother's sister Mary the wife of Clopas, and Mary Magdalene—and only one disciple, the beloved John (John 19:25). Heartbroken, half dead with sorrow, *they were there in love.*

They never deserted Him. They loved Him too much for that. Trustful women were later to become the heart of the Church—and still are.

So He died, while these watched. As He "gave up the ghost," the veil of the Temple was "rent,"—torn aside. This veil was a curtain that shut off the Holy of Holies in the Temple into which no man could go but the chief priests, and even these could go but once a year. The cross tore open the veil, so that *any* man could pass to God. No longer was God hidden by any curtain. That was why Jesus did not even try to save Himself; He died to put the keys of the Kingdom in the hands of men; He opened the way.

He died at three o'clock on a Friday afternoon; the next day was the Sabbath, a day in which no work could be done. Anointing the dead was work and forbidden on that day. But "When the Sabbath was past, Mary Magdalene, and Mary the mother of James, and Salome . . . brought sweet spices, that they might come and anoint him" (Mark 16:1). The women, again! Three women came before any disciple came to the tomb where He had been laid at sunrise. They came still torn by grief, still bewildered. The body had been placed in a tomb and the door of the tomb was sealed by a round stone as large as a cartwheel. The women worried: who could open the door of that tomb, that they might go in?

Mark's account of the Resurrection is brief. He was an artist in condensing his words, in giving only the facts of whatever happened to or through Jesus. He simply states here that the loving women found the door of the sepulchre open, and a young man in white sitting inside the empty tomb. They had come to anoint a dead body, but the body was not there. "He is risen; he is not here!"

We once knew a good woman who lost her husband; every day, for weeks on end, she went out to the cemetery to sit at his graveside and weep. But—poor soul that she was—she did not know that her husband was not there but risen. We pity her in her sorrow, but we wish that she might have reached out her hand above that grave to take the hand of a Christ who left this word for her: "Let not your heart be troubled . . . And if I go and prepare a place for you, I will come again, and receive you unto myself; that where I am, there ye may be also" (John 14:1, 3).

So this is the Resurrection. This is the great central core of the Christian faith. It had to be, for if this Jesus had not been crucified and had He not then risen from the dead, we would never have heard of Him. It was His Resurrection that changed weak, despairing men into men afire with God's love.

Peter was a man of despair immediately following the Crucifixion. He thought it was all over, finished. He was wrong. The young man in white, sitting in the tomb, gave the women who came a message for Peter: "Go and tell his disciples *and Peter* that he (Christ, risen) would see him again, in Galilee." How that must have shaken Peter who had denied Him thrice. But never again did the fisherman deny his Lord: he, too, died on a cross.

The word is *Go.* He meant that for us, as well as for Peter. Go, teach, preach, witness. He will go with us, not as a dead Christ but a Living Presence who had conquered death. He is alive, *now.*

SUGGESTIONS TO TEACHERS

"Were you there when they crucified my Lord . . . ?"

The words of the old spiritual are also a question to each of us. The only answer, of course, is, "Yes, we were there."

We were there in the person of all those who were party to or present at the Crucifixion. We were also there at the empty tomb. The Cross and the Resurrection were for us as well as for the participants. Most important, we can continue to meet the Risen Lord 1,900 years later!

Mold this Easter morning lesson to behold Jesus crucified and raised through the eyes of those participants. Discuss what the Cross and Resurrection meant to them, and, most important, what these events mean to us.

1. *"CRUCIFIED...."* Among the cast of characters you may talk about are:
   A. *PILATE.* What similarities do those in your class have to this man of authority and responsibility? When are those in your class most inclined to make compromises or excuse themselves?
   B. *THE CROWD.* Why does the voice of the group around us, those we work with, those we bowl with, and party with, our "crowd," carry such weight? In what ways is the crowd we run with prone to reject Christ? A Christian must sometimes choose between the Christ and the crowd!
   C. *THE SOLDIERS.* Remind your class of the violent streak in our temperament and throughout our society. Even some of our most popular sports glorify violence. The mentality of the soldiers still prevails!
   D. *SIMON OF CYRENE.* Devote some class time on this man who was forced to carry the cross and thereby missed celebrating the Passover holiday. Discuss what forms of cross-bearing each member of your class may be expected to undertake.

2. *"... AND RAISED FROM DEATH."*
   A. *JOSEPH OF ARIMATHEA.* Relate the story of this member of the Sanhedrin who appears occasionally throughout Jesus' career (John 3:1–15; 7:50). What would have prompted this respectable member of the Council to take the risks and endure the indignities of removing Jesus' body except that he was profoundly affected by Jesus' death on the Cross. Do your people feel the same?
   B. *THE WOMEN.* Look at the earliest participants in the Easter story. Remark on the ways in which they were transformed from funeral folk to resurrected revolutionaries.
   C. *ELEVEN DISCIPLES AT TABLE.* The Risen Lord surprised some of His followers when they least expected Him. Point out that the Living Christ continues to encounter us in ways and places we aren't expecting Him. He presents Himself also when we are at worship and at His Table! Emphasize the importance of remaining within the fellowship of fellow believers and at the place of worship, especially in those times when the Lord may not seem very real or near!

TOPIC FOR ADULTS

HE HAS RISEN!

Alive in the World! "Just across the valley of Hinnom from the Scots kirk in Jerusalem are the supposed sites of the Crucifixion of Jesus. The word *sites* is plural because there are two. One—and the more authentic—is that now covered by the Church of the Holy Sepulchre, set in the middle of the Old City and reached by a walk through the throng and bustle of the market with its traders, visitors, pilgrims, and shoppers all making a multicoloured, multiracial kaleidoscope of people and things. The church itself is a vast, rambling building, shared by several Christian Churches (with Ethiopian monks in a roof church) and covering the site both of Calvary and of the Easter Garden. It's all very busy and noisy and populous.

"The other site is the place known as "Gordon's Calvary." This is a small garden where the visitor can see a real rock tomb of the kind in which Jesus was laid; and just beside the garden is a small hill the contours of which look remarkably like a human skull. This garden site has no archaeological authenticity but it is a quiet secluded place.

"Whatever be the rights and wrongs of the identification of sites, it is perhaps good that there are these two possible places, because each in its own way speaks of Easter. There is the personal, introverted aspect of the Easter story which calls on each of us to make the events our own. We have needed the garden with its solitariness and its peacefulness to sort ourselves out. That is one side of Easter.

"There is also, however, the message of Easter which speaks of the risen power of Christ alive and at work in the world. None of Jesus' followers stayed long beside the empty tomb; once they saw that Jesus was not there, they went their ways into the world. Indeed for the New Testament, the tomb is largely irrelevant; the evidence of the Resurrection was not that the tomb was empty but that the risen power of Jesus was real and evident and at work in the lives of men and women. Nobody asked the question: 'Who moved the stone?'; but all disciples and the others with them eventfully shouted with joy the exclamation: 'Jesus lives!'

"It was St. Paul who put this truth at its most profound when he asked the question: 'When you stand by the Cross and look at the events of Good Friday and Easter Day, what do you see?' And he answered by saying that what you see is that God was in Christ reconciling the world unto Himself.

"That is why it is appropriate and spiritually authentic that the Church of the Holy Sepulchre should be right in the middle of all the noise of the Jerusalem marketplace, for it is in the places where people of all races and creeds and political persuasions meet that Christ is present in His risen power. It is in the world of trade and money and gain and loss that God is at work reconciling the world, bringing all humankind into that unity which is the ultimate purpose of His creation. It is therefore in that world that His followers are called to live by the power of the Resurrection!"—W. B. Johnston, "An Easter Meditation," *Life and Work*, April 1980.

Hints of Hope. "In the early days of World War II, I used to feel annoyed by newspapers describing how the Japanese were taking country after country and island after island. Why dwell on that, I complained. I was absolutely certain that America and its allies would win the war. So the only really significant news, it seemed to me, would be news of whatever victories, however small, we were beginning to achieve. Our successes were what would be permanent, what would be the first steps toward the final victory.

"In the war with Satan, it is the same way. Ever since Easter we have known that we are on the winning side."—W. M. Ramsay, *Presbyterian Outlook* (512 E. Main St., Richmond, VA 23219), November 9, 1981.

Believe in the Dawn. Do you recall reading the inscription of the hunted Jewish refugees during the Nazi terror? Written on the walls of their secret refuge underneath Cologne Cathedral were these words: "I believe in the dawn, even though it be dark; I believe in God, even though He be silent." This is the Easter conviction. This is what we learn when we "live ourselves into the story" and find our hearts warmed by His invisible presence.

Questions for Pupils on the Next Lesson. 1. What, in your opinion, is *wisdom?* 2. Should Christians expect to be exempt from difficulties? 3. Why must sincere religion include both knowledge and action? 4. Who are the persons with special needs in your class and in your congregation? How is your church ministering to them? 5. As far as you can know yourself, where are the main differences between the values you profess and the values you live by?

TOPIC FOR YOUTH
DEATH DEFEATED!

Christ Is Alive. "Would you like a prescription for a brighter outlook, a sunnier disposition, and a happier day?

"Here it is: Before reading or listening to the bad news in your newspaper or on your radio, read a portion of the Good News in God's Word and in your favorite daily devotional guide.

"Early one morning as I sat down with my cup of coffee, the daily newspaper was on my left, and my Bible and some devotional literature were on my right. Would I start my day by reading of man's inhumanity to man, or would I begin the day by reading of God's inexhaustible love for man and His ever-present love within man?

"Although the front page headlines of the newspaper tempted me, these words on the cover of *Decision,* a widely-circulated Christian magazine, completely captured my attention: 'Christ Is Alive Today.'

"Some newspaper editors make a special effort to print more and more stories of good news, reporting the positive, heroic deeds and achievements of young people and adults. We should encourage more of our editors to do likewise.

"In the meantime, may we not forget to start each day by turning our attention to the original Good News: Christ Is Alive Today. He Is Risen. He Is Here Among Us"—W. A. Ward, *Quote,* April 6, 1975.

Release the Birds! On the Isle of Capri in the Bay of Naples, members of the local Christian parish have a traditional ceremony every Easter which is a powerful symbol of all that Christ's Resurrection means. Each family gathering for the early Sunday morning Easter celebration carries a bird cage. The crowded church and the plaza outside are jammed with the people of Capri carrying cages. After the benediction, all of the cages are opened and the birds are released to the gleeful shouts that Christ has risen!

Do you feel such a sense of release and jubilation because of the Resurrection? Death has been defeated! Sins are forgiven! Your hopes may soar!

More Than a Talking Tombstone. From Sunnyvale, California, comes word that Stan Zelazny, a thirty-seven-year-old manufacturing engineer, has invented a tombstone that plays back a ninety-minute recorded message from the deceased. It seems Zelazny is disturbed because everyone at a funeral has something to say except the "guest of honor." The talking tombstone is guaranteed for forty years.

God has done more than send us prerecorded messages from the tomb. He has raised up Christ alive! God guarantees that the Living Lord speaks not for forty years but forever!

Sentence Sermon to Remember: Belief in the resurrection is not an appendage to the Christian faith; it is the Christian Faith.—John S. Whale.

Questions for Pupils on the Next Lesson. 1. Why do we feel critical of people who don't do what they claim they will do? 2. Who is the wisest person you know? Why do you look up to this person for his or her wisdom? 3. Will difficulties happen to a devout Christian? 4. Who are the persons in need that you know best? Is your church reaching out to them?

THE LETTER OF JAMES
(5 LESSONS)

LESSON IX—APRIL 29

BE A DOER OF THE WORD

Background Scripture: James 1
Devotional Reading: James 1:12–18

KING JAMES VERSION	REVISED STANDARD VERSION

KING JAMES VERSION

JAMES 1 1 James, a servant of God and of the Lord Jesus Christ, to the twelve tribes which are scattered abroad, greeting.

2 My brethren, count it all joy when ye fall into divers temptations;

3 Knowing *this*, that the trying of your faith worketh patience.

4 But let patience have *her* perfect work, that ye may be perfect and entire, wanting nothing.

5 If any of you lack wisdom, let him ask of God, that giveth to all *men* liberally, and upbraideth not; and it shall be given him.

6 But let him ask in faith, nothing wavering. For he that wavereth is like a wave of the sea driven with the wind and tossed.

19 Wherefore, my beloved brethren, let every man be swift to hear, slow to speak, slow to wrath:

20 For the wrath of man worketh not the righteousness of God.

21 Wherefore lay apart all filthiness and superfluity of naughtiness, and receive with meekness the engrafted word, which is able to save your souls.

22 But be ye doers of the word, and not hearers only, deceiving your own selves.

23 For if any be a hearer of the word, and not a doer, he is like unto a man beholding his natural face in a glass:

24 For he beholdeth himself, and goeth his way, and straightway forgetteth what manner of man he was.

25 But whoso looketh into the perfect law of liberty, and continueth *therein*, he being not a forgetful hearer, but a doer of the work, this man shall be blessed in his deed.

26 If any man among you seem to be religious, and bridleth not his tongue, but deceiveth his own heart, this man's religion *is* vain.

27 Pure religion and undefiled before God and the Father is this, To visit the fatherless and widows in their affliction, *and* to keep himself unspotted from the world.

REVISED STANDARD VERSION

JAMES 1 1 James, a servant of God and of the Lord Jesus Christ,

To the twelve tribes in the Dispersion: Greeting.

2 Count it all joy, my brethren, when you meet various trials, 3 for you know that the testing of your faith produces steadfastness. 4 And let steadfastness have its full effect, that you may be perfect and complete, lacking in nothing.

5 If any of you lacks wisdom, let him ask God, who gives to all men generously and without reproaching, and it will be given him. 6 But let him ask in faith, with no doubting, for he who doubts is like a wave of the sea that is driven and tossed by the wind.

19 Know this, my beloved brethren. Let every man be quick to hear, slow to speak, slow to anger, 20 for the anger of man does not work the righteousness of God. 21 Therefore put away all filthiness and rank growth of wickedness and receive with meekness the implanted word, which is able to save your souls.

22 But be doers of the word, and not hearers only, deceiving yourselves. 23 For if any one is a hearer of the word and not a doer, he is like a man who observes his natural face in a mirror; 24 for he observes himself and goes away and at once forgets what he was like. 25 But he who looks into the perfect law, the law of liberty, and perseveres, being no hearer that forgets but a doer that acts, he shall be blessed in his doing.

26 If any one thinks he is religious, and does not bridle his tongue but deceives his heart, this man's religion is vain. 27 Religion that is pure and undefiled before God and the Father is this: to visit orphans and widows in their affliction, and to keep oneself unstained from the world.

KEY VERSE: But be ye doers of the word, and not hearers only. . . . James 1:22.

HOME DAILY BIBLE READINGS

Apr. 23. M. *James the Brother of Jesus.* Matthew 13:53–58.
Apr. 24. T. *James's Leadership.* Acts 15:12–21.
Apr. 25. W. *Faith and Trials.* James 1:1–8.
Apr. 26. T. *Being Poor Is Rich.* James 1:2–11.
Apr. 27. F. *Words of Hope.* Isaiah 40:3–8.
Apr. 28. S. *Being Tested.* James 1:12–18.
Apr. 29. S. *Hearing and Doing.* James 1:19–27.

BACKGROUND

Now, having finished our study of the lifework of Jesus, we turn to study a letter written after Jesus had gone, sometime about A.D. 50. The writer is James. But *which* James? There are four with that name in the Gospel story, and there has been a long, long debate over which one of them wrote this letter, the earliest letter of the New Testament. It is useless to argue about that. Generally speaking, and traditionally, this was James the brother or step-brother of Jesus, the first bishop of Jerusalem.

Not only has the authorship of this letter been disputed; its value has been questioned. Even the great Martin Luther (who believed in salvation by faith alone) called it "a right strawy epistle." Some others have described it as "an ethical scrapbook." But it is still one of the most dramatic—and disturbing—epistles ever directed at all Christians. James believed that while a man must be saved by faith, he must *prove* his salvation by way of good works. Faith *and* works was his formula.

While he does not write at length about doctrine, he bases his whole epistle upon—salvation!

NOTES ON THE PRINTED TEXT

Salvation from *what?* This lesson begins with the teaching of James that it is salvation from life's trials and temptations. James wrote as a man on his knees, almost overwhelmed by troubles; it was said of him that he spent so much time on his knees that his knees were as hard and calloused as a camel's. He was martyred for his faith about A.D. 62.

James makes an arresting suggestion at the very beginning of his letter: he says that we should *bless* our trials and temptations! That sounds ridiculous to the casual reader, but there is great truth in it. Trials test us and make us strong enough to overcome them. The strongest Christians are those who have faced all this, and with God's help, conquered it.

As one Christian scholar put it, "The Christian must *expect* to be jostled by trials on the Christian way."

Jesus never promised us that if we became His followers, we would, *presto*, be "living in a bed of roses." He did promise us what Winston Churchill called "blood, sweat, and tears." Think of it in terms of an athlete who is put through a period of gruelling, exhausting preparation before he goes out to race against strong opposition. He *must* face the rigors of training before the race starts if he is to win. A famous football coach said that the first question he always asked himself about a new, young, untried athlete was, "How long will he *last*, when the heat is on?"

"Where there is no temptation," wrote William Hickling Prescott, "there can be little claim to virtue." Thank God for tribulation: it is a great strengthener.

Verses 1:19–27 could well be called, "A Practical Guide to Practical Christianity." Having laid down the doctrine that "the word of truth" (God's Word) is the foundation of man's redemption, he proceeds to tell us what is required of man by way of response. To gain that redemption, man has to do more than only believe; his life must be shot through with actions that prove his belief. It looks like "just too much to expect from the average man," but the true Christian is *not* the average man. He is a new man in Christ, and he follows Christ's admonitions in his practical everyday life.

If you honestly want to be a Christian, James says, then *act* like a Christian. Don't talk too much; *listen constantly* to the Word, for that is what can save your soul. Be patient; Rome wasn't built in a day, and neither is the Kingdom. Don't blow up in anger; only those who have lost their heads do that. Control your tongue; loose tongues are as dangerous as loose dynamite. Don't be like a man who looks in a mirror and then walks away and forgets what he looks like! Look endlessly into God's Word and law, and you will know what He intended you to look like—as a Christian.

But the real "clincher," the deep, underlying truth in all this is found in James's words: "But be ye doers of the word, and not hearers only . . ." (verse 22). How easy it is for us to go to church and listen to the expounding of the Word, and feel that by merely coming and listening we have "done our duty." James cries out, "No! That is not enough." What is read or heard in church must be done in life. The Lamb's Book of Life is in no wise copied from church records.

There is an old story that is told about a very rich Russian lass who went to church one freezing winter day. She enjoyed the service a bit too long. When she came out of the cathedral, she found her coachman frozen to death on the seat of her carriage. She had not asked him to go into the warm cathedral, and so he died. An exaggeration? Maybe. But how many of us invite to sit with us in church the poor who live in freezing tenements?

Now read James 1:27. No—memorize it, for it is the finest definition of true religion that you will ever read. (And read Micah 6:8 for another good definition.) Says James: "Pure religion and undefiled before God and the Father is this, To visit the fatherless and widows in their affliction, and to keep himself unspotted from the world." Amen, and Amen!

Faith *and* works: this is the message of James. The words fit him like a well-made cloak.

SUGGESTIONS TO TEACHERS

The Interfaith Meeting featured a panel of Jewish and Christian leaders. After presentations by each panel participant, the session was thrown open to comments and questions. A rabbi spoke. "Frankly speaking, all I read and hear from you Christians is your emphasis on right doctrine. With all due respect, however, I must point out that with us Jews, the emphasis is also on right deeds." The rabbi gently chided Christian church people for stressing the believing at the expense of the doing.

Which is it: Doctrines or Deeds?

The Letter of James insists that it's both, not one or the other. Beginning with today's lesson, your assignment as teacher is to remind Christians in your class that the rabbi's criticism must not apply to *your* church. Christians must be doers of the Word!

1. *TESTED.* James's letter deals with practical problems which Christians face today in their attempt to be doers as well as hearers of the Word. Among these problems are the trials and testing every believer experiences. James advises those who take Christ seriously to count these a cause of joy! Reflect with your class what the benefits of such an attitude may be.

2. *TRUSTING.* James calls for a balanced emphasis on personal spiritual development and responsible redemptive activity in the world. He calls for faith,

but says it must be tested and proved by actions. Remind your people that there is no such thing as "faith" in the abstract. Faith means trusting the Lord in very specific ways in particular situations.

3. *TRANSITORY*. James offers a wholesome reminder that life is brief, and the person who boasts in riches will discover "as the flower of the grass he shall pass away" (1:10). It is appropriate to have each person ask himself or herself what he/she is living for, for the transitory or for the eternal.

4. *TEMPTED*. Every believer has his/her own peculiar temptation. Some temptations are common to all Christians. Have your students state what some of these are, and how Christians may cope with them.

5. *TACITURN*. James 1:10 and 26 warns against loose, careless talk by Christians. James urges each Christian to be "quick to hear, slow to speak," and to "bridle his tongue." Reflect on this in the light of everyone's delight in gossip.

6. *TRANSPARENT*. Consider with your class James's admonition to see beyond yourself and not see yourself mirrored, as is the case if you are merely a hearer of God's Word (1:23–25). The person who is a hearer but not a doer of God's Word "deceives himself," and doesn't truly see others. Is life all mirrors or is it also windows for those in your class? Christ intends us to be hearers *and* doers!

7. *TURNING*. Doctrine must be translated into deeds. And this means turning toward the oppressed. Allow plenty of time to consider the meaning of James 1:27, pondering its meaning for your people in your church in these times.

TOPIC FOR ADULTS
BE A DOER OF THE WORD

Continuing the Music. In 1924, the great Italian operatic composer, Giacomo Puccini, was told that he had cancer. He was at work on the score of the opera *Turandot*. When the opera was about half finished, Puccini's cancer became critical and death stopped his writing. His disciples finished the scores. One of his pupils was Arturo Toscanini, who consented to direct the orchestra and opera the first time it was presented. Toscanini stopped the orchestra on the last note that Puccini had written when death interrupted. Turning to the audience with tears in his eyes, Toscanini said, "Thus far the master wrote and he died." And then Toscanini added: "But his disciples finished the master's music."

Theory and Practice. "One of the tragedies of the modern liberal is the illusion that theory and practice, the ideal and the real, can be separated from each other. The Hindu poet is right—'Thou hast to churn the milk, O, Disciple, if thou desirest the taste of butter.'"—Howard Thurman, *Deep Is the Hunger*, Harper & Brothers, New York.

Doers Will Suffer, yet Live! "Calvary speaks the truth that if people live honestly and in love, they are bound to suffer and experience death. Jesus remained true to himself and his principles, and at Calvary he was crucified as a traitor. Dying is experienced not only in corporal death but also in the death of relationships, and in the death of visions in the face of harsh realities. Calvary says that death is not shameful or ignoble. Worldly power and success are not essential to what is whole and complete, because there on the cross, in total impotence, was fulfilled the most perfect and complete expression of human life ever lived."—James Wilkes, *The Gift of Courage*, Philadelphia: Westminster, 1981.

Questions for Pupils on the Next Lesson. 1. Why are economic status and success so important to people in our culture? 2. How is Abraham an example of a person who combined faith and works? 3. Why is it morally wrong to treat others on the basis of their economic status? 4. How do you measure the integrity of others? 5. Why is it never enough simply to have feelings of concern for others?

TOPIC FOR YOUTH
BELIEVING MEANS DOING

They Are Hungry, Too. "Few people have not heard of the faith and courage of that modern apostle of love, Mother Teresa of Calcutta. It is told how Mother Teresa was called urgently to the hovel where a woman with several small children was starving to death. She took a small bag of rice and with one of her assistants hurried to the home. While she was attending to the pitifully emaciated children, she placed the rice on the floor. When she looked up a little later, she noticed the rice and the mother had disappeared. A little later the woman was back, but the quantity of rice had shrunk to half its former size. When she asked the woman where it had gone, the woman looked at her quietly and said, 'They are hungry too.'

"They were a Muslim family living next door—also perilously close to death. The woman was Hindu. Mother Teresa taught her that believing means doing.

True Heresy. "I was quite astonished that one sentence in an address twelve years ago was more often quoted than any other I have ever spoken or written. I said: 'It must become clear that church members who deny in fact their responsibility for the needy in any part of the world, are just as much guilty of heresy as those who deny this or that article of faith. . . .' The echo of that phrase made me wonder whether it had been misunderstood. So I said a few years later: 'Church members who deny that God has reconciled men to himself in Christ are just as much guilty of heresy as those who refuse to be involved in the struggle for justice and freedom in the world and who do nothing to help their brethren in need.' "—W. A. Visser't Hooft. Reprinted by permission from CONTEXT (March 15, 1981) of Claretian Publication, 221 W. Madison, Chicago, IL 60606.

Believing and Doing! "In England a century ago, a group of committed Christians at the Clapham Church in London learned personally that believing means doing. These believers spearheaded social change in Britain, such as the end of slavery.

"In the Clapham church, lay persons were spending three hours daily for the work of the kingdom and giving much of their income toward its building. Lord Shaftesbury commented, 'No man, depend upon it, can persist from the beginning of his life to the end of it in a course of generosity . . . unless he is drawing from the fountain of Our Lord Himself.' When his son asked him how he could manage so many reforming initiatives at once, he answered, 'By hearty prayer to Almighty God before I begin, by entering into it with faith and zeal, and by making my end to be His glory and the good of mankind.' "—Florence M. G. Higham: *Lord Shaftesbury, A Portrait*, London: SCM Press, 1945.

Sentence Sermon to Remember: There cannot be a more glorious object in creation than a human being replete with benevolence, mediating in what manner he may render himself most acceptable to the Creator by doing good to His creatures.—Henry Fielding.

Questions for Pupils on the Next Lesson. 1. Why do people in our society seem to place so much importance on economic status and success? 2. What are the major inconsistencies between your beliefs and your actions? 3. Who are the adults you know who seem to show that both faith and works are important? 4. Why is it true that "actions speak louder than words"? 5. Who are the hurting people with whom you are able to empathize most readily?

LESSON X—MAY 6

SHOWING YOUR FAITH THROUGH WORKS

Background Scripture: James 2
Devotional Reading: Leviticus 19:15–18

KING JAMES VERSION

JAMES 2   1 My brethren, have not the faith of our Lord Jesus Christ, *the Lord* of glory, with respect of persons.

2 For if there come unto your assembly a man with a gold ring, in goodly apparel, and there come in also a poor man in vile raiment;

3 And ye have respect to him that weareth the gay clothing, and say unto him, Sit thou here in a good place; and say to the poor, Stand thou there, or sit here under my footstool:

4 Are ye not then partial in yourselves, and are become judges of evil thoughts?

5 Hearken, my beloved brethren, Hath not God chosen the poor of this world rich in faith, and heirs of the kingdom which he hath promised to them that love him?

6 But ye have despised the poor. Do not rich men oppress you, and draw you before the judgment seats?

7 Do not they blaspheme that worthy name by the which ye are called?

14 What *doth it* profit, my brethren, though a man say he hath faith, and have not works? can faith save him?

15 If a brother or sister be naked, and destitute of daily food,

16 And one of you say unto them, Depart in peace, be *ye* warmed and filled; notwithstanding ye give them not those things which are needful to the body; what *doth it* profit?

17 Even so faith, if it hath not works, is dead, being alone.

18 Yea, a man may say, Thou hast faith, and I have works: shew me thy faith without thy works, and I will shew thee my faith by my works.

19 Thou believest that there is one God; thou doest well: the devils also believe, and tremble.

20 But wilt thou know, O vain man, that faith without works is dead?

21 Was not Abraham our father justified by works, when he had offered Isaac his son upon the altar?

22 Seest thou how faith wrought with his works, and by works was faith made perfect?

23 And the scripture was fulfilled which saith, Abraham believed God, and it was imputed unto him for righteousness: and he was called the Friend of God.

24 Ye see then how that by works a man is justified, and not by faith only.

REVISED STANDARD VERSION

JAMES 2   1 My brethren, show no partiality as you hold the faith of our Lord Jesus Christ, the Lord of glory. 2 For if a man with gold rings and in fine clothing comes into your assembly, and a poor man in shabby clothing also comes in, 3 and you pay attention to the one who wears the fine clothing and say, "Have a seat here, please," while you say to the poor man, "Stand there," or, "Sit at my feet," 4 have you not made distinctions among yourselves, and become judges with evil thoughts? 5 Listen, my beloved brethren. Has not God chosen those who are poor in the world to be rich in faith and heirs of the kingdom which he has promised to those who love him? 6 But you have dishonored the poor man. Is it not the rich who oppress you, is it not they who drag you into court? 7 Is it not they who blaspheme the honorable name which was invoked over you?

14 What does it profit, my brethren, if a man says he has faith but has not works? Can his faith save him? 15 If a brother or sister is ill-clad and in lack of daily food, 16 and one of you says to them, "Go in peace, be warmed and filled," without giving them the things needed for the body, what does it profit? 17 So faith by itself, if it has no works, is dead.

18 But some one will say, "You have faith and I have works." Show me your faith apart from your works, and I by my works will show you my faith. 19 You believe that God is one; you do well. Even the demons believe—and shudder. 20 Do you want to be shown, you foolish fellow, that faith apart from works is barren? 21 Was not Abraham our father justified by works, when he offered his son Isaac upon the altar? 22 You see that faith was active along with his works, and faith was completed by works, 23 and the scripture was fulfilled which says, "Abraham believed God, and it was reckoned to him as righteousness"; and he was called the friend of God. 24 You see that a man is justified by works and not by faith alone.

KEY VERSE: So faith by itself, if it has no works, is dead. James 2:17 (RSV).

HOME DAILY BIBLE READINGS

Apr. 30. M. *Don't Be Prejudiced.* James 2:1–7.
May. 1. T. *Love Your Neighbor.* James 2:8–13.
May. 2. W. *Laws of Justice.* Leviticus 19:13–18.
May. 3. T. *Faith and Actions.* James 2:14–18.
May. 4. F. *Abraham and Rahab's Actions.* James 2:19–26.
May. 5. S. *Abraham Obeys God.* Genesis 22:1–14.
May. 6. S. *Rahab's Good Deed.* Joshua 2:1–14.

BACKGROUND

The Church, in its earliest days, was a poor Church, founded by One whose earthly possessions were limited to the gown He wore, sustained, largely, by men of little means. But as time wore on, it is apparent that men and women of means were attracted and became members. James saw a lurking danger in that. Someone has said that it is *always* dangerous for a Church to become "respectable."

But James was not trying to scold the Church because it had a few men of wealth and prominence in its congregation; he was only warning them that it must never follow the worldly custom of considering the rich and the prominent as a different, higher breed than the poor. There is no sin in making a millionaire a member of the Church, but there is a sin involved when we put him on an invisible throne and almost worship him.

The General Epistle of James may have been a sort of religious essay widely distributed by its author, or it may have been a sermon preached by James as he traveled his circuit among non-Christian Jews. If it was a sermon, it must have "rocked the boat." Many a preacher has lost his job for preaching what he found in James. . . .

NOTES ON THE PRINTED TEXT

James starts out by saying that they must not show any partiality "as you hold the faith of our Lord Jesus Christ." Jesus and God are no respecters of men; they have no favorites, no "pets." To drive in that ideal, he gives his hearers a little parable. There were two men who came to church. One was a wealthy man, rich in raiment and with his fingers covered with gold rings. The other was a poor man, a "lower class" man in rags and wearing no gold. What should we do, in our churches, with these two? Should we bow and scrape before the rich one, give him the best seat in the house, treating him like a king who comes to visit us, while we tell the poor man to "stand over there," out of sight, even to sit at the wealthy brother's feet? Who are we, to do a thing like that? Judge not, that ye be not judged! That must have been hard to take for masters and slaves who came to worship a God who despised discrimination sitting side by side. It was a new idea; it was dynamite. But it was also Christ's way.

We remember one Sunday in our local church when an ex-convict came to our morning service. He was led to an obscure seat in the last row. When we came to celebrate the communion supper, he did not move out of his pew; he cringed, and cried—until the most prominent elder of the church came and put his arms around him, and led him to the altar rail. James would have loved that.

And we remember Henry Sloane Coffin, who was once pastor of a swank church in New York City. Coffin saw to it that a tug-boat captain was elected leader of the church's Session, its governing body. Did he get that idea from James?

Verses 14–24, in our Scripture lesson, is an enlargement of the "Be Doers" idea of James which we considered last week. Maybe James felt that he needed to add a more detailed description of what he meant by that. His explanation here makes good sense.

He puts great emphasis on works—so much so that many must have felt that he was disagreeing with the great Paul on this subject. This is not true. James was only repeating what John the Baptist meant when he said that men must bring forth fruits (works) "meet for repentance," or what Jesus meant when he said that men should so live that the world might see their good works and give the glory to God. And though Paul held the belief that men were saved by faith, he also stressed the ethical *effects* of Christianity which must follow the belief. He said that God will render to every man according to his deeds (Romans 2:6). Every man, he said, shall receive his own reward according to his labor (1 Corinthians 3:8).

No, Paul and James did not contradict each other. They complemented each other. They both believed in faith and works; the only difference between them is that they emphasized different *aspects* of belief. There are two kinds of belief: one is found in *intellectual* acceptance of the saving Gospel of Christ. The second form lies in the conviction that action should come after the faith is accepted, as a demonstration of its truth. The Christian needs to believe in both of these ways.

James gives two illustrations of this. He offers the picture of Abraham as a man of great faith—and whose faith was *proved* by his willingness to sacrifice his son; that was a "work" which made him The Friend of God. That was a great honor. Later, in verse 25, James speaks of Rahab the harlot who, driven by faith, saved the lives of two Israelite spies sent out by Joshua (Joshua 2:1–14). Without that faith, she could never have undertaken such a perilous work; because of it, she is mentioned with honor in the Scriptures (Psalms 87:4; Hebrews 11:31) and she is also listed in Matthew's geneology of Boaz and Jesus. Faith—*and* works!

Karl Marx laid down the infamous suggestion that "Religion is the opium of the people." We detest that; we hate Marx for saying it. But, much as we disagree with it, can it not be true that for *some* people, religion does seem to have the *effect* of opium? To these "some," conversion leaves them in a daze or a dreamy state of mind which prevents them from applying their new-found faith in every walk of human life. James insists that justice and mercy—the good works of faith—*must* characterize those who profess to serve the Lord. Is James wrong?

Only you can answer that question.

Only yesterday, we found the pastor of our church visiting the sick in a hospital on Easter Sunday—*before* he preached two sermons on his busiest day of the year. He preached several good sermons in that hospital, without saying a word.

SUGGESTIONS TO TEACHERS

"Don't talk to me of love—show me!" runs the line of a popular song a few years go. Aphorisms, such as "Actions speak louder than words" and "What you are speaks louder than what you say," may be found in every language. This lesson is meant to be more than a rehash of familiar folksayings like these.

The Letter of James reminds us that God has done more than talk; He has acted. James insists that Christians in turn, must do more than talk. This is the thrust of your lesson for this Sunday.

James always quickly gets down to cases. Take your cues from James's Letter in this lesson on "Showing Your Faith Through Works" by discussing the following:

1. *DISTINCTION DANGERS.* James reminds us that we are easily impressed with wealth. To us, money means power. Wealth, in our society, confers respect. We are apt to find ourselves partial to the well-dressed person with the big portfolio and fat wallet.

A. *GOD'S PARTIALITY TOWARD THE POOR.* Your class may find it disconcerting to hear that Scripture shows God has a bias toward the penniless and the oppressed. As teacher, you may have to remind your people of the persistent theme throughout the Bible of God's preoccupation with the widows, the orphans, the strangers—all of whom were usually neglected or forgotten.

B. *RICH'S PROPENSITY TOWARD PRIDE.* James bluntly states that wealth has dangers. The rich person easily slips into thinking that he/she accrued his/her wealth by his/her own efforts. Also, the rich man or woman easily falls into the error of assuming that he/she deserves what he/she owns! Your class members will as a matter of course reject any notion that any of them are wealthy. Remind them, however, that compared with the rest of the world's people, they *are* rich!

C. *CHRISTIAN'S POSSIBILITY FOR PERISHING.* This lesson may help smoke out some of the old perceptions about the Gospel and wealth that some hold, such as "Keep it spiritual, and don't talk about such sordid stuff as money." Remind your hearers that such deceit can (and has) led many church folk to ruin their faith.

2. *DOUBLE DUTIES: FAITH AND WORKS.*

A. *PRACTICE OF PEACE.* Suggest that James's words in 2:15–17 be memorized. A Christian cannot merely say, "Go in peace" to a brother or sister. If one is to share Christ's peace (or *Shalom*), it means bringing harmony and wholeness (the meaning of *Shalom*) among everyone.

B. *PARITY OF PLENTY AND PRACTICE.* Take some lesson time to let your class discuss the tension between faith and works, especially since many think that it must be one or the other. Be sure to let James get in the last word, namely that faith and works must go together!

TOPIC FOR ADULTS
BE FAITHFUL THROUGH WORKS

Acting His Faith. Shortly after the close of the Civil War, in a fashionable Richmond Church, members of the congregation were invited to come to the altar rail to receive Holy Communion. After several rows of worshipers came and left after receiving the Sacrament side by side, a black man walked down the aisle toward the altar. A tense silence gripped everyone. No one got up to come down to receive the bread and wine, although many in the church had not yet received Communion. The black man started to kneel—alone. Quietly, a tall, greying man with a military bearing stood up and strode down the aisle to the black man's side. Together, they knelt. Before the officiating clergyman could continue, people recognized that the person kneeling beside the black man without showing any distinction was General Robert E. Lee. Although Lee said nothing, everyone realized he had shown his faith through his act of joining that lonely black worshiper at the altar rail.

Medicine as Ministry. The Reverend Malcolm Marshall, who conducts healing services at St. Margaret's Episcopal Church in Washington, D.C., says, "I don't precede the word *healing* with qualifications such as 'faith' or 'spiritual.' It's healing. Doctors have their approach to healing. So do we. We're all working to the same end."

Dr. Marshall notes that it was a physician, Dr. Richard C. Cabot, who was instrumental in helping develop the modern healing movement in the Episcopal Church. In the 1930s, Dr. Cabot, then at Harvard Medical School, and the Rev. Russell L. Dicks, chaplain at Massachusetts General Hospital, became interested in the role of faith in healing. "Their thesis was that the body itself heals, that this is a part of God's creation," says Dr. Marshall.

He speaks of the surgeon who refuses to operate on a patient who thinks he will die during surgery. "If surgeons thus recognize the place of fear, then they must also recognize that of faith and let the patient move into surgery confident in God, confident in the surgeon, and confident in the care and love that will surely be given him," says Dr. Marshall. "I don't call this miraculous. It's as common and ordinary as eating and drinking. It's the action of God."

One surgeon who appears to see things this way is Dr. William S. Reed of Tampa, Florida, whose preoperative prayer is always essentially the same: "Dear Lord, help us in this to do your perfect will in the name of Jesus Christ. Amen."

Dr. Reed emphasizes the need for a positive approach in the OR. "If your conversation or attitudes during the operation are negative, then the patient will respond negatively," he maintains. "We treat the patient as if he were awake. Spiritually speaking, the patient is never anesthetized. I am against conducting an operation as though it were an autopsy. I hold that the patient has put his faith in me, and I respond by in effect saying, 'You are ours to the end. We'll pray for you all the way.' In many ways medicine is a ministry; we're more than just doctors."—*Medical World News*, December 25, 1978.

Love in Practice Versus Love in Dreams. It's not difficult to love in theory, but, as Dostoevski reminded us, "Love in practice is a harsh and terrible thing compared with love in dreams."

Questions for Pupils on the Next Lesson. 1. Why is teaching in Church as elsewhere such a serious responsibility? 2. Why does what you say have such power for good or evil? 3. What examples can you give of the importance of trustworthy communications? 4. How do people sometimes give verbal and nonverbal messages that may not agree? 5. Why is unselfish service a demonstration of what the Bible calls "true wisdom"?

TOPIC FOR YOUTH
LET YOUR ACTION DO THE TALKING

Why Don't You Act? Our expressions of devotion to God or our fellowmen are seen for what they are by the degree to which we back them up with positive action. A little girl was standing in the lobby of a hotel with her parents when she noticed a famous actress standing nearby. With typical childlike audacity, she walked up to the woman and asked: "Aren't you an actress?" The woman nodded her head affirmatively, but the little girl kept standing there as if she were expecting something more. After a noticeable pause, the child said: "Well, why don't you act then?" This question is more than applicable to our spiritual life. As Christians, we express our love through our emotions and through our actions.

What Actions Say. The dean of a church-related college received a telephone call from an irate parent early in the fall term shortly after students gathered. The caller took the dean to task for placing her WASP daughter with a black roommate. "How could you do such a thing as assigning my Jennifer Sue a roommate who is black?" the mother exploded. "We thought by choosing a Christian school we could avoid this kind of a problem!"

How would you have answered this parent if you had been the dean? How would you have handled the situation if you lived on the same floor as these two girls? The two roommates, incidentally, insisted on staying together and thanked the dean for helping them to learn more what a Christian community can mean.

Showing Your Faith Through Your Works to Others. John Hunter, the distinguished eighteenth-century Glasgow doctor, used to say to his students, "Never perform an operation on another person which under similar circumstances you would not perform on yourself." How marriage and industrial relationships would be enriched if husbands and wives, employers and employees, would treat each other as they would want to be treated if the roles were reversed!

Even on the highways and streets when driving, "Honk unto others as you would have them honk unto you." The Golden Rule is showing your faith through your works to others.

Sentence Sermon to Remember: When God wanted sponges and oysters, He made them, and put one on a rock, and the other in the mud. When He made man, He did not make him to be a sponge or an oyster. He made him with feet and hands and head, and heart, and vital blood, and a place to use them, and said, "Go, work!"—Henry Ward Beecher.

Questions for Pupils on the Next Lesson. 1. What experiences have you had or heard about in which somebody was hurt through gossip? 2. Why do hypocrisy and dishonesty cause such damage in the long run? 3. In what ways does speech influence you and does your speech influence others? 4. How do people's verbal messages sometimes not agree with their nonverbal messages? 5. What is your definition of "true wisdom," and what is the definition of such wisdom in James's Letter?

LESSON XI—MAY 13

BE CAREFUL WHAT YOU SAY

Background Scripture: James 3
Devotional Reading: Ezekiel 33:1–9

KING JAMES VERSION

JAMES 3 1 My brethren, be not many masters, knowing that we shall receive the greater condemnation.

2 For in many things we offend all. If any man offend not in word, the same *is* a perfect man, *and* able also to bridle the whole body.

3 Behold, we put bits in the horses' mouths, that they may obey us; and we turn about their whole body.

4 Behold also the ships, which though *they be* so great, and *are* driven of fierce winds, yet are they turned about with a very small helm, whithersoever the governor listeth.

5 Even so the tongue is a little member, and boasteth great things. Behold, how great a matter a little fire kindleth!

6 And the tongue *is* a fire, a world of iniquity: so is the tongue among our members, that it defileth the whole body, and setteth on fire the course of nature; and it is set on fire of hell.

7 For every kind of beasts, and of birds, and of serpents, and of things in the sea, is tamed, and hath been tamed of mankind:

8 But the tongue can no man tame; *it is* an unruly evil, full of deadly poison.

9 Therewith bless we God, even the Father; and therewith curse we men, which are made after the similitude of God.

10 Out of the same mouth proceedeth blessing and cursing. My brethren, these things ought not so to be.

13 Who *is* a wise man and endued with knowledge among you? let him shew out of a good conversation his works with meekness of wisdom.

14 But if ye have bitter envying and strife in your hearts, glory not; and lie not against the truth.

15 This wisdom descendeth not from above, but *is* earthly, sensual, devilish.

16 For where envying and strife *is*, there *is* confusion and every evil work.

17 But the wisdom that is from above is first pure, then peaceable, gentle, *and* easy to be intreated, full of mercy and good fruits, without partiality, and without hypocrisy.

18 And the fruit of righteousness is sown in peace of them that make peace.

REVISED STANDARD VERSION

JAMES 3 1 Let not many of you become teachers, my brethren, for you know that we who teach shall be judged with greater strictness. 2 For we all make many mistakes, and if any one makes no mistakes in what he says he is a perfect man, able to bridle the whole body also. 3 If we put bits into the mouths of horses that they may obey us, we guide their whole bodies. 4 Look at the ships also; though they are so great and are driven by strong winds, they are guided by a very small rudder wherever the will of the pilot directs. 5 So the tongue is a little member and boasts of great things. How great a forest is set ablaze by a small fire!

6 And the tongue is a fire. The tongue is an unrighteous world among our members, staining the whole body, setting on fire the cycle of nature, and set on fire by hell. 7 For every kind of beast and bird, of reptile and sea creature, can be tamed and has been tamed by humankind, 8 but no human being can tame the tongue—a restless evil, full of deadly poison. 9 With it we bless the Lord and Father, and with it we curse men, who are made in the likeness of God. 10 From the same mouth come blessing and cursing. My brethren, this ought not to be so.

13 Who is wise and understanding among you? By his good life let him show his works in the meekness of wisdom. 14 But if you have bitter jealousy and selfish ambition in your hearts, do not boast and be false to the truth. 15 This wisdom is not such as comes down from above, but is earthly, unspiritual, devilish. 16 For where jealousy and selfish ambition exist, there will be disorder and every vile practice. 17 But the wisdom from above is first pure, then peaceable, gentle, open to reason, full of mercy and good fruits, without uncertainty or insincerity. 18 And the harvest of righteousness is sown in peace by those who make peace.

KEY VERSE: Death and life are in the power of the tongue, and those who love it will eat its fruits. Proverbs 18:21 (RSV).

HOME DAILY BIBLE READINGS

May 7. M. *Mistakenly Speaking.* James 3:1–5.
May 8. T. *Speaking Can Hurt.* James 3:6–12.
May 9. W. *Ezekiel Is a Watchman.* Ezekiel 33:1–9.
May 10. T. *Accepting Consequences of Words.* Proverbs 18:17–21.
May 11. F. *Warning Against Arrogance.* James 3:13–18.
May 12. S. *Example of a Loving Heart.* 1 Thessalonians 3:6–13.
May 13. S. *Boasting for the Lord.* 1 Corinthians 1:26–31.

BACKGROUND

This lesson is aimed straight at *teachers* (*see* James 3:1, RSV), and the church school teacher may wonder if it is meant "for teachers only." No, it is not. We are all teachers, professional and amateurs though we may be. Parents are teachers in Christianity. Friends are teachers. All men who write books are teachers. James speaks to all these.

In Judaism, long before Christ came, the teaching Rabbi was highly honored. In Old Testament days, if a Rabbi and parents needed help, the Rabbi was helped *first.* He was a most important man in that society. In the times of Jesus and in the Early Church, teachers were also of prime importance. The disciples and the apostles, like the prophets of old, were constantly on the move. It was their responsibility to make clear the meaning of the Gospel, and they were well respected men.

James, a good teacher himself, warned his brother teachers to be careful of what they *said* to the new converts of the Church. He told them that teaching was a highly dangerous business. The teacher can either make or break the faith of those to whom he speaks.

Watch what you say. Watch your *tongue.*

NOTES ON THE PRINTED TEXT

The tongue is such a *little* thing! You cannot even see it, but, when we open our mouths to speak, that tongue becomes either an organ of blessing or a curse. God, in the beginning, gave man dominion "over the fish of the sea, and over the fowl of the air, and over every living thing that moveth upon the earth" (Genesis 1:28). "But the tongue can no man tame" (James 3:8).

James offers three illustrations here about the use of the tongue. He says that we put bits in horses mouths; the bit is probably the smallest part of the harness of a horse, but it is the most important. With this bit, we can control every movement of the horse; a mere tug on it can send him in the way we want him to go; it can move his whole body in any direction. What he is saying here is that if we can somehow control our tongues, we can control our whole minds and bodies.

Or the tongue in our mouths is like the rudder on a ship. What a tiny thing that rudder is! You can't see it down there in the water, hidden. The passengers on a ship may not even know what a rudder is, but this tiny mechanism moves the whole ship; without it the ship would be completely out of control, staggering helplessly and going nowhere.

Again, James compares the tongue with a forest fire. Have you ever seen a forest fire? Have you ever seen a man drop a match that was still burning—and see it kindle a fire that will burn thousands of acres? The *range* of the fire is unbelievable. So is the range of a poisonous word spoken in slander against a neighbor. It can reach from New York to California. Many an innocent man has had his reputation—and his life—ruined by a casual gossiper.

And many a young convert can be lost to Christ by a teacher who does not think before he speaks. The teacher can distort Scripture; he can teach falsely or *carelessly.* We once knew a teacher who murdered a potential Christian—a young boy who asked him how he could prove there was a God. The teacher had a chance there with a boy with nerve enough to ask such a question, but the teacher "blew it"—sent the boy home after scolding him bitterly. The boy never came back.

Watch that tongue, Christian. Use it to bless God, and never to curse man.

Now, having "laid down the law" about the use of the tongue, James goes on to trace both the tongue and the words it utters back to two possible sources. He talks about wisdom. One of the sources of wisdom is "wisdom from above"; a second wisdom is the wisdom that springs out of man's selfish nature. God's wisdom and man's! The divine wisdom is "first pure, then peaceable, gentle, open to reason, full of mercy and good fruits, without uncertainty or insincerity" (verse 17). Man's wisdom, on the other hand, is apt to be centered in jealousy and ambition—self-centered and *selfish*. We should be careful of the "wisdom" we circulate with our tongues. Let it be "the harvest of righteousness . . . sown in peace by those who make peace" (verse 18). Let the tongue speak peace, peace born out of righteousness, out *of God's* wisdom. Let us speak in this divine wisdom, as we can understand it, in humility and peace, and *never* in boasting.

Yes, man has demonstrated a great wisdom, but, like a tongue gone astray, it can be a wisdom gone astray. Man has been smart enough to invent the airplane—and he uses it to drop bombs! Man created the automobile so that we might "get there faster"; getting there faster, we kill about 50,000 people a year! Man has taught himself to read, and that seems good, but a prominent publisher tells us that a book has to have a "sex slant" if it is to be successful! Konrad Adenauer, with his tongue in his cheek, wrote: "The good Lord set definite limits on man's wisdom, but set no limits on his stupidity—and that's just not fair." William Cowper put it more charitably: "God never meant that man should scale the heavens by strides of human wisdom."

Hold your tongue, Christian, until it is ready to speak God's wisdom.

SUGGESTIONS TO TEACHERS

During World War II, civilians and military alike were warned to be careful what they said. Posters screamed "A SLIP OF THE LIP MAY SINK A SHIP!" in huge block letters. The Allies discovered that the enemy was so eagerly listening to what people were saying that misinformation was deliberately leaked, such as in June, 1944, when people talked about the D-Day landings occurring near Calais, thereby luring Nazi concentration to the wrong part of the French coast before the invasion. Words are weapons!

James's Letter stresses the power and danger of speech. What you say can destroy! As a Christian who is called to build up, you soon discover that your tongue can easily and quickly tear down others and rip apart a community.

1. *PERIL OF A TEACHER.* You as a leader in the Christian Church carry a particularly heavy burden of responsibility. Like a preacher, you soon become aware of what your tongue may do. Share this burden with your class by bringing out all the solemn warnings of James 3 to teachers. Probably many, if not most, in your class have not given much thought to the frighteningly serious responsibility you as a teacher have to live with! Since Christians must help bear each others' burdens, remind the class members that they may help you by praying for you regularly, and by forgiving you for your inadequate presentations of the Gospel.

2. *POWER OF THE TONGUE.* Make certain that your class understands each of the metaphors which James uses for the human tongue, including the bit which controls a horse, a rudder which steers a ship, and a match which ignites a forest fire. Although the tongue, like a bit or rudder or match, appears insignificant, what terrible destruction it can cause! Permit your class to share instances from personal experience in which careless words or idle gossip brought hurt or harm to others.

3. *PROBLEMS OF ITS TAMING.* How does a Christian control his or her speech? Here, James offers great insights and help. The words that come out of a person's mouth are actually the product of a person's heart! In other words, a person's speech must be "converted" each day by dedicating one's tongue, heart, mind, and soul to Christ.

4. *PERSONALITY OF THE TRULY WISE.* Ask your class members to state what each thinks defines a "wise" person. Or, have each tell about the wisest man or woman he or she has ever met, and why that person is considered "wise." Give careful attention to James at this point, especially 3:13–18, where James describes the "meekness of wisdom." Ask if your members' talk is along the lines of James's thoughts about the "meekness" of wisdom.

TOPIC FOR ADULTS
BE CAREFUL WHAT YOU SAY

Watch Your Tongue! John Wesley always grew upset with people who relished criticizing others. Wesley especially became disturbed by persons who took a delight in making personal comments about teachers, preachers, and others in church work. One time, Wesley was preaching to a congregation in which there was a lady who was well known for her critical attitude. He noticed that this woman seemed to be paying particular attention to his necktie. After the service, Wesley greeted her cordially. The woman, however, snapped, "Mr. Wesley, the strings on your tie are much too long. It is an offense to me."

Wesley calmly asked if any of the women present happened to have a pair of scissors with them. One lady found a pair of shears in her purse and handed them to Wesley. Wesley passed them to the critical woman and suggested that she trim his necktie to the length she preferred. The woman eagerly snatched the scissors and snipped Wesley's tie close to his collar.

"Are you sure the length is all right now?" Wesley asked graciously.

"Yes," the critical woman said sharply, "that is much better."

"Then may I have those shears a moment," Wesley continued. "I'm sure you won't mind if I also gave you a bit of correction. I don't want to be cruel, I must tell you that your tongue is an offense to me. It's too long. Please stick it out so I can take some off."

Wesley of course was only trying to make a point and didn't mean to harm the woman. He helped her to see, however, that Christians must guard their speech.

Jesus' Teacher. A parish Church of the Greek Catholics is built in Nazareth on the site of the traditional synagogue. The foundation stones are still there—30' x 26'. Synagogue sites were not readily changed. Nazareth, exclusively Jewish for centuries after Jesus' life, probably kept the same spot for a synagogue. The Pilgrim of Piacenza mentions this synagogue on his visit in the sixth century.

Jesus here learned at the feet of some teacher. Josephus, governor of Galilee thirty-some years after Jesus lived there, wrote that the Jews recognized their duty to educate children in customs and commands of fathers "that they may imitate them, and being nourished up in them may neither transgress them, nor have any excuse for ignorance of them."

It's interesting to speculate who was the teacher? What he was like, how he and the pupil Jesus got along. His instruction must have kindled and his friendship must have encouraged Jesus.

Possibly James, the brother of Jesus, who wrote the Letter we are using as the basis of these lessons, also studied under that same teacher. James and Jesus were profoundly influenced by the teaching of some now-unknown person or persons. Obviously, this teacher or these teachers had been careful in what they had said and had been aware of their responsibilities.

"Every Sunday School teacher is just as much called of God as a missionary to the heart of Africa. He needs to prepare just as diligently—he needs to labor just as earnestly—as if he were carrying the Gospel to the most remote spot on the globe."—Billy Graham.

Questions for Pupils on the Next Lesson. 1. What is the cause of most enmity and strife? 2. Why does James insist that every Christian must choose between friendship with "the world" and friendship with God? 3. What must we do if we truly wish to have a sense of God in our hearts? 4. How would you define sin? 5. In planning for the future, why is it important to bear in mind both God's will and human limitations?

TOPIC FOR YOUTH
WATCH YOUR WORD

Knowing How To Say No. "Fiorello LaGuardia, flamboyant mayor of New York City from 1934 to 1945, in his premayoral days was assigned as judge of the night court. The inspector in charge of the antiprostitution division of the Immigration Service was a man by the name of Andrew Tedesco.

"LaGuardia said that when he first sat on the bench at night court, Tedesco said to him, 'You can get experience in this job, or you can make a great deal of money. I don't think you'll take the money. But remember, the test is if you hesitate. Unless you say "No!" right off, the first time an offer comes your way, you're gone.' "—*A Second Reader's Notebook,* Gerald Kennedy, New York: Harper & Brothers.

Gossip as Stealing. "Isn't malicious gossip and slander eating away at a person's character and reputation really stealing? How different was the attitude of General Robert E. Lee! He was asked his opinion of one of his severest critics. Lee gave him a very high rating. The man to whom Lee spoke expressed great surprise and told the general the particular person held a low opinion of Lee. Lee replied that he had been asked to give his opinion of his opponent, not his opponent's opinion of him."—Church Management: *The Clergy Journal,* September 1977.

Speed of Words. "I haven't figured it out, but I have it on good authority that if two persons, after exchanging a false rumor, each told his rumor to two more people within fifteen minutes and then those four people, on hearing it, would pass it on to each of two more within fifteen minutes, and this process kept going, that soon the number would reach that of the population of the United States.

"How long do you think it would take theoretically for this to happen? We might try to guess. We won't keep you in suspense. The answer is that in less than six hours and forty-five minutes the rumor would make the rounds of our entire country. There is a moral to this little announcement, but I know that it's not necessary to tell you what it is."—Walter McPeek, *The Scout Law in Action,* Nashville: Abingdon.

Sentence Sermon to Remember: Never believe anything bad about anybody unless you feel that it is absolutely necessary—and that God is listening while you tell it.—Henry Van Dyke.

Questions for Pupils on the Next Lesson. 1. What is the cause for the strife and enmity in our world? 2. How does a person go about getting close to God? 3. What makes human relationships meaningful? 4. In what ways do you feel the influence of our society and its values to be in conflict with what God wants? 5. In what areas do you find it most difficult to accept responsibility?

LESSON XII—MAY 20

BE RESPONSIBLE TO GOD

Background Scripture: James 4
Devotional Reading: 1 Peter 4:7–19

KING JAMES VERSION

JAMES 4 1 From whence *come* wars and fightings among you? *come they* not hence, *even* of your lusts that war in your members?

2 Ye lust, and have not: ye kill, and desire to have, and cannot obtain: ye fight and war, yet ye have not, because ye ask not.

3 Ye ask, and receive not, because ye ask amiss, that ye may consume *it* upon your lusts.

4 Ye adulterers and adulteresses, know ye not that the friendship of the world is enmity with God? whosoever therefore will be a friend of the world is the enemy of God.

5 Do ye think that the scripture saith in vain, The spirit that dwelleth in us lusteth to envy?

6 But he giveth more grace. Wherefore he saith, God resisteth the proud, but giveth grace unto the humble.

7 Submit yourselves therefore to God. Resist the devil, and he will flee from you.

8 Draw nigh to God, and he will draw nigh to you. Cleanse *your* hands, *ye* sinners; and purify *your* hearts, *ye* double minded.

9 Be afflicted, and mourn, and weep: let your laughter be turned to mourning, and *your* joy to heaviness.

10 Humble yourselves in the sight of the Lord, and he shall lift you up.

13 Go to now, ye that say, To day or to morrow we will go into such a city, and continue there a year, and buy and sell, and get gain:

14 Whereas ye know not what *shall be* on the morrow. For what *is* your life? It is even a vapour, that appeareth for a little time, and then vanisheth away.

15 For that ye *ought* to say, If the Lord will, we shall live, and do this, or that.

16 But now ye rejoice in your boastings: all such rejoicing is evil.

17 Therefore to him that knoweth to do good, and doeth *it* not, to him it is sin.

REVISED STANDARD VERSION

JAMES 4 1 What causes wars, and what causes fightings among you? Is it not your passions that are at war in your members? 2 You desire and do not have; so you kill. And you covet and cannot obtain; so you fight and wage war. You do not have, because you do not ask. 3 You ask and do not receive, because you ask wrongly, to spend it on your passions. 4 Unfaithful creatures! Do you not know that friendship with the world is enmity with God? Therefore whoever wishes to be a friend of the world makes himself an enemy of God. 5 Or do you suppose it is in vain that the scripture says, "He yearns jealously over the spirit which he has made to dwell in us"? 6 But he gives more grace; therefore it says, "God opposes the proud, but gives grace to the humble." 7 Submit yourselves therefore to God. Resist the devil and he will flee from you. 8 Draw near to God and he will draw near to you. Cleanse your hands, you sinners, and purify your hearts, you men of double mind. 9 Be wretched and mourn and weep. Let your laughter be turned to mourning and your joy to dejection. 10 Humble yourselves before the Lord and he will exalt you.

13 Come now, you who say, "Today or tomorrow we will go into such and such a town and spend a year there and trade and get gain"; 14 whereas you do not know about tomorrow. What is your life? For you are a mist that appears for a little time and then vanishes. 15 Instead you ought to say, "If the Lord wills, we shall live and we shall do this or that." 16 As it is, you boast in your arrogance. All such boasting is evil. 17 Whoever knows what is right to do and fails to do it, for him it is sin.

KEY VERSE: Draw near to God and he will draw near to you. . . . James 4:8 (RSV).

HOME DAILY BIBLE READINGS

May 14. M. *Source of Quarrels and Fights.* James 4:1–6.
May 15. T. *Selfish Human Desires.* Romans 7:5–12.
May 16. W. *Managing God's Gifts.* 1 Peter 4:7–19.
May 17. T. *Come Near to God.* James 4:7–12.
May 18. F. *Humility Is Greatness.* Matthew 23:1–12.
May 19. S. *Be Examples to the Flock.* 1 Peter 5:1–7.
May 20. S. *Trusting in God.* James 4:13–17.

BACKGROUND

The little General Epistle of James almost *didn't* get into the New Testament; its acceptance as Scripture came only after a long, hard fight. That is not hard to understand. James did not write what many people wanted to hear; he never showed any ambition to become "the author of the year." But he wrote fearlessly what he believed *had* to be written to and about the Christians of his day. Of course, the scribes and the Pharisees hated him; they put him to death.

Perhaps the trouble was that he got too *personal* about Christianity. Where, in last week's lesson, he was scholarly in talking about wisdom, in today's lesson, he becomes emotional, "het up" about certain things that were going on among the new Christians. Someone has written in our time, that many people become Methodists because "they like a fire under the boiler." There was fire in James. He was like the seraphim who came to Isaiah (Isaiah 6:6) with a live coal in his hand. He preached and wrote a flaming faith given to him by his Christ, and there were many who did *not* want that.

NOTES ON THE PRINTED TEXT

He begins with a "shocker": "From whence come wars and fightings among you?" (verse 1). Wars! The world of the Early Church was a world at war. Soldiers were marching everywhere; Rome was wielding a fearful sword. Rome took whatever Rome wanted, killing mercilessly to get it. There had always been war, ever since Cain killed Abel, and many there are among us who spurn the Prince of Peace and say that there will always be war between nations until the last battle of Armageddon is fought.

But James here is not speaking of nations at war, but of individuals at war with each other. "Is it not your (individual) passions that are at war *in your members?*" (Is there not a continuing struggle between good and evil going on among people? Or, as *The Living Bible* has it, "Isn't it because there is a whole army of evil desires *within* you?"

There is. Men, like nations, want something they don't have—and they will kill to get it. Men without money will destroy those who have it. Combinations of men "team up" to drive the small competitor to the wall. Here in our twentieth century, men in the high places of government (men already wealthy) stand convicted of bribery and other corruptions. Men, seemingly good men, ally themselves with gangsters; there is big money in that! That's the way of the world, and it is a vicious way.

Ah, says James, "Do you not know that friendship with the world is enmity with God?" (verse 4, RSV). Don't you see that this is *adultery?* The reference is not to physical adultery, but *spiritual* adultery—being unfaithful to God just as a wife or husband may be unfaithful to his or her mate.

Get wise, Christian! Remember that God "resisteth the proud but giveth grace unto the humble" (verse 6). If we enjoy evil pleasures in this world and count ourselves as being favored of God because we are rich, then we are no friends of God. God gives *strength* to the humble because He *loves* them.

Wash your hands, you proud sinners. Be clean. Originally, the washing of hands was a religious ritual with the Jews, so that a man might be ceremonially clean before he went to worship God. James gives it another meaning; he calls for a cleansing of the heart, for only the pure in heart shall see God (Matthew 5:8).

Humility! When Samuel Morse invented the telegraph, the first message that he sent over the wires was a most humble one: "What hath God wrought!" He made no fortune out of it; he gave the glory to God. When Jonas Salk produced his cure for infantile paralysis, he made no big money out of it; he *gave* it to humanity. When James—and Jesus—died, they left no "estates" but love of man for God, and love for men. Humility!

In verses 8–10, James calls upon his Christian brothers to get busy about their Father's business—*now*. Tomorrow may be too late, and one can never tell what tomorrow will bring. How do you know what will happen tomorrow, or next week, or next year? The days of your life are numbered, but you do not *know* how many more days you have. Don't fool yourselves by saying that life is a wandering in a fog, uncertain, capricious, baffling—now you have it, now it's gone. Don't brag about *your* plans to do this or that on some tomorrow. Live now as though God were guiding that life, working His will. His plan is far more important than yours.

We once toured the world with a tourist party. One in that party was a fine woman who told us that she and her husband had long planned such a tour together—but her husband died suddenly, and she moaned every time she saw some spot they had planned to visit together, "If only Jack were here to see it with me!" It ruined her trip. Tomorrow never came for her.

Then there was a little lady undergoing a serious operation. She said to her pastor, "I may not come out of this, but so what? Whatever is right for God is all right for me." She made it, and for that she thanked God.

He who lives selfishly, who makes his own plans, lives poorly. He who lives knowing that God has a plan for every minute of our living lives well.

SUGGESTIONS TO TEACHERS

Many in-depth surveys report that people long for a "sense of the Transcendant." Prayer and devotional books are perennial best-sellers in the religious book field. Young people, although turned off by the institutional and traditional forms of religion such as your Church, continue to show a strong interest in meditation and programs emphasizing spirituality. Apparently many people are seeking a sense of inner peace.

Your lesson for this Sunday is to keep these people in mind. In a sense, this includes everyone in your class, including you the teacher. Use the Epistle of James, chapter 4, and help everyone in your group to delve deeper into the promise of God's peace.

1. *CAUSE OF DISCORD.* Everyone sometimes feels like a "walking civil war," as one person described his inner feelings. Every person must deal with the greed and the anger and other destructive forces trying to take over his or her thinking. The root cause of all strife—personal, marital, community, national, industrial, international—is within each person. War begins with you and me. Bear down on the need for peace within oneself in this lesson. You may want to have your class break into groups of two or three, and discuss frankly what the barriers to inner peace seem to be in each person's life.

2. *CONFORMITY TO THE WORLD?* Remind your class of the powerful pressures each person is under to conform to the norms of our society, and how hard it is to conform to God's will. James calls Christians to draw near to God and His will. You may wish to continue the small groups and have these talk over the areas in the lives of each in your class where it is most difficult to conform to God's will. With some, it will be at work, or at school. With others, it may be in understanding what God's will is. Remind everyone that the clamor by the society to conform often drowns out God's whisper.

3. *CLARITY OF WILL.* James insists that believers must "cleanse your hands and purify your hearts" in order to know God's will. There can be no double-mindedness! A person's life must conscientiously center itself on living each day consistent with Jesus Christ's life. This means purity in thinking, speaking, and doing.

4. *CONTRITE IN WORSHIP.* The Scripture in James 4:9, 10 states that attitude in worship is essential if God is to be real in a person's life. Unless a person recognizes his or her need of mercy and sincerely turns to the Lord in worship, there is not a hope of peace within. Does worship in your church help people to have such a sense of contrition?

5. *COMPASSION TOWARD THE WEAKER.* Finally, James has blunt words about how one must feel and act toward others within the Christian family. As you and your class already know, often the hardest group to be patient with is your own congregation! Those nearest us, especially fellow Christians, seem to get under our skin the most! Be sure to look hard at James 4:11, 12. What does his teaching have to do with the attitude of your class members toward each other, toward others in your congregation, toward other churches in your area, toward Roman Catholics and others with whom you have points of disagreement?

TOPIC FOR ADULTS
DRAW NEAR TO GOD

Bring Up the Regiment! In the Civil War battle of Corinth, a certain regiment of Wisconsin infantry was under fire for the first time. They were ordered to advance and hold a certain ridge. Their color sergeant was a fresh young college boy named Jerome Davis, later to become a great Congregational missionary to Japan. Sgt. Davis marched ahead with his flag as ordered, until he was on the ridge. Crouching behind a stump he looked back. The regiment was not there. Far down the slope he saw their line, ragged and wavering and threatening to break as the enemy bullets whined about them and a few men fell. But Sgt. Davis held his ground. In a few minutes, an orderly came crawling forward on his stomach. When near enough he shouted in a lull in the firing, "Davis, bring back the colors." Davis shouted back, "The colors are where they belong! Bring up the regiment!" This they did, helping to win the battle.

This is where the colors belong: the banner of the Son of God. Bring up the regiment. We often want to pull the colors back. We must go forward.

Need for Whistle Blowing. Federal employees have abundant knowledge of illegal and wasteful government activities, but the majority of them don't report such activities because they believe nothing would be done to correct the situation according to a government survey in 1981. The survey was distributed to 13,000 federal employees in fifteen different agencies, and more than 8,500 responses were received. The survey, conducted by the U.S. Merit Systems Protection Board, reported that 45 percent of those questioned said they had personally observed fraud, waste or mismanagement in their agencies within the past year. One quarter of these activities consisted of waste caused by unnecessary or deficient goods or services, but also included were cases of government employees stealing federal property or funds, the use of official positions for personal benefit, and employees tolerating situations that posed a danger to the health and safety of the public.

But officials at the board said the most surprising finding was that 73 percent of the employees who had witnessed such activity and not reported it said they hadn't spoken up because nothing would be done about it. Only 19 percent cited the fear of reprisal as their reason for keeping quiet.

"This concern is buttressed by our finding that 43 percent of those employees who actually came forward to report wrongdoing said the reported abuses were not corrected," said Ruth T. Prokop, chairman of the board.

The survey discovered that of the 30 percent who reported such activity, one fifth felt they had been victims of reprisal due to their disclosures.

Those who blow the whistle on illegal and wasteful practices are showing responsibility to their country—and also to God. Drawing near to God means being responsible to others. Although our society does not always encourage such a sense of responsibility to government or to God, as this survey reveals, Christians know that they serve not because of a desire to be rewarded!

Draw Near to God! "The instruments through which God works in the church are human beings. If our hearts and minds are not properly transformed, we are like musicians playing untuned instruments, or engineers working with broken and ill-programmed computers. The attunement of the heart is essential to the outflow of grace. This is not to emphasize faith and experience over works, thought, and social action. We must aim at building the structures of God's kingdom but recognize that we will only create these through the transformation of our experience. Concentration on reformation without revival leads to skins without wine; concentration on revival without reformation soon loses the wine for want of skins."—Richard A. Lovelace, *Dynamics of Spiritual Life.*

Questions for Pupils on the Next Lesson. 1. What are you doing to make your prayer life more significant? 2. Where do you find you can share your joys and sorrows? 3. What experiences have you had recently which have required you to be patient? 4. Is your congregation a praying community? 5. What promises has God made to you and this class?

TOPIC FOR YOUTH
GETTING CLOSE TO GOD

Why Are They There? "One gets the distinct impression, observing us preachers berating our parishioners from the pulpit . . . and watching our congregations grovel about on their knees, that if Christ ever stood in the midst of our worship and said, 'Rise, your sins are forgiven,' we would stone Him for blasphemously interrupting our humility! Few gifts of God are more threatening than the gift of forgiveness. One doesn't need a psychiatrist to understand the subtle self-gratification and stubborn pride that lurks behind our Sunday morning humility. On our knees, with our heads bowed low, we are still only looking at ourselves. . . .

"We pastors would be wise, every so often, to spend a moment at the beginning of worship looking out over our assembled congregations and asking, 'Why are they here?' . . . . They may be there on Sunday morning, week-in-and-week-out—in spite of all the good modern reasons for not being there, in spite of all the good modern endeavors that the church does not do well, in spite of all our shortcomings as worship leaders and fellow worshipers—because they are looking for God. Or perhaps they are there because, like Augustine before them, they have the notion that God is looking for them. Perhaps they are there seeking, or more accurately, perhaps they are there hoping to be found. Perhaps they assemble for nothing more than, in the words of the old Calvinists, 'to glorify God and enjoy Him forever.' What more revolutionary, subversive activity could one undertake in this 'Me Generation' than to be caught singing a doxology?"—William H. Willimon, *The Bible: A Sustaining Presence in Worship.* Valley Forge: Judson Press, 1981. Used by permission of Judson Press.

Greatest Question. "The greatest question of our time is not communism versus individualism, not Europe versus America, not even East versus West: it is whether man can bear to live without God."—Will Durant, *Quote,* October 1, 1981.

Where Are All the Bessie Gwynns Today? "I suppose this is a secular smuggled-in item, but it feels religious. Black columnist Carl Rowan recently paid tribute to 'Miss Bessie,' who died at age eighty-five. She taught him Chaucer, Shakespeare, and Milton—there you find me again slipping into a portrayal of better, older days! This was all four decades ago in a little Jim Crow high school in McMinnville, Tennessee. Bessie taught Rowan about simile and metaphor and hyperbole, often by kerosene lamp. 'Bessie Gwynn was stern, insisting that what we put in our heads could not be taken away by the Ku Klux Klan. Still, she knew compassion and humor.'

"Here's Miss Bessie's best gift to Rowan, or, I wish, to us or our teens: 'You don't have to bend to every destructive peer group pressure!' Rowan liked to use 'ain'ts' and 'deses' and 'doses' to show he was tough enough to be on the football team. 'Boy, you'll make first-string only because you have guts and can play football. But do you know what really takes guts? Saying to yourself you've got to live and be somebody fifty years after the football games are over.' Now: 'God, how I hope a lot of young black teachers are socking it to kids of potential, making them believe that, in order to be a hitter in football or a playmaker in basketball, you don't have to play dumb.' Or yes, this is a religion item: 'I just give thanks that the Good Lord let Bessie Gwynn live long enough to teach me, my mother, my brothers, and sisters, and hundreds more. She made this a much better society.' For a first moment I thought, 'I wish I'd known her.' On second thought, now I do."— Martin Marty. Reprinted by permission from CONTEXT (January 15, 1981) of Claretian Publication, 221 W. Madison, Chicago, IL 60606.

Sentence Sermon to Remember: Ability involves responsibility.—Alexander MacLaren.

Questions for Pupils on the Next Lesson. 1. Do you have much hope for the future? Why or why not? 2. Who has made promises to you, and to whom have you made promises? Why were these promises made? Are they being kept? 3. Has God made any promises to you? How do you know He will keep them? 4. When have you experienced the power of prayer in your life?

LESSON XIII—MAY 27

BE PATIENT BEFORE GOD

Background Scripture: James 5
Devotional Reading: 1 Timothy 6:3–10

KING JAMES VERSION

JAMES 5 7 Be patient therefore, brethren, unto the coming of the Lord. Behold, the husbandman waiteth for the precious fruit of the earth, and hath long patience for it, until he receive the early and latter rain.

8 Be ye also patient; stablish your hearts: for the coming of the Lord draweth nigh.

9 Grudge not one against another, brethren, lest ye be condemned: behold, the judge standeth before the door.

10 Take, my brethren, the prophets, who have spoken in the name of the Lord, for an example of suffering affliction, and of patience.

11 Behold, we count them happy which endure. Ye have heard of the patience of Job, and have seen the end of the Lord; that the Lord is very pitiful, and of tender mercy.

12 But above all things, my brethren, swear not, neither by heaven, neither by the earth, neither by any other oath: but let your yea be yea; and *your* nay, nay; lest ye fall into condemnation.

13 Is any among you afflicted? let him pray. Is any merry? let him sing psalms.

14 Is any sick among you? let him call for the elders of the church; and let them pray over him, anointing him with oil in the name of the Lord:

15 And the prayer of faith shall save the sick, and the Lord shall raise him up; and if he have committed sins, they shall be forgiven him.

16 Confess *your* faults one to another, and pray one for another, that ye may be healed. The effectual fervent prayer of a righteous man availeth much.

17 Elias was a man subject to like passions as we are, and he prayed earnestly that it might not rain: and it rained not on the earth by the space of three years and six months.

18 And he prayed again, and the heaven gave rain, and the earth brought forth her fruit.

REVISED STANDARD VERSION

JAMES 5 7 Be patient, therefore, brethren, until the coming of the Lord. Behold, the farmer waits for the precious fruit of the earth, being patient over it until it receives the early and the late rain. 8 You also be patient. Establish your hearts, for the coming of the Lord is at hand. 9 Do not grumble, brethren, against one another, that you may not be judged; behold, the Judge is standing at the doors. 10 As an example of suffering and patience, brethren, take the prophets who spoke in the name of the Lord. 11 Behold, we call those happy who were steadfast. You have heard of the steadfastness of Job, and you have seen the purpose of the Lord, how the Lord is compassionate and merciful.

12 But above all, my brethren, do not swear, either by heaven or by earth or with any other oath, but let your yes be yes and your no be no, that you may not fall under condemnation.

13 Is any one among you suffering? Let him pray. Is any cheerful? Let him sing praise. 14 Is any among you sick? Let him call for the elders of the church, and let them pray over him, anointing him with oil in the name of the Lord; 15 and the prayer of faith will save the sick man, and the Lord will raise him up; and if he has committed sins, he will be forgiven. 16 Therefore confess your sins to one another, and pray for one another, that you may be healed. The prayer of a righteous man has great power in its effects. 17 Elijah was a man of like nature with ourselves and he prayed fervently that it might not rain, and for three years and six months it did not rain on the earth. 18 Then he prayed again and the heaven gave rain, and the earth brought forth its fruit.

KEY VERSE: *The prayer of a righteous man has great power in its effects.* James 5:16 (RSV).

HOME DAILY BIBLE READINGS

May 21.	M.	*The Folly of Riches.* James 5:1–6.
May 22.	T.	*Be Fair to the Poor.* Deuteronomy 24:10–15.
May 23.	W.	*Rich in Faith.* 1 Timothy 6:3–10.
May 24.	T.	*Endure Patiently.* James 5:7–11.
May 25.	F.	*Job's Patience.* Job 1:13–22.
May 26.	S.	*Power of Prayer.* James 5:12–20.
May 27.	S.	*Speak Honestly.* Matthew 5:33–37.

BACKGROUND

James writes his last word on his Epistle in Chapter 5, and he bases what he has to say on the teaching of the Second Coming of Jesus. That belief was widespread in the days of James. The Christians believed with all their hearts that He would come very soon: "Behold, the judge standeth before the door" (verse 4). But no Christian of that hour could say exactly *when* He would come. There were guesses made about it, and even today there are perfectly sincere Christians who believe and say that the time of the Coming is near, even *right now.* Many times, small sects in the Church have sold their worldly goods and gone out on some hilltop to await the appearance of Jesus. But He has not yet appeared. Even Jesus Himself said that He did not know when the promised divine event would occur: "But of that day and hour knoweth no man, no, nor the angels of heaven, but my Father only" (Matthew 24:36).

So—what was the young Church to do about this Coming? James may have seen some indication among the people of the Church that they might just sit down and do nothing—they might just *wait.* Why do anything, if the Lord is to come tomorrow and change everything? James forestalled that by telling them what they must do while they waited.

NOTES ON THE PRINTED TEXT

The first thing they had to do was to display a little *patience.* No man hurries the hand of God. No man sets God's timetable. James's friend Peter wrote that "one day is with the Lord as a thousand years, and a thousand years as one day" (2 Peter 3:8). God's idea of time is not man's idea. God in His own good time will do what He had promised. Stop worrying, Christian—be patient. Take a lesson from the farmer who sows his seed, confident that God will send rain that will make a harvest out of a seed. Should we have less faith in Christ and God than the humble farmer has in his seed? Believe—and be patient in belief.

Don't just wait; live like a Christian, quietly, peacefully, confident that whatever God does is for our sake and therefore good. Don't grumble and complain if it doesn't work out all *your* way. And don't complain about your petty afflictions. People who lived before you and people who will live after you will suffer afflictions. Some people fear afflictions; others make good use of them.

James suggests that his Christians take time out to read the story of Job in the Old Testament. Job was one of the most afflicted men in all of the Scriptures and the most heroic in overcoming his afflictions. He was a righteous, God-fearing man who for no reason at all was afflicted with boils, a shrewish wife, seven sons who died, flocks of sheep killed by lightening, and a house destroyed in a hurricane—yet he rose above it all with a triumphant shout: "Though he (God) slay me, yet will I trust in him." James suggests that a church about to suffer at the hands of its enemies might do well to imitate Job.

There was already opposition developing against the Church; from the very start there was opposition, and that opposition would grow as time marched on. What *kind* of Church should it be, James asks, to win out over opposition that would become persecution? First of all, it would be, must be made up of men of sterling character, faith, and reputation—men who were so committed to truth that they need not swear to tell the truth in court. (Many of our Quakers still believe that.) Let his every word (every yea and nay) be "as good as his bond." Let him be a man well known and one held in high respect. Such a man is Christianity's best advertisement.

Let this Church be a singing church (verse 13). They accepted that idea; the early Church *was* a singing church, singing in the very face of peril. Its members sang in the catacombs of Rome, sang as they were martyred, sang—almost everywhere. They were likely to burst into song at the least provocation. And the Church they sang in came singing down the centuries; from the beginning to now, it has been a Church singing for joy, a Church so happy that it just *had* to burst into song. The Christians learned early in the day that happy churches thrived, while dour churches had a habit of suffering sudden death.

Let the Church be a *healing* Church. Is there any sick among you? Visit him! "Let him call for the elders of the church" (as our sick call for their ministers). The Church, lest we forget it, is the mother of the modern hospital. Care for the sick was an inheritance from Judaism; when a Jew fell ill, it was not a doctor but a Rabbi that was called upon for help, and to anoint the sick with oil ("Oil," said Galen the great Greek doctor, "is the best of all medicines"). The Church has always sought out the sick, and the sick have always sought the helping hand of the Church. Few of any of the other institutions in modern society can make that claim.

Last but never least, let it be a *praying* Church. The Jews taught that sickness is due to sin, and that before a man could be healed of his sickness he had to be forgiven by God. Hence the petition of prayer—those moments in which we strive for a better relationship with God. We have found it good—no, *necessary*—to report in prayer to God at least once a week, to have our hearts and minds scrubbed clean. We *must* pray in complete sincerity, and in full confidence that God is *listening*—as He listened to a man named Elijah . . . read what prayer did for him in James 5:17–18.

Given such a Church, we shall have a Church of which we will never be ashamed.

SUGGESTIONS TO TEACHERS

Suppose each Christian had to write a one-page set of guidelines of what is expected of every Christian church member. What would your list include? What do you think your class would list?

To get your lesson off the ground this Sunday, you may wish to pass out paper and pencils and ask every person in your class to prepare such a set of basic suggestions for the folks in your congregation. After writing their lists, your people could benefit by looking again at James 5. What items appear in James that aren't on your class members' lists, and vice versa? Using the fifth chapter of James as a checklist, help your people to consider the following:

1. *PATHOS OF THE WEALTHY.* Ask your people why James and all Christian leaders keep warning against the dangers of possessions. Point out that it's not that money is evil in itself; it's what it can do to a person. According to James, those who have more than is needed for basic health and comfort are in peril! Luxury and pleasure have a corrupting effect. In every Christian's set of guidelines, therefore, should be stern warnings against deceit, cheating, fraud, and greed. There also must be equally strong insistence on simple life-style and concern for the poor.

2. *PATIENCE IN THE WAIT.* Every Christian must take into consideration the fact of suffering. James assures his readers that the Lord is coming and urges them to remain steadfast. Judgment is at hand always, but "establish your hearts," he pleads. In the interim before Christ's return, how does your class understand the meaning of hardship and problems?

3. *POSITIVE IN WITNESS.* James 5:12 discusses oath-taking, remembering that God consistently keeps His promises. Christians keep their word also. Truth is a hallmark of Christian character. In light of such a call for honesty in speech and action, ask your class if there is any place for the "little white lie," the shading of facts, the discreet silence, the exaggerated advertising claims, the strident rhetoric, the simplistic propaganda which are so common in our culture?

4. *PRAYER FOR THE WEAK.* "Prayer seems to be the lost word," wrote George Buttrick about the Christian Church a generation ago. Some say this is still true. Would your class agree? James 5:13 calls for serious praying for the sick and the suffering in each band of believers. How is your class mobilized to pray for others? Does your church have prayer circles? Are your people praying regularly—and by name—for one another?

5. *PERSEVERANCE WITH WANDERERS.* Every church has its backsliders. Actually, of course, each of us is a backslider in many ways, but here and in James 5:19 we are thinking of those who have wandered away from the Gospel and from the fellowship of Christians. Note the urgency James feels in bringing such "wanderers" back to the truth. How does your class reach out to those who are inactive? What could your congregation do for those who have dropped out or are fringe members? Why should Christians have such a concern for these?

TOPIC FOR ADULTS
BE PATIENT AND STEADFAST

Like a Basket of Sand. We are prone to criticize others and are eager to rebuke them. Even in the Church, we find ourselves being impatient with each other.

One of the early Christian desert monastic leaders was named Abbot Moses. Abbot Moses was an enormous black man whose generosity toward others was as big as his huge body. One day in the Egyptian desert where he lived, he and the other monks were called together to sit in judgment on an erring brother and to join in a communal reproof. Other monks with grim expressions had gathered, impatient to get on with a trial and eager to pronounce a severe sentence. Abbot Moses had not arrived. Grumbling, the others waited. Finally, the gentle giant walked into the solemn assembly. Abbot Moses was carrying a basket of sand, letting the sand run out through the many holes. Facing the glowering circle of startled monks, he said quietly, "My own sins are running out like this sand, and yet I come to judge the sins of another."

Abbot Moses knew God's patience with us. And the great abbot also knew that we had to be patient before God with each other.

Christianity's Hardest Problem. "The hardest problem of Christianity is the problem of the church. We cannot live without it, and we cannot live with it. . . . However bad the church may be in practice, it is the necessary vehicle for Christ's penetration of the world. However much it may at times become adulterated, the church is now, as always, the only saving salt we have in this world. The intelligent plan, then, is never to abandon the church, for then we have lost it all. Instead, rather, we must find some way of restoring the salt to greater purity and thus to more effective preserving quality and, if possible, though this is not so necessary as the other, to better savor to our palate. . . . When a Christian expresses sadness about the church, it is always the sadness of a lover."—Elton Trueblood, *The Incendiary Fellowship.*

The Listening Christian. Speaking of the need for regular times of praying, Mark Gibbard writes, "I have known this in theory for I do not know how long. But to experience its reality has been my great discovery these last few years. If nowadays I have occasionally to miss it, I don't worry too much, I don't get upset. Yet to miss it is like missing the visit of a friend. Even now this quiet, contemplative time hasn't always the same quality, the same depth—neither have all the meetings with a friend. But frequency builds up intimacy. If you can't find quiet where you live, can't you find a silent church, a park to walk in or a quiet reading-room in a library? Madeleine Delbrel was sometimes driven to find her time in a metro journey of five stops. You may have to use your ingenuity to find it, but love has its own ingenuity.

"Coming to God in this way quietly and receptively should spill over into our relationships with others and help us to meet them sensitively and receptively. This is so important, for one of the great needs of today is to listen to others—and not with half an ear. Dietrich Bonhoeffer, as we have seen, wrote about this and added its converse: 'He who can no longer listen to his brother will soon be no longer listening to God either.' "—Mark Gibbard, *Twentieth Century Men of Prayer,* London: SCM Press, 1974.

Questions for Pupils on the Next Lesson. 1. Why was Samuel not in favor of a king for Israel? 2. Why did the people want a king? 3. What were the requirements which Samuel insisted that the king fulfill? 4. Is it possible to have the best motives and yet make poor decisions? 5. Is it true that disobeying God will ultimately result in destroying the nation?

TOPIC FOR YOUTH
YOU ARE RESPONSIBLE

Why Are They Cheating? "In the dark of night, Gary sneaks inside a University of Maryland building here and spirits away a copy of his forthcoming economics test. Later, he passes it on to friends. 'A lot of these kids, their fathers work in business or whatever they do, they get a shortcut the other guy doesn't. That's the way to get what you get,' he reasons.

"In the light of day, John—son of a corporation president, pre-med student, academic star—shuffles into a crowded lecture hall, slips into a seat and begins taking a math test under the name of an academically sliding fraternity brother. 'Nobody's afraid about saying they do it,' he shrugs.

"Gary and John (those aren't their real names) are cheating, which itself is hardly new on college campuses. But educators fear they see some disturbing new trends among modern cheaters like these.

" 'They seem to feel it's part of the game; they feel less guilty about it,' says Richard Conway, who has taught English at several colleges, most recently Colorado's Lamar Community College. Educators say such students rationalize their cheating by citing such pressures as grade inflation, overcrowded campuses, intensified competition for graduate degrees, and the presence of professional cheating mills. And the cheaters use more sophisticated methods than their predecessors."—Reprinted by permission of the *Wall Street Journal* © Dow Jones & Company, Inc., 1980. All Rights Reserved.

As a Christian, you are responsible to God and others, regardless of the pressures or the excuses of others. Do you see your responsibility applying also to the classroom?

Responsible for Jailbirds. Being patient before God is not easy. John Erwin of Chicago, however, carries out his responsibilities patiently. A few years ago, Erwin, Director of the PACE Institute, a skills program in Chicago's tough Cook County prison, heard that one of the inmates was going to be released. Erwin patiently sought work for the man, and finally located a job for him in downtown Chicago. A couple of weeks later, John Erwin telephoned the boss of the man who had been released to ask how the inmate was doing. To his surprise, Erwin learned that the ex-prisoner had not even shown up for work after he had been released.

Erwin could have let it drop. After all, many of the convicts only return to crime after being turned loose. Erwin could have told himself that he had already done a lot for the man and didn't need to do any more if his efforts weren't more appreciated.

John Erwin did not blow up. Nor did he forget the former inmate or write him off as "hopeless." Instead, he went to the ex-con's home. He asked the man why he had not shown up for work. He learned that the man could not read English well enough to tell which bus to get to the job. Erwin then began a program of teaching the former inmate how to read well enough to recognize signs and simple instructions. To his satisfaction, Erwin watched the man start the job and continue it as a reliable employee.

Out of this, John Erwin started a special program for prisoners called PACE (Programmed Activities for Correctional Education) to teach prison inmates to read, write, and learn the skills to assist them to hold a job when they are discharged from jail.

Sentence Sermon to Remember:

> Let us be content in work
> To do the thing we can, and not presume
> To fret because it's little.
> —Elizabeth Barrett Browning

Questions for Pupils on the Next Lesson. 1. What is the difference between authority and authoritarianism? 2. Why is it so important to study the story of rulers of Israel? 3. What happens when a person or a nation disobeys God? 4. As long as your motives are good, won't your decisions be good? 5. What are the chief risks you have to take in life?

JUNE, JULY, AUGUST, 1984

THE RISE AND FALL OF A NATION

LESSON I—JUNE 3

THE PEOPLE'S DEMAND FOR MONARCHY

Background Scripture: 1 Samuel 8; 12
Devotional Reading: 1 Samuel 8:4–9

KING JAMES VERSION	REVISED STANDARD VERSION

KING JAMES VERSION

1 SAMUEL 12 14 If ye will fear the LORD, and serve him, and obey his voice, and not rebel against the commandment of the LORD, then shall both ye and also the king that reigneth over you continue following the LORD your God:

15 But if ye will not obey the voice of the LORD, but rebel against the commandment of the LORD; then shall the hand of the LORD be against you, as *it was* against your fathers.

16 Now therefore stand and see this great thing, which the LORD will do before your eyes.

17 *Is it* not wheat harvest today? I will call unto the LORD, and he shall send thunder and rain; that ye may perceive and see that your wickedness *is* great, which ye have done in the sight of the LORD, in asking you a king.

18 So Samuel called unto the LORD; and the LORD sent thunder and rain that day: and all the people greatly feared the LORD and Samuel.

19 And all the people said unto Samuel, Pray for thy servants unto the LORD thy God, that we die not: for we have added unto all our sins *this* evil, to ask us a king.

20 And Samuel said unto the people, Fear not: ye have done all this wickedness: yet turn not aside from following the LORD, but serve the LORD with all your heart;

21 And turn ye not aside: for *then should ye go* after vain *things,* which cannot profit nor deliver; for they *are* vain.

22 For the LORD will not forsake his people for his great name's sake: because it hath pleased the LORD to make you his people.

23 Moreover as for me, God forbid that I should sin against the LORD in ceasing to pray for you: but I will teach you the good and the right way:

24 Only fear the LORD, and serve him in truth with all your heart: for consider how great *things* he hath done for you.

25 But if ye shall still do wickedly, ye shall be consumed, both ye and your king.

REVISED STANDARD VERSION

1 SAMUEL 12 14 If you will fear the LORD and serve him and hearken to his voice and not rebel against the commandment of the LORD, and if both you and the king who reigns over you will follow the LORD your God, it will be well; 15 but if you will not hearken to the voice of the LORD, but rebel against the commandment of the LORD, then the hand of the LORD will be against you and your king. 16 Now therefore stand still and see this great thing, which the LORD will do before your eyes. 17 Is it not wheat harvest today? I will call upon the LORD, that he may send thunder and rain; and you shall know and see that your wickedness is great, which you have done in the sight of the LORD, in asking for yourselves a king." 18 So Samuel called upon the LORD, and the LORD sent thunder and rain that day; and all the people greatly feared the LORD and Samuel.

19 And all the people said to Samuel, "Pray for your servants to the LORD your God, that we may not die; for we have added to all our sins this evil, to ask for ourselves a king." 20 And Samuel said to the people, "Fear not; you have done all this evil, yet do not turn aside from following the LORD, but serve the LORD with all your heart; 21 and do not turn aside after vain things which cannot profit or save, for they are vain. 22 For the LORD will not cast away his people, for his great name's sake, because it has pleased the LORD to make you a people for himself. 23 Moreover as for me, far be it from me that I should sin against the LORD by ceasing to pray for you; and I will instruct you in the good and the right way. 24 Only fear the LORD, and serve him faithfully with all your heart; for consider what great things he has done for you. 25 But if you still do wickedly, you shall be swept away, both you and your king."

KEY VERSE: Only fear the Lord, and serve him faithfully with all your heart; for consider what great things he has done for you. 1 Samuel 12:24 (RSV).

HOME DAILY BIBLE READINGS

May 28.	M.	*The People's Request for a King.* 1 Samuel 8:4–9.
May 29.	T.	*The Secret Choice of Saul.* 1 Samuel 9:24–10:1.
May 30.	W.	*Saul's Initiatory Religious Experience.* 1 Samuel 10:1–13.
May 31.	T.	*The Choice of Saul by Lot.* 1 Samuel 10:17–27.
June 1.	F.	*Saul's Maintenance of National Security.* 1 Samuel 11:1–11.
June 2.	S.	*Public Choice of Saul.* 1 Samuel 11:12–15.
June 3.	S.	*Samuel's Farewell Address.* 1 Samuel 12:14–25.

BACKGROUND

Now we take a long jump, in these lessons, back from James and the New Testament to the early history of Israel in the Old Testament—an Israel ruled by kings good and not so good. We start, today, with the first of these kings.

For 410 years before the first king appeared, Israel was a loosely bound group of tribes, each of which had its elected leader, or "judge." Many of them were poorly equipped chieftains, respected only by their own tribes. But there were at least fourteen of these judges who were good and able men; the last of them was a man, a priest and a judge and a *born* leader, whose name was Samuel.

He was old, and he was tired; so were his people tired. They had to fight off the pagan tribes of Canaan and, being separated from each other as they were, they knew that they had a slim chance of ever conquering these enemies unless they could merge into one state and one army led by a capable *military* leader. They came to Samuel with a request that stunned the old man: "Now make us a king to judge (rule) us like all the nations" (1 Samuel 8:5). Samuel didn't think much of kings, but the Lord spoke unto Samuel and the old priest changed his mind.

NOTES ON THE PRINTED TEXT

It wasn't that Samuel despised the kings of his time because they were kings; he only felt that the tribes of Israel *needed* no king. For long, long years, Israel had depended upon God alone as their king. Why change that, Samuel asked; hadn't their God guided them every step of the way into the Promised Land? Were they not a people different from any other people, a peculiarly *chosen* people, responsible only to God—and not to any earthly king?

But the people refused to listen to that. They kept shouting, like a mob, "Give us a king." All right, said God to Samuel, let them have their king. Let them find out what fools they are the hard way. But this king shall rule only so long as he rules *under the guidance of God.* Let him hear the voice of God *and obey it;* if he doesn't obey, then he *and you* will find the hand of the Lord against yourselves. So said Samuel to his people. The Lord God approved of what he said; God demonstrated His approval in a giant clap of thunder, and the falling of rain—and "all the people greatly feared the Lord and Samuel."

And so Samuel put his hands upon the head of young Saul, son of the Benjaminite Kish, and named him the first king of Israel.

Saul! Young. Tall. Handsome. Strong. Every inch a king. At the sight of him all Israel shouted, "God save the king." God tried to but He couldn't. Saul was destined to destroy himself, and almost to destroy Israel. But at the start of his reign, he *seemed* to be a great and good king. He was likeable and loyal, he conquered the enemies of his people, and he was fairly faithful to the God of his people. In him, this monarchy, which was installed the moment Saul was anointed by Samuel, seemed to be a good instrument of God. The inference is plain: Samuel, in this sermon or address to his people, demanded that they as well as their ap-

pointed king must "fear the Lord, and serve him in truth with all your hearts ...
But if ye shall still do wickedly, ye shall be *consumed....*"

It applies to us as much as it applied to the first Israelites in Canaan. We still
have kings. Literally, even we Americans have a love for the pomp of kings, even
though we live under a democracy and not under a monarchy. But there are not
many kings left in our world; in their places, we put elected presidents (and
sometimes, dictators!). We "anoint" these presidents with great power—a power
that can either make us a great nation or a puny one. They are "the choice of the
people" just as King Saul was the people's choice. But if they are not watched
carefully, if *we* do not put in these high places of rulership men *fit* to rule *righ-
teously,* then we are asking for trouble—fatal trouble, often resulting in revolutions that execute bad kings.

Do we really look at our "rulers" and measure them by a yardstick of righteousness—or do we go to the polls and vote blindly for someone who happens to
belong to *our* party? Do we elect our rulers because they are only good politicians? If we do, we will *not* elect good rulers; we will get not kingdoms that God
can love but kingdoms He must despise.

Speaking of kingdoms, Mr. T. Z. Koo, a fine Chinese statesman who knew well
the tyranny of wicked rulers in his homeland, said this: "The Kingdom of God
does not exist because of your effort or mine. It exists because God reigns. Our
part is to enter this Kingdom and bring our own life under His sovereign will."

In the long view of history, Mr. Koo is painfully right. We will never get any
kingdom on earth that even approximates the Kingdom Jesus talked about until
we do what Samuel tells us to do: *live under the rule of God and His righteousness.*

SUGGESTIONS TO TEACHERS

When a person suffers from the loss of memory, confusion results. Institutions
also can suffer the effects of amnesia. When a nation or the Church forgets its
past, it soon loses a sense of identity in the present and lacks a direction for the
future.

The lessons for this Quarter are designed to help your class to remember its
past as part of God's people. The story of the rise and fall of the Old Testament
nation of Israel is more than a look at the ancient past. It is the account of sin and
obedience, corruption and reform which have shaped us.

The first five lessons discuss the establishment of the monarchy, beginning in
1020 B.C. Today's material focuses on God's response to the insistence of the people for a king. In this lesson and the ones to follow, keep in mind that you are not
merely "teaching history" but helping your class members to avert spiritual amnesia.

1. *REJECTING AND RUINING.* You and your class should take careful note
of the ways in which God's people turned from the Lord. Even "clergy" such as
Samuel's sons descended into greed and dishonesty. The political leaders wanted
to compete with other countries and have a king in order to be like other nations.
Corruption and ambition, according to 1 Samuel 8, displeased God and planted
the seeds which ultimately destroyed Israel. Remind your people that these same
seeds are present in the life of God's community today and can bring ruin to the
Church. In the case of a nation, ambition and corruption also spell problems and
eventual doom. Take note of the Prophet Samuel's warnings of loss of freedom
and high costs when a people turn from trusting in God and obeying Him.

2. *REMEMBERING AND REALIZING.* Take plenty of time in your lesson to
study Samuel's "Farewell Address" (1 Samuel 12). Samuel reminds his hearers of
their past; he retells their story. In remembering Moses and the Exodus, the
Judges and the prophets, Samuel knew that they would recall God's involvement

in history. One Samuel 12:9 has a line you should emphasize: "But they forgot the Lord their God. . . ." And trouble followed. But when they remembered the Lord, He sent leaders to deliver them. Have your class remember ways in which God has guided your congregation through its ups and downs. Encourage members to recall occasions in which God has revived the Church when Christians recovered their sense of memory of Jesus Christ. You should also remind your class that at the altar at the time of Holy Communion, the words of Jesus are always repeated, "This do in remembrance of me." Discuss what remembering Him may mean for your church.

3. *RESPONDING AND RISING.* Critics through the ages have written off God's people. Voltaire and the French philosophers, Bishop Butler and eighteenth-century English churchmen, and present-day seers of doom and gloom sing their requiems over the Church. Some in your class are undoubtedly pessimistic about the future of the Church. Samuel's closing words (1 Samuel 12:19–25) could well be read aloud. Some of these sentences apply particularly to you as teacher: "Far be it from me that I should sin against the Lord by ceasing to pray for you; and I will instruct you in the good and the right way." You and your class may wish to renew your pact with each other—and with the Lord to "fear the Lord, and serve him faithfully with all your heart."

TOPIC FOR ADULTS
THE PEOPLE'S CHOICE

Cut Out God. According to biographers, at first Charles Darwin was a believer in God and that, in his first edition of *Origin of Species,* he spoke frankly of God as the Director of evolution. His book, however, was received with such enthusiasm by the German materialists that Darwin became intoxicated with his success and cut out God in the second edition. In our churches, in our nation, and in our personal lives, we can become so impressed with our accomplishments that we leave out God. We often start with faith but end in folly because of our pride.

The story of the monarchs of the Old Testament is such a record. Read it as God's Word to us in our times!

True to Designer's Intention. In an old cathedral in Europe, there is a metal plate on the floor on a certain place where, once a year, the light shines on it through an iron ring on a window. If the building is still plumb and true, the light will come through the iron ring onto the metal plate. The builder had designed this as a means of checking on whether the structure was in danger of collapsing.

God has designed the human community to conform with His intentions. In the stories of the Old Testament monarchs, He instructed them to check whether or not their lives and the life of their nation was true to His Design by the light of His word. We are given similar opportunity to determine whether our lives are true to what God intends by the light of Jesus Christ.

Forces Which Make for Life and Death in Our Society. "We must try to remember that the enemy is as human as we are, and not an animal or a devil. Finally, we must be reminded of the way we ourselves tend to operate, the significance of the secret forces that rise up within us and dictate fatal decisions of prejudice and hate. We must be reminded of objective moral standards, and of the wisdom which goes into every judgment, every choice, every political act that deserves to be called civilized. We cannot think this way unless we shake off our passive irresponsibility, renounce our fatalistic submission to economic and social forces, and give up the unquestioning belief in machines and processes which characterizes the mass mind. History is ours to make; now above all we must try to recover our freedom, our moral autonomy, our capacity to control the forces that make for life and death in our society."—Thomas Merton, ed., *Breakthrough to Peace,* New Directions, 1963.

Questions for Pupils on the Next Lesson. 1. What can fear and suspicion do to a person's thinking and behavior? 2. What happens when some persons are not granted the recognition and appreciation they desire? 3. Describe an occasion in your life when you experienced jealousy. 4. Why is reconciliation essential if adults are to live harmoniously together? 5. How can the fear of the loss of status cause estrangement between persons?

TOPIC FOR YOUTH
THE PEOPLE'S CHOICE

What He Intended. A famous composer who was also a gifted violinist happened to be walking along a city street one day and overheard a street-corner fiddler begging for coins by trying to play one of the composer's best-known pieces. The composer stopped and listened to the awkward squeals. When the fiddler had finished, the composer stepped forward, dropped a coin in the player's cap, and asked if he could borrow the instrument for a moment. He then played the piece magnificently, pouring forth such beauty and harmony that the fiddler's rendition a few minutes earlier sounded like a different piece. When he played his composition, the great artist handed back the violin and added quietly, "That is what I intended that piece to be."

Through the scriptural story, we understand what God has intended His creation to be. The accounts of the kings of Israel help us to remember how we are to "play the piece" as the Lord has meant it to be played.

Contentment With the Universe. "John Gunther's son Johnny, who was a better philosopher at seventeen when he died of meningitis than some will be at seventy, left behind a private notebook in which he jotted down one day the lines:

" 'Contentment with the universe.

" 'Discontent with the World.

" 'If a person is at peace with the universe, at one with his Creator, attuned to reality, sure of his place and purpose within the large scheme of things, then he is free to be discontented, creatively discontented, with the domestic arrangements here on earth. If he is rooted in some central stabilities and nourished by a few great convictions, he can be profitably, even happily, discontented with things as they are. But if he is merely critical, merely dissatisfied, then he stands the risk of being merely edgy and querulous.' When Robert Frost the poet came to die, he asked that there should be engraved on his tombstone the words, 'I had a lover's quarrel with the world.' He nagged and chided the world not, as too often happens, because he disliked and distrusted it, but because he longed to see its rich possibilities realized, its promise fulfilled, and its goodness evoked. But then, you see, Robert Frost had not forgotten his resting-place. After a period of initial uncertainty, he had found his vocation. He knew what he had been called to do and so had no necessity to go scrambling from mountain to hill."—W.B.J. Martin, *Little Sins, Big Consequences,* Abingdon, 1982.

Limits Needed. Little four-year-old Billy was dissatisfied with everyone and everything. Finally, he announced to his mother, "Mummy, I am running away!" His mother was extraordinarily wise. "All right, Billy, you may run away but you cannot go farther than the driveway." Billy took off, but stopped at the end of the driveway, then sat and sulked for a few minutes. When Mummy called a few minutes later, "Billy, I love you. Won't you come home again?" he got up and walked back to the welcoming arms.

God handles us the same way. In our rebelliousness, we want to run away from Him. But He puts limits on us, even on our fleeing Him. More important, He welcomes us back to His presence.

The story of the monarchy in the Old Testament is similar to Billy's running away and returning. It is also the tale of your attempt to establish your little kingdom in the light of God's rule.

Sentence Sermon to Remember: As long as we work on God's line, He will aid us. When we attempt to work on our own lines, He rebukes us with failure.— Theodore Ledyard Cuyler.

Questions for Pupils on the Next Lesson. 1. How has jealousy ruined friendships among people you have known? 2. What makes us jealous of others? 3. What leadership qualities do you see in yourself? 4. Do you appreciate any leadership qualities in your Sunday-School teachers, your pastor, your church officers? 5. How can adults live together in harmony?

LESSON II—JUNE 10

WHEN JEALOUSY DOMINATES

Background Scripture: 1 Samuel 18:1–29
Devotional Reading: Genesis 37:12–24

KING JAMES VERSION

1 SAMUEL 18 5 And David went out whithersoever Saul sent him, *and* behaved himself wisely: and Saul set him over the men of war, and he was accepted in the sight of all the people, and also in the sight of Saul's servants.

6 And it came to pass as they came, when David was returned from the slaughter of the Philistine, that the women came out of all cities of Israel, singing and dancing, to meet king Saul, with tabrets, with joy, and with instruments of music.

7 And the women answered *one another* as they played, and said, Saul hath slain his thousands, and David his ten thousands.

8 And Saul was very wroth, and the saying displeased him; and he said, They have ascribed unto David ten thousands, and to me they have ascribed *but* thousands: and *what* can he have more but the kingdom?

9 And Saul eyed David from that day and forward.

10 And it came to pass on the morrow, that the evil spirit from God came upon Saul, and he prophesied in the midst of the house: and David played with his hand, as at other times: and *there was* a javelin in Saul's hand.

11 And Saul cast the javelin; for he said, I will smite David even to the wall *with it.* And David avoided out of his presence twice.

12 And Saul was afraid of David, because the LORD was with him, and was departed from Saul.

13 Therefore Saul removed him from him, and made him his captain over a thousand; and he went out and came in before the people.

14 And David behaved himself wisely in all his ways; and the LORD *was* with him.

15 Wherefore when Saul saw that he behaved himself very wisely, he was afraid of him.

16 But all Israel and Judah loved David, because he went out and came in before them.

REVISED STANDARD VERSION

1 SAMUEL 18 5 And David went out and was successful wherever Saul sent him; so that Saul set him over the men of war. And this was good in the sight of all the people and also in the sight of Saul's servants.

6 As they were coming home, when David returned from slaying the Philistine, the women came out of all the cities of Israel, singing and dancing, to meet King Saul, with timbrels, with songs of joy, and with instruments of music.

7 And the women sang to one another as they made merry,
"Saul has slain his thousands,
And David his ten thousands."

8 And Saul was very angry, and this saying displeased him; he said, "They have ascribed to David ten thousands, and to me they have ascribed thousands; and what more can he have but the kingdom?" 9 And Saul eyed David from that day on.

10 And on the morrow an evil spirit from God rushed upon Saul, and he raved within his house, while David was playing the lyre, as he did day by day. Saul had his spear in his hand;
11 and Saul cast the spear, for he thought, "I will pin David to the wall." But David evaded him twice.

12 Saul was afraid of David, because the LORD was with him but had departed from Saul. 13 So Saul removed him from his presence, and made him a commander of a thousand; and he went out and came in before the people. 14 And David had success in all his undertakings; for the LORD was with him. 15 And when Saul saw that he had great success, he stood in awe of him. 16 But all Israel and Judah loved David; for he went out and came in before them.

KEY VERSE: "Saul has slain his thousands, and David his ten thousands." 1 Samuel 18:7 (RSV).

HOME DAILY BIBLE READINGS

June 4.	M.	War With the Philistines. 1 Samuel 13:1–7.
June 5.	T.	The Breach Between Saul and Samuel. 1 Samuel 13:8–15.
June 6.	W.	The Rejection of Saul. 1 Samuel 15:7–22.
June 7.	T.	The Anointing of David. 1 Samuel 16:1–13.
June 8.	F.	David's Position at Saul's Court. 1 Samuel 16:14–23.
June 9.	S.	David's Slaying of Goliath. 1 Samuel 17:41–51.
June 10.	S.	Saul's Jealousy of David. 1 Samuel 18:5–16.

BACKGROUND

Saul, as a young man and a young king, "had everything going for him." He came from a wealthy family; he need never worry about money and so never became a corrupt leader in Israel. He had a most imposing presence, standing head and shoulders above any of his men. He was a man of deep religious nature (*see* 1 Samuel 9:2–6). He had great power as a military leader; he whipped the Canaanites and chased them from their land. He also had another noticeable gift, if we can call it a gift: Saul was mysteriously *temperamental*, alternating between bursts of energy and fits of depression. (Was it Mark Twain who said that *temperamental* was nine tenths temper and one tenth mental?) From the day of his birth, he was a boy and a man quick to anger, impulsive, wanting his own way and fierce with anyone who challenged him or his authority. Given the post and power of king only intensified this nature of the inner man in Saul. The time came when the men around him, frightened at his spasmodic fits of anger, talked him into sending for a young shepherd boy in Bethlehem to come to court and bring his harp. The boy David was good on the harp, and he just might soothe the kingly heart with his music. The boy came, bringing his harp—and a slingshot with which he had just killed a giant named Goliath.

NOTES ON THE PRINTED TEXT

Now, with David's arrival at Saul's court, begins one of the most fascinating stories in the Bible. Two stories unfold here: one dealing with the rise and fall of a king whom God first approved and then abandoned, and the other with the rising star of a boy whom God prospered and guided through the pitfalls and intrigues of the influential persons surrounding the king.

As the story is told, David "made it"—or found quick success as a military leader. The victory over Goliath was overshadowed by a whole series of victories won by the soldiers under the command of David. Saul was a good soldier; David was a spectacular soldier. It was not long before the people were singing his praises in the streets—especially the *women*, who not only sang but danced in praise of the new hero come to Israel. King Saul didn't like that at all. Homage should be given to the king, not to this young usurper from Bethlehem. Saul sulked; these women singing that Saul had slain his thousands but David had slain his tens of thousands made him angry, then furious, then insanely *jealous*.

·t *started* with jealousy, which was so common that it was not listed among the seven *deadly* sins. Mere jealousy seemed like a small thing—but it was as subtle and deadly as a cancer. Here was a very young David, with the humble background of a shepherd, capturing the applause of a crowd of fickle women (a cheering public must be watched; it changes its mind quickly about its heroes) who put this upstart on a pedestal, while the rich, young, brilliant Saul has to stand and watch it. Naturally, he was jealous—but a bit *too* jealous. We can watch the development of jealousy into envy, and the envy develop into fear, and fear drives him into hatred. Slowly the brilliant king, who at first was only jealous, plots to take the life of this David.

David is not greatly disturbed by this turn of events; he keeps his head, remains calm, does his job as a commander of the forces of the king. While Saul's mind crumbled and the taint of insanity grew strong enough to kill him, David did what God sent him to do—he grew in the knowledge of God and prepared himself for the kingship and never once attempted to kill his mad enemy Saul.

How often do we see it, in the long history of man! All through the early history of Israel, the kings killed one another in their lust to rule. Not one of the first eighteen popes in the Roman Church died in bed; they were murdered one way or another by other jealous, envious, hating men who wanted that top job! All the way down in European history, both kings and emperors were guilty of murder in their quest for power. In gentler ways, men striving for power and position have fought to rid themselves of their competition.

While all this has gone on and on, another brand of men have condemned the murders, striven calmly and quietly to establish better rulers on their thrones and a better way of life. There is an old German proverb about envy that rings a bell in our minds: "Envy is the sorrow of fools." Brilliant as he was, Saul was a fool in king's robes when he decided to kill innocent David: the more desperate he became, the more David's popularity grew. It ended in suicide for Saul, and David taking his place on Israel's throne.

Historians have not been very kind to Saul; most of them scold or deride him as something less than a man. That is too harsh, for Saul had his good points, and he is more to be pitied than condemned. He had two great faults that destroyed him: he sinned and didn't care what God thought about it, and he never had the courage to confess it to God (he lived and died as a man without a God); and, second, he summed it all up in words of his own when he admitted, "I have played the fool" (1 Samuel 26:21). That was the only confession he ever made, and that one came too late.

It was not a very auspicious start for the monarchy in Israel.

SUGGESTIONS TO TEACHERS

Jealousy is different from all the other forms of sin. Each of the other sins points to an end or a goal that is not in itself evil. Gluttony, for example, is a sin, but no one would tell us not to eat. Lust may be a sin, but we are not told not to reproduce the species. Greed, sloth, pride, and wrath also result from goals which are not in themselves wicked but which have been done wrongly. Jealousy seems to be wrong in itself.

In the case of Saul, Israel's first king, jealousy came to dominate his life and finally caused him to deteriorate to the point of self-destruction. Your lesson draws upon Saul's story as a case history of jealousy at work. Because everyone must struggle with jealousy, your lesson for this Sunday has great urgency. You have an opportunity to affect people "where they live."

1. *FEEBLE.* Have your class pick out examples of times when Saul showed his insecurity. Why did he seek applause and acclaim? Note the times when he seemed to require reinforcement. Why? Saul felt insecure. Point out to your class that our only true security lies with God. Apart from the Lord, we are feeble.

2. *FRIGHTENED.* Saul was threatened by a younger, abler person and became afraid of David's popularity. Talk with your class how each person is made to feel that he or she must compete with others in our society and is made to feel frightened. Ask if God intends us to feel that we must compete constantly with others. Remind them that the Lord desires compassion, not competition.

3. *FURIOUS.* Saul's temper tantrums degenerate into violent outbursts, and he finally tries to spear David. Jealousy makes us see others as rivals and can result in murder. This is a good place to discuss the deep feelings of anger present in each person as a result of jealousy. Have your class think together of the ways each person may be helped to find healing from the virus of destructive jealousy.

4. *FICKLE.* Using Saul as your "Case Study," trace the continuing deterioration of his character as he descends from angry outbursts to cunning plots against David. Saul turns devious. He schemes to have David slain in battle. Jealousy, if unchecked, warps a personality. Saul's jealousy so consumed him that he used all of his creative energies to try to destroy his rival David. And what a waste!

5. *FALSE.* Saul's life finally turns into a monstrous lie. He repeatedly goes back on his word to David and to the Lord. His jealousy makes him so suspicious that he deceives himself. Trace the way that falsehood grows out of Saul's jealousy

with the end in mind of showing that any in your class can be twisted into such a deceitful monster through jealousy.

TOPIC FOR ADULTS
WHEN JEALOUSY DOMINATES

The Cost of Jealousy. Jealousy must be crushed right in the beginning else it will lead us to mean and low things in order to thwart the success of those of whom we are jealous.

Not long ago I heard a terrifying story on the evil effects of jealousy. It appears there was a surgeon in a rural town who had built up a wonderful reputation over the years. As sometimes happens in small towns, another surgeon set up his practice, and before long, the newcomer was more and more in demand. A bitter jealousy grew up in the heart of the old-time surgeon—a jealousy so evil that it caused a thing that he probably will regret until the day he dies. The newcomer was to perform a particularly dangerous and delicate operation which the old-timer himself would not undertake and so he hated to think of another's possible success. And what happened? On the night before the operation the old-timer arranged to have his rival called by telephone several times during the night. As a result, the newcomer had hardly any sleep and the operation which he performed was a complete failure. His patient died on the table.

Gruesome Pictures. "It is interesting to note that medieval poetry and drama portraying the seven deadly sins very often give their most lurid portrayals in treating the evils represented by the sin of envy. In *Piers Plowman*, Langland personifies the seven deadly sins and describes their confession. He pictures Envy 'pale as a pellet,' with a knife by his side and a long lean face. His body is swollen, and words come out like those of 'an adder's tongue.' His confession is filled with reference to his neighbors and members of his family, so 'that all my body folneth for bitter of my galle.' Chaucer's parson in the *Canterbury Tales* declares, 'In the devil's furnace are forged three cursed wicked words, then standeth Envie and holdeth the hot iron on the heart of man with a pair of long tongs of long rancour.' In Spenser's *Faerie Queene*, Envy rides on a wolf in the procession of the sins. He is chewing a toad from which poisonous juices run down his face. He is wearing a 'discolored kirtle, "full of eyes." ' In his bosom curls a snake."—Lance Webb, *Conquering the Seven Deadly Sins.*

Maiming Effect. "Fatal or not, jealousy maims the spirit, paralyzes the will. At its most intense, the emotion can not be sustained: one can let it simmer to a consumptively querulous suspiciousness, kill its object, or get over it. Jealousy, however heated, ultimately becomes dull because it begins and ends with *self.* One's jealousy of someone has only to do with oneself; it touches not even tangentially the intrinsic peculiar worth of either its object or its instigator."—Joan Didion, "Jealousy—Is It a Curable Illness?", *Vogue*, June 1961.

Questions for Pupils on the Next Lesson. 1. What kind of work brings you most satisfaction and significance? 2. Did being king relieve David of his responsibility to God? 3. Why does the need for security often block a person's ability to listen? 4. Do you feel a need to get immediate gratification, or are you able to make sacrifices in order to realize a dream? 5. What are you doing to care for future generations?

TOPIC FOR YOUTH
CONTROLLED BY JEALOUSY

Jealous Wish Granted. An American automobile dealer grew jealous of his competitors selling foreign cars. Unfortunately, his business continued to slip. Finally, he went bankrupt and lost his business. His troubles continued. Bitterly, he began to drink. He turned into a wino and wandered the streets. He continued to blame all of his problems on competition by foreign cars and grew increasingly jealous and bitter of successful foreign car dealers. One day, in a boozy haze, he found a bottle with the cork still in it. Pulling out the cork, he was surprised to find a genie pop out. The genie thanked the former auto dealer for freeing her and offered to grant him any one wish he could think of. The ex-car man pondered deeply and remembered that foreign car dealers were making out well. He answered, "My wish is that I be a foreign car dealer in a big city." When he awoke, he found that the genie had granted him his wish: he had become a Chrysler dealer in Tokyo.

Like Contagious Infection. "If you were to find the germs of TB lurking in your body, you would spare no time, effort, or money in ruling them out. And yet many people are addicted with this deadly venomous envy and they are doing nothing about it."—Billy Graham, *Quote*, November 29, 1970.

Painful Effects. In Dante's *Inferno,* a medieval classic describing the effects of wrong-doing in this world, Lucia, who symbolizes the light of God's grace, conducts the poet on a tour of hell. On the second terrace, Dante is shown the people who have lived enviously of others. These unfortunates are clad in sackcloth and have the eyes repeatedly sewn up with iron threads. Dante in his epic is trying to warn his readers against looking on others with envy.

Sentence Sermon to Remember: Jealousy is the jaundice of the soul.—John Dryden.

Questions for Pupils on the Next Lesson. 1. Why did God select David to be the king? 2. What happened when David forgot that he was responsible to God? 3. What are your responsibilities to the groups you belong to? Your school? Your church? 4. Why does a community benefit or suffer from a leader's work? 5. In what ways are your nation's leaders showing or shirking responsibility?

LESSON III—JUNE 17

AN ANOINTED SHEPHERD

Background Scripture: 2 Samuel 5–7
Devotional Reading: Psalm 23

KING JAMES VERSION

2 SAMUEL 5 1 Then came all the tribes of Israel to David unto Hebron, and spake, saying, Behold, we *are* thy bone and thy flesh.

2 Also in time past, when Saul was king over us, thou wast he that leddest out and broughtest in Israel: and the LORD said to thee, Thou shalt feed my people Israel, and thou shalt be a captain over Israel.

3 So all the elders of Israel came to the king of Hebron; and king David made a league with them in Hebron before the LORD: and they anointed David king over Israel.

7 8 Now therefore so shalt thou say unto my servant David, Thus saith the LORD of hosts, I took thee from the sheepcote, from following the sheep, to be ruler over my people, over Israel:

9 And I was with thee whithersoever thou wentest, and have cut off all thine enemies out of thy sight, and have made thee a great name, like unto the name of the great *men* that *are* in the earth.

10 Moreover I will appoint a place for my people Israel, and will plant them, that they may dwell in a place of their own, and move no more; neither shall the children of wickedness afflict them any more, as beforetime.

11 And as since the time that I commanded judges *to be* over my people Israel, and have caused thee to rest from all thine enemies. Also the LORD telleth thee that he will make thee a house.

12 And when thy days be fulfilled, and thou shalt sleep with thy fathers, I will set up thy seed after thee, which shall proceed out of thy bowels, and I will establish his kingdom.

13 He shall build a house for my name, and I will stablish the throne of his kingdom for ever.

14 I will be his father, and he shall be my son. If he commit iniquity, I will chasten him with the rod of men, and with the stripes of the children of men:

15 But my mercy shall not depart away from him, as I took *it* from Saul, whom I put away before thee.

16 And thine house and thy kingdom shall be established for ever before thee: thy throne shall be established for ever.

REVISED STANDARD VERSION

2 SAMUEL 5 1 Then all the tribes of Israel came to David at Hebron, and said, "Behold, we are your bone and flesh. 2 In times past, when Saul was king over us, it was you that led out and brought in Israel; and the LORD said to you, 'You shall be shepherd of my people Israel, and you shall be prince over Israel.' " 3 So all the elders of Israel came to the king at Hebron; and King David made a covenant with them at Hebron before the LORD, and they anointed David king over Israel.

7 8 Now therefore thus you shall say to my servant David, 'Thus says the LORD of hosts, I took you from the pasture, from following the sheep, that you should be prince over my people Israel; 9 and I have been with you wherever you went, and have cut off all your enemies from before you; and I will make for you a great name, like the name of the great ones of the earth. 10 And I will appoint a place for my people Israel, and will plant them, that they may dwell in their own place, and be disturbed no more; and violent men shall afflict them no more, as formerly, 11 from the time that I appointed judges over my people Israel; and I will give you rest from all your enemies. Moreover the LORD declares to you that the LORD will make you a house. 12 When your days are fulfilled and you lie down with your fathers, I will raise up your offspring after you, who shall come forth from your body, and I will establish his kingdom. 13 He shall build a house for my name, and I will establish the throne of his kingdom for ever. 14 I will be his father, and he shall be my son. When he commits iniquity, I will chasten him with the rod of men, with the stripes of the sons of men; 15 but I will not take my steadfast love from him, as I took it from Saul, whom I put away from before you. 16 And your house and your kingdom shall be made sure for ever before me; your throne shall be established for ever.' "

KEY VERSE: " *'I took you from the pasture, from following the sheep, that you should be prince over my people Israel.'* " 2 Samuel 7:8 (RSV).

255

HOME DAILY BIBLE READINGS

June 11. M. *David's Elegy Over Saul and Jonathan.* 2 Samuel 1:17–27.
June 12. T. *David's Punishment of Ish-bosheth's Murderers.* 2 Samuel 4:1–12.
June 13. W. *David King Over All Israel.* 2 Samuel 5:1–5.
June 14. T. *Establishment of Jerusalem as Capital.* 2 Samuel 5:6–16.
June 15. F. *War With Philistines.* 2 Samuel 5:17–25.
June 16. S. *Bringing the Ark to Jerusalem.* 2 Samuel 6:1–15.
June 17. S. *Establishment of David's House.* 2 Samuel 7:8–16.

BACKGROUND

At Mount Gilboa, Saul, first king of Israel, found the end of his road: he and three of his sons were killed by the Philistines. Taunting the defeated Israelites, the Philistines hung Saul's body on the walls of Beth-shan. What now, Israel, with your king dead and gone? The Israelites came by night and took the body down and buried it . . . they fasted seven days, then they made Saul's fourth son, Ishbosheth, their second king. Ishbosheth was murdered almost before he had time to sit down on the throne, and that was the beginning and the end of the dynasty of Saul.

Now what? Now whom? Now they turned to one who had stood head and shoulders above Saul and the sons of Saul: they turned to David, the strange little shepherd boy who had established himself as a leader even before Saul died by his own hand.

Was this a case of *God,* by His hand alone, establishing a ruler over Israel?

NOTES ON THE PRINTED TEXT

Young David had much to commend him in the eyes of the people of Israel. He was a winner of battles, yet he did not strut in pride; being born a shepherd on an obscure farm, he grew up as one of the people; he was also born with a tremendous talent as a military leader—so necessary in those days of war. He was a good executive. And he was passionately loyal to the God of Hosts of Israel. He sinned seldom during his reign—and unlike Saul he confessed those sins and begged forgiveness.

Perhaps it was this passionate faith that found the eye and the approval of Israel's God. It had taken long years before the men of Israel could come to name a man for king in whom they felt that they could *completely* trust. They had cheered him as a youth; they had fought under his command on the battlefields of Canaan, and even when they lost a battle, they still trusted him, *just as he trusted God.* They saw in him a patient persevering and an all-out confidence that God's purpose would prevail. It would take seven long years before the tribes of Israel could be firmly melted into one, but the faith of the people in their David matched his faith in God, and they were unified. It was worth waiting for.

They made a good second start with David: they feared God and honored the king (1 Peter 2:17).

In 2 Samuel 7:1–16, we find a David well established as king of Israel. His old enemies have been conquered; there is no war to worry him, but he *is* worried over something that had nothing to do with war. He came to the Prophet Nathan with a problem, which dealt with the presence of God among his people. He tells Nathan that it does not seem right for him (the king) to be living in a beautiful palace made of cedar while the precious ark of his people is kept in a tent! Nathan shuns the question; he tells David to just go ahead doing what he had to do as king, and the Lord would take care of the rest. It wasn't much of an answer. It was really an evasion—and God promptly put a better answer on the lips of his prophet, and Nathan relays it to David.

There are two points of emphasis in Nathan's speech. First, God puts strong emphasis upon the declaration that He, God, needs no beautiful house in which to live. All He wants is a house (place) in the hearts of His people wherever they are and wherever they are going. Had God not been with them in their long trek through the wilderness? Had He not been a cloud by day and a pillar of fire in the night, *leading them?* He had no need of a house in the wilderness, any more than *they* needed houses. He had set His presence in the midst of His people—*in their hearts.* (For the Christians, did not Jesus say that the important thing was to worship Him in spirit and in truth, *wherever* they were?)

Jesus wasn't condemning all temples; He went into them more than once in His ministry, to enjoy the *atmosphere* of worship, but He also believed that where two or three were gathered together in His name, He would be in their midst. The important thing about worship is not *where* we worship, but *how*. Great cathedrals are an inspiration; we love them and rightly. But the lesser cathedrals of the soul are places "where the action is," where things happen.

The second emphasis in this passage is the promise that David's seed (descendants) will rule from his throne *forever*. A Covenant is made here between David, his sons and his God; God's steadfast love will dwell in them, they shall rule under His direction—and some of them may be doomed to punishment for their iniquity. But good or bad, David's "house" would be a dwelling-place for God, and God would build a great dynasty through which He rewarded or punished both king and people, when they *needed* punishment.

Ultimately, this passage suggests, it all depends upon the consciousness in the hearts of their kings that their God is indeed the God and King of them all. If God be worshiped in their kingly hearts, if they turn to Him for guidance, turn to Him in spirit and in truth, their reigns will be good. If not?

David, until the day he died, longed to build a great "house" for God. That was denied him, that was not to be. But his son would build that great temple in Jerusalem: the shadow of Solomon is in these verses.

David learned his lesson on the whole, he was Israel's greatest king, because he listened most closely to his God.

SUGGESTIONS TO TEACHERS

Your lesson today is to look at David as an anointed shepherd. Many in your class will have seen David only as a monument, not as a man. Your task is not to be a debunker, however. You should try to portray this anointed one as a forerunner of The Anointed One, and to point out that every person is responsible to the Lord.

1. *HALLOWS HIS LIFE.* Begin your lesson by showing how David realized that God had established him as king. David sensed that God had plans for him. David dedicated himself to the Lord: David hallowed his life to be God's anointed ruler. This provides you an opportunity to talk seriously with your students about the way each of them belongs to God. Prompt each person to consider his or her calling as God's person. Encourage your class members to reflect on the plans the Lord has in mind for each. Does your church help each one to grow in awareness of God's call and God's plans?

2. *HARKENS TO GOD.* David tried to listen to the Lord's voice. He asked if he should attack the Philistines (2 Samuel 5:19). Hearing an affirmative answer, David took action and won a victory. He remembered, however, to give the credit to God, not to himself. This is a good place to talk about ways of listening for God's instructions today. David tried to sensitize himself to hear the "sound of marching in the tops of the balsam trees" (2 Samuel 5:24), or to catch the faintest whispers from the Lord. How many Christians learn to listen for God?

3. *HONORS THE LORD.* A dancing David brings the Ark of the Covenant back to Jerusalem. Dancing was his way of worshiping. Someone pointed out that

the shout *Hallelujah* means "Hooray for God!" as a way of honoring the Lord. David's leaps and shouts as the Ark is trundled into Jerusalem are expressions of joy and thanks. Worship is basically honoring God. Although not every Christian can dance or leap, there must be an authentic desire to honor God.

4. *HARMONIZES HIS LIVING.* David fervently desired to build the Temple. However, the Lord denied David's wish. David accepts God's "No." David learned to live with limits. He realized he was not allowed to do everything he wanted. You should use enough lesson time to help your students to understand that every person must learn to harmonize his or her life within the limits set by God. Have your class members offer examples of the boundaries of turn-downs which the Lord has put on their lives, and how they are handling these in a positive way.

5. *HUMBLES HIS THRONE.* You should not try to portray David as a saint, yet not focus exclusively on the sordid details of his life. The Bathsheba episode cannot be glossed over, but it is not the last word about David. Lead your class to the scene where David "went in and sat before the Lord" in repentance (2 Samuel 7:18) and recalls humbly God's goodness and greatness. Have your class consider the words of David's moving prayer (2 Samuel 7:18–29). Remind your people that this prayer must also be theirs.

TOPIC FOR ADULTS
GOD'S CHOICE OF A LEADER

Mirror Self. One practical joker produced a book that looked like any ordinary book, with his title on the outside, *Wild Animals I Have Known.* When anybody opened the book, the would-be reader found himself staring into a mirror. The Bible is like that. You can find yourself in it somewhere. There are characters like everybody in the world today in the Bible. The story of David, God's anointed shepherd, describes you. Through the accounts of the lives of the personalities of Scripture, you discover yourself. God speaks to us about us as well as about Himself.

Saw Transcending Moral Issues. David was a great king. His people remembered him as the nation's greatest ruler. The question arises: What makes David—or any person a great leader?

James MacGregor Burns, in his engaging study, *Leadership,* tells about Franklin D. Roosevelt clashing with Joseph Kennedy. "The two never got along especially well, yet they needed one another to realize their ambitions. Kennedy had votes that Roosevelt needed to defeat Wilkie in 1940. Roosevelt could appoint Kennedy to office, as he did when Kennedy went to England as ambassador.

"Kennedy became an impediment to Roosevelt because he did not believe that England could withstand Hitler. F.D.R. manipulated him out of office by apparently promising him a vice-presidential nomination that never materialized in exchange for the 1940 votes that Kennedy delivered. Kennedy lacked vision. Burns puts it this way: Kennedy never seemed to see a transcending moral issue in the war. Because Roosevelt did, he was able to act with moral impact—to act with power."—*Leadership,* Harper & Row, 1978.

A Sense of Vocation. "A man can stand a lot of boredom and routine if he knows that the fundamental orientation of his life is right. The more deeply satisfying a man's job is, the less extrinsic excitement he craves. Every profession and trade has its stretches of sheer boring and monotonous routine; but if a man has a sense of vocation, he can absorb them. But where there is no sense of vocation, no dignity, or worthwhileness within his lifework, it has to be sought for in 'kicks' and cookouts."—W.J.B. Martin, *Little Sins, Big Consequences,* Abingdon, 1982.

Questions for Pupils on the Next Lesson. 1. How did David's lapses from responsibility to God and others affect his family? 2. What happened to persons in the scriptural accounts for this lesson who compromised their principles for social and political esteem? 3. Why do caring parents have to know how to teach their children discipline? 4. How would you describe the character of Absalom? 5. What do you think the major family problems are today?

TOPIC FOR YOUTH
THE NUMBER ONE CHOICE

Actor With Principles. Alan Alda, recognized and honored for his acting skills, is also a person with deep convictions. When he was signed on for the award-winning "M*A*S*H" television series, Alda was residing with his family on the East Coast. Even when he realized the show would survive a second year, Alda resisted moving to California—he didn't like the idea of uprooting his family. So his children have all gone to public schools in New Jersey, and Alda has maintained his exhausting coast-to-coast commute.

His first screenplay, *Senator,* is about a politician who loses touch with himself under the strain of his work. "It's a movie about how success puts pressure on a family," Alda explains. "We say we value our families and our integrity. On the other hand, we say success is the most important thing. People make compromises. They use their families."

There must be something positive in a film for Alda to appear in it. "I won't do a conventional war movie in which the excitement of war is the main adventure. In 'M*A*S*H' we show the effects of the war, not the fighting itself." Alda once turned down a commercial for cigarettes when he was $50,000 in debt and the money would have covered the whole thing. "I'm not going to ask somebody to get lung cancer so I can make $50,000."

The "So-What" Club. Fifty men gather on the second Thursday night of each month in a Nashville restaurant for a meeting of a strange club. They call themselves the So-What Club. They meet primarily to swap bawdy jokes, drink beer, and enjoy each other's rowdy fellowship. They have no work projects, support no charities, and undertake no worthwhile ventures in the community. The motto is simply "So-What?" Members pay their $35 dues every six months and show up for meetings if they feel like it. Nobody asks any questions about qualifications to join. The only requirements are that members must be males who will uphold the motto.

Actually, the So-What Club extends beyond Nashville, and has millions of secret members who wholeheartedly subscribe to its motto but who may not be carried on the Nashville club's roster. Some are on the rolls of every church.

God's people, however, can never take "So What?" for their watchword. Instead, like David, they realize that they have responsibilities to one another, and, most of all, responsibilities to God.

Expensive Butter. "In a certain bank, there was a trust department in which four young men and one older man were employed. It was decided by the directors that they would promote the older employee and also promote one of the younger men to have charge of the trust department after the older gentleman was removed to his new position. After considering the merits of each of the men, a certain one of the four younger men was selected for the new position and to receive a substantial increase in salary. It was decided to notify him of the promotion that afternoon at four o'clock. At the noon hour, the young man went to a cafeteria for lunch. One of the directors was behind him in the line with several other customers in between them. The director saw the young man select his food including a small piece of butter. The butter, he flipped on his plate, and threw some food on top of it to hide it from the cashier. In this way he lied to the cashier about what was on his plate. That afternoon the directors met to notify the young man that they had intended giving him the promotion, but because of what had been seen in the cafeteria, they must discharge him. They felt that they could not have as the head of their trust department one who would lie and steal. 'Honesty is the best policy' both in natural things and in spiritual things."—*The Free Will Baptist*, PULPIT HELPS, October 1977.

Sentence Sermon to Remember: Being "called," in the Christian sense, means simply being called to recognize a spiritual need in humanity and doing something about it.—Herman Melrose.

Questions for Pupils on the Next Lesson. 1. What are the areas of tension in your family? Why are these present? 2. What are you doing to bring reconciliation when such tensions occur? 3. What value systems are you considering? Why? 4. What is it that your parents and other elders do that disillusions you most about their religious commitment?

LESSON IV—JUNE 24

FAMILY REBELLION

Background Scripture: 2 Samuel 13:20–18:16
Devotional Reading: 2 Samuel 14:25–33

KING JAMES VERSION

2 SAMUEL 15 2 And Absalom rose up early, and stood beside the way of the gate: and it was *so*, that when any man that had a controversy came to the king for judgment, then Absalom called unto him, and said, Of what city *art* thou? And he said, Thy servant *is* of one of the tribes of Israel.

3 And Absalom said unto him, See, thy matters *are* good and right; but *there is* no man *deputed* of the king to hear thee.

4 Absalom said moreover, Oh that I were made judge in the land, that every man which hath any suit or cause might come unto me, and I would do him justice!

5 And it was *so*, that when any man came nigh *to him* to do him obeisance, he put forth his hand, and took him, and kissed him.

6 And on this manner did Absalom to all Israel that came to the king for judgment: so Absalom stole the hearts of the men of Israel.

7 And it came to pass after forty years, that Absalom said unto the king, I pray thee, let me go and pay my vow, which I have vowed unto the LORD, in Hebron.

8 For thy servant vowed a vow while I abode at Geshur in Syria, saying, If the LORD shall bring me again indeed to Jerusalem, then I will serve the LORD.

9 And the king said unto him, Go in peace. So he arose, and went to Hebron.

10 But Absalom sent spies throughout all the tribes of Israel, saying, As soon as ye hear the sound of the trumpet, then ye shall say, Absalom reigneth in Hebron.

11 And with Absalom went two hundred men out of Jerusalem, *that were* called; and they went in their simplicity, and they knew not any thing.

12 And Absalom sent for Ahithophel the Gilonite, David's counselor, from his city, *even* from Giloh, while he offered sacrifices. And the conspiracy was strong; for the people increased continually with Absalom.

REVISED STANDARD VERSION

2 SAMUEL 15 2 And Absalom used to rise early and stand beside the way of the gate; and when any man had a suit to come before the king for judgment, Absalom would call to him, and say, "From what city are you?" And when he said, "Your servant is of such and such a tribe in Israel," 3 Absalom would say to him, "See, your claims are good and right; but there is no man deputed by the king to hear you." 4 Absalom said moreover, "Oh that I were judge in the land! Then every man with a suit or cause might come to me, and I would give him justice." 5 And whenever a man came near to do obeisance to him, he would put out his hand, and take hold of him, and kiss him. 6 Thus Absalom did to all of Israel who came to the king for judgment; so Absalom stole the hearts of the men of Israel.

7 And at the end of four years Absalom said to the king, "Pray let me go and pay my vow, which I have vowed to the LORD, in Hebron. 8 For your servant vowed a vow while I dwelt at Geshur in Aram, saying, 'If the LORD will indeed bring me back to Jerusalem, then I will offer worship to the LORD.'" 9 The king said to him, "Go in peace." So he arose, and went to Hebron. 10 But Absalom sent secret messengers throughout all the tribes of Israel, saying, "As soon as you hear the sound of the trumpet, then say, 'Absalom is king at Hebron!'" 11 With Absalom went two hundred men from Jerusalem who were invited guests, and they went in their simplicity, and knew nothing. 12 And while Absalom was offering the sacrifices, he sent for Ahithophel the Gilonite, David's counselor, from his city Giloh. And the conspiracy grew strong, and the people with Absalom kept increasing.

KEY VERSE: Absalom stole the hearts of the men of Israel. 2 Samuel 15:6.

HOME DAILY BIBLE READINGS

June 18.	M.	David's Prayer of Gratitude. 2 Samuel 7:18–29.
June 19.	T.	David's Wars and Victories. 2 Samuel 8:1–14.
June 20.	W.	David's Kindness to Mephibosheth. 2 Samuel 9:1–13.
June 21.	T.	A Rebuke by the Prophet Nathan. 2 Samuel 12:1–7.
June 22.	F.	Festivities of Sheepshearing Time. 2 Samuel 13:22–29.
June 23.	S.	Absalom's Estrangement from David. 2 Samuel 14:28–33.
June 24.	S.	The Revolt of Absalom. 2 Samuel 15:1–14.

BACKGROUND

King David raised quite a family; from 2 Samuel 5, we learn that he "took him more concubines and wives out of Jerusalem, after he was come from Hebron; and there were yet sons and daughters born to David." At least eleven of his sons and daughters were born in Hebron, but that is about all we know about them save one named Solomon. They were apparently a mediocre lot. Only two of his offspring had any claim to fame: Solomon, his son by Bathsheba, and Absalom his son by Maachah. This flock of children is to be pitied; it is always difficult and sometimes impossible for the children of great men to get out of the shadow of their famous fathers. If often takes two or three generations for another "great" to be born.

Of these royal children, Absalom was by far the most attractive. "In all Israel there was none to be so much praised as Absalom for his beauty: from the sole of his foot even to the crown of his head there was no blemish in him" (2 Samuel 14:25). He had a glorious head of hair; he took better care of that hair than he did of his soul.

Handsome he was, but there was one little flaw that finally killed him: Absalom had the dirtiest heart in Israel. That was sad, because without such a heart he might have become king of Israel with a loyal and admiring people as his subjects.

NOTES ON THE PRINTED TEXT

Just when the trouble started, we cannot be sure, but it must have come when young Absalom looked into his mirror and discovered that he was good-looking—more so than his brothers and sisters. Or on another day, when he realized that he had a great talent for persuading people to see things his way. It was a way which at first seemed to be a clever way, but it was a way thoroughly evil and murderously selfish. Absalom would get up early in the morning and go down to the gate of the city where he met people coming into the city to participate in trials near the gate. He was smooth, gracious, and apparently sympathetic with these people, and anxious to help them "get justice." He wouldn't let them bow to him; he shook hands with them. The people liked that: this prince of the house of David was one of them and anxious to see that they received good treatment—he called it "justice." Such a *nice* young man!

He flattered them; he patted them on their backs; And as their protector, he "stole their hearts." He did not win their affections with any logical argument; he deceived and *beguiled* them, led them down the path to disaster by way of plain lies and false promises. By the time they discovered that they were being "taken" by a clever demagogue, it was too late.

There are many sons of Absalom in our midst. We have clever demagogues who tour the country promising to "turn the country around," bring justice to the oppressed, do away with all crime—the great friend of the people who will work miracles for them "if and when I am elected." A demagogue, by definition, is "a leader who seeks to make capital of social discontent and gain political influence." Yes, Absalom is still with us. Beware of him!

"Every dictator has arisen by these self-same methods. How different are the means employed by God in Christ to win the world! Jesus was crucified because He refused the trappings of power and refused to promise all men falsely that His Kingdom would bring automatic redress for every personal injustice, real or fancied. A lasting kingdom can be built only upon the hearts of free men freely drawn to the truth. Amid all the changes of time and space, history asserts this central fact."—Ganse Little in *The Interpreter's Bible*, vol. 2, by permission of Abingdon Press, publishers.

What Absalom wanted was not justice for the poor, but David's kingdom, ruled by Absalom. He got not that, but disaster and death; his troops were no match for the dedicated commanders of David, and, losing his battle, Absalom ran for his life through a thick woods, was snatched from his mule by his long, beautiful hair, and died strangled by it in the overhanging branch of a tree. How ignominious for a man who might have been king!

There was evidently little weeping and wailing over the death of Absalom. More than likely, those who had been deluded into following him might have said what Booth said when he shot Abraham Lincoln: *"Sic semper tyrannus."* They could say it in a better sense than Booth said it: a wicked man who longed to be leader had perished and that was good. But there was one man almost broken with grief when it was all over. This was David the father of Absalom, crying out of a broken heart, "If only I could have died for you! O Absalom, my son, my son." This is what we mean when we speak of a love that passes all understanding. If only Absalom had had just a little of this love, he might be remembered as one of Israel's great.

We honor David as a king honored of God. We would like to forget Absalom if we could.

SUGGESTIONS TO TEACHERS

The American family is in trouble. No Sunday-School teacher needs statistics to prove how serious the trouble is. You have enough sad stories of family problems within your church to provide plots for a dozen soap operas. Today's lesson addresses the issue of family relationships. As teacher, however, devote most emphasis not on what's wrong, but on what God intends. Use the biblical accounts of the rebellions in David's family as examples of how things go wrong.

1. *IRRELIGIOUS AND INDULGENT.* David's personal behavior in his disgraceful affair with Bathsheba had countless unforeseen side effects. "Like father, like son." David's son Ammon connives to carry out his lustful feelings. Ammon rapes his half-sister, Tamar, triggering a terrible chain of tragedies. Your lesson should focus on the causes of infidelity, not the sordid details. The root of all sexual misbehavior is an irreligious and indulgent attitude. Both David and Ammon provide prime examples.

2. *IRATE AND INDECENT.* Evil takes on a life of its own, and Ammon's evil action infects others. Tamar's brother vows vengeance and hatches a murder plot against Ammon. Anger toward family members must be handled in constructive ways immediately. Otherwise, destruction inevitably follows. Talk with your class about ways in which Christians deal with anger within a family circle.

3. *IRRESOLUTE AND INEFFECTIVE.* David is a poor role model for his children. Furthermore, he can neither discipline them nor show affection toward them satisfactorily. He seems to ignore his sons' need of boundaries and their need for acceptance. David does not discipline Ammon, and, later he will not be reconciled to Absalom. Depending on the make-up of your class, you may use some lesson time profitably to discuss the responsibilities of both parents and children in a Christian home.

4. *IRRESPONSIBLE AND INDIFFERENT.* God actively concerns Himself in our lives, and is the model for every human parent. People who act in irresponsible and indifferent ways toward others are ones who have neglected their faith. Trace the examples of this fact in the scriptural material for today's lesson, such as David's casual attitude toward his sons and Absalom's arrogant attempt to take over his father's throne. Point out to your class that it is not until David remembers his faith after being forced to flee from Jerusalem that he finally is able to mobilize efforts to quell the revolt. Tragically, however, it's too late; David loses a son who had talents and promise. As teacher, encourage your class to recognize

the urgency for mending broken family relationships and living responsibly before God.

TOPIC FOR ADULTS
FAMILY REBELLION

Out of the Mouths of Delinquents. Five delinquent boys in the Eldora, Iowa, training school were recently asked what they will do to keep their children out of the kind of trouble into which they had fallen. Their replies, published in the school magazine, are a rebuke to most American homes, parents, and public schools. Out of their stern experiences with the law came their request for a training which most parents and guardians have denied their children or have been unwilling to impose on them. Their program included: religious training; proper education; wholesome companionship in the home; discipline; and respect for property, law, and parental authority. Even when we discount these answers as an effort to cajole the authorities of the school, they still stand as a judgment against the climate of indifference and indulgence in which many of our young people grow up. Perhaps an even more enlightening and reliable rebuke is evident in the fact that the authority and the discipline which our homes have refused to provide, the delinquent youth of our cities seek and require in their gangs and clubs. We are paying the penalty for our disregard of the biblical injunction that we should "train up a child in the way he should go." Our children are warning us, not only by their delinquency but also by their recoil from the consequences of their misfeasance, that there is something amiss in our philosophies of child training. If we continue setting our children adrift upon the wild seas of our time without rigorous training, without compass or star, we can expect increasing human wreckage.

Hurry Home. Dr. Carl Menninger of Topeka, Kansas, was giving a talk to young mothers on helping the child form creative attitudes toward life. After the address, one of the mothers came up to Dr. Menninger and asked him when she should begin to teach these attitudes to the child.

"How old is your child?" asked the doctor.

"Three years," said the mother.

"Well," said Dr. Menninger, "hurry home as fast as you can. You already are three years late."

Already Religious Institution. Elton Trueblood says in *The Recovery of Family Life* that "it is not necessary to invent a religious program for the home, because the home is intrinsically a religious institution. Sometimes the religion inculcated in the family is bad religion, self-centered and contemptuous of others, sometimes it is a secular religion, as in the case of Marxism, but in any case the home is the place where most people receive their earliest and deepest convictions about that which they are committed."

Questions for Pupils on the Next Lesson. 1. What is Solomon's failure? 2. How did Solomon's policies lead to God's judgment on the nation? 3. What decisions in your life have had long-term consequences for good or bad? 4. How is your church seeking to build for future generations? 5. Does disobeying God's covenant bring dire consequences in our times?

TOPIC FOR YOUTH
TROUBLE IN THE MAKING

The Common Life. "On a small scale, . . . the home has all the problems and all the opportunities of the community at large. For its closely knit members, it is a society in embryo: a combination church, state, court, hospital, schoolroom, and playground all in one. It provided the young with a safe place for moulding character and gaining experience. Here they can learn to love and be loved, to trust and be trusted, to obey and be obeyed, to forgive and be forgiven. Consequently, although it dare never end there, the home is truly the right place for Christian charity to begin.

"Thus it is true, as men say, that parents, although they had nothing else to do, could attain salvation by training their own children. If they rightly train them to God's service, they will indeed have both hands full of good works to do. For what else are the hungry, thirsty, naked, imprisoned, sick, strangers, than the souls of your own children? With them God makes of your house a hospital, and sets you over them as chief nurse, to wait on them, to give them good words and works as meat and drink, that they may learn to trust, believe, and fear God. . . . O what a pleased marriage and home were that where such parents were to be found! Truly it would be a real church, a chosen cloister, yea, a paradise."— William H. Lazareth, *Luther On The Christian Home.*

Parable of a Penknife. At a museum in Alexandria, Virginia, is displayed a penknife which George Washington's mother is said to have given him for honoring her wish when, in his fifteenth year, he was eager to become a seaman. The story is related in several forms but, according to the ablest biographers, the true form is probably as follows. Young George had an opportunity to become a midshipman on a river packet, though some say it was a British warship. In spite of his mother's disapproval, he had carried the matter so far that his trunk and clothing had been put aboard the vessel. As he bade his mother good-by, she told him that he was leaving without her consent. Her words took effect. He removed his belongings from the ship, returned home, went back to school, and started upon the career which made him eventually "the father of his country." Think what both he and the nation might have lost if he had not honored his mother's judgment.

Home-Made Religion. A mother and father peer through the door to their children's room; three tykes bow in worship before an idol fashioned of clothes, hockey sticks, arrows, etc. Their oblation: a doll, a token of infant sacrifice. Says mother to father: "Well, you were the one who said we shouldn't force religion on them—that they'd find it for themselves."

Sentence Sermon to Remember: A house without a roof can scarcely be a more different home than a family unsheltered by God's friendship, and the sense of being always rested in His providential care and guidance—Horace Bushnell.

Questions for Pupils on the Next Lesson. 1. What happened when Solomon failed to obey what God commanded? 2. Does disobeying God have dire consequences in the life of a nation in our times? 3. What do we mean by "God's judgment upon the nation"? 4. What happens to a community or to a nation when leaders betray public trust? 5. Are you aware of character weaknesses within yourself which can lead to personal defeat?

LESSON V—JULY 1

SOWING SEEDS OF DESTRUCTION

Background Scripture: 1 Kings 9:1–11:13
Devotional Reading: 2 Peter 2:17–21

KING JAMES VERSION

1 KINGS 9 1 And it came to pass, when Solomon had finished the building of the house of the LORD, and the king's house, and all Solomon's desire which he was pleased to do,

2 That the LORD appeared to Solomon the second time, as he had appeared unto him at Gibeon.

3 And the LORD said unto him, I have heard thy prayer and thy supplication, that thou hast made before me: I have hallowed this house, which thou hast built, to put my name there for ever; and mine eyes and mine heart shall be there perpetually.

4 And if thou wilt walk before me, as David thy father walked, in integrity of heart, and in uprightness, to do according to all that I have commanded thee, *and* wilt keep my statutes and my judgments;

5 Then I will establish the throne of thy kingdom upon Israel for ever, as I promised to David thy father, saying, There shall not fail thee a man upon the throne of Israel.

6 *But* if ye shall at all turn from following me, ye or your children, and will not keep my commandments *and* my statutes which I have set before you, but go and serve other gods, and worship them;

7 Then will I cut off Israel out of the land which I have given them; and this house, which I have hallowed for my name, will I cast out of my sight; and Israel shall be a proverb and a byword among all people:

11 9 And the LORD was angry with Solomon, because his heart was turned from the LORD God of Israel, which had appeared unto him twice,

10 And had commanded him concerning this thing, that he should not go after other gods: but he kept not that which the LORD commanded.

11 Wherefore the LORD said unto Solomon, Forasmuch as this is done of thee, and thou hast not kept my covenant and my statutes, which I have commanded thee, I will surely rend the kingdom from thee, and will give it to thy servant.

12 Notwithstanding, in thy days I will not do it for David thy father's sake: *but* I will rend it out of the hand of thy son.

REVISED STANDARD VERSION

1 KINGS 9 1 When Solomon had finished building the house of the LORD and the king's house and all that Solomon desired to build, 2 the LORD appeared to Solomon a second time, as he had appeared to him at Gibeon. 3 And the LORD said to him, "I have heard your prayer and your supplication, which you have made before me; I have consecrated this house which you have built, and put my name there for ever; my eyes and my heart will be there for all time. 4 And as for you, if you will walk before me, as David your father walked, with integrity of heart and uprightness, doing according to all that I have commanded you, and keeping my statutes and my ordinances, 5 then I will establish your royal throne over Israel for ever, as I promised David your father, saying, 'There shall not fail you a man upon the throne of Israel.' 6 But if you turn aside from following me, you or your children, and do not keep my commandments and my statutes which I have set before you, but go and serve other gods and worship them, 7 then I will cut off Israel from the land which I have given them; and the house which I have consecrated for my name I will cast out of my sight; and Israel will become a proverb and a byword among all peoples.

11 9 And the LORD was angry with Solomon, because his heart had turned away from the LORD, the God of Israel, who had appeared to him twice, 10 and had commanded him concerning this thing, that he should not go after other gods; but he did not keep what the LORD commanded. 11 Therefore the LORD said to Solomon, "Since this has been your mind and you have not kept my covenant and my statutes which I have commanded you, I will surely tear the kingdom from you and give it to your servant. 12 Yet for the sake of David your father I will not do it in your days, but I will tear it out of the hand of your son.

KEY VERSE: But if you turn aside from following me, you or your children . . . then I will cut off Israel from the land which I have given them. . . . 1 Kings 9:6, 7 (RSV).

HOME DAILY BIBLE READINGS

June 25. M. *Solomon's Prayer for Wisdom.* 1 Kings 3:3–15.
June 26. T. *Solomon's Vision.* 1 Kings 9:1–9.
June 27. W. *The Forced Levy.* 1 Kings 9:15–22.
June 28. T. *Visit of the Queen of Sheba.* 1 Kings 10:1–13.
June 29. F. *Solomon's Wealth.* 1 Kings 10:14–25.
June 30. S. *Solomon's Business Enterprises.* 1 Kings 10:26–29.
July   1. S. *Judgment on Solomon.* 1 Kings 11:1–13.

BACKGROUND

Solomon, son of David, was born with the proverbial golden spoon in his mouth. Of all the sons of David, he stands out as the wisest and best of them all. As his father's reign came to an end, young Solomon was named king of Israel, and Israel rejoiced. David might have appointed his older son Adonijah who as the eldest son had a claim to the throne, but Adonijah was much less a man than Solomon. It was a fateful choice and a wise one, for Solomon, in spite of his fall from grace and popularity in later years, lifted Israel to its highest place in the history of the land. He started well on his knees at Gibeon. In a dream, God spoke to him. Already a king, Solomon had great need to hear that voice, for he trembled in fear when he thought of the responsibilities he was to face as king. "I am but a little child: I know not how to go out or come in. . . . Give therefore thy servant an understanding heart . . . that I may discern between good and bad" (1 Kings 3:7, 9). At that moment, Solomon was magnificent and well on his way to a high place in the Almighty's Hall of Fame.

NOTES ON THE PRINTED TEXT

He was the prime builder-king; it is difficult to count the number of fine buildings he sponsored, made of imported stone and cedars from Lebanon. His famous Temple was regarded as the most magnificent temple of his times; only 100 feet long by 30 feet wide, it was smaller than many churches built in *our* times, but the people of Israel looked upon it as the most beautiful of all buildings in the world. Solomon built it not for his own use but for God, and God "hallowed this house, and put his name upon it for ever." The king was indeed wise when he built that temple; it outlived him by many years.

He built palaces for himself; he spent thirteen years building one of them. This "palace" was really a whole group of buildings housing government offices and shelters for himself—and for his harem. He constructed a whole string of "store and chariot" cities to defend his trade with foreign countries and to protect his capital, Jerusalem. Solomon was indeed a great builder.

He was wise in directing his government and his people; wise in judgments—as in the famous case of the disputed baby; wise in beautifying his country, in enriching it with vineyards and gardens; wise in his developments of learning and the arts. He wrote (or is believed to have written) three thousand Proverbs, and his Songs were a thousand and five. He was a botanist, a poet, a philosopher, an architect!

Alas, as it is with so many of us, Solomon had his weaknesses, hidden though they were by his great accomplishments. He was foolish and unwise for *himself*, though he never seemed to know it. He married a heathen (Egyptian) princess; he had, besides this, seven *hundred* wives and three *hundred* concubines. (Polygamy was not forbidden, in those days; the marrying of other than Jewish women *was* forbidden.) These foreign women brought their pagan gods to Jerusalem, and Solomon encouraged that. Little by little, he was turning away from the God for whom he had built the Temple.

He spent money as though it came from a bottomless well: he financed 12,000 horsemen and 1,400 chariots, fortresses, fleets, swords, spears—all necessary for "national defense." His spectacular buildings were built by a people enslaved in forced labor. They paid outrageous taxes; he lived in a palace gleaming with cedar and gold and seldom if ever helped the poor. They groaned; he called for more cedar palaces, more golden drinking cups. Just before he died, his glorious Jerusalem was almost bankrupt. Yet he went on writing Songs and Proverbs. His Songs reveal him in the days of his youthful innocence, his Proverbs in the days of his wisdom and moral strength, his Ecclesiastes in the days of his bitter, aged disenchantment. "All is vanity" was his Great Amen.

What had happened to this great and unfortunate Solomon? What do we learn from him?

We learn that men need more than Lebanon cedars to build a good and lasting nation. They need God. Solomon knew God once; then, perhaps unwittingly, forgot Him as he went about the merry business of constructing buildings that were destined to be destroyed by a future enemy. God had made it plainer than plain: if Solomon as king would walk before God as David his father had walked, and live in integrity and righteousness, then God would put him on a throne forever as one of David's line. But if he failed to walk like that, then God would cut off not only Solomon but all Israel as well. For the sake of David, loved of God, God would not take the kingdom away from Solomon his son, but from Solomon's son.

Some biblical writers and commentators tell us that since the final edition of the Book of Kings was published during the Babylonian Exile, this account of Solomon's tragic failure must have been written long after he died. It is a moot question as yet unanswered and unsolved. Be that as it may, this is the tragedy that really did happen, a prophecy that was actually fulfilled. When it happened is of little interest; how and why it happened should be sending out signals to us in a day when we put very little trust in God and very much in bombs that can wipe out all of the great cities in our world in an hour's time!

SUGGESTIONS TO TEACHERS

After most disasters, formal investigations are conducted. Authorities and the general public want to know why a certain dam collapsed, or why an airplane crashed, or why an offshore drilling rig capsized. Nearly always, the causes are shown to be apparently insignificant flaws, such as an inferior grade of material which no one thought important in the dam's construction, or a build-up of ice on the wings of the airplane which no one regarded as dangerous, or a weakness in design which no one considered dangerous when an oil rig was anchored in the Atlantic. In retrospect, experts point out that the disaster was inevitable.

Your lesson is to examine the causes of the breakup of Solomon's great kingdom. You will find that the biblical writer in this lesson and the next lessons seems to be conducting a "court of inquiry." Although the kingdom under Solomon seemed to be permanent and flourishing, the seeds of destruction were being sown. Your task as teacher is not only to have your pupils examine the reasons for Solomon's great kingdom to decline, but to have them consider the implications of these findings for their own nation and community and church.

1. CONDITIONS OF HALLOWING. "Obey—or else!" seems to be the blunt way the Bible writers speak for God. The people which remain faithful to the Lord will prevail. Mention that Solomon knew this, and stated this lesson in his impressive prayer when his magnificent Temple was dedicated. God never automatically blesses any group with His presence. Do people in our country not sometimes think that our policies are always to be equated with God's?

2. COMPROMISE WITH HERITAGE. Point out the ways in which Solomon went back on his great Hebrew heritage by instituting forced-labor gangs to carry out his ambitious building schemes. God had once delivered His people from the

Pharaoh's slave crews, and Solomon seemed to be turning the clock back to pre-Exodus times. When a nation or a Church fails to live up to its own ideals and history, trouble follows.

3. *COMFORT FOR HIGHEST.* Solomon's dazzling splendor impressed even the Queen of Sheba who was used to high living herself. When the leaders lounge in luxury, however, especially when the rank-and-file complain in pain, a revolt will fester. Are the disparities between the upper and lower classes in our nation cause for concern? What would the biblical writers say about the luxury and the poverty in our communities?

4. *COST OF HEDONISM.* Point out to your class the exorbitant expenses and ostentation in Solomon's court, such as the gold-and-ivory throne and the 1,400 chariots. What happens to a country which comes to rely on wealth and power? What results when a culture puts pleasure ahead of duty? What parallels are there between the biblical story and our times?

5. *COLLAPSE OF HUMILITY.* Solomon's "playboy philosophy" led him to liaisons with 700 foreign princesses and 300 concubines. These women, mostly pagan, introduced various cults and rival religions. Solomon personally dabbled in these, forsaking the Lord he had promised to serve. The king who was warned to be faithful to God and who had warned others to remain loyal defiantly turned from the Covenant. A proud people stand in mortal danger!

TOPIC FOR ADULTS
SOWING SEEDS OF DESTRUCTION

"Secure" Car. Recently, CCS Communications Control offered for sale what it called the most advanced, most secure automobile ever manufactured. It's bullet-proof and blast-proof. Among other "extras," the 1979 car has machine gun mounts, tear gas vents, radar, and an antikidnaping electronic system. All for just $245,000 with no estimated miles per gallon specified.

Why is this "secure" car being offered for sale? Who ordered it in the first place?

This fancy car, with its security devices, was ordered by Shah Mohammed Reza Pahlavi, the Shah of Iran who was driven out by the revolutionary forces of Ayatollah Khomeini. The Shah had lived in a luxury similar to Solomon. He had disregarded the pleas for reform from among his people and permitted repressive measures. The seeds of destruction were sown years before his overthrow. That elegant $245,000 car symbolizes the failure of a once-strong ruler. It might have been built powerfully enough to withstand assassins' fire, but it could not prevent the seeds of destruction from growing within his kingdom.

Danish Spider's Forgetfulness. There is an old Danish fable which tells how a spider slid down a single filament of web from the lofty timbers of a barn and established himself on a lower level. There he spread his web, caught flies, grew sleek, and prospered. One Sunday afternoon, wandering about his premises, he saw the thread that stretched up into the dark unseen above him, and thought: "How useless!" He snapped it. His web collapsed and soon was trodden under foot.

Whenever a person forgets the thread of God's care and judgment which supports him or her, that person brings his or her downfall swiftly.

Planting a Tree. Speaking of the need to think of future generations, D. Elton Trueblood, educator, author says, "A man has made at least a start on discovering the meaning of human life when he plants shade trees under which he knows full well he will never sit."

Questions for Pupils on the Next Lesson. 1. Why was the nation of Israel taken from Solomon's family? 2. What happened to the tribe of Judah? 3. Who was Rehoboam and who was Jeroboam? 4. Why must we express civic and social responsibility in assessing and choosing national leaders? 5. As a Christian, what are ways in which you can best serve your nation?

TOPIC FOR YOUTH
WRONG CHOICE!

Collapse of the Great Wall. Most of you have seen pictures of the Great Wall of ancient China. Historians tell us that it was erected centuries before the time of Christ to protect the advanced Chinese civilization from barbarians beyond the border. We are also told that within a year after the wall was completed, it was breached three times. The wall was not destroyed by some new superior military weapon or superladder or catapult. It was breached because the gate keepers were bribed. Ancient China did not fall because of military weakness but because of a breakdown in morality and character.

Come to the Senses, Clemens. "Clemens has his head full of imaginary piety. He is often proposing to himself what he would do if he had a great estate. He would outdo all charitable men that are gone before him, he would retire from the world, he would have no equipage, he would allow himself only necessaries, that widows and orphans, the sick and distressed, might find relief out of his estate. He tells you that all other ways of spending an estate is folly and madness.

"Now, Clemens has at present a moderate estate, which he spends upon himself in the same vanities and indulgences as other people do.

"He might live upon one-third of his fortune and make the rest the support of the poor; but he does nothing of all this that is in his power, but pleases himself with what he would do if his power was greater.

"Come to thy senses, Clemens. Do not talk what thou wouldst do if thou wast an angel, but consider what thou canst do as thou art a man. Make the best use of thy present state, do now as thou thinkest thou wouldst do with a great estate, be sparing, deny thyself, abstain from all vanities, that the poor may be better maintained, and then thou art as charitable as thou canst be in any estate. Remember the poor widow's mite."—William Law.

Deadline for Decision. There comes a time when every person must make a decision whether or not to take God's offer of hope seriously. There finally comes a time when it is too late to respond. The lack of decision and response proves costly.

A businessman who had become a Christian published in the newspaper an advertisement that if anyone would come to him the next day before 12 o'clock noon and bring to him a list of all his debts, he would pay the entire indebtedness for him. As you can imagine, everybody in town talked about it, but nobody believed it. They thought it was a new advertising gag—just a joke. Why, who would believe such nonsense? All morning he sat in his office, and no one came, until finally, at 11:50 one man came. Of course, he looked around to see that nobody was watching him, because he didn't want to appear like a fool, but he came in to see if this wasn't so. It was so, but he was kept in the office. A couple other people came in, and they, too, had their debts taken care of. Then at 12 o'clock, they were permitted to go out, and as the word spread everybody wanted to get in, but it was too late. The deadline had been passed.

Sentence Sermon to Remember: The fear of the Lord is the beginning of wisdom.—Psalms 111:10.

Questions for Pupils on the Next Lesson. 1. What happened to his nation when Rehoboam was unresponsive to pleas for relief? 2. What was the effect of Solomon's worshiping false gods? 3. How can one person's foolish decisions bring ruin to an entire nation? 4. Does God hold our nation responsible? 5. What are the responsibilities of a Christian to the nation?

LESSON VI—JULY 8

WHY DIVISION CAME

Background Scripture: 1 Kings 11:26–14:31
Devotional Reading: 1 Kings 12:1–11

KING JAMES VERSION

1 KINGS 11 29 And it came to pass at that time when Jeroboam went out of Jerusalem, that the prophet Ahijah the Shilonite found him in the way; and he had clad himself with a new garment; and they two *were* alone in the field:

30 And Ahijah caught the new garment that *was* on him, and rent it *in* twelve pieces:

31 And he said to Jeroboam, Take thee ten pieces: for thus saith the LORD, the God of Israel, Behold, I will rend the kingdom out of the hand of Solomon, and will give ten tribes to thee:

32 (But he shall have one tribe for my servant David's sake, and for Jerusalem's sake, the city which I have chosen out of all the tribes of Israel:)

33 Because that they have forsaken me, and have worshipped Ashtoreth the goddess of the Zi-donians, Chemosh the god of the Moabites, and Milcom the god of the children of Ammon, and have not walked in my ways, to do *that which is* right in mine eyes, and *to keep* my statutes and my judgments, as *did* David his father.

12 15 Wherefore the king hearkened not unto the people; for the cause was from the LORD, that he might perform his saying, which the LORD spake by Ahijah the Shilonite unto Jeroboam the son of Nebat.

16 So when all Israel saw that the king hearkened not unto them, the people answered the king, saying, What portion have we in David? neither *have we* inheritance in the son of Jesse: to your tents, O Israel: now see to thine own house, David. So Israel departed unto their tents.

REVISED STANDARD VERSION

1 KINGS 11 29 And at that time, when Jeroboam went out of Jerusalem, the prophet Ahijah the Shilonite found him on the road. Now Ahijah had clad himself with a new garment; and the two of them were alone in the open country. 30 Then Ahijah laid hold of the new garment that was on him, and tore it into twelve pieces. 31 And he said to Jeroboam, "Take for yourself ten pieces; for thus says the LORD, the God of Israel, 'Behold, I am about to tear the kingdom from the hand of Solomon, and will give you ten tribes 32 (but he shall have one tribe, for the sake of my servant David and for the sake of Jerusalem, the city which I have chosen out of all the tribes of Israel), 33 because he has forsaken me, and worshiped Ashtoreth the goddess of the Sidonians, Chemosh the god of Moab, and Milcom the god of the Ammonites, and has not walked in my ways, doing what is right in my sight and keeping my statutes and my ordinances, as David his father did.' "

12 15 So the king did not hearken to the people; for it was a turn of affairs brought about by the LORD that he might fulfil his word, which the LORD spoke by Ahijah the Shilonite to Jeroboam the son of Nebat.

16 And when all Israel saw that the king did not hearken to them, the people answered the king,
"What portion have we in David?
    We have no inheritance in the
        son of Jesse.
To your tents, O Israel!
    Look now to your own house,
        David."
So Israel departed to their tents.

KEY VERSE: ". . . for thus says the Lord, the God of Israel, 'Behold, I am about to tear the kingdom from the hand of Solomon, and will give you ten tribes . . . because he has forsaken me. . . .' " 1 Kings 11:31, 33 (RSV).

HOME DAILY BIBLE READINGS

July 2.   M.   *Hadad, Adversary of Solomon.* 1 Kings 11:14–22.
July 3.   T.   *Jeroboam, Adversary of Solomon.* 1 Kings 11:26–40.
July 4.   W.   *Withdrawal of Israel From Judah.* 1 Kings 12:16–20.
July 5.   T.   *Jeroboam's Idolatry.* 1 Kings 12:25–33.
July 6.   F.   *Judgment Against Jeroboam.* 1 Kings 13:1–5.
July 7.   S.   *Conflicting Counsel.* 1 Kings 12:1–11.
July 8.   S.   *Rehoboam's Tragic Decision.* 1 Kings 12:12–15.

BACKGROUND

The last days of King Solomon were bitter days for a king who knew that he had failed; old, tired, weak, he must have welcomed death. At his death, his son Rehoboam was named as king. It was a sad choice: this Rehoboam was a simpleton, a man with a child's mind. He was a king only because he happened to be the son of a king.

The resentment and threat of rebellion that had been brewing in Solomon's kingdom boiled over when his feeble successor presented himself at Shechem for confirmation of his succession. Shechem was the main religious and political center of the northern tribes—those tribes living north of Jerusalem. The northerners had a right to complain that they had no place of authority in the government located in Jerusalem; they were taxed "without representation": their people were often forced into hard labor for the benefit of the *southern* kingdom. The stage was set for an explosive uprising, and it came, blowing the ten tribes in the north apart from two tribes—Judah and Benjamin—in the south. The famed "United Kingdom" lasted only from Saul to David, and it was never to be reunited after two strange men met on the road to Jerusalem.

NOTES ON THE PRINTED TEXT

One of these strangers was a prophet named Ahijah, an obscure little prophet who often had the nerve to protest against the extravagances of Solomon and against the influence of the foreign gods upon whom Solomon smiled—right to the king's face. That made him anything but popular with the king, but probably popular with the suffering people. The other stranger was a man named Jeroboam, a rebel born; he was Solomon's secretary of labor and taxes when he met Ahijah.

The story of their meeting on the Jerusalem road is highly dramatized by whoever wrote it into the Book of Kings. Jeroboam, according to the story, was on his way with a delegation of northern protesters en route to seek relief from the new king. Rehoboam had a chance, here, to bring peace and justice to his kingdom and to establish himself in the favor of his people. But, fool that he was, he disregarded the advice of the older aides at his court and followed the suggestion of a group of young, untried, intolerant, radical young men. He told those who sought relief from oppression that they should be quiet and behave themselves; his father Solomon had chastised them with whips, but he, Rehoboam, would chastise them with scorpions unless they quieted down and did what he, their king, told them to do.

In a moment of outraged anger, the little prophet reached out and tore the cloak off the back of Jeroboam. He ripped that cloak into twelve pieces; he put ten pieces in the hands of Jeroboam, with the explanation that the rebel adventurer was to rule over the ten tribes in the north—to rule as their first king. That left only two other pieces, representing the two southern tribes of Judah and Benjamin to be ruled by Rehoboam. The greatest event of centuries had happened here: the kingdom of David was no more; there was no "unity"; there were only two kingdoms ruled by men unworthy and incompetent.

Why?

Read verse 33 in 1 Kings 11, and you will know why. Solomon had turned his back on God. He had welcomed the worshipers of pagan gods into his kingdom; he had bent the knee to Ashtoreth, the goddess of the Sidonians, and the gods of Moab and the Ammonites. Rehoboam ran for his life to the hills of Jerusalem as the fighting turned against him; there until he died, he insulted his father's God at every turn of the road. The worship of graven heathen images spread from hovel to palace; he established groves for illicit worship, and led his people into an immorality scarce even in those early times. He was a total failure.

So was Jeroboam, who fled to Egypt when his resistance movement failed. He returned later (about 922 B.C.) to become the first king of Israel, and to take up the fight against domination by Rehoboam. The old battle yell, "To your tents, O Israel" (which meant "to your *arms*") was heard again in the land. Jeroboam reigned and fought over a period of twenty-two years, and then he died, leaving in his wake countless dead from both north and south and a string of idols and golden calves worshiped between Dan and Bethel. But he never ruled Jerusalem. He led Israel in the worship of false gods, and he helped a nation to lose its soul, and then he died. He set no value on God's favor; God set no value on him.

Actually, this splitting of the kingdom goes all the way back to the early days in Canaan. The people in the south and those in the north always seemed to be somehow different and "separated" from one another. They never quite reached a state of perfect unity, and, weakened by the excesses of Solomon's days, it was inevitable that a revolution should come to drive them even farther apart. It need never have happened; it would not have happened had they kept their covenant to walk with God.

Revolutions, says someone, never come because of what the people want but because of what their rulers are. That is true in our time. Much of our world is ruled by dictators or terrorists who are so determined to rule that they would kill every last one of their poor "subjects" to attain that end. "The people" of old Israel and the people of our world cannot be blamed for disasters rained upon them by godless, oppressive kings. Only a revolution in the hearts of the people will change that process of decay and disaster and give us leaders worthy of our admiration and respect.

SUGGESTIONS TO TEACHERS

The breakup of a family brings trauma to each member. When a national "family" splits, the wound-shock is also felt by every citizen. The division of Solomon's kingdom into two separate nations introduced a love-hate relationship between the people of Israel and Judah for as long as the two lasted. The lesson for today examines why division came and is part of a four-lesson unit on the two kingdoms.

Remember as always that you are not turning your lesson into a history class, but listening for God's whispers for these times through Scripture.

1. *IRON WILL FULLNESS.* The biblical account shows the corruption and disobedience during Solomon's reign. In addition, it shows the crushing tax burdens and forced-labor gangs which Solomon's administrators laid on the people. Unfortunately, Rehoboam, Solomon's successor, showed a heavy-handed attitude toward his people. When a leader is unwilling to listen, especially to hurting people in his own country, the danger lights soon flash. Point your lesson toward the responsibilities of leaders, whether in government, in church, or in any organization. Remind your class members that because they are Christians, they are automatically called as leaders in our society, and therefore have responsibilities to the oppressed. Are they heeding the cries of these in the community?

2. *GOLD BULLS.* Review the career of Jeroboam. Although he began his reign with immense promise, he drifted into apostasy. He dabbled in pagan ceremonies. His example caused his people to fall away from the Lord. The result: the disintegration of worship and the moral fiber of Israel. Point out the way the nameless prophet warned Jeroboam, and the occasion in which prophet Ahijah warned of dire consequences to Jeroboam's family because of the king's willful rejection of God for golden bulls. Remind your class that Christians and the Church must often speak an unpopular word to leaders and to society. God's

spokesmen and spokeswomen—the meaning of *prophet*—protest "golden bulls" in every generation.

3. *BRASS SHIELD*. Also review the career of Rehoboam. Like Jeroboam, his rival in the north, this king thought it fashionable and expedient to forsake the Lord and go along with foreign cults. The spiritual and ethical tone of Judah declined. When Shishak invaded, Rehoboam bought him off by replacing Solomon's gold shields with less-expensive brass models. Rehoboam sold out his heritage. Discuss how easy it is to think that we can substitute cheap, attractive practices which quickly tarnish for priceless, permanent moral values. For example, the current fads of sexual permissiveness have replaced the ideal of faithfulness in marriage for many, even in religious circles.

4. *STEELY DESTRUCTIVENESS*. Have your class note the constant, debilitating warfare between Israel and Judah recorded in 1 Kings. The cost of such mutual suspicion and hostility was beyond measure. This offers your class a fine opportunity to talk about the effects of conflict in any community, including the church. You can profitably guide your class through a discussion on ways whereby Christians deal with disagreements and differing viewpoints in constructive rather than destructive ways.

TOPIC FOR ADULTS
REVOLTS AGAINST OPPRESSION

Verdict of History. Eighty years ago, the British *raj* in India was at the height of its power and glory. In the year 1903, Lord Curzon was viceroy of India. He organized an immense *durbar* in Delhi, to celebrate the recent accession of Edward VII. Curzon was a man of great ability, with an immense capacity for attention to detail. He exercised this latter gift in close supervision of every aspect of the preparations for the *durbar*. A Christian service was planned, and Curzon called, in advance, for a copy of the Order of Service. He found that one of the hymns proposed was "Onward Christian Soldiers," and forthwith he placed a vice-regal veto on it. He did not do so for the quite plausible reason that most of the soldiers on view at the *durbar* would be Muslims and Hindus, but on the more Curzonian ground that the hymn contained the lines:

> Crowns and thrones may perish,
> Kingdoms rise and wane.

Lord Curzon could not, apparently, envisage a state of affairs in which the crown which he represented and the empire which he served with such distinction could possibly wane. Yet within less than eighty years, the Indian Empire has given place to a sovereign republic.

The Restraint of Sin. One primary principle of Christian social ethics has been traditionally formulated as "the restraint and remedy of sin." This essential aspect of Christian social policy is no less important because it is negative. In fact, this formula sums up in large part the way Christians understand the nature of social institutions and justify their existence. The simplest social institutions with their surrounding customs regulating human behavior give illustration of the need for "restraining and remedying sin." Consider the coin boxes on public transportation buses: the driver checks whether the passengers put in their fares; and passengers put their own money in the box, rather than giving it to the driver, lest he be led into too great temptation. None of our markets where economic goods and services are exchanged are arranged as if only righteous men, or wholly righteous men, were engaged in them. All are arranged in part to anticipate and restrain sin. James Madison said the same thing of properly arranged political institutions.

"What is government itself, but the greatest of all reflections on human nature?

If men were angels, no government would be necessary. If angels were to govern men, neither external nor internal controls on government would be necessary. In framing a government which is to be administered by men over men, the great difficulty lies in this: you must first enable the government to control the governed; and in the next place oblige it to control itself.

"A dependence on the people is, no doubt, the primary control on the government; but experience has taught mankind the necessity of auxiliary precautions. . . ."—Paul Ramsay, *Basic Christian Ethics*.

Ruined Garden. In 1938, after a visit to the Holy Land, a certain minister dreamed a dream. He wanted to erect a garden, a place of prayer, a chapel, in his home town of Covington, Kentucky. His dream was to bring the Holy Land to all those who would never see it.

Land was purchased. Flowers and trees came from twenty-four countries. Many individuals contributed toward the project. A chapel was erected for prayer and meditation. There was a carpenter's shop, and tools from the village of Nazareth. A replica of the open tomb was built. Overlooking the entire project, a huge statue of Christ stood, and could be seen for many, many miles.

In 1959, the minister opened his beautiful park to the public. It was called, appropriately, "The Garden of Hope."

Almost immediately, "The Garden of Hope" met with difficulty. Most of the plants and trees, brought from all over the world, could not stand the Kentucky climate. One after another, they died. The garden did not have the visitors that were expected. Bills could not be paid, and the park went into debt.

For twenty-one years, a minister had planned and dreamed about this "Garden of Hope" before it had finally become a reality. But his dream failed.

The park is a sad and tragic site today. Weeds have grown up everywhere, the chapel is padlocked, and the lonely statue of Christ is unkempt. Beer cans litter the entire area. "The Garden of Hope," in Covington, Kentucky, is a failure.

God planted this world as a "Garden of Hope," but we allow it to become a place of ruin. Our corruption and disobedience can turn every dream-community into a wasteland. The story of Israel and Judah may become our stories!

Questions for Pupils on the Next Lesson. 1. Why are many people concerned about their nation's involvement with other nations? 2. Do you think that your national and local leaders are concerned about national morality as well as national politics? 3. Why is it so easy to rationalize evil? 4. How did Jezebel exert an evil influence on Israel? 5. How did Elijah oppose Baal worship in Israel?

TOPIC FOR YOUTH
LET'S SPLIT

Opium. British merchants such as Jardine, Matheson, Dent, and Joseph Henry found a substitute currency for gold in opium grown in India. They were soon landing the drug at the Pearl River estuary at the rate of 6 million pounds a year. They defended themselves morally by calling opium "a harmless luxury and a precious medicine except to those who abuse it," took the business line that if they did not sell it to the Chinese, someone else would.

The Chinese government reacted with moral lectures, then seized and burned British opium stocks at Canton. In the Opium War following, the flimsy Chinese navy was sunk, the feudal armies scattered. In the peace treaty, the humiliated emperor was forced to grant free trade at five ports, pay $21 million indemnity, hand over Hong Kong to the British. Opium was not officially outlawed in Hong Kong until 1945!

Relations between the European or Western nations and the Chinese were deeply affected by the self-interest of merchants and governments which exploited the Chinese. Part of the harsh feelings by Chinese toward outsiders has been their anger against the treatment given them in the nineteenth century. Conflict results when injustice and oppression continues.

Robber Bands Big and Small. "Set justice aside and what are kingdoms but large robber bands, and what are robber bands but little kingdoms? . . . Excellent and elegant was the pirate's answer to the great Macedonian Alexander, who had taken him. The king asking him how he durst molest the seas so, he replied with a free spirit, 'How darest thou molest the whole world? But because I do it with a little ship only, I am called a thief; thou doing it with great navy art called a conqueror' "—St. Augustine.

Government the Teacher. Almost fifty years ago, Mr. Justice Brandeis warned against governmental misconduct, saying: ". . . Our government is the potent, the omnipresent teacher. For good or for ill, it teaches the whole people by its example. Crime is contagious. If the government becomes a law-breaker, it breeds contempt for law; it invites every man to become a law unto himself; it invites anarchy."

Sentence Sermon to Remember: If men be good, government cannot be bad.— William Penn.

Questions for Pupils on the Next Lesson. 1. Do you sometimes find it difficult to do the right thing in all circumstances? 2. How do you avoid yielding to peer pressure in making your decisions? 3. Are you tempted to use your skills and strengths for personal advantage? 4. What effect did Queen Jezebel have on her nation? 5. What did Elijah do to oppose Baal worship in Israel?

LESSON VII—JULY 15

AN ERA OF EVIL

Background Scripture: 1 Kings 16:15–22:40
Devotional Reading: 1 Kings 19:9–18

KING JAMES VERSION

1 KINGS 16   21 Then were people of Israel divided into two parts: half of the people followed Tibni the son of Ginath, to make him king; and half followed Omri.

22 But the people that followed Omri prevailed against the people that followed Tibni the son of Ginath: so Tibni died, and Omri reigned.

23 In the thirty and first year of Asa king of Judah began Omri to reign over Israel, twelve years: six years reigned he in Tirzah.

24 And he bought the hill Samaria of Shemer for two talents of silver, and built on the hill, and called the name of the city which he built, after the name of Shemer, owner of the hill, Samaria.

25 But Omri wrought evil in the eyes of the LORD, and did worse than all that *were* before him.

29 And in the thirty and eighth year of Asa king of Judah began Ahab the son of Omri to reign over Israel: and Ahab the son of Omri reigned over Israel in Samaria twenty and two years.

30 And Ahab the son of Omri did evil in the sight of the LORD above all that *were* before him.

31 And it came to pass, as if it had been a light thing for him to walk in the sins of Jeroboam the son of Nebat, that he took to wife Jezebel the daughter of Ethbaal king of the Zidonians, and went and served Baal, and worshipped him.

32 And he reared up an altar for Baal in the house of Baal, which he had built in Samaria.

33 And Ahab made a grove; and Ahab did more to provoke the LORD God of Israel to anger than all the kings of Israel that were before him.

22   37 So the king died, and was brought to Samaria; and they buried the king in Samaria.

38 And *one* washed the chariot in the pool of Samaria; and the dogs licked up his blood; and they washed his armour; according unto the word of the LORD which he spake.

39 Now the rest of the acts of Ahab, and all that he did, and the ivory house which he made, and all the cities that he built, *are* they not written in the book of the Chronicles of the kings of Israel?

REVISED STANDARD VERSION

1 KINGS 16   21 Then the people of Israel were divided into two parts; half of the people followed Tibni the son of Ginath, to make him king, and half followed Omri. 22 But the people who followed Omri overcame the people who followed Tibni the son of Ginath; so Tibni died, and Omri became king. 23 In the thirty-first year of Asa king of Judah, Omri began to reign over Israel and he reigned for twelve years; six years he reigned in Tirzah. 24 He bought the hill of Samaria from Shemer for two talents of silver; and he fortified the hill, and called the name of the city which he built, Samaria, after the name of Shemer, the owner of the hill.

25 Omri did what was evil in the sight of the LORD, and did more evil than all who were before him.

29 In the thirty-eighth year of Asa king of Judah, Ahab the son of Omri began to reign over Israel, and Ahab the son of Omri reigned over Israel in Samaria twenty-two years. 30 And Ahab the son of Omri did evil in the sight of the LORD more than all that were before him. 31 And as if it had been a light thing for him to walk in the sins of Jeroboam the son of Nebat, he took for wife Jezebel the daughter of Ethbaal king of the Sidonians, and went and served Baal, and worshiped him. 32 He erected an altar for Baal in the house of Baal, which he built in Samaria. 33 And Ahab made an Asherah. Ahab did more to provoke the LORD, the God of Israel, to anger than all the kings of Israel who were before him.

22   37 So the king died, and was brought to Samaria; and they buried the king in Samaria. 38 And they washed the chariot by the pool of Samaria, and the dogs licked up his blood, and the harlots washed themselves in it, according to the word of the LORD which he had spoken. 39 Now the rest of the acts of Ahab, and all that he did, and the ivory house which he built, and all the cities that he built, are they not written in the Book of Chronicles of the Kings of Israel?

KEY VERSE: *"How long will you go limping with two different opinions? If the Lord is God, follow him; but if Baal, then follow him."* 1 Kings 18:21 (RSV).

HOME DAILY BIBLE READINGS

July 9. M. Reign of Nadab of Israel. 1 Kings 15:25–32.
July 10. T. Reign of Baasha of Israel. 1 Kings 15:33–16:7.
July 11. W. Reign of Elah of Israel. 1 Kings 16:8–14.
July 12. T. Consequences of Zimri's Coup. 1 Kings 16:15–22.
July 13. F. Reign of Amri of Israel. 1 Kings 16:23–28.
July 14. S. Reign of Ahab of Israel. 1 Kings 16:29–34.
July 15. S. The Death of Ahab. 1 Kings 22:30–40.

BACKGROUND

Now we have two lines of kings to trace, in order to understand the rise and fall of the nation of Israel. One line ruled in Judah, the other in northern Israel. To bring it up to date: after Rehoboam, in Judah, came Abijah his son, who tried to recover the Ten Tribes, failed and died after only three years on the Judean throne. Then Asa who was really a fine king; he loved to smash idols and was merciless against the enemies of Jehovah; he swept the kingdom clean and died too soon, loved and honored, because he never walked in his father's sins. After Asa, there was Jehoshaphat who, believe it or not, was an improvement on his distinguished father. Asa built well, fought well, separated church and state, and sent out missionaries of the faith; he was one of the few fit to be a king.

Meanwhile, in Israel, Jeroboam was followed by Nahab, who supervised a short (2 years) and evil reign and was slain by Baasha, a vicious man born with a sword in his hand. Baasha swam to power in a river of blood and finally drowned in it, conquered by Asa. Then one named Elah (2 years, again) was murdered while drunk by one Zimri. Zimri lasted just one week; he was succeeded by Omri—a good general and a good man who arrived on the scene a bit too late. His religious record was weak and sometimes bad, but he had one great accomplishment to his credit: we call it Samaria.

NOTES ON THE PRINTED TEXT

In tracing these kings and their reigns, there does seem to be an overabundance of weak, poor, and evil kings. We must be sensible about judging them and remember that they must be judged against the backgrounds of their times. They lived in brutal times which made them brutal men. They lived by the sword: so did every other nation and king in their world.

Now the men who wrote down their histories in the Book of Kings, very often wrote in an effort to color their accounts with an appeal to religious faith. They believed that if a king lacked a good faith in Israel's God, and lived an evil, godless life, then all Israel would pay for his apostasy in disaster. If the king were a sincere worshiper of God, then God blessed him and his people. This concept runs through the whole Old Testament.

But to get back to Omri: the historians and writers of the Old Testament were not quite fair to Omri, probably because he inspired no real religious reforms or movements during his reign. But he accomplished much for Israel in other areas: he conquered the land of Moab and added it to Israel: he founded a dynasty that lived for forty years: he defended his country and defended it well; Assyrians who fought him called his country "The Land of Omri." He established good business alliances with other nations. And he bought a fine high hill owned by a man named Shemer and there built a city which he called Samaria (named for the owner, Shemer). It was a city that spread out from that hill, that was destined to become one of the great cities of Palestine, a capital city with the commanding importance of Jerusalem. Its name eventually was applied to the whole territory of northern Israel. The Samaritans had a liberal attitude toward their neighbors —which the Jewish people of Jerusalem did not like. Samaritans and Jews never got along well together; to the people of Judah, the people of Samaria were different and dangerous!

Omri did, however, make one sad mistake. He married off his eldest son, Ahab, to the Phoenician Jezebel, daughter of the king of Tyre, and there was the crack of doom in their wedding-bells.

Ahab! Famous and infamous. Cynic and penitent, bully and truckling. Sulky. Envious. Effeminate. Inconsequent. Omri's son. Ahab, worse than all previous sinner-kings put together!

Jezebel! Haughty of bearing. Unconquerable of will and temper. Religious fanatic. Antiquity's Lady Macbeth. *Jezebel!*

What a pair they were! Jezebel crushed Ahab into the status of a whimpering, whipped dog or a spineless, craven slave. She ruled the land. She built temples of worship for Baal, Melkarth, and lewd Astarte, pagans all! Even the great Elijah ran from her fury. Ahab stumbled along through a "reign" of twenty or twenty-two years, then mercifully died. Never a king and born a coward, he threw not only his body but his life and his people to the dogs.

Literally, Jezebel was thrown from her palace window to the street below, where the dogs came and licked up her blood. Israel hated her with good reason; she was the worst and most wicked woman ever born—but she had a courage that Ahab never had. She ruled Israel with an iron hand; even on the day of her death, over sixty, she was queen of Israel. It was bad enough that this aggressive queen made her husband a Baal-worshiper; it was worse that she initiated a religious movement which transformed an entire nation into a nation of Baal-worshipers.

Why, may we be wondering, did not God stop it, prevent it before it gained any strength. Perhaps it was because a king who could have been a God-worshiping, good king chose to be something less. God did not arrange this drama of life and death in war; the kings and the inhabitants of the land arranged that without consulting God at all! "All that is necessary for the triumph of evil," said Edmund Burke, "is that good men do nothing." The people of Israel did nothing to stop the holocaust that was coming their way; they even encouraged it.

We have many of the sons and daughters of Ahab and Jezebel living in our midst. We have murderous tyrants galore, and lesser evil ones who would kill to get possession of a nation, or of a strip of sand in a Middle-Eastern desert. They thrive because the people are too weak to cut them down. Too weak—or too evil? When Frederich Nietzsche was asked what evil was, he said, "Whatever springs from weakness is evil." If a man who did not believe in either Christ or Christianity can believe that, why do we not believe it? And what should we be doing about it, before any nation has to fall?

SUGGESTIONS TO TEACHERS

Today's lesson covers such a big block of Scripture and such an event-filled era that it is easy to get lost in the dozens of subplots. As teacher, you will have to keep everyone's eyes on the main themes. You will be talking about many different human actors including powerful rulers like Jezebel and Ahab, but remember that the real power is the Lord. You will also note that the real heroes are the few faithful spokesmen for the Lord. It may be helpful to build your lesson around some few of the vignettes in today's Scripture readings. Here are a few.

1. *SACRIFICE BY A WIDOW.* Have your class consider the faith of a poor but devout widow who shares her meager food supply with the Prophet Elijah during a time of desperate hardship (*see* 1 Kings 17:9–15). Somehow, when she shares, there is still enough for her and her son. Is not this miracle still true for God's faithful people? Point out to your class that although we don't know the woman's name, she is one of the Lord's "great people." Anyone who sacrifices for others is blessed! Furthermore, when she faces the loss of her son, both she and Elijah learn

at firsthand the power of prayer. God brings new life! This episode is a preview of God's resurrecting demonstrated by and through Jesus.

2. *SHOWDOWN ON CARMEL.* Although the leaders denounce Elijah as a "troublemaker," Elijah continues his lonely crusade. Sometimes God's people must endure accusations. In fact, every Christian will be denounced as a troublemaker whenever he or she takes God seriously. Elijah boldly tells King Ahab that *he* is the troublemaker because he ignores the Lord's requirements. He follows up with the stirring challenge to the king and his hired religious yes-men on Mt. Carmel. Let your class appreciate the drama of the fire-building contest between Elijah and the prophets of Baal.

3. *STILLNESS AT SINAI.* Elijah faces the dangers as well as denunciations. His victory on Carmel brings a death-threat by Jezebel, and he flees for his life. Remind your class that serving the Lord does not mean winning popularity contests. In fact, being a prophet for God usually brings one suffering! Jesus, who is The Prophet, warns us that we must be prepared for the worst. Prophets also sometimes feel lonely and depressed. Have your class relate times when being a faithful Christian caused them loneliness and depression. Above all, remind your people that the Lord strengthens His people and sends them back refreshed to serve.

4. *STUPIDITY OF AHAB.* Ahab wins a victory but foolishly and carelessly lets Benhadad, his adversary, get away (1 Kings 20:20). Elijah warns him that his irresponsibility will cost him his throne. Winning one dramatic victory is never enough. Living responsibly afterward in the undramatic also counts. Otherwise, the effects of the victory are offset by foolishness.

5. *STAND AGAINST GREED.* The seizure of Naboth's vineyard (1 Kings 21) by the greedy, unscrupulous monarchs brings down the wrath of Elijah, who predicts the extinction of Ahab's family. Have your class think about the way evil often seems to go unchecked. Remind your people, however, that greed and cruelty never continue unchecked. We still live in a moral universe.

6. *STEADFAST BEFORE KINGS.* Allow time in your lesson to review the courageous way Micaiah stood up to Ahab and Jehoshaphat, the rulers, and to Zedekiah and the false prophets (2 Chronicles 18). Sometimes the Micaiahs are a persecuted minority because they speak the truth! In your lesson, urge your class members to tell of times when they felt like a Micaiah for their stands for truth or justice.

TOPIC FOR ADULTS
BAD TIMES FOR GOD'S PEOPLE

The God of Jesus Christ. "Even before his death on the cross, Jesus was aware of all the evil in the world, all the injustice, wickedness, cruelty, all the suffering, all the pain, all the grief. But, in the face of all the evil, Jesus did not give any philosophical or theological justification of God, any theodicy. His answer has a practical orientation; it points to God as Father: God as the Father who in his active providence and solicitude looks after every sparrow and every hair, who knows our needs before we ask him, makes our worries seem superfluous; God as the Father who knows about everything in this far from perfect world and without whom nothing happens, whom man can absolutely trust and on whom he can completely rely even in suffering, injustice, sin and death.

"This, then, is Jesus' practical answer to the question of theodicy. . . . This is not a God at an ominous, transcendent distance, but close in incomprehensible goodness; he is a God who does not make empty phrases about the hereafter or minimize the present darkness, futility and meaninglessness. Instead, in darkness, futility and meaninglessness, he invites us to the venture of hope. In regard to him, man does not have to protect his freedom. God's rule and man's activity are not mutually exclusive. The problem . . . of divine predestination and human freedom of choice, of the divine and the human will, is obviously no problem for Jesus . . ."—From DOES GOD EXIST? by Hans Kung. Copyright © 1978, 1979, 1980 by Doubleday & Company, Inc.

God's People in Bad Times. "Being a lover of freedom, when the revolution came to Germany, I looked to the universities to defend it, knowing that they had always boasted of their devotion to the cause of truth; but no, the universities were immediately silenced. Then I looked to the great editors of the newspapers, but they, like the universities, were silenced in few short weeks. Then I looked to the individual writers, but they too were mute. Only the Church stood squarely across the path of Hitler's campaign for suppressing the truth. I never had any great interest in the Church before. But now I feel a great affection and admiration because the Church alone had the courage and persistence to stand for intellectual truth and moral freedom. I am forced to confess that what I once despised I now praise unreservedly."—Albert Einstein.

Soldier's Sacrifice in Evil Era. "Goch is a small German town in North-Rhine Westphalia, and in its long and varied history it has been the center of many invading or defending armies. The tower which now stands near the center of the bustling community was once the entrance to a walled city, built as a fortress in the middle ages.

"Goch was an important strategic position during the advance of the Allied armies into the German homeland in 1944–45, and the historic tower was partly demolished by intensive shelling. Once the headquarters of the Hitler Youth Movement, the tower is now part of a municipal museum that has been built up since the war years, and hanging on the wall in the main room is a photograph of a British major killed in action in 1945.

"He was Major Ronald Edmond Balfour, a lecturer from King's College, Cambridge, seconded to the First Canadian Army as an advisor in history and archaeology. As the army advanced, he identified centers of historical importance and mapped them so that as little damage as possible would be inflicted. He was killed by a German shell as he was saving some Roman artefacts.

"In grateful memory of his work and sacrifice, the township of Goch placed his photograph in the museum alongside that of their own dignitaries who have been of exceptional service to the community.

"On Remembrance Day I shall remember this act of sacrifice—and the act of reconciliation that brings two people closer together.

"Major Balfour knew the futility of war, and was able to use his academic and scholastic gifts in preserving for the victors and the vanquished a heritage that united them both.

"I shall thank God for Major Ronald Edmond Balfour, King's College, Cambridge, who in the midst of battle, worked for a vision of a world at peace with itself and at peace with God."—George Grubb in *Life and Work*, November 1981, article, "Remembrance is Reconciliation."

Questions for Pupils on the Next Lesson. 1. How did Jehu fail to follow the Lord's purposes? 2. What does the word *Jezreel* mean, and why did Hosea name his child this name? 3. Why do many people do whatever an authority figure tells them to do? 4. When do you find yourself tempted to agree with the ethic that "Might makes right"? 5. Do you feel that your convictions have a positive influence in all facets of living?

TOPIC FOR YOUTH
BAD TIMES FOR GOD'S PEOPLE

"In mid-1968, a research team in the social psychology program at Columbia University Teachers College was conducting an experiment in lower Manhattan.

We were dropping wallets on the street, and learning that about 45 percent of the people who found the wallets returned them to their owners within a couple of days. Our research had been in progress some time, and this return rate had become a reliable average.

"Then an extraordinary thing happened. Not a single one of the wallets dropped on June 4 was returned. During that night, a young man named Sirhan Sirhan fired a bullet through the head of Robert F. Kennedy. The bullet had killed him, as the public soon learned through the news media. But it did something else as well. It damaged whatever social bonds had caused people to return those lost wallets. It demoralized people and made them socially irresponsible.

"Since that tragic day, we have conducted extensive research into the effects of news broadcasts on people's willingness to help others. Our findings are unmistakable and highly important, in our view. They suggest not only that the media influence our daily moral actions, but, more generally, that altruism in individuals probably rises or falls with the altruism, or lack of it, in social events that may not touch us directly.

"Far from just imparting facts, news stories about morality or immorality in action impress us, at least temporarily, with corresponding views of human nature—views that tend to move us, quite unconsciously, to behave in ways appropriate to such views. At worst, as we have seen, newscasts can break down the kinds of group ties that cause people to help and trust their fellows."—John H. Hayes, *Quote*, January 2, 1977.

World's Third Largest Airforce. Over 4,000 airplanes and helicopters may be found in the 3,000 acres of the Military Aircraft Storage and Disposition Center at Davis-Monthan Air Base in Tucson, Arizona. Together, these Voodoos, Phantoms, Stratojets, Shooting Stars, B-52s, and Super Constellations make up the third largest airforce in the world. However, they are all grounded. Few of them will ever fly again. They rest in the sun and sagebrush to be stripped for spare parts or sold for scrap. After World War II, $3.9 billion worth of aircraft became $6.5 billion worth of scrap metal.

What price glory? The long lines of old propellers tell us that military considerations meant sacrificing other things.

Consider what might have been: six low-cost houses instead of one Huey helicopter; twenty full college scholarships instead of one B-52 sortie in Vietnam; a 100 percent increase in federal funds for solar energy instead of twenty-two F-15 fighters. Like most graveyards, this is a place for contemplation.

What Makes Our Nation Great. Here's what Alexis de Tocqueville saw in America on his visit a century ago: "I sought for the greatness and genius of America in her commodious harbours and her ample rivers, and it was not there; in the fertile fields and boundless prairies, and it was not there; in her rich mines and her vast world commerce, and it was not there. Not until I went into the churches of America, and heard her pulpits aflame with righteousness, did I understand the secret of her genius and power. America is great because she is good, and if America ever ceases to be good, America will cease to be great."

Sentence Sermon to Remember: Blessed are they which do hunger and thirst after righteousness: for they shall be filled.—Matthew 5:6.

Questions for Pupils on the Next Lesson. 1. Why did Jehu not turn out to be a good king? 2. Does the end ever justify the means? 3. How do you answer those who claim that might makes right? 4. Who are the authority figures you respect the most? Why? 5. How do your convictions help give you a sense of personal identity?

LESSON VIII—JULY 22

REFORM: BY FORCE?

Background Scripture: 2 Kings 9, 10; Hosea 1:4, 5
Devotional Reading: Psalms 37:1–9

KING JAMES VERSION

2 KINGS 10 18 And Jehu gathered all the people together, and said unto them, Ahab served Baal a little; *but* Jehu shall serve him much.

19 Now therefore call unto me all the prophets of Baal, all his servants, and all his priests; let none be wanting: for I have a great sacrifice *to do* to Baal; whosoever shall be wanting, he shall not live. But Jehu did *it* in subtilty, to the intent that he might destroy the worshippers of Baal.

24 And when they went in to offer sacrifices and burnt offerings, Jehu appointed fourscore men without, and said, *If* any of the men whom I have brought into your hands escape, *he that letteth him go,* his life *shall be* for the life of him.

25 And it came to pass, as soon as he had made an end of offering the burnt offering, that Jehu said to the guard and to the captains, Go in, *and* slay them; let none come forth. And they smote them with the edge of the sword; and the guard and the captains cast *them* out, and went to the city of the house of Baal.

26 And they brought forth the images out of the house of Baal, and burned them.

27 And they brake down the image of Baal, and brake down the house of Baal, and made it a draught house unto this day.

28 Thus Jehu destroyed Baal out of Israel.

29 Howbeit, *from* the sins of Jeroboam the son of Nebat, who made Israel to sin, Jehu departed not from after them, *to wit,* the golden calves that *were* in Bethel, and that *were* in Dan.

30 And the LORD said unto Jehu, Because thou hast done well in executing *that which is* right in mine eyes, *and* hast done unto the house of Ahab according to all that *was* in mine heart, thy children of the fourth *generation* shall sit on the throne of Israel.

31 But Jehu took no heed to walk in the law of the LORD God of Israel with all his heart: for he departed not from the sins of Jeroboam, which made Israel to sin.

REVISED STANDARD VERSION

2 KINGS 10 18 Then Jehu assembled all the people, and said to them, "Ahab served Baal a little; but Jehu will serve him much. 19 Now therefore call to me all the prophets of Baal, all his worshipers and all his priests; let none be missing, for I have a great sacrifice to offer to Baal; whoever is missing shall not live." But Jehu did it with cunning in order to destroy the worshipers of Baal.

24 Then he went in to offer sacrifices and burnt offerings.

Now Jehu had stationed eighty men outside, and said, "The man who allows any of those whom I give into your hands to escape shall forfeit his life." 25 So as soon as he had made an end of offering the burnt offering, Jehu said to the guard and to the officers, "Go in and slay them; let not a man escape." So when they put them to the sword, the guard and the officers cast them out and went into the inner room of the house of Baal 26 and they brought out the pillar that was in the house of Baal, and burned it. 27 And they demolished the pillar of Baal, and demolished the house of Baal, and made it a latrine to this day.

28 Thus Jehu wiped out Baal from Israel. 29 But Jehu did not turn aside from the sins of Jeroboam the son of Nebat, which he made Israel to sin, the golden calves that were in Bethel, and in Dan. 30 And the LORD said to Jehu, "Because you have done well in carrying out what is right in my eyes, and have done to the house of Ahab according to all that was in my heart, your sons of the fourth generation shall sit on the throne of Israel."

31 But Jehu was not careful to walk in the law of the LORD the God of Israel with all his heart; he did not turn from the sins of Jeroboam, which he made Israel to sin.

KEY VERSE: A wise man is mightier than a strong man, and a man of knowledge than he who has strength. Proverbs 24:5 (RSV).

HOME DAILY BIBLE READINGS

July 16. M. *Fomenting a Political Revolution.* 1 Kings 19:14–21.
July 17. T. *Condemning the Oppressive Dynasty.* 1 Kings 21:17–24.
July 18. W. *Anointing of Jehu in Israel.* 2 Kings 9:1–13.
July 19. T. *Assassination of Joram and Aniaziah.* 2 Kings 9:17–29.
July 20. F. *Assassination of Jezebel.* 2 Kings 9:30–37.

July 21.   S.   Extermination of House of Amri. 2 Kings 10:1–17.
July 22.   S.   Massacre of Baal Worshipers. 2 Kings 10:18–31.

BACKGROUND

The end of Jezebel was the end of a dynasty and the end of an era. Enough was enough: Israel was ripe for a revolution, and revolution came thundering in the person of a wild and fearless chariot-driver who had Jezebel thrown to her death from a window, and then drove his horses and his chariot wheels over her dead body. Many cheered Jehu for doing that; nobody objected. Nobody dared to object to anything Jehu did or said. Having ridden rough-shod over the body of Jezebel, he proceeded to ride like a madman over every enemy of Israel—even any *suspected* enemy was crushed to death. Israel had never seen anything like it.

Ghastly as it was, it made Jehu powerful and head of the longest-lived dynasty in Israel, but at what a cost!

NOTES ON THE PRINTED TEXT

Generally speaking, there are two roads to any revolution. One road is that of quiet, behind-the-scenes planning and execution in which good minds in good, peaceful men do what has to be done. The other road is the way of violence and terror. The revolution led by Jehu is remarkable in that it included both quiet planning *and* violence. Elisha and Elijah, the two great prophets of the era, had long stood out against the cruelty and corruption of the kingdom of Ahab, Jezebel, and Omri. It was Elisha who arranged the crowning of Jehu as king of Israel, while Jehoram, the last of the house of Omri, was still king. Jehu took care of that, quickly: he had Jehoram killed, and had himself properly anointed king, with the approval of the old conservative, prophetic party of Elisha and Elijah.

That murder was only the beginning. The mad charioteer ordered and executed the slaying of seventy of the princes of Samaria, Ahaziah of Judah and forty-two of his kinsmen, and Jezebel the queen. As a final blow against the enemies of the heathen worshipers of Baal in the country, he gathered all the Baalites he could find into one great pagan temple and massacred them, removing with this one blow the heathen population of the kingdom. Few other rulers in the history of the world can match that record.

Was there any defense, any reason, for such a bloody character as Jehu to be anointed as king of God's Chosen People? Any justification? Any reason why we should "honor" him because he happens to be a biblical character?

Certainly Jehu accomplished the overthrow of Baal in Israel. That conquest was not, however, complete, for Baal-worship continued in some sections of the land. But it was never strong again. Certainly Jehu finished off and destroyed the house of Ahab and wiped out the debased and formless religion for which Ahab and Jezebel had stood, insofar as a form of religion sponsored by a royal house was concerned. That much of it was good, for the religion of Baal held nothing good for Israel; it contributed nothing to bringing about a close relationship between men and a God of love, and morally it was despicable. In this sense, we might say that the *cause* of Israel, if not its Jehu, won out over the degenerate cause of paganism. Jehu also left a strong dynasty to rule Israel after he was gone.

But all this does not in any way excuse the abhorrent use of duplicity and murder to attain such an end. Actually Jehu had no love for God; he only pretended to have that. He allied himself with the people and the prophets of the true God only to further his own end which was the attainment of kingship. It may have been good that the nobler, more inspiring view of God conquered the less admirable teachings of Baal, but no God—or concerned man—can possibly believe that this Jehu in any way was approved of God in his massacres of Israel's enemies. Though we might not like to hear it, it is still not true that "the end justifies the means." Jehu's purpose was power at any cost, and he did his best to "get God on his side." In the end, he was a miserable failure. His reign as king was anything but good. He had rid himself of Ahab, but the gods of Jezebel still spoke from the bull-images of Dan and Bethel. And, still putting his faith in the violence of war, Jehu sought the help of kings who knew not God. Those who wrote about him later had nothing good to say about him; they only wrote that there were signs of crisis ahead for Israel while Jehu reigned, but Jehu missed them.

In the end, he left his kingdom weak, and the prey of stronger nations. His wholesale slaughterings and violence sapped the nation's strength, and before he died he was paying tribute to a new kingdom on the Euphrates. The shadow of Assyria lay full across the land. He who lives by the sword has a way of perishing by the sword.

Not long ago, we saw a fight in a street in Shanghai. Two Chinese men shouted at each other like raving maniacs, and a crowd around them howled its approval. Then one of them slapped the other in the face—and the crowd murmured its disapproval and walked away. To them, when a man ran out of arguments and turned to using his fists, he had lost the fight. That was the wrong thing to do.

Violence may *seem* to win battles, but in the end it brings only calamity. This was in the handwriting on the walls of Jehu's palace, but he was so blind with the lust for power that he never saw it. When he died, calamity was just around the corner for his Israel.

SUGGESTIONS TO TEACHERS

After you read the background Scripture for today's lesson, you will probably have two reactions: (1) What gory stuff! and (2) Why is this record of so much bloodshed in the Bible? You may also ask yourself how you can shape a Sunday-School lesson out of such material.

Start by remembering that our God deals with real life, with the events of this world. The world that God gets involved in is often not a pretty world. It is a world of cruel tyrants and brutality and bloodshed. God, however, chooses to concern Himself with this world.

Furthermore, remember that God's people are not necessarily "nice" people. Don't fret because persons in the Bible are shown with the dark side to their nature. You need not worry because the scriptural material in today's lesson doesn't hold up admirable examples. The Bible is the story of Israel and Judah—and also the people of your town. Most important, Jesus, not Jehu, is God's Good News!

You can also profitably discuss these issues in your lesson:

1. *PEACE WITH CONDITIONS.* "How can there be peace when we still have all the witchcraft and idolatry that your mother Jezebel started?" asked Jehu (2 Kings 9:22 TEV). God's *shalom* can be known and received only when our living is firmly rooted in Him. This means there is no place for superstitions or folk-religion, immorality or unethical behavior. Today's lesson offers your class a chance to examine the harmony or *shalom* in each person's life and within the life of your congregation. Is there need for reform?

2. *PROBLEM OF COERCION.* Jehu tries to bring reform by force. Like many others through history, he has the mistaken notion that he can compel people to amend their ways. This idea still persists whenever religious people determine to make others be holy. Jesus never pushed others around. Especially, Jesus never brutalized anyone for the sake of the faith. The Crusades and the Inquisition and other examples of conversion-by-coercion or goodness-by-the-gun are shameful blots in the Church's history.

3. *PERIL OF CARELESSNESS.* Have your class take particular notice of 2 Kings 10:31 ("But Jehu was not careful to walk in the law of the Lord ... with all his heart"). How many well-meaning people have stumbled because they were

not careful to obey God with all their heart! Emphasize the need of every Christian to be mindful constantly of walking in God's ways. Ask for suggestions as to how to be more careful to live obediently.

4. *PREDICTABILITY OF GOD.* Hosea, who lived in Israel during this bloody period of history, named one of his children *Jezreel,* meaning "God sows." The message applies for this day as well as for Hosea's: God brings to pass His plans, and will ultimately see the fruition of what He began. In spite of frightening times, God may be trusted!

TOPIC FOR ADULTS
REFORM: BY FORCE?

Ominous Songs. In August, 1981, a group calling itself Young Americans for Freedom held a convention in Boston. The Young Americans for Freedom are determined to reform the world by force, at least judging by some of their songs. According to newspaper accounts, the delegates knew by heart and sang enthusiastically to the tune of "Deck the Halls with Boughs of Holly" the following words:

> Deck the halls with Commie corpses
> Fala-la-lala-lala-la
> 'Tis the time to be remorseless
> Fala-la-lala-lala-la
> Wield we now our sharp stilletti
> Fala-la-lala-lala-la
> Carve the pinks into confetti.

Some newspaper reporters with long memories detected attitudes reminiscent of Hitler's youth movement.

Although everyone is for freedom, and everyone is for young Americans to be committed to ideals of reforming our world and preserving our democracy, such lyrics betray a dangerous attitude. Reform never comes from "decking the halls with Commie corpses." In fact, we betray our heritage and veer toward fascism when we remorselessly seek to carve the enemy into confetti.

God's Last Word. "The question is not whether God has spoken through the Scripture, but, rather, what God's last word is. Of old there was the law, administered by the priests; the mature counsels of wise men; oracles spoken by prophets. But God's last word is Jesus. Wars in the Old Testament do not mean that God teaches us in these days that national policy should revolve around armaments that deprive the poor of bread, nor depend upon weapons capable of wiping out the human race. If Deborah can sing, 'The Lord is a man of war,' the early church could proclaim of Jesus, 'He is our peace.'"—J. Carter Swaim, *War, Peace, and the Bible,* Orbis Books, 1982.

Not Meetings but Meeting. "... In today's world, the hunger for deepened spiritual life is apparent in both churches and secular culture. Many leave the church to find 'turn-ons' in a variety of experiences. They turn to Eastern religions and meditation techniques because they promise direct connectedness with the ultimate source of life in place of what they regard as the wordy hearsay of Protestantism. One layperson, a woman, long active and involved in her church and its wider judicatories said, 'What I want now is not meetings but meeting, meeting in terms of spiritual presence and direction.' Evangelical, pentecostal, and charismatic renewal groups seem to many mainline church members to offer more in terms of an experience of faith, an immediate felt contact with the Holy Spirit. ..."—Roy W. Fairchild, on the occasion of his installation as Professor of Spiritual Life and Psychology at San Francisco Seminary, February 3-6, 1982.

Questions for Pupils on the Next Lesson. 1. How would you describe the relationship between Israel and Judah as described in 2 Kings 14? 2. What happens when a nation takes inordinate pride in its military prowess? 3. Why do some people and nations boast of their achievements? 4. How is conflict often a way of trying to gain status? 5. Why are most people reluctant to accept advice?

TOPIC FOR YOUTH
REFORM: BY FORCE?

Parish Peacemaking. "Buckhorn is a small community in Eastern Kentucky where 80 percent of the residents live below the U.S. poverty level. The county seat of Hazard is more than forty-five minutes away on mountain roads, and thus law enforcement and emergency medical facilities are practically nil.

"During the past few years, Perry County has had a higher homicide rate than New York City. Buckhorn alone witnessed five killings in a period of eighteen months. Fear, anxiety and anger were mounting during this period and many of these feelings were heightened when a jury acquitted five members of a family charged with the shooting of two deputy sheriffs in front of the church. One deputy was killed. The typical response to any form of confrontation has been to get a gun.

"The session of our church felt that they had one of two paths to take: they could resign themselves to the belief that 'that's just the way things are done around here,' or they could meet the violence, despair, and apathy head-on with the demands of love and peace. They chose the latter.

"The pastor preached a series of sermons on 'The Things That Make for Peace.' Towards the end of the series, a community meeting was held at the church to discuss our concerns, and feelings. About twenty people were expected, but sixty showed up, including the family involved in the shooting of the sheriffs, whom we made a special effort to invite. Fears and frustrations were expressed, and plans of action were formulated, including making suggestions about ways to work with the parents of the young people who had been causing problems. The world was not changed by this meeting, but for the first time people were voicing what had been said only in private and were listening to each other.

"The following Sunday was World Communion Sunday. Through the peacemaking offering, the church pledged to continue to be serious about peacemaking as we gathered around the Table.

"It is also important to add that a minister cannot be serious about peacemaking unless he or she is first a pastor to the people. Much behind-the-scenes pastoral work has been necessary to lay the groundwork.

"The Buckhorn Church has come to see that working for peace can begin in our church, our families, and our communities."—Stephen R. Montgomery, pastor, Buckhorn Lake Area Church, Buckhorn, Kentucky, *Monday Morning,* November 16, 1981.

Farewell of Father of Nuclear Navy. In 1982, after sixty-three years in uniform and three decades after Congress saved him from forced retirement, Admiral Hyman G. Rickover stepped down. The man, who gained fame as the father of the atomic submarine and founder of the nuclear navy, Rickover was both revered and feared on Capitol Hill where he built a power base that made him invulnerable to pressure from the navy, the Department of Defense, the White House, or the ship-building industry. He was hated in private shipyards where he prowled all hours of the day and night, demanding of executives and welders alike the same commitment he placed upon himself. He was held in awe by his lieutenants and deeply mistrusted by officials who crossed swords with him over the years. In farewell, Rickover attacked shipbuilding contractors, ridiculed the Department of Defense bureaucracy, and philosophized on the virtues of capital-ism. He said he thought the country was spending too much on defense, that the navy had too many admirals, and that in an all-out war the new nuclear-powered aircraft carriers would survive about "two days."

Nuclear power for both military and peaceful uses should be outlawed, Rickover said, because radioactivity poses an inherent danger.

"We must expect that when war breaks out again, we will use the weapons available," he said. "I think we'll probably destroy ourselves.

"I'm not proud of the part I played in fostering the nuclear navy," Rickover said.

There is no reform by force—not even nuclear powered navies.

Cellars Are Filling. Today, as never before, there is a seller's market for Christian truth. On all hands, we have evidence of the search for spiritual assurance. Consider the multiplicity of religious exercises provided in every big city at this moment—Hinduism, Zen and Sufi, Pyramidology and Process, Atlanteans, Subuds, Druidism, and witchcraft. I suspect you have to pay your money. You can certainly take your choice. "The churches may be emptying," writes Timeri Murari, author of *Route Maps to Salvation,* "but the cellars are filling."

Sentence Sermon to Remember: Not by might, nor by power, but by my spirit, saith the Lord of hosts.—Zechariah 4:6.

Questions for Pupils on the Next Lesson. 1. Why does our society seem to glorify violence? 2. Do you sometimes find yourself allowing others to push you into doing things you later regret? 3. When do you most frequently act rashly and impulsively? 4. What happens when people you know try to intimidate others? 5. How would you sum up 2 Kings 14?

LESSON IX—JULY 29

WAR BETWEEN THE KINGDOMS

Background Scripture: 2 Kings 14
Devotional Reading: Deuteronomy 24:16–22

KING JAMES VERSION

2 KINGS 14 1 In the second year of Joash son of Jehoahaz king of Israel reigned Amaziah the son of Joash king of Judah.

2 He was twenty and five years old when he began to reign, and reigned twenty and nine years in Jerusalem. And his mother's name *was* Jehoad-dan of Jerusalem.

3 And he did *that which was* right in the sight of the LORD, yet not like David his father: he did according to all things as Joash his father did.

8 Then Amaziah sent messengers to Jehoash, the son of Jehoahaz son of Jehu, king of Israel, saying, Come, let us look one another in the face.

9 And Jehoash the king of Israel sent to Amaziah king of Judah, saying, The thistle that *was* in Lebanon sent to the cedar that *was* in Lebanon, saying, Give thy daughter to my son to wife: and there passed by a wild beast that *was* in Lebanon, and trode down the thistle.

10 Thou hast indeed smitten Edom, and thine heart hath lifted thee up: glory *of this*, and tarry at home: for why shouldest thou meddle to *thy* hurt, that thou shouldest fall, *even* thou, and Judah with thee?

11 But Amaziah would not hear. Therefore Jehoash king of Israel went up; and he and Amaziah king of Judah looked one another in the face at Beth-shemesh, which *belongeth* to Judah.

12 And Judah was put to the worse before Israel; and they fled every man to their tents.

13 And Jehoash king of Israel took Amaziah king of Judah, the son of Jehoash the son of Ahaziah, at Beth-shemesh, and came to Jerusalem, and brake down the wall of Jerusalem from the gate of Ephraim unto the corner gate, four hundred cubits.

14 And he took all the gold and silver, and all the vessels that were found in the house of the LORD, and in the treasures of the king's house, and hostages, and returned to Samaria.

REVISED STANDARD VERSION

2 KINGS 14 1 In the second year of Joash the son of Joahaz, king of Israel, Amaziah the son of Joash, king of Judah, began to reign. 2 He was twenty-five years old when he began to reign, and he reigned twenty-nine years in Jerusalem. His mother's name was Jeho-addin of Jerusalem. 3 And he did what was right in the eyes of the LORD, yet not like David his father; he did in all things as Joash his father had done.

8 Then Amaziah sent messengers to Jehoash the son of Jehoahaz, son of Jehu, king of Israel, saying, "Come, let us look one another in the face." 9 And Jehoash king of Israel sent word to Amaziah king of Judah, "A thistle on Lebanon sent to a cedar on Lebanon, saying, 'Give your daughter to my son for a wife'; and a wild beast of Lebanon passed by and trampled down the thistle. 10 You have indeed smitten Edom, and your heart has lifted you up. Be content with your glory, and stay at home; for why should you provoke trouble so that you fall, you and Judah with you?"

11 But Amaziah would not listen. So Jehoash king of Israel went up, and he and Amaziah king of Judah faced one another in battle at Beth-shemesh, which belongs to Judah. 12 And Judah was defeated by Israel, and every man fled to his home. 13 And Jehoash king of Israel captured Amaziah king of Judah, the son of Jehoash, son of Ahaziah, at Beth-shemesh, and came to Jerusalem, and broke down the wall of Jerusalem for four hundred cubits, from the Ephraim Gate to the Corner Gate. 14 And he seized all the gold and silver, and all the vessels that were found in the house of the LORD and in the treasuries of the king's house, also hostages, and he returned to Samaria.

KEY VERSE: *Pride goes before destruction, and a haughty spirit before a fall.* Proverbs 16:18 (RSV).

HOME DAILY BIBLE READINGS

July 23. M. *The Reign of Jehu in Israel.* 2 Kings 10:28–36.
July 24. T. *The Reign of Athaliah.* 2 Kings 11:9–20.
July 25. W. *The Reign of Jehoash in Judah.* 2 Kings 12:17–21.
July 26. T. *The Reign of Jehoahaz in Israel.* 2 Kings 13:1–9.
July 27. F. *The Reign of Joash in Israel.* 2 Kings 13:10–25.

July 28. S.   Ambition of Amaziah in Judah. 2 Kings 14:1-7.
July 29. S.   Defeat of Amaziah by Israel. 2 Kings 14:8-14.

BACKGROUND

While Jehu was wreaking his madness upon Israel, important things were happening in southern Judah. All signs pointed to a grim fact: the two kingdoms, which so sadly had separated from one another, were now slowly heading for trouble between themselves.

In Judah, the eighth king, Joash, did fairly well in very troublous times (837–800 B.C.), then lapsed into a moral and spiritual degeneration. He was finally removed from the throne by the popular method of murder, and his son Amaziah was crowned the ninth king, and his first royal decision marked him as one who might live in the memory of Judah as one of her finest rulers.

Amaziah punished the murderers of his father, "but the children of the murderers he slew not." That was something new. Up to this point, it was expected that the children of a condemned criminal were to be executed with him. To pardon the children meant that Judah had a king with the courage to defy custom in favor of mercy. It was a good start for Amaziah.

Having avenged his father's murderers, he threw an army of 100,000 *Israelite* mercenaries against an old enemy—the Edomites. They crushed Edom, and both Judah and Israel were glad to see that happen. But not for long. The victory went to Amaziah's head.

NOTES ON THE PRINTED TEXT

Like a little boy who had won one little fight, Amaziah, flushed with his victory over the Edomites, "looked around for other enemies to conquer." For some years now, Judah had been little more than a vassal of the stronger Israel—so, Amaziah told himself, Israel must be an "enemy" to be conquered. So he threw out a challenge to King Joash of Israel to mobilize his army and come out and fight! It was the gesture of a very little man drunk with sight of power. Joash tried to save him from his own folly by telling him, as one tells a joke, that such a war would be nonsense and fatal to little Judah—it would be like a great cedar of Lebanon fighting a little thistle that could be crushed by any passing beast. It was a warning. Amaziah ignored it, marched out to meet the armies of Israel at Bethshemesh, a few miles west of Jerusalem. Israel won the battle. It was like a giant stepping on an egg. Joash broke through Jerusalem's wall, robbed the Temple of its treasures and went home to Samaria with a train of hostages. Exit Amaziah. Pity Jerusalem. It was a totally unnecessary war, a petty war that should never have been fought. All it accomplished was to demonstrate that most wars are unnecessary and alien to the purposes of God.

David Howarth, writing of the battle between England and Spain in a book entitled *The Voyage of the Armada*, tells us why that unnecessary battle had been fought. The Spaniards, he says, fought that battle only because they had been offered loot if they won: "Plunder if they succeed and heaven if they fail: all through history this dual promise has been used to drive men into battle." There is truth in that, if not the whole of truth why mankind places its trust in war.

It remains true after thousands of years. We fought a most regrettable Civil War in our country; many historians tell us that it might have been prevented if only hotheads on both sides had been silenced in time—there need not have been that war! We are told the same thing about other wars of our time. If only the fools who like war and the wise who hate it could sit down like intelligent beings and settle their disputes before a shot could be fired!

It may be a hard lesson for us to learn and a difficult principle to understand, but it is pure truth: men will never stop fighting unnecessary and deliberately provoked wars until they have the courage and the common sense to put their faith in cooperation, mutual helpfulness, and brotherhood. *There is no other way to peace.*

"The very same motives which impelled Amaziah to embark so rashly on his ill-fated adventure against Joash are at the heart of the world's disorder today. And unless we have learned better ways by catastrophes which have overtaken our modern world, only the ruin which overtook those two little Jewish kingdoms is in store for us."—Raymond Calkins in *The Interpreters Bible,* vol. 3, by permission of Abingdon Press, publishers.

An unknown author says the same thing in fewer words: "Men will carry guns until they learn to carry the cross."

SUGGESTIONS TO TEACHERS

"Today's youth seem to think that all history began when they were born and will end tomorrow before breakfast," a professor remarked to a group of colleagues. Most of us, including those in your Sunday-School class, have such a short-term and self-centered view of history. Your lesson for this Sunday is meant to broaden your horizons.

At first glance, you may dismiss the 2 Kings 14 passage as a tedious jumble of trivial events. The Bible as "sacred history" is more than records of the "long ago and faraway." Through the Scripture story, God tells us about *our* story. He especially tells us how to preserve a perspective about ourselves as a church and as a nation.

1. *CONNECT.* Tell your class about the way Amaziah spared the children of his father's murderers because he saw the connection between the Lord's law in Scripture and his personal life. Amaziah could have followed the usual brutal practice of having the entire family of an assassin wiped out, but he understood the tie between what he knew in Scripture and what he did. Do your class members understand that connection? Do they take the Bible seriously enough to try to relate its message to how they live?

2. *CONTENT.* Unfortunately, Amaziah became arrogant after some minor military successes. Puffed up after defeating the Edomites, he began to think he was invincible. A silly nationalism gripped Judah. His neighbor to the north advised him, "Be content with your glory" (2 Kings 14:10). Amaziah refused to be content and itched for more power, more glory, more territory. Your lesson can serve a constructive purpose at this point by having your people ponder carefully the dangers of a rampant nationalism.

3. *CONTEMPT.* "But Amaziah would not listen" (2 Kings 14:11). His inability to listen made him contemptuous of other kings. He mobilized his nation for war. Moving against his kinfolk in the neighboring kingdom to the north, he suffered a disgraceful defeat. When a person refuses to listen, whether to God or others, he or she begins to act with contempt toward the world. Ultimately, of course, there will be a day of reckoning!

4. *CONSENT.* "They made a conspiracy against him . . . and he fled" (2 Kings 14:19). Amaziah became forgetful of his people and lost the consent of his subjects to serve as their leader. Leadership is a sacred trust, and it must be carried out with the interests of the group as its main concern. Rulers from Amaziah to Richard Nixon have learned to their dismay that breaking trust with their people brings their downfall. Ask your class what leaders and the led need to do in these times to build greater trust.

TOPIC FOR ADULTS
BOASTING IN MILITARY MIGHT

A Modest Proposal. In "A Modest Proposal," an adaptation of the address accepting the Einstein Peace Prize, George Kennan reminds us that for the past thirty-six years many far-seeing people have warned us about the dangers of war

in our time under the nuclear doomsday machine. In light of our failure to deal
with the problems of arms and arms control, despite professions and efforts of
president after president, he notes a certain "discouragement, resignation, perhaps even despair" about the peacemaking process. Coming at this matter from
the perspective of a distinguished diplomatic historian, as well as a former ambassador to Moscow, he sees, . . . "this same phenomenon playing its fateful part
in the relations among the great European powers as much as a century ago, I see
this competitive buildup of armaments conceived initially as a means to an end,
soon becoming the end in itself. I see it taking possession of men's imagination
and behavior, becoming a force in its own right, detaching itself from the political differences that initially inspired it, and then leading both parties invariably
and inexorably, to the war they no longer know how to avoid."

This compulsion today is brewed out of many components, for which the
United States as well as the Russians must share responsibility. The only way,
Kennan suggests, that we may be able to break out of the vicious circle is by a
"bold and sweeping departure." Kennan himself suggests that the United States
and Soviet governments engage in an immediate across-the-board reduction by
50 percent of the nuclear arsenals now being maintained by the superpowers.

Parable on Arrogance. "A cruel, selfish man," the story goes, "died and went
where he belonged. He found his bed in hell very uncomfortable. He bore it
hardly. Finally he cried out with a loud voice: 'I want to get out of here. Get me
out of this place.' At length an angel came and asked him what he had ever done
to make him deserve a better place. He spent much time thinking and then he
said, 'Oh, I know, once I gave a carrot to a half-starved donkey.' 'Good,' said the
angel. 'We will see.' Pretty soon an immense carrot was let down from heaven
and a Voice said, 'Lay hold of the carrot and you will be saved.' The man seized
the carrot and was being carried up to heaven. Hundreds of souls saw it and ran
out and got hold of the carrot and were going up with him. But his old nature
asserted itself and he shouted, 'Let go there; this is my carrot.' Immediately the
carrot dropped and the man has been where he belonged ever since."

Symbolic Power. "At one time I was a guest in a country that had a World War
II cruiser with eight-inch gun mounts and I was entertained aboard that ship. As I
was departing, in custom of naval tradition I asked the captain if I could inspect
the ship. He became somewhat nervous and my naval aide gently pulled me to
the side to ask me not to pursue it. So I didn't inspect the ship. That night I was
told that that particular ship, which was standing majestically in the harbor of
this nation, had a totally inoperative boiler room. In fact, I think it had been gut-
ted. At night, the ship was towed around in the harbor at various spots. But
everybody in that country looked upon that ship as its guardian."—John W.
Warner, undersecretary, U.S. Navy.

So much of the boasting of military might by nations is such useless show and a
pompous pose.

Questions for Pupils on the Next Lesson. 1. In what specific way did the nation
of Israel disregard the warnings of the prophets? 2. What resulted? 3. Are there
always dire consequences for our disobedience, or can we "get away with it"
after all? 4. What changes should our culture make to conform more to God's
will? 5. Why do we often prefer to make others responsible rather than risk vul-
nerability?

TOPIC FOR YOUTH
I DARE YOU!

How Do We Make Peace? ". . . And that leads me to confront the vital question
of disarmament. There are Christians whose conscience leads them to advocate a
total renunciation of armaments of any kind. Others, with equal conviction, be-

lieve that this is not the way to ensure peace. I am not going into all the arguments that have resounded among Christians for many years—except to say that, whatever decision we come to, we should be aware of the terrible consequences that may result. What concerns me now is that many church members seem to feel that if they are not radical pacifists there is nothing they can do or say about the cause of disarmament. We seem to have bred a kind of sullen acquiescence in an armaments race that is a blasphemy in our hungry world and any recommendation for restraint is seen as defeatist and unpatriotic. The General Assembly of our church, which is not dominated by pacifists, has called for an arms freeze to be agreed upon by the superpowers—a moratorium on the building of new weapons by the U.S.A. and the Soviet Union. This is totally different from unilateral disarmament. Yet one of our members, seeking signatures for such a proposal found it easier to get them in Central Park than among our church members here! Have we been so brainwashed that we shy away from anything that bears the word *Peace?*"—David H. C. Read, sermon at Madison Avenue Church, New York City, October 4, 1981.

Danger to Democracy. Alexis de Tocqueville left us a warning in his *Democracy in America*, as appropriate today as when he published it in 1835. "No protracted war," he wrote, in his famous book of observations about the United States, "can fail to endanger the freedom of a democratic country." He continued: "War does not always give over democratic communities to military government, but it must invariably and immeasurably increase the powers of civil government; it must also compulsorily concentrate the direction of all men and the management of all things in the hands of the administration. If it does not lead to despotism by sudden violence, it prepares men for it more gently by their habits. All those who seek to destroy the liberties of a democratic nation ought to know that war is the surest and the shortest means to accomplish it."

Dare to Read! John Wycliffe, the Englishman who first translated Scripture into English, was known as the "morning-star of the Reformation" because of his opposition to military might in Church or State and insistence that Christ is Head of all rulers. His translation of the Bible in 1384 was intended to place the Scriptures in the language of the common person. He dared to persevere with his translation in spite of fierce opposition by church authorities and rulers. On the flyleaf of his new English Bible, Wycliffe inscribed the words: "This Bible is translated and shall make possible government of people, by people, for people."

It is no wonder that the Bible is the first casualty under dictatorships. Are you daring to read it?

Sentence Sermon to Remember: There have been three historic scourges: famine, pestilence, and war. The first two have been slain by science. The last one science cannot kill. War can be abolished only by love.—Charles E. Jefferson.

Questions for Pupils on the Next Lesson. 1. What happens when a nation persists in defying God's will? 2. What were the warnings of God's prophets to Israel? 3. What happened to Israel? 4. Do evil acts always bring on evil consequences? 5. Do you always feel responsible for your actions?

LESSON X—AUGUST 5

LAST DAYS OF A KINGDOM

Background Scripture: 2 Kings 16, 17
Devotional Reading: 2 Kings 17:34–41

KING JAMES VERSION

2 KINGS 17 5 Then the king of Assyria came up throughout all the land, and went up to Samaria, and besieged it three years.

6 In the ninth year of Hoshea the king of Assyria took Samaria, and carried Israel away into Assyria, and placed them in Halah and in Habor *by* the river of Gozan, and in the cities of the Medes.

7 For *so* it was, that the children of Israel had sinned against the LORD their God, which had brought them up out of the land of Egypt, from under the hand of Pharaoh king of Egypt, and had feared other gods,

8 And walked in the statutes of the heathen, whom the LORD cast out from before the children of Israel, and of the kings of Israel, which they had made.

9 And the children of Israel did secretly *those* things that *were* not right against the LORD their God, and they built them high places in all their cities, from the tower of the watchmen to the fenced city.

11 And there they burnt incense in all the high places, as *did* the heathen whom the LORD carried away before them; and wrought wicked things to provoke the LORD to anger:

12 For they served idols, whereof the LORD had said unto them, Ye shall not do this thing.

13 Yet the LORD testified against Israel, and against Judah, by all the prophets, *and by* all the seers, saying, Turn ye from your evil ways, and keep my commandments *and* my statutes, according to all the law which I commanded your fathers, and which I sent to you by my servants and prophets.

14 Notwithstanding, they would not hear, but hardened their necks, like to the neck of their fathers, that did not believe in the LORD their God.

15 And they rejected his statutes, and his covenant that he made with their fathers, and his testimonies which he testified against them; and they followed vanity, and became vain, and went after the heathen that *were* round about them, *concerning* whom the LORD had charged them, that they should not do like them.

17 And they caused their sons and their daughters to pass through the fire, and used divination and enchantments, and sold themselves to do evil in the sight of the LORD, to provoke him to anger.

18 Therefore the LORD was very angry with Israel, and removed them out of his sight: there was none left but the tribe of Judah only.

REVISED STANDARD VERSION

2 KINGS 17 5 Then the king of Assyria invaded all the land and came to Samaria, and for three years he besieged it. 6 In the ninth year of Hoshea the king of Assyria captured Samaria, and he carried the Israelites away to Assyria, and placed them in Halah, and on the Habor, the river of Gozan, and in the cities of the Medes.

7 And this was so, because the people of Israel had sinned against the LORD their God, who had brought them up out of the land of Egypt from under the hand of Pharaoh king of Egypt, and had feared other gods 8 and walked in the customs of the nations whom the LORD drove out before the people of Israel, and in the customs which the kings of Israel had introduced. 9 And the people of Israel did secretly against the LORD their God things that were not right. They built for themselves high places at all their towns, from watch tower to fortified city; 11 and there they burned incense on all the high places, as the nations did whom the LORD carried away before them. And they did wicked things, provoking the LORD to anger, 12 and they served idols, of which the LORD had said to them, "You shall not do this." 13 Yet the LORD warned Israel and Judah by every prophet and every seer, saying, "Turn from your evil ways and keep my commandments and my statutes, in accordance with all the law which I commanded your fathers, and which I sent to you by my servants the prophets." 14 But they would not listen, but were stubborn, as their fathers had been, who did not believe in the LORD their God. 15 They despised his statutes, and his covenant that he made with their fathers, and the warnings which he gave them. They went after false idols, and became false, and they followed nations that were round about them, concerning whom the LORD had commanded them that they should not do like them. 17 And they burned their sons and their daughters as offerings, and used divination and sorcery, and sold themselves to do evil in the sight of the Lord, provoking him to anger. 18 Therefore the LORD was very angry with Israel, and removed them out of his sight; none was left but the tribe of Judah only.

KEY VERSE: Therefore the Lord was very angry with Israel, and removed them out of his sight; none was left but the tribe of Judah only. 2 Kings 17:18 (RSV).

HOME DAILY BIBLE READINGS

July 30.	M.	*The Reign of Shallum in Israel.* 2 Kings 15:13–22.
July 31.	T.	*The Reign of Pekahiah in Israel.* 2 Kings 15:23–26.
Aug. 1.	W.	*The Reign of Pekah in Israel.* 2 Kings 15:27–31.
Aug. 2.	T.	*The Reign of Jotham in Judah.* 2 Kings 15:32–38.
Aug. 3.	F.	*The Reign of Ahaz in Judah.* 2 Kings 16:5–20.
Aug. 4.	S.	*The Reign of Hoshea in Israel.* 2 Kings 17:1–6.
Aug. 5.	S.	*The End of the Northern Kingdom.* 2 Kings 17:7–18.

BACKGROUND

We go back to Israel, today, for a quick look at what was happening to those northern people while things were going from bad to worse in Judah after Amaziah. The same pattern was being followed in northern Israel. Jeroboam II succeeded Joash on the throne, and ruled for forty-one years; on the whole, he was a good king, but not quite good enough to stem the rising tide of disaster sweeping toward Israel.

But look at the next six kings. Zechariah (ruled six months) was bad; so were Shallum (one month), Menahem (eight years), Pekahiah (two years), Pekah (six years), and Hoshea (nine years). It was a sad parade of men not fit to be kings, and made king, often, by way of murder. It does seem, as we come to the end of the lineage of Israel's kings, that there were far more bad or inefficient men on that throne than there were men through whom God might have saved the nation from extinction.

But as we look carefully at the records as they appear in the Bible, it would seem that there were other reasons for the debacle, other errors and "sins" which cannot be laid at their feet.

Just why did Israel finally fall, and whose fault was it?

NOTES ON THE PRINTED TEXT

The Old Testament authors, at times, oversimplify the reasons behind the final collapse of Israel; they blame it all upon the unfaithfulness of Israel's kings. But there was more to it than that.

Israel, if you look at your maps, will be found caught in between two great nations which were aspiring to rule their world: one was Egypt, and the other was Assyria. Poor Israel and Judah bounced back and forth between these two powers, trying to make up their minds as to whether they would look for aid to Egypt or to Assyria. It was the old game of international alliances, and it was a grim and finally fatal game.

Hoshea, the last king of Israel, became king with the help and blessing of Assyria (2 Kings 15:29, 30). But the sly Egyptians convinced King Hoshea that with their help he could gain freedom from the Assyrians. That was a bad move; King Shalmaneser (the Fifth) threw his armies against the Israelites; he wanted to keep open the road that ran through Israel from Assyria to Egypt. For three long years, the Israelites fought—and lost. The city of Samaria fell, and the best of her population was marched off to slavery in Assyria. The ten tribes were never heard of again: they became "the ten lost tribes." There have been attempts to identify these lost tribes with the British people or the American Indians, but there is no foundation in historical fact for such an idea.

So Samaria fell; thanks to that fatal alliance with Assyria, Israel was no more. Her scattered people might have wished that they had put no trust in princes, but it was too late now to worry about that. Alliances are always dangerous, tricky and (like armaments) likely to be turned back upon those who create them. Our own President Washington warned us against becoming involved in "foreign entanglements," and we have profited by his advice.

We cannot, however, put all the blame upon the kings of Israel for becoming entangled with foreign powers; to give them credit, they were at least trying to save their nation, but the means they used were wrong. But back of this alliance confusion, there was a more basic cause of the disaster in Samaria. There was a prosperity that sapped their strength. During the reign of Jeroboam, for instance, the country was called "a stubborn heifer" in its pursuit of wealth and luxury, and "a band of drunkards." "His people sold the righteous for silver, and the poor for a pair of shoes" (Amos 2:6). They were so repulsive morally and so extravagant in their sacrifices that the Lord hated the feast days (5:21). They were far from being worthy of the help and love of their God.

Prosperity! The worship of Mammon! It has cut out the heart of many a nation. This passion for more, more, more, even when we have enough to live comfortably, has brought many a man and many a nation down into ruin.

In times of prosperity, we have a habit of crowing from the rooftops that we are "successful," so successful that we really don't need God's help any more. It is like the little boy who was asked if he prayed to God; "Yes," said the youngster, "I pray only at night-time, but not in the day. I don't need His help during the day." Funny, no, not funny. It is a grim philosophy hidden in many of our hearts: "We can take care of ourselves." That's what Samaria thought, but Samaria found out too late that she had taken the wrong road.

It is easy to blame the kings for the fall of Israel, but according to the Bible records, the people of the land were equally to blame for their fall. A king, or a president, is only as good or bad as his people are good or bad. To the author or authors of 2 Kings, the people of Israel are often to be condemned along with the kings; they, as well as their king, were to be punished for *their* long record of disloyalty to God. What these authors wrote in 2 Kings 17 is a dirge sung over a corpse named Samaria; it was written to show that loyalty to God is the one great principle that should guide people as well as monarchs. The fall of Israel, say these writers, proves that this is so.

SUGGESTIONS TO TEACHERS

You can probably recall knowing someone who had such exceptional gifts that everyone predicted a brilliant future for that person. Perhaps it was in sports, maybe in music or acting or painting. You and others were certain that person would soar to fame. However, instead of fulfilling all the dreams everyone had for that person, he or she faltered and finally failed because of a fatal inner flaw. Your lesson this Sunday is like watching the decline and death of a once-promising athlete or artist. The last days of Israel has tones of a Shakespearean tragedy, but it is not your task to wallow in sadness or what-might-have-been. Instead, consider what went wrong, and what does this mean for us in our times?

1. *DALLYING WITH CULTS.* The rulers and his subjects persisted in setting aside their commitment to the Lord and participating in pagan cults. King Ahaz even went so far as to sacrifice his own infant son in a disgusting ritualistic orgy. Leaders are examples in every community. As they think and act, others follow suit. In Israel, the leaders' continuing immorality infected the nation. They thought they were being chic and clever by imitating the practices of the "in" groups of Assyria, Egypt, Syria, and Canaan. They dismissed traditional Yahweh worship as "prudish" and "irrelevant." As teacher, you should urge your class to pick out similarities to Israel's morality (or lack of it) to the outlook in our culture.

2. *DESTROYING THE COVENANT.* The prophets criticized the leaders of Is-

rael for conniving with the Assyrians and the Egyptians because their "deals" with these superpowers meant covenanting with them. And covenanting with Assyria or Egypt meant repudiating the covenant with the Lord. Your lesson should give time to what the covenant God has through Jesus Christ with us, His people means in these times. Are there times when we break covenant with God? Are there dangers in us covenanting with other "powers," such as success, or comfort?

3. *DEGRADING THE COMMUNITY.* A group takes on the character of what it takes most seriously or worships. Two Kings 17:15 says it well, in describing the Israelites who "worshipped worthless idols, became worthless themselves." *Worship* means "worth-ship." True worth-ship comes only from placing the Lord in the center of life. Trying to find such value in life from idols merely degrades personalities and the community. Have your class consider the values which are idol-ized in our society. What is worship of these idols doing to people?

4. *DEFYING THE CREATOR.* They worshipped the Lord but they also worshipped their own gods (*see* 2 Kings 17:33, 41). The Israelites tried to have it both ways—a little faith and a lot of phony religion. God will have no rivals. The Lord demands complete allegiance. When His people persist in turning from Him, they bring on their own destruction! Israel, and later, Judah, learned this. Have we?

TOPIC FOR ADULTS
REFUSING TO FACE THE CONSEQUENCES

Ignoring the Consequences. King George III in his earlier years was an enlightened politician and patron of the arts. His learning and taste showed he had good ideas when he was in his twenties and thirties. He bought Buckingham Palace when he was only twenty-four. Previously, he had been tutored by some of England's finest minds. He understood architecture, astronomy, engineering, music, book-binding, and the crafts involved in most of the fine arts. He particularly was fascinated by clocks and maintained a large and fascinating collection of timepieces showing the hours, the tides and sunrises in many parts of the world. Later, however, George III became more preoccupied with the royal furnishings than with government of his American colonies. His scientific interest in clocks informed him about the sunset in Peking and the high tide at Amsterdam, but he refused to heed the signs of the time from Boston and Philadelphia. Refusing to face the consequences of his selfish obsessions, he lost the thirteen colonies in the New World from his Empire.

Once Beautiful Names. "We later civilizations, we, too, know now that we are mortal," Paul Valery said in discussing "The Crisis of the Mind" in Western civilization.

"We had long heard tell of whole worlds that had vanished, of empires sunk without a trace, gone down with all their men and all their machines into the unexplorable depths of the centuries.

"We were aware that the visible earth is made of ashes, and that ashes signify something. Elam, Nineveh, Babylon were but beautiful vague names, and the total ruin of those worlds had as little significance for us as their very existence. But France, England, Russia—these too would be beautiful names. Lusitania, too, is a beautiful name. And we see now that the abyss of history is deep enough to hold us all. We are aware that a civilization has the same fragility as a life."— James Reston, *New York Times,* October 31, 1976. © 1976 by The New York Times Company. Reprinted by permission.

Facing the Consequences. "Neither party expected for the war, the magnitude, or the duration which it has already attained. Neither anticipated that the cause of the conflict might cease with, or even before, the conflict itself should cease.

Each looked for an easier triumph, and a result less fundamental and astounding. Both read the same Bible, and pray to the same God; and each invokes His aid against the other. It may seem strange that any men should dare to ask a just God's assistance in wringing their bread from the sweat of other men's faces; but let us judge not that we be not judged. The prayers of both could not be answered, that of neither has been answered fully. The Almighty has His own purposes. 'Woe unto the world because of offences! for it must needs be that offences come; but woe to that man by whom the offence cometh!' If we shall suppose that American Slavery is one of these offences which, in the providence of God, must needs come, but which, having continued through His appointed time, He now wills to remove, and that He gives to both North and South, this terrible war, as the woe due to those by whom the offence came, shall we discern therein any departure from those divine attributes which the believers in a Living God always ascribe to Him? Fondly do we hope—fervently do we pray—that this mighty scourge of war may speedily pass away. Yet, if God wills that it continue, until all the wealth piled by the bond-man's two hundred and fifty years of unrequited toil shall be sunk, and until every drop of blood drawn with the lash, shall be paid by another drawn with the sword, as was said three thousand years ago, so still it must be said 'the judgments of the Lord, are true and righteous altogether.'

"With malice toward none; with charity for all; with firmness in the right, as God gives us to see the right, let us strive on to the finish the work we are in; to bind up the nation's wounds; to care for him who shall have borne the battle, and for his widow, and his orphan—to do all which may achieve and cherish a just, and a lasting peace, among ourselves, and with all nations."—Abraham Lincoln, Second Inaugural Address, March 4, 1865.

Questions for Pupils on the Next Lesson. 1. Who was Hezekiah and what did he do? 2. Do you long for a sense of heritage and belonging? 3. When you experienced crises, who gave you the support you needed? 4. How do you act out your commitments to Christ and others? 5. Have you experienced times when you questioned religious symbols?

TOPIC FOR YOUTH
FACING THE CONSEQUENCES

Throwing Out the Jewels. In September, 1979, a Bethlehem, Pennsylvania woman stashed $15,000 worth of jewels in a garbage bag for safekeeping while the family was on vacation, but lost the jewelry when the bag was inadvertently put outside, picked up by the garbage collector and dumped in the city landfill. The uninsured jewelry belonged to Betsy Duga. The jewelry was apparently thrown out in the garbage but the loss wasn't noticed until a week later. City Public Works Director Alex Panik said a search at the landfill which took four hours and covered a 50-by-50-foot area, turned up nothing. The effort was like trying to find a "needle in a haystack," Panik said, since the jewels would have been buried under a week's worth of compacted garbage.

Many persons treat their Christian heritage or Christian values just as carelessly. Somehow, often without being noticed, these jewels got thrown out. When we treat Christian morals and ideals as merely another bit of junk or garbage, we can easily lose the faith. And, we must face the consequences just as did ancient Israelites.

National Warning. "Observe good faith and justice toward all nations. Cultivate peace and harmony with all.

"Nothing is more essential than that permanent, inveterate antipathies against particular nations and passionate attachment for others should be excluded, and that in place of them, just and amicable feelings toward all should be cultivated.

The nation which indulges toward another an habitual hatred or an habitual fondness, is in some degree a slave. It is a slave to its animosity or to its affection, either of which is sufficient to lead it astray from its duty and its interest. Antipathy in one nation against another disposes each more readily to offer insult and injury, to lay hold of slight cause to umbrage, and to be haughty and intractable when accidental or trifling occasions of dispute occur."—George Washington, from his Farewell Address, 1796.

"I have lived a long time, sir, and the longer I live the more convincing proof I see of this truth, that God governs in the affairs of men. And if a sparrow cannot fall to the ground without His notice, is it probable that an empire can rise without His aid? We have been assured, sir, in the sacred writings that 'except the Lord build the house, they labor in vain that build it.' I firmly believe this and I also believe that without His concurring aid we shall succeed in this political building no better than the builders of Babel."—Spoken by Ben Franklin, eighty-one years old at the Constitutional Convention.

Sentence Sermon to Remember: An undivided heart, which worships God alone, and trusts Him as it should, is raised above all anxiety for earthy wants.—James Cunningham Geikie.

Questions for Pupils on the Next Lesson. 1. What was Hezekiah remembered for? 2. Who were the Assyrians? 3. When have you felt a sense of belonging? 4. Do you feel such a sense of belonging in your church? Why or why not? 5. Who gives you the best support when you're having difficulties?

LESSON XI—AUGUST 12

REFORM IN RELIGION

Background Scripture: 2 Kings 18–20
Devotional Reading: Isaiah 1:18–20

KING JAMES VERSION

2 KINGS 18 1 Now it came to pass in the third year of Hoshea son of Elah king of Israel, *that* Hezekiah the son of Ahaz king of Judah began to reign.

2 Twenty and five years old was he when he began to reign; and he reigned twenty and nine years in Jerusalem. His mother's name also *was* Abi, the daughter of Zachariah.

3 And he did *that which was* right in the sight of the LORD, according to all that David his father did.

4 He removed the high places, and brake the images, and cut down the groves, and brake in pieces the brazen serpent that Moses had made: for unto those days the children of Israel did burn incense to it: and he called it Nehushtan.

5 He trusted in the LORD God of Israel; so that after him was none like him among all the kings of Judah, nor *any* that were before him.

6 For he clave to the LORD, *and* departed not from following him, but kept his commandments, which the LORD commanded Moses.

7 And the LORD was with him; *and* he prospered whithersoever he went forth: and he rebelled against the king of Assyria, and served him not.

8 He smote the Philistines, *even* unto Gaza, and the borders thereof, from the tower of the watchmen to the fenced city.

19 29 And this *shall* be a sign unto thee, Ye shall eat this year such things as grow of themselves, and in the second year that which springeth of the same; and in the third year sow ye, and reap, and plant vineyards, and eat the fruits thereof.

30 And the remnant that is escaped of the house of Judah shall yet again take root downward, and bear fruit upward.

31 For out of Jerusalem shall go forth a remnant, and they that escape out of mount Zion: the zeal of the LORD *of hosts* shall do this.

20 20 And the rest of the acts of Hezekiah, and all his might, and how he made a pool, and a conduit, and brought water into the city, *are* they not written in the book of the chronicles of the kings of Judah?

REVISED STANDARD VERSION

2 KINGS 18 1 In the third year of Hoshea son of Elah, king of Israel, Hezekiah the son of Ahaz, king of Judah, began to reign. 2 He was twenty-five years old when he began to reign, and he reigned twenty-nine years in Jerusalem. His mother's name was Abi the daughter of Zechariah. 3 And he did what was right in the eyes of the LORD, according to all that David his father had done. 4 He removed the high places, and broke the pillars, and cut down the Asherah. And he broke in pieces the bronze serpent that Moses had made, for until those days the people of Israel had burned incense to it; it was called Nehushtan. 5 He trusted in the LORD the God of Israel; so that there was none like him among all the kings of Judah after him, nor among those who were before him. 6 For he held fast to the LORD; he did not depart from following him, but kept the commandments which the LORD commanded Moses. 7 And the LORD was with him; wherever he went forth, he prospered. He rebelled against the king of Assyria, and would not serve him. 8 He smote the Philistines as far as Gaza and its territory, from watchtower to fortified city.

19 29 "And this shall be the sign for you: this year you shall eat what grows of itself, and in the second year what springs of the same; then in the third year sow, and reap, and plant vineyards, and eat their fruit. 30 And the surviving remnant of the house of Judah shall again take root downward, and bear fruit upward; 31 for out of Jerusalem shall go forth a remnant, and out of Mount Zion a band of survivors. The zeal of the LORD will do this."

20 20 The rest of the deeds of Hezekiah, and all his might, and how he made the pool and the conduit and brought water into the city, are they not written in the Book of the Chronicles of the Kings of Judah?

KEY VERSE: "And the surviving remnant of the house of Judah shall again take root downward, and bear fruit upward." 2 Kings 19:30 (RSV).

HOME DAILY BIBLE READINGS

Aug. 6. M. Hezekiah's Reforms. 2 Kings 18:1–12.
Aug. 7. T. Invasion of Sennacherib's Army. 2 Kings 18:13–18.
Aug. 8. W. Call for Unconditional Surrender. 2 Kings 18:28–39.
Aug. 9. T. Isaiah's Counsel. 2 Kings 19:1–7.
Aug. 10. F. Sennacherib's Message to Hezekiah. 2 Kings 19:10–19.
Aug. 11. S. Deliverance of Jerusalem. 2 Kings 19:32–37.
Aug. 12. S. Isaiah's Protest Against Babylonian Negotiations. 2 Kings 20:12–19.

BACKGROUND

While Israel was stumbling down the road to oblivion, little Judah was not stumbling; it seemed that Judah might outlast the storms of war that swept around her. It seemed so during the reign of Uzziah (783–742 B.C.), who did *not* desert God. His reign was the finest since Solomon's; he strengthened the military defenses of Jerusalem, he encouraged agriculture; in the hills, he had many a flock of sheep. The people loved him. In one bad moment of pride, he outraged the priests by offering incense himself, and for that he was punished with death—by leprosy!

Jothan followed him as king; Jothan meant well, but he was no Uzziah; he tried too much to imitate his father. He left the country fairly wealthy, fairly safe, and walked off the stage in death just as the Assyrians were closing in on Judah. He died, and his son Ahaz snatched the scepter. Ahaz was a case of walking depravity. He had no honor, no courage, no reverence for anyone or anything except himself. He put Judah in a state of vassalege under Assyria, strangled the faith of his fathers, locked the Temple doors, and put out the ancient lamps. Lights out! Vision was dead—almost. Had it not been for the coming of Hezekiah, the end of Judah might have been right at this moment.

Hezekiah stood for one brave moment against the flames of total disaster: he came as the righteous son of an unbelievably wicked father, and he held the torch high for twenty-nine years.

NOTES ON THE PRINTED TEXT

Hezekiah was still young when he took over the throne of Judah: twenty-five years old and wise beyond his years. He turned out to be a statesman, a poet, a fighter, and above all, a determined and successful reformer. His reforms were of two varieties.

Religious reform came first in his plans for Judah, possibly because the young king saw that unless there was immediate religious reform there was no hope at all for Judah. That was typical Jewish thinking: without God, nothing! So he set about restoring the damage that had been done by Ahaz his father. The Temple was reopened and restored; the lamps were relighted. The cleansing took sixteen days, at the end of the sixteenth day, the Levites reported to him: "We have cleansed all the House of the Lord." This was the beginning of his reforms.

He "removed" (smashed) every pagan idol he could find, including what was said to be the brazen serpent that Moses had made. He cleansed a dirty house of religion and in that process began the cleansing of the hearts of Judah. The Judeans knew all too well that they had deserted the God who had led them through the Wilderness, and they cheered their young monarch for telling them so.

Second, there were economic and agricultural reforms. The barns of Judah's farmers were filled to capacity; a famous new tunnel was dug to bring the water of Gihon Spring into Jerusalem—an adequate water supply in case Jerusalem might be besieged. (Read James Michener's dramatic description of the digging of that tunnel in his book, *The Source.*)

Hezekiah got along fairly well with the Assyrians, who still ruled a conquered Judah—until he somehow got to thinking that an alliance with Egypt might help him overcome the Assyrians. He paid dearly for that: the Assyrians swept down upon him "like a wolf on the fold," overran Jerusalem and Judah, and penned up Hezekiah "like a bird in a cage." The wolf was Sennacherib, who collected a heavy tribute from his royal prisoner. Hardly had Sennacherib gone back home to Assyria when Hezekiah began to arm Judah for another attack on the Assyrians. Sennacherib came back this time to meet defeat. He never fought Judah again.

Hezekiah lived only about a year to enjoy his well-earned peace and glory, and then he "slept with his fathers" after a reign of twenty-nine years—aged fifty-six. He had indeed won great glory. When everything seemed hopeless for Judah, he restored her faith. He turned hopelessness into new hope. Greatest of all was *this* hope: out of Jerusalem, even though she might lay in ruins, there would come a *remnant*, a band of survivors who would later become strong in the restored city. At the moment, there wasn't much left to salvage in Jerusalem, even with Sennacherib out of the way, but there were to be enough survivors to keep the faith alive all down through the uncertain future. Other Sennacheribs might come and strut their little day in future battles, but they would die as Sennacherib had died, and God would go on working out His purpose with a faithful remnant. That was Lesson Number One, taught by the rise and fall of Hezekiah: kings and military leaders may come and go, but the power of moral ideals based upon spiritual devotion are always stronger than secular power.

Lesson Number Two was this: irreligion is the basic cause of national decay and disaster. If we would save the nation, we must first prevent the decay of religious faith, and if, today, religion is to reform our national life, we will need to smash the little idols dependent upon wealth and military arms and stop telling the world that, "We are *the* people" and start crying, "We are *God's* people,"—and live and do as such a Father would have us live and do.

There are no shortcuts to the Kingdom of God—it is a long, hard road, but He walks it with those who have the faith and the courage to walk on through tears and trouble to the promised end.

SUGGESTIONS TO TEACHERS

King Louis XVI ruled France at the time the French Revolution erupted. Unable or unwilling to understand what was happening to his people and his nation, he spent most of his time amusing himself with stag hunts and lavish parties with the nobility. His diary often carried a one-word entry: *Rien,* meaning "Nothing," even on the day the Revolution broke out in 1789. The injustices suffered by his subjects and the outbreak which followed were not understood.

Many in Judah and Israel probably would have written "nothing happened" during the twilight of these two nations. This final series of three lessons traces the final days of both countries. Through the eyes of faith, however, the writers of God's "diary" in 2 Kings never state *Rien* in describing those happenings.

Likewise, as teacher, you are to interpret the events of the reigns of Hezekiah, Manassah, Josiah, and the last Judean kings. Lots was happening with God. Lots is still happening.

1. *INAUGURATION TRIUMPHS.* Hezekiah opens his rule with an attempt to clean up the disgusting moral and worship practices in Judea. The period of civic and religious renewal which followed were a brief triumph for righteousness. Have your class pay careful attention to the words in the Scripture about the greatness of a nation resting upon their faithfulness. Remind your class that this still holds true.

2. *ISRAEL TOTTERS.* You may wish to draw a time line on the blackboard to help your class understand the sequence of events during the days of the united

kingdom, the division which followed Solomon, and the final collapse of the northern nation Israel. More important than memorizing the date of Israel's capture (721 B.C.) by the Assyrians is remembering the cause. Israel would not listen to the Lord or obey. Do we?

3. *INVADER TAUNTS.* Your class should enjoy the drama of 2 Kings 18, 19, in which the Assyrians taunt the defenders of Jerusalem. You can easily make this scene very vivid by pointing out how invincible and cruel the Assyrian war machine was. Ask your class how God's people today stand up to stress and taunts. Many Christians feel "under siege" and find it hard not to surrender to the threats and blandishments of the hostile society around them.

4. *ISAIAH TELLS.* Make certain that the Prophet Isaiah's words of counsel are examined in this lesson. His confidence in the midst of a deadly siege and his message about God and humans steadied Hezekiah and can also steady us!

5. *INDISCRETION TORMENTS.* King Hezekiah foolishly allowed himself to be flattered by Babylonian visitors and showed them all the wealth of his treasury. Failure to put the security of his kingdom ahead of personal pride meant that the Babylonians greedily eyed his gold. Your class is offered another example of the way personal acts of irresponsibility can cost dearly.

TOPIC FOR ADULTS
REFORM IN RELIGION

Resolve, Reform, and Religion. When Hezekiah was a young man, he resolved to reform the religious and moral practices in his realm. Another young man, William Booth, also resolved to reform the religious and moral practices in England in the last century. Booth succeeded in establishing what came to be known as the Salvation Army, and brought great change within his country in the 1800s. Here is the list of resolutions he drew up when he was a young man of only twenty. As you read them, reflect on Hezekiah's reforms, and also reflect on what resolutions for reform in religion you have made recently.

"I do promise, my God helping—

"Firstly, that I will rise every morning sufficiently early to wash, dress, and have a few minutes, not less than five, in private prayer.

"Secondly, that I will, as much as possible, avoid all that babbling and idle talk in which I have lately so sinfully indulged.

"Thirdly, that I will endeavor in my deportment and conduct before the world and my fellow servants especially to conduct myself as a humble, meek, and zealous follower of the bleeding Lamb, and, by serious conversation and warning, endeavor to lead them to think of their immortal souls.

"Fourthly, that I will not read less than four chapters in God's Word every day.

"Fifthly, that I will strive to live closer to God, and to seek after holiness of heart, and leave providential events with God.

"Sixthly, that I will read this over every day or at least twice a week. God help me, enable me to cultivate a spirit of self-denial and to yield myself a prisoner of love to the Redeemer of the world. Amen and Amen. William Booth. I feel my own weakness, and without God's help, I shall not keep these resolutions a day."

Moral of Abscam. Harrison A. Williams was a twenty-three-year veteran of the United States Senate when he was caught in Abscam, the F.B.I. undercover scam, for agreeing to use his influence to obtain government contracts for a titanium mine and processing plant in which he had a concealed financial interest and to improperly smooth the way for a supposed Arab sheik investor to immigrate to the U.S. Williams was convicted on a federal charge of conspiracy and bribery, sentenced to serve three years in prison and fined $50,000. When senators convened to debate whether or not to expell him from the Senate, Williams insisted that he had been unjustly framed and offered no apologies. He tried to fight expulsion by claiming that it was unfair for the F.B.I. to catch corrupt politicians, and called for investigation of the F.B.I. The Senate was spared from a vote when Williams finally resigned in March, 1982. Williams, however, never explained why he had not turned his back on temptation. As Senator Howell Heflin of Alabama, of the Senate Ethics Committee, said, "Put most simply, Harrison Williams traded on his office. At any point in this drawn-out, sordid affair, Senator Williams could have said, 'Wait a minute. What you're proposing is wrong.' But he didn't. He stayed, he discussed, he agreed, he promised, he pledged, all this to abuse his public trust."

Senators and common citizens alike have a duty to keep reform in mind in all of their dealings. Unless we continually are intent to bring renewal and reform to every level of public and private life, our society is doomed.

Difference Between a Civilization and a Jungle. "Self-discipline, not externally applied discipline, is the only avenue to morality. It is what individuals do when alone, when no one is looking, and when they know they won't get caught, that makes the difference between a civilization and a jungle."—Balfour Brickner, rabbi of the Stephen Wise Free Synagogue, in *The New York Times,* March 7, 1982.

Questions for Pupils on the Next Lesson. 1. Why was Josiah considered a good king? 2. What did Josiah do when the scroll was discovered in the House of the Lord? 3. What do some adults do in order to be accepted by their peers? 4. Are the leaders of our nation and your church concerned about the proper issues? 5. What does it mean for a community to be "covenanted"?

TOPIC FOR YOUTH
CHANGING DIRECTIONS

Inner Braces. Reform and changing directions in life cannot be done only because of outside pressure. Nor can we blame outside pressures for the bad directions we sometimes find ourselves taking.

A minister once met a man who had become involved in a corrupt practice in the community. The minister rebuked the man for having so little moral backbone, especially since he had known what he had been doing.

"You don't know what the outside pressure was," the man lamely explained.

"Outside pressure, outside pressure," the minister indignantly declared. "Where were your inner braces?"

Where are your inner braces? Do you change direction with every whiff of outside pressure?

Change in Direction. "The greatest need of mankind today—socially and individually—is a true sense of direction. Our world is like an Atlantic liner deprived of rudder, compass, sextant, charts, and wireless tackle, yet compelled to go full steam ahead. There is magnificence, comfort, pulsating power; but whither are we going? Does that depend solely on the accident of circumstance and the ever-changing balance of conflicting interests and ambitions? Or is there available for man, if he so will, guidance on his dark and dangerous course from some Wisdom higher than his own?"—B. H. Streeter, *The God Who Speaks.*

Jesus the Direction-Changer. "The Korean poet-playwright Kim Chi Ha is a committed Christian who has suffered greatly under repressive regimes in Korea because of his unrelenting cry for justice and an uncompromising commitment to the search for truth. Repeatedly jailed and tortured by the regime of Park Chung Hee for his eloquent criticism of oppression in South Korea, Kim Chi Ha was sentenced to life imprisonment in 1976. Yet his spirit remains firm and his hope undaunted, for beyond his own suffering and the suffering of his people, he sees the suffering of Jesus Christ. In his play, *The Gold-Crowned Jesus,* a leper, the most despised of social outcasts in Korea, encounters Jesus imprisoned in concrete by government, business, and church officials. The leper asks, 'What can be done to free you, Jesus, to make you live again so that you can come to us?' and Jesus replied: 'My power alone is not enough. People like you must help to liberate me. Those who seek only the comforts, wealth, honor, and power of this world, who wish entry to the kingdom of heaven for themselves only and ignore the poor . . . cannot give me life again. . . . Only those, though very poor and suffering like yourself, who are generous in spirit and seek to help the poor and the wretched can give me life again. You have helped to give me life again. You removed the gold crown from my head and so freed my lips to speak. People like you will be my liberators' "—Reprinted by permission from *Sojourners* Magazine, Box 29272, Washington, D.C. 20017.

Sentence Sermon to Remember: Tomorrow I'll reform, the fool doth say; today's too late; the wise did that yesterday.—Benjamin Franklin in *Poor Richard's Almanac.*

Questions for Pupils on the Next Lesson. 1. Who was King Josiah? 2. Who was Huldah? 3. Have you ever felt alienated from others because of your wrongdoing? 4. Are you aware that nations have been destroyed because leaders have ceased serving the best interests of their people? 5. Who are your authorities for your behavior?

LESSON XII—AUGUST 19

MEASURED BY THE WORD

Background Scripture: 2 Kings 21:1-23; 30
Devotional Reading: 2 Kings 21:1-9

KING JAMES VERSION

2 KINGS 22 10 And Shaphan the scribe showed the king, saying, Hilkiah the priest hath delivered me a book. And Shaphan read it before the king.

11 And it came to pass, when the king had heard the words of the book of the law, that he rent his clothes.

12 And the king commanded Hilkiah the priest, and Ahikam the son of Shaphan, and Achbor the son of Michaiah, and Shaphan the scribe, and Asahiah a servant of the king's, saying,

13 Go ye, inquire of the LORD for me, and for the people, and for all Judah, concerning the words of this book that is found: for great *is* the wrath of the LORD that is kindled against us, because our fathers have not hearkened unto the words of this book, to do according unto all that which is written concerning us.

15 And she said unto them, Thus saith the LORD God of Israel, Tell the man that sent you to me,

16 Thus saith the LORD, Behold, I will bring evil upon this place, and upon the inhabitants thereof, *even* all the words of the book which the king of Judah hath read:

23 1 And the king sent, and they gathered unto him all the elders of Judah and of Jerusalem.

2 And the king went up into the house of the LORD, and all the men of Judah and all the inhabitants of Jerusalem with him, and the priests, and the prophets, and all the people, both small and great: and he read in their ears all the words of the book of the covenant which was found in the house of the LORD.

3 And the king stood by a pillar, and made a covenant before the LORD, to walk after the LORD, and to keep his commandments and his testimonies and his statutes with all *their* heart and all *their* soul, to perform the words of this covenant that were written in this book. And all the people stood to the covenant.

REVISED STANDARD VERSION

2 KINGS 22 10 Then Shaphan the secretary told the king, "Hilkiah the priest has given me a book." And Shaphan read it before the king.

11 And when the king heard the words of the book of the law, he rent his clothes. 12 And the king commanded Hilkiah the priest, and Ahikam the son of Shaphan, and Achbor the son of Micaiah, and Shaphan the secretary, and Asaiah the king's servant, saying, 13 "Go, inquire of the LORD for me, and for the people, and for all Judah, concerning the words of this book that has been found; for great is the wrath of the LORD that is kindled against us, because our fathers have not obeyed the words of this book, to do according to all that is written concerning us."

15 And she said to them, "Thus says the LORD, the God of Israel: 'Tell the man who sent you to me, 16 Thus says the LORD, Behold, I will bring evil upon this place and upon its inhabitants, all the words of the book which the king of Judah has read.'"

23 1 Then the king sent, and all the elders of Judah and Jerusalem were gathered to him. 2 And the king went up to the house of the LORD, and with him all the men of Judah and all the inhabitants of Jerusalem, and the priests and the prophets, all the people, both small and great; and he read in their hearing all the words of the book of the covenant which had been found in the house of the LORD. 3 And the king stood by the pillar and made a covenant before the LORD, to walk after the LORD and to keep his commandments and his testimonies and his statutes, with all his heart and all his soul, to perform the words of this covenant that were written in this book; and all the people joined in the covenant.

KEY VERSE: *I have found the book of the law in the house of the Lord.* 2 Kings 22:8 (RSV).

HOME DAILY BIBLE READINGS

Aug. 13.   M.   *The Wicked Reign of Manasseh.* 2 Kings 21:1-15.
Aug. 14.   T.   *The Wicked Reign of Amon.* 2 Kings 21:19-26.
Aug. 15.   W.   *Discovery of the Book of the Law.* 2 Kings 22:1-10.
Aug. 16.   T.   *Consultation With Huldah.* 2 Kings 22:11-20.

Aug. 17.   F.   *Josiah's Religious Reforms.* 2 Kings 23:1–14.
Aug. 18.   S.   *Extension of Reforms to Northern Kingdom.* 2 Kings 23:15–20.
Aug. 19.   S.   *Final Days of Josiah.* 2 Kings 23:21–30.

BACKGROUND

When Hezekiah died his son Manasseh reigned; he has been called "the most wicked king of Judah," and he probably was. But he also enjoyed the longest reign of any king of Judah (forty-five years), and he did many good things for his people. But to the people who really knew him, he was Manasseh the Mad, unclean, unworthy, unwanted. His son Amon was not much better; as king, he was so bad that he was murdered in his own palace by his own servants. That made Josiah, son of Amon, king by way of the approval of "the people of the land." Josiah was eight years old when the people picked him. It was a lucky and a providential choice, for this boy became a Hezekiah reborn, the most blameless of them all, perhaps the noblest of them all. His reign, good and godly though it was, was also the sunset, the last ray of hope for Judah.

NOTES ON THE PRINTED TEXT

Nothing much happened during the first eighteen years on the throne of Josiah; that was probably because a regency ruled the land until the boy grew up and became king in his own right at the age of twenty-six. Then things really began to happen. Josiah at twenty-six had few of the old problems with Assyria that his predecessors had; Assyria had had her day in the sun, and her control over the small states she had conquered became weaker and weaker. As Assyria declined, the fortunes and faith of Judah grew stronger—thanks to the leadership of a courageous King Josiah.

Josiah inherited a bad situation from Amon; all we have to do to understand how bad it was is to look at what was left of the holy Temple in Jerusalem. Its dilapidation started with Manasseh and continued through Amon's brief reign, and now it was nothing more than a sad wreck. The evil kings had opened its doors to Baal and offered sacrifices and incense to the sun, the moon, and the twelve signs of the zodiac. They persecuted the prophets; Manasseh killed the aging Isaiah. To call it a shambles is to underestimate its influence upon the people of the land.

Like a torch flaming up suddenly in a dark night, Josiah stood before his people and began a reformation that swept all across Judah. First, he restored, or rebuilt, the Temple. Helping him were Shaphan the scribe and Hilkiah the high priest—both highly placed in the religious organization of Jerusalem. He appealed to a people far from rich for money, and they gave it joyfully. To the Jewish people, this Temple enshrined their faith; it was the visible incarnation of their religion. When Josiah restored that Temple, he built new temples of hope in the hearts of his people. He had great help; this was the era of three great prophets: Jeremiah, Zephaniah, and (a rather unattractive) Nahum.

The Temple building had top priority in Josiah's plan of reform. The Temple came first, for without a strong Temple, mere people could do nothing. The Temple first, above all!

The Church first, above all! How many of us still believe that? There was a time in our country when the Church was the heart of the community—when, as in old New England, the town was built *around* "the little church on the green." That's gone, now. Every "main line" Church in the United States is showing an annual *loss* in membership, and therefore in the mission of the Church. We build skyscrapers, gigantic dams, palatial governmental buildings, great temples of finance and industry—but few, too few, new churches.

What Josiah tells us is that the Temple has to be at the heart of it all, or our religion will fade and die and the nation with it. "At no time and nowhere has religion existed without incorporating itself in institutional form."—Raymond Calkins. Right, or wrong? If this is right, why is church membership falling and why is the Church only a building to which we go to pray—occasionally?

The amazing reformation of Josiah was built upon two foundations: the restoration of the Temple, and the discovery of the book of the law. A "book of the covenant . . . was found in the house of the Lord" (23:2). What was this book? It was, quite probably, made up of the material which we find in the Book of Deuteronomy—a compendium of ancient laws edited and revised during Manasseh's reign and hidden in the Temple in the hope that, some day, it might inspire a reformation. It did just that. Its discovery and publication inspired the most thorough reformation of worship in the history of Judah. Josiah's reformation was based upon this finding of the law.

What Josiah read in this book frightened him: the book said that the wrath of God would surely descend upon the people of Judah unless they turned to obey this law. In a fit of fear, Josiah consulted a prophetess named Huldah, who verified the verdict that the end of Judah was imminent because of her disloyalty to God and her failure to live by the laws of the book. That sent Josiah on a crusade to *force* his people into strict obedience—and that was a mistake.

The basic truth here is that no one can be *forced* into obedience to God or into love for Him. Josiah's idea was good but his means (force) were bad, and so he failed as his fathers had failed. Reform wrought by violence is not good reform; the means are *not* justified by the ends. Ruthless zeal can and does often destroy the finest of reforms. If Josiah had only proceeded with a gentler hand, he might have won. As it worked out, he lost: he perished in a battle at Megiddo, fighting back at Neco of Egypt. Great was the lamentation of Judah over the death of her godliest king.

But Judah still had the book. Judah saved us this *portion* of our Book, our Bible. For centuries, as it was with Josiah, the Book, our Bible, was a lost Book, existing only in ancient manuscripts which have long since been lost, too. But in the Protestant Reformation (beginning early in the sixteenth century) the Bible was rediscovered, released from the chains which bound it and kept it from the common man—set free for all to read and love. In the rediscovery of the Book in this Reformation, the religion and morality of Europe was changed for the better, and the roots of our democracy were laid.

Just so have the lives of men been changed, in the opening of the Book, the reading of it, the practice of its precepts and commands. The discovery of the Bible has been a turning point in many a man's life.

Have we lost it—lost our use of and our interest in the Book of Books? God help us, if we have, for only He can help. Over us, in our modern world, lies the long shadow of *international* disaster—disaster by the bomb. If we move too far away from His Law, His Book, His love, even He cannot save us!

Josiah warned Judah. He did the work of ten men in his effort to save his Judah, but save her he could not. The long shadow of a new world power hung over Judah, but she never saw it—the shadow of a new world power called Babylon, and Babylon's Nebuchadnezzar.

SUGGESTIONS TO TEACHERS

Like a dying star growing fainter in its final descent, then suddenly flaring with a brilliant light for a brief period before plunging into the void, Judah's decline was interrupted in the brief era of King Josiah's reign. You will be tracing the next-to-last years of Judah in this lesson. Focus your teaching on the impact of Josiah and his reform.

1. *RETURN TO DESTRUCTION.* Point out that after King Hezekiah's time, a

horrible period followed under King Manasseh. Two Kings 21:11 flatly states that this evil monarch promoted practices which even out-sinned the Canaanites! The worst offenses were the ruthless destruction of human lives through violence and cults. As teacher, you may refer to Manasseh's callous disregard for human beings by murdering them and offering up his own child as a human sacrifice. Take this opportunity to foster discussion on the dangers of violence and cults in our society. Have your class take heed of the prophets' warnings on the morality of a Manasseh.

2. *RESPITE FROM DISOBEDIENCE.* You will have to allude to the events in Judah after Manasseh, including Amon's murder, but move the lesson toward considering the boy-king Josiah and his accomplishments. You should point out the circumstances behind Josiah's reform and particularly set out the significance of the book discovered during the renovations of the Temple. That book, as you know, is Deuteronomy. You must spend a few minutes informing your class about the importance of this part of Scripture and its message to God's people. State to the class that Deuteronomy, like all of the Bible, is God's yardstick or set of standards, and that believers are still measured by God's Word.

3. *RENEWAL OF DEDICATION.* Relate to your class the impact that the discovery of the "second law" book (the literal meaning of Deuteronomy) had on Josiah and Judah. A complete clean-up followed. Josiah and the priests eradicated the pagan practices and instituted a proper Passover in Jerusalem. Most important, they renewed the Covenant. Ask your class to comment on the meaning of God's Covenant in their lives. What commitments do they understand that God makes to us? How do they know that God keeps His Word? You can profitably use a chunk of the lesson time to reflect on God's Covenant with us through Jesus Christ.

4. *REPRIEVE FROM DOOM.* Josiah's reform bought time. This noble-minded ruler temporarily arrested the decline of his nation. Although Judah's years of disobedience meant that the nation would ultimately crumble, Josiah saved Judah for a time. This offers you an opportunity to comment on the power of one person's moral example. Ask your pupils if they realize the enormous responsibility they carry as members of God's people, and, therefore, leaders in society. Remind your people that they, like Josiah, may bring reprieve from doom in our society. When they realize that they are measured by God's Word, they can bring His saving vitality to bear on society.

TOPIC FOR ADULTS
MEASURED BY THE WORD

In Solitude or in Society? The great philosopher Alfred North Whitehead once defined religion as "what a man does with his solitariness." Interesting though this definition may appear, it is not the way the Bible described faith. In fact, the Old Testament and the New both insist that faith in the God of Israel is just the opposite. Religion is what a man or a woman does under pressure and in actual events as they interact with other people in daily life. Religion is being measured by God's Word in the activities of this world, not in the cloister of solitude.

Blackbeard's Goal. Reading the story of Manasseh and other Old Testament kings whose code seemed to be cruelty and catastrophe to others brings to mind an episode from the life of Edward Teach, the "most ruthless, bloodthirsty and defiant of all, and determined to win at everything" pirate remembered as "Blackbeard." Teach, master of a captured vessel named *Queen Anne's Revenge,* sported an enormous bushy beard which reached to his chest and was festooned with bright ribbons. Before going into battle, he lighted matches and pieces of hemp dipped in saltpeter and stuck them in his matted hair to make himself more terrifying. He seemed to thrive on brutality. Once he challenged his crew, "let's make a hell out of this world and see how long we can bear it." He then had the hatches closed and quantities of sulphur lighted. Blackbeard and the crew members seated themselves in the hold, seeing who would hold out the longest before asking for the hatches to be opened. The pirate gang was forced to endure the horrid, choking smoke until they began to sicken and pass out. Finally, Blackbeard threw open the hatches, laughing fiendishly because he was unaffected.

Certain rulers like Manasseh also seemed determined to make a hell out of this world to see how long they could bear it. Tragically, they brought incalculable pain and grief to others. In a sense, the human story is a record of trying to make a hell out of God's beautiful world, and God's patient efforts to reclaim it as His world.

Measure of a Nation. "Every nation in the world, however small and however large, must make greater endeavors to preserve the honor and dignity of the human race and its labors, however humble. Nations must be wise enough to retain only that which is good and true value; bold and ruthless enough to discard false customs, prejudices, and traditions. A nation must be sincere and honest in purpose in its endeavors to help and understand another nation's problems. These good principles and endeavors, sincerity of purpose will not be forthcoming from any nation unless each and every one of us, as individuals and families collectively, play our part. There is no such thing as isolation in the world today."— Jane W. Baldwin, in "Australia Today," *Pakistan Horizon,* vol. XXI, no. 4.

Questions for Pupils on the Next Lesson. 1. How would you describe the leadership in Judah during its final days? 2. What happened to the people of Judah when the Babylonians captured Jerusalem? 3. Is God's judgment sometimes carried out by people or nations that do not revere Him? 4. How are some people able to keep going on with life after the worst of disasters? 5. Why are some people forced to suffer because of the decisions and behavior of others?

TOPIC FOR YOUTH
LIVING BY THE BOOK

In George Bernard Shaw's *Saint Joan,* after the coronation Joan tells the king that she has heard divine voices bidding her lead on to victory. Charles the king, surrounded by the splendor and glory of his court, seems vexed that Joan can hear voices and he cannot. He asks Joan why the voices do not come to him. Joan tells the king that the voices do come to him but that he doesn't hear them because he will not listen. She chides him for crossing himself when the Angelus rings but not continuing to pray from his heart; for being so hasty as to hurry away when he ought to listen to the bells after they stop ringing. Joan insists that the king could hear the voices as well as she if he would listen.

Josiah was a king who tried to hear God's voice by living by the Book. Like Joan and others of God's realm, he heeded the divine voice. Are you listening to the message in God's Word?

Russian Proverb. Many young people see no point in reading the Bible. Many especially claim to be bored by the history passages and say, "This Book is a waste of time."

The Russian writer Alexander Solzhenitsyn points out how vitally important it is to be aware of God's presence and plans through His Book. Solzhenitsyn quotes an old Russian folk proverb in the preface of his volume, *The Gulag Archipelago:* "Dwell on the past and you'll lose an eye; forget the past and you'll lose both eyes."

If you forget the past, especially the biblical story, you end by being blind to deeper realities of God and yourself!

National Strength. "But the greatest strength of any nation is in its human and spiritual resources. Christians everywhere are sustained and inspired by the ideal of the brotherhood of man and the commandment to love one another. They can set an example of Service and self-sacrifice, of reconciliation and unity, so as to make the world a better place for all.

"For the people of this country which has achieved so much, there remains a powerful underlying sense of community and of direct links with generations past and still to come. In this fast changing temporal world, it is the task of the Church, by fresh inspiration and new understanding, to awaken and renew this sense of common stewardship.

"Over the centuries perhaps the greatest moments in the history of our country have been in times of great adversity when the nation has stood alone, when we have been faced by the threat of more powerful material forces, but have been sustained by the strength of our own moral and spiritual conviction. Under God's will, we can still achieve that truer greatness in our own generation. For it is part of the Christian message that 'time and chance happeneth to all men.'

"Opportunity lies with each and every generation in the circumstances of its day provided it acts with faith, courage and perseverance."—Queen Elizabeth in Address to Church of Scotland, 1978.

Sentence Sermon to Remember: God's Road Map—the Bible.—Kenyon A. Palmer.

Questions for Pupils on the Next Lesson. 1. Do your acts of wrongdoing always have bad results or can you "get away with it?" 2. Why do wrongdoings make a person alienated from the larger group? 3. What happened to the people of Jerusalem when the Babylonians captured the city? 4. What exactly is meant by God's judgment? 5. Are nations as well as individuals responsible to God?

LESSON XIII—AUGUST 26

INTO EXILE

Background Scripture: 2 Kings 24; 25
Devotional Reading: Jeremiah 12:8-16

KING JAMES VERSION

2 KINGS 25 1 And it came to pass in the ninth year of his reign, in the tenth month, in the tenth *day* of the month, *that* Nebuchadnezzar king of Babylon came, he, and all his host, against Jerusalem, and pitched against it; and they built forts against it round about.

2 And the city was besieged unto the eleventh year of king Zedekiah.

3 And on the ninth *day* of the *fourth* month the famine prevailed in the city, and there was no bread for the people of the land.

4 And the city was broken up, and all the men of war *fled* by night by the way of the gate between two walls, which *is* by the king's garden: (now the Chaldees *were* against the city round about:) and *the king* went the way toward the plain.

5 And the army of Chaldees pursued after the king, and overtook him in the plains of Jericho: and all his army were scattered from him.

6 So they took the king, and brought him up to the king of Babylon to Riblah; and they gave judgment upon him.

7 And they slew the sons of Zedekiah before his eyes, and put out the eyes of Zedekiah, and bound him with fetters of brass, and carried him to Babylon.

8 And in the fifth month, on the seventh *day* of the month, which *is* the nineteenth year of king Nebuchadnezzar king of Babylon, came Nebuzaradan, captain of the guard, a servant of the king of Babylon, unto Jerusalem:

9 And he burnt the house of the LORD, and the king's house, and all the houses of Jerusalem, and every great *man's* house burnt he with fire.

10 And all the army of the Chaldees, that *were with* the captain of the guard, brake down the walls of Jerusalem round about.

11 Now the rest of the people that were left in the city, and the fugitives that fell away to the king of Babylon, with the remnant of the multitude, did Nebuzaradan the captain of the guard carry away.

12 But the captain of the guard left of the poor of the land *to be* vinedressers and husbandmen.

REVISED STANDARD VERSION

2 KINGS 25 1 And in the ninth year of his reign, in the tenth month, on the tenth day of the month, Nebuchadnezzar king of Babylon came with all his army against Jerusalem, and laid siege to it; and they built siegeworks against it round about. 2 So the city was besieged till the eleventh year of King Zedekiah. 3 On the ninth day of the fourth month the famine was so severe in the city that there was no food for the people of the land. 4 Then a breach was made in the city; the king with all the men of war fled by night by the way of the gate between the two walls, by the king's garden, though the Chaldeans were around the city. And they went in the direction of the Arabah. 5 But the army of the Chaldeans pursued the king, and overtook him in the plains of Jericho; and all his army was scattered from him. 6 Then they captured the king, and brought him up to the king of Babylon at Riblah, who passed sentence upon him. 7 They slew the sons of Zedekiah before his eyes, and put out the eyes of Zedekiah, and bound him in fetters, and took him to Babylon.

8 In the fifth month, on the seventh day of the month—which was the nineteenth year of King Nebuchadnezzar, king of Babylon—Nebuzaradan, the captain of the bodyguard, a servant of the king of Babylon, came to Jerusalem. 9 And he burned the house of the LORD, and the king's house and all the houses of Jerusalem; every great house he burned down. 10 And all the army of the Chaldeans, who were with the captain of the guard, broke down the walls around Jerusalem. 11 And the rest of the people who were left in the city and the deserters who had deserted to the king of Babylon, together with the rest of the multitude, Nebuzaradan the captain of the guard carried into exile. 12 But the captain of the guard left some of the poorest of the land to be vinedressers and plowmen.

KEY VERSE: For because of the anger of the Lord it came to the point in Jerusalem and Judah that he cast them out from his presence. 2 Kings 24:20 (RSV).

HOME DAILY BIBLE READINGS

Aug. 20. M. *The Reign of Jehoiakim in Judah.* 2 Kings 23:36–24:7.
Aug. 21. T. *First Deportation under Jehoiachin.* 2 Kings 24:8–17.

Aug. 22. W. *Siege of Jerusalem under Zedekiah.* 2 Kings 24:18–25:7.
Aug. 23. T.   *The Sack of Jerusalem.* 2 Kings 25:8–21.
Aug. 24. F.   *The Murder of Gedaliah.* 2 Kings 25:22–26.
Aug. 25. S.   *The Pardon of Jehoiachin.* 2 Kings 25:27–30.
Aug. 26. S.   *Prayer for God's Blessing on the King.* Psalms 72:1–15.

BACKGROUND

Little Judah stumbled on for nearly 150 years after Israel fell, living out those years under the rule of foreign kings. Jehoahaz II, son of Josiah, managed to stay on the throne for three months; he gets very little attention in Jewish history, mainly because "he did much that was evil in the eye of the Lord." He was succeeded by Jehoiakim, the second of Josiah's sons, who followed the same evil road that Jehoahaz had trod, but managed to stay a king for eleven years; he gave up the scepter to Jehoiachin, son of Jehoiakim, who held on for three months plus ten days, following which the great Nebuchadnezzar carried him off to Babylon, where he died.

Now came a gleam of light in the person of Zedekiah, who was something of a pet of Nebuchadnezzar, who thought he might do something to quiet down those restless Jews in Jerusalem. The people of Jerusalem may have thought that at long last they had a king they could trust. There was nothing wicked about Zedekiah, but he seemed a bit weak whenever he faced a crisis, and when he was forced to make a decision that would please or displease either Nebuchadnezzar or his own, in Jerusalem. The job of being king of Judah was "no bed of roses," as Zedekiah soon discovered. But he made an oath of allegiance to the king of Babylon, and was given permission to sit down and be king of Judah.

NOTES ON THE PRINTED TEXT

At first, Zedekiah had a great chance to save Judah from destruction. He was, physically, "every inch a king." He was likable and well-intentioned—so much so that he was treated by the great Prophet Jeremiah with a deference that prophet never extended to other kings. Jeremiah was a real power in Judah—a behind-the-scenes prophet and statesman who had great influence.

There was murmuring in Judah, at this time, among the people, who wanted freedom from the rule of Babylon; they talked endlessly about it, almost pleading for war with a nation a hundred times stronger than she was! Jeremiah opposed them, and he led King Zedekiah to oppose it, too, and settle down to live in peace for a few years without a war with Babylon. He and Zedekiah were like-minded on this.

But like all kings and presidents and would-be rulers of any people, Zedekiah heard those mutterings—and wondered what he should do about it all. His conscience told him to stand for peace—yes, at any price, even at the price of submission to Nebuchadnezzar. Zedekiah decided on the wrong solution to his problem: he broke the solemn oath he had made to Babylon's king and rebelled against Nebuchadnezzar. The rest is a story of pure horror. Nebuchadnezzar crushed Judah like an egg; he left not a house standing, not an inch of the old walls—nothing but a howling waste. It reminds us of the remark of General Sheridan, in our Civil War, about what he planned to do in the Shenandoah Valley. "I will leave it so barren that a crow will have to carry his own rations if he flies over the Valley." That is what happened to Jerusalem. Only a few poor vine dressers and husbandmen were left; the rest were driven down the road to exile in Babylon.

We may blame Zedekiah for it; we may call him a fool to think he could whip Babylon. But we should think twice before we do that. Look at the problem that faced him! On the one hand, he had Jeremiah and his conscience, whispering to him that he take the way of peace and save his people; on the other hand, he heard the screaming for rebellion in the streets on the part of his people—the part of the howling mob which would have killed Jeremiah if they could. Zedekiah had only one of two choices: to go with the crowd, or to go with God and Jeremiah. He went with the crowd. That was not only morally wrong; it was morally and physically and spiritually futile.

The lessons are clear. No nation wins anything when it defies God. No nation, in the end, wins anything by way of violence. It is not difficult to draw up a list of seemingly great nations which went all-out in an effort to control the world, and ended in death and disaster. The world will never be won that way; it will be won only from the inside-out, from the heart of love that conquers all.

There is another reason why we should not condemn but pity Zedekiah: his own people helped to destroy him. *They* wanted war. They *demanded* war. The voice of the mob is too often stupid and dangerous; the voice of God in the human heart is infinitely stronger: God and Zedekiah *alone* might have brought peace. Pity any king or president who is put in power by a fickle people who expect kings and presidents to solve problems which they themselves cannot solve. They expect miracles of their rulers to accomplish the impossible. Pity our rulers: they sit in the middle of a deluge of demands from all sides—demands all of which are often impossible to meet.

We can take this one step further: isn't there something of Zedekiah in all of us? How often do we reenact his tragedy, as common men! How often are we caught in a situation which calls for making a decision between the good and the bad, and how often do we listen to the roar of the crowd and *not* to the still small voice of our God! Each man chooses for himself the way he will go—the high road or the low. Before we deliberately choose to walk the wrong way, we might be smart to read again the story of Zedekiah's choice, and to consider the price he paid for his sad decision.

SUGGESTIONS TO TEACHERS

The end of the nation of Judah was more than a date in history. Your class needs to understand that it was a traumatic event in the story of God's people. Your class should also remember that the Lord felt the anguish that a parent feels when a son or daughter persistently disobeys and gets into serious trouble. Throughout your lesson today, keep in mind the feelings of both the people of Judah and God. There were tears. Remember, however, that defeat and death was not the end of God's story. After Exile, God brought a remnant back to Jerusalem! And after Calvary, God raised up Jesus alive! The final word, tell your people, is God's victory! With the hope which Christians have, develop your lesson around the following themes from 2 Kings 24, 25.

1. *REFUSALS AND REMINDER.* Have your class take note of the main plot of the story of God's people's dealings with their Lord, namely their refusal to live trustingly and obediently before Him. In spite of the pleas of the prophets, the people of Judah (as had their neighbors in the nation of Israel to the north) refused to keep trust with God and refused to follow His commandments. "The Great Refusal" could be the description of Judah's attitude. As teacher, assist your class to be aware of the same danger for God's people today. The Bible is written as a reminder of that danger to your class and to all of God's family in every age.

2. *REVOLUTIONS AND RECESSIONAL.* The quick succession of rulers, each indifferent to moral realities and ethical responsibilities, hastened the end of the nation. Tragically, none of them seemed to realize what was going on in the world at the time he lived. Do we? Are the members of your class conscious of

what God is doing in these times? Guide the class discussion toward remembering that this is still a moral universe. God will not be mocked or checkmated! God is and always will be the Lord of history. He is at work carrying out His purposes, even in bad times for humans. What are His purposes today?

3. *RULES AND RELEVANCE.* Two Kings 24:20 refers to "the anger of the Lord." Get your class to talk about the meaning of this phrase. Does this mean that God flies into a rage when He is crossed, or that He gets miffed when things don't go right for Him? Or, on the other hand, is God a benign, senile great-grandfather-like figure who has no feelings? Remember as teacher that God had disclosed His personality completely in the person of Jesus Christ.

4. *REVOLT AND REQUIEM.* Do not overlook or minimize the wound-shock of the fall of Jerusalem and the deportation of Judah's leaders. The events of the final days of the nation, the destruction of the Temple, the exile in Babylon of God's people left permanent scars on the collective memory of the biblical people down to our day. Have your class list the main lessons the fall of Jerusalem taught to God's people in the era before Christ. Also have the class consider ways in which God's people in these times sometimes feel they are captives or living in exile.

TOPIC FOR ADULTS
INTO EXILE

Inscribed on the Heart. That great Irishman of letters, James Joyce, wrote: "There was an English queen who said that when she died the word *Calais* would be written on her heart. *Dublin* will be found on mine."

For the people of Judah, "Jerusalem" seemed to be inscribed on their hearts. From the time of David, it had been the beautiful capital of the nation and location of the Temple and proud center of the faith. Furthermore, it symbolized a relationship between the Lord and His people. Somehow, these people believed, God would never let anything wipe out Jerusalem.

God's judgment on His disobedient people meant permitting the unthinkable to happen: letting Jerusalem be captured and allowing its people to be carried away into exile in Babylon.

Sometimes, we think that the magnificent cities of our cultures are engraved on God's heart and that He is the guardian or mascot who will protect them regardless of what their peoples may do. Remember Jerusalem!

Possibility of Divine Judgment. Americans seemed to have the illusion that they enjoyed some special dispensation. It did not occur to them that the rules which governed the rest of mankind also applied to them. Other nations rose and fell, but the United States seemed to possess the happy illusion of immortality. "There is no special Providence for us. We are not a chosen people that I know of. If we are, we deserve it as little as the Jews. . . . We must and shall go the way of the earth. We ought to contend, to swim though against the wind and tide, as long as we can; and the poor, injured, deceived, mocked, and insulted people will struggle till battles and victories and conquests dazzle the majority into adoration of idols. Then come popes and emperors, kingdoms and hierarchies."—*John Adams, A Biography.*

Exile for Our World? "We now have nuclear weapons equivalent to at least 30 billion tons of TNT and it may be ten times that much, which means there are at least ten tons of TNT equivalent destructive power for every man, every woman, and every child on the face of this globe. If it could be put in the form of TNT and packed into freight cars, it would respresent a string of freight cars that would reach from the earth to the moon and back fifteen times.

"Since everyone's head seems to be filled with space these days, the question is constantly asked, 'Is there intelligent life on other planets?' What some of us want to know is, 'Is there intelligent life on this planet?' or was George Bernard Shaw right when he said, 'If there is intelligent life on other planets, they are undoubtedly using this planet as their insane asylum.'

"Is there any hope for our world? For those of us who are Christians, we believe that hope begins with God who twenty centuries ago 'in the fullness of time' came to us in the person of Jesus Christ, the Prince of Peace. It was Jesus Christ who said in the Sermon on the Mount, 'Blessed are the peacemakers, for they shall be called the children of God.' "—William G. Rusch, *Newsletter,* Synod of the Trinity, January, 1982.

Questions for Pupils on the Next Lesson. 1. Why did Saul journey to Damascus? 2. What previous experience with the gospel had Saul had before his conversion? 3. Exactly what does conversion to Jesus Christ mean? 4. Must every Christian have a life-changing experience? 5. Has your faith in Jesus Christ ever helped you resolve inner conflicts?

TOPIC FOR YOUTH
WITHOUT A HOME

The Little Apple Trees. Someone once asked Martin Luther what he would do if he knew his judging God was coming to meet him in a few minutes.

"Well, I would go out to water my little apple tree," said Luther, "if my little apple tree needed watering."

Luther was not being flippant. He was so much at home with the Lord that he could "hang loose" with his earthly home's possessions. He knew that God's judgment was not a distant possibility but a daily reality. Therefore, Luther had no terror of the end. Look at the words of his great hymn, "A Mighty Fortress Is Our God!" In the threat of exile, Martin Luther would not panic but would go out and water his little apple tree.

Remembering God's Hand. "We have forgotten the gracious Hand which has preserved us in peace and multiplied and enriched and strengthened us, and have vainly imagined in the deceitfulness of our hearts that all those blessings were produced by some superior wisdom and virtue of our own. Intoxicated with unbroken success, we have become too self-sufficient to feel the necessity of redeeming and preserving Grace, too proud to pray to the God who made us."—Abraham Lincoln, 1863.

A National Home. "A great nation is more than a geographical location; it lives in the hearts and minds of its people. Its life blood is nationalism, which is pumped through its veins by its heart, which is patriotism. Real honest-to-goodness Americans will keep faith with our heritage and, in time, the spasm of internal strife and divisions among us will pass. This nation will resume its pursuit of greatness. That is our destiny."—John Macray Baker, *Hanover Evening Sun.*

With a Home! At a time when some think that there is no future or hope for the world, including our nation, and that we are to be without a home, we can recall another bleak era, the grim days of the American colonies in the eighteenth century. The prayer given at the First Continental Congress on September 4, 1774 by the Rev. Jacob Duche could be prayed at every meeting in every town or city this week.

"Be thou present, O God of wisdom, and direct the councils of this honorable assembly, enable them to settle on the best and surest foundation, that the scene of blood may be speedily closed; that order, harmony, and peace may be effectually restored, and truth and justice, religion and piety prevail and flourish among the people."

Sentence Sermon to Remember: The world will be safe and secure in its peace only when nations adopt the principles of Christ and play fair with them.—William Pearson Merrill.

Questions for Pupils on the Next Lesson. 1. How would you describe the conversion of Saul? 2. How would you describe your own conversion as a Christian? 3. How important is it for a person to make a personal commitment to Jesus Christ? 4. Does your desire to please peers ever cause you to do what you feel you should not do or not to do what you feel you should? 5. Do you sometimes feel that you are searching for a cause to which you can commit yourself? If so, how do you respond to the challenge of Jesus Christ to you to follow Him?